D1525777

Pitt and Popularity

William Beckford as Lord Mayor of London

He holds in his left hand the Bill of Rights. Beside his right hand is 'Magna Charta'
and under it the text of the famous speech he delivered to the King on 23 May 1770,
on the occasion of the presentation of a City Remonstrance arising out of the
Middlesex dispute. Beckford died barely a month later.

The Statue of the Elder Pitt in the Guildhall of the City of London
[For the inscription see page vi.]

PITT AND POPULARITY

The Patriot Minister and London
Opinion during the Seven Years'
War

MARIE PETERS

CLARENDON PRESS · OXFORD
1980

Oxford University Press; Walton Street, Oxford OX2 6DP

OXFORD LONDON GLASGOW

NEW YORK TORONTO MELBOURNE WELLINGTON

KUALA LUMPUR SINGAPORE JAKARTA HONG KONG TOKYO

DELHI BOMBAY CALCUTTA MADRAS KARACHI

NAIROBI DAR ES SALAAM CAPE TOWN

Published in the United States
by Oxford University Press, New York

British Library Cataloguing in Publication Data

Peters, Marie
  Pitt and popularity.
  1. Pitt, William, *Earl of Chatham*
  2. Seven Years' War, 1756–1763 – Public opinion
  – Great Britain
  3. Public opinion – Great Britain – History
  – 18th century
  I. Title
  941.07'2'0924   DA483.P6   79–41672

  ISBN 0–19–822498–2

Text set in 10/12 pt VIP Baskerville, printed and bound
in Great Britain at The Pitman Press, Bath

FOR MY MOTHER AND FATHER

The inscription to the Statue of the Elder Pitt on the frontispiece reads

IN GRATEFUL ACKNOWLEDGMENT TO THE SUPREME DISPOSER OF EVENTS; WHO INTENDING TO ADVANCE THIS NATION, FOR SUCH TIME AS TO HIS WISDOM SEEM'D GOOD, TO AN HIGH PITCH OF PROSPERITY AND GLORY; BY UNANIMITY AT HOME; – BY CONFIDENCE AND REPUTATION ABROAD; – BY ALLIANCES WISELY CHOSEN AND FAITHFULLY OBSERVED; – BY COLONIES UNITED AND PROTECTED; – BY DECISIVE VICTORIES BY SEA AND LAND; – BY CONQUESTS MADE BY ARMS AND GENEROSITY IN EVERY PART OF THE GLOBE; – BY COMMERCE FOR THE FIRST TIME UNITED WITH, AND MADE TO FLOURISH BY WAR: – WAS PLEASED TO RAISE UP AS A PRINCIPAL INSTRUMENT IN THIS MEMORABLE WORK,

WILLIAM PITT

THE MAYOR, ALDERMEN AND COMMON COUNCIL, MINDFUL OF THE BENEFITS WHICH THE CITY OF LONDON RECEIVED IN HER AMPLE SHARE IN THE GENERAL PROSPERITY, HAVE ERECTED TO THE MEMORY OF THIS EMINENT STATESMAN AND POWERFUL ORATOR, THIS MONUMENT IN HER GUILDHALL; THAT HER CITIZENS MAY NEVER MEET FOR THE TRANSACTION OF THEIR AFFAIRS, WITHOUT BEING REMINDED THAT THE MEANS BY WHICH PROVIDENCE RAISES A NATION TO GREATNESS, ARE THE VIRTUES INFUSED INTO GREAT MEN; AND THAT TO WITHHOLD FROM THOSE VIRTUES, EITHER OF THE LIVING OR THE DEAD, THE TRIBUTE OF ESTEEM AND VENERATION, IS TO DENY TO THEMSELVES THE MEANS OF HAPPINESS AND HONOUR.

THIS DISTINGUISHED PERSON, FOR THE SERVICES RENDERED TO KING GEORGE THE SECOND AND TO KING GEORGE THE THIRD, WAS CREATED

EARL OF CHATHAM

THE BRITISH NATION HONOURED HIS MEMORY WITH A PUBLIC FUNERAL, AND A PUBLIC MONUMENT AMONGST HER ILLUSTRIOUS MEN IN WESTMINSTER ABBEY.

Preface

This book is about the public reputation of one of the greatest eighteenth-century English statesmen at the height of his career. It has been written in the conviction that historians can make good use of the growing volume of propaganda generated by eighteenth-century politics. Such propaganda appears, at first, to have little merit; it reflects fable and prejudice more than truth. Yet, when carefully analysed, it provides rich evidence of the modes of thinking, the hopes and fears, of people beyond the heart of politics in Parliament, Cabinet, and Closet. What these people thought about politics could powerfully influence events when circumstances were ripe.

In recent years, the work of several historians has brought back to life this wider political nation. The purpose of my work is to show the connections between its opinions and concerns and the political fortunes of a leading statesman. These connections undermine even further the 'questionable assumption' to which Professor Plumb drew attention some years ago, the notion that there were

two worlds of politics in the eighteenth century—a tight political establishment, linked to small groups of powerful political managers in the provinces, who controlled parliament, the executive and all that was effective in the nation, and outside this an amorphous mass of political sentiment that found expression in occasional hysteria and impotent polemic, but whose effective voice in the nation was negligible.[1]

Contemporary opinion about Pitt cannot be measured precisely, but it was far from an 'amorphous mass'. It was certainly neither 'impotent' nor 'negligible' in influence.

This study also makes some contribution to a political history of the City of London during the Seven Years' War. It throws new light on relations within that remarkable concentration of political power, the

---

[1] *Man versus Society in Eighteenth-Century Britain. Six Points of View*, ed. James L. Clifford, Cambridge, 1968, p. 12.

coalition Ministry of Newcastle and Pitt. On these matters, however, it does not attempt to be comprehensive. Each is important but subsidiary to the main purpose. Nor is the book intended to make anything but an incidental contribution to the much-needed new history of the press in the eighteenth century. Some useful material on political content has been brought together, but major gaps remain, especially on authorship, management, and patronage. I hope this study may provide some basis for further work in these fields.

My work would not have been possible without the help of many people. Dame Lucy Sutherland first suggested the *Monitor* to me as worth investigation. It provided an excellent introduction to this wider study and I have greatly benefited from her continued interest and encouragement. Professor N. C. Phillips introduced me to the eighteenth century and supervised the earliest stages of this work. He has always been a rigorous, constructive, and encouraging critic. To Paul Langford, who read my typescript in its first draft and made many valuable suggestions, I am especially grateful for mitigating the effects of isolation from others working in the field. My Head of Department, Otway Woodward, and several colleagues gave me valuable support. John Cookson read part of the initial draft. David McIntyre helped to remove from the final draft the effects of too much reading of long-winded pamphlets. Many librarians in Great Britain, North America, Australia, and New Zealand have given patient and expert assistance. The Reference and Acquisitions Librarians of the University of Canterbury deserve my special thanks. My work could not have been undertaken without generous research grants from the New Zealand University Grants Committee and the University of Canterbury, or without the study leave I was given in 1972–3. It would never have seen the light of day without the patience and skill of several typists, especially Michele Downer and Merilyn Johnson. And it could not have been completed without my son's cheerful tolerance of his mother's idiosyncrasies. To all who have helped me in so many ways I am warmly grateful.

University of Canterbury   Marie Peters
New Zealand.
April 1979

Contents

List of Maps

List of Illustrations

Abbreviations and References

Add. MSS	British Library Additional Manuscripts
Eg.	British Library Egerton Manuscripts
HMC	Historical Manuscripts Commission
PRO	Public Record Office
DNB	*Dictionary of National Biography*
AR	*The Annual Register*
GM	*The Gentleman's Magazine*
LM	*The London Magazine*
CR	*The Critical Review*
MR	*The Monthly Review*
Gaz.	*The Gazetteer*
LC	*The London Chronicle*
LEP	*The London Evening Post*
Lloyd's EP	*Lloyd's Evening Post*
Mon.	*The Monitor*
OWC	*Owen's Weekly Chronicle*
PA	*The Public Advertiser*
PL	*The Public Ledger*
RWJ	*Read's Weekly Journal*
St. JC	*The St. James's Chronicle*
UC	*The Universal Chronicle*

Abbreviated titles for other works are established by the use of square brackets at the first reference where necessary for clarity or to distinguish different works by the same author.

The titles of pamphlets are given in the shortest comprehensible form in the footnotes. Full titles appear in the bibliography.

Publication details are given for pamphlets sighted; for others, references to the *Monthly Review* and *Critical Review* are given, with the title only if the pamphlet is of some importance.

In quotations, abbreviations have been expanded, but the original spelling and punctuation have been retained, except where excessive capitalization becomes intrusive.

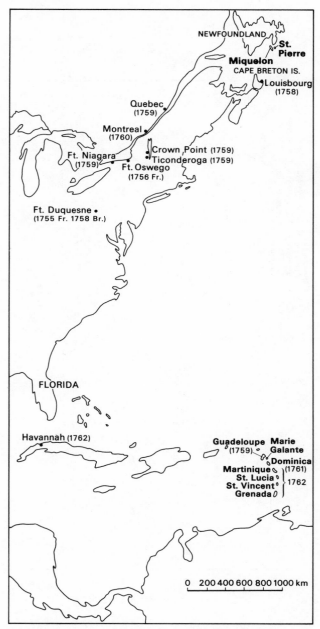

NEWFOUNDLAND
St. Pierre
Miquelon
CAPE BRETON IS.
Louisbourg (1758)
Quebec (1759)
Montreal (1760)
Crown Point (1759)
Ft. Niagara (1759)
Ticonderoga (1759)
Ft. Oswego (1756 Fr.)
Ft. Duquesne • (1755 Fr. 1758 Br.)
FLORIDA
Havannah (1762)
Guadeloupe (1759)
Marie Galante
Dominica (1761)
Martinique
St. Lucia
St. Vincent } 1762
Grenada

0 200 400 600 800 1000 km

North America and the West Indies: engagements mentioned
in the text.

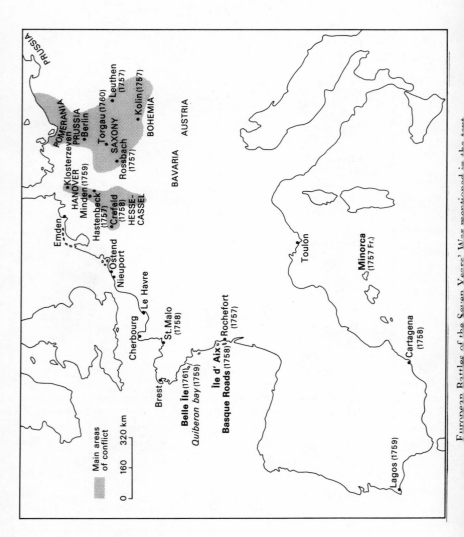

European Battles of the Seven Years' War mentioned in the text

INTRODUCTION
Pitt and Popularity

William Pitt the Elder is unique among politicians of the eighteenth century, not least because a claim to 'popularity' was a substantial element of his political strength. He began his political career and won his first acclaim in opposition to Walpole. He forced himself on the attention of the Pelhams in the early 1740s by his virulent anti-Hanoverianism. Such opposition brought some measure of popular standing. Then, quite suddenly in the mid-1750s, these scattered seeds unexpectedly bore fruit in an unusual popular reputation. Thereafter this reputation, which attained unprecedented heights from 1759 after the marvellous victories of war, was to play a powerful part in shaping his career. His earlier years were reinterpreted in the light of it; later he was both materially aided, and, at other times, much perplexed by it.

Yet the genesis of this reputation, its nature, and its influence on Pitt's political standing have never been fully explained. Earlier historians, in so far as they paid it much attention, accepted his popularity as a natural effect on the spirit of the nation of his oratory and his success, or promise of success, as a war minister. They looked no further for an explanation and took for granted the importance of popularity in his political career. Later, for the generation whose view of politics was dominated by the great work of Sir Lewis Namier, such a basis for political strength fitted uneasily into their assumptions. Perhaps, with the repellent force of Pitt's strange arrogant character, this is why none of them has attempted a complete political biography. When they looked at parts of his career, they explained his rise to high office in the 1750s almost entirely in terms of his securing the support of Leicester House and, while sometimes admitting his oratorical and popular appeal, regarded it only as window-dressing for the realities of power.

Yet those more perceptive of the wider context of politics still recognized that 'popularity', while not Pitt's only support, did contribute substantially to his hold on high office in 1756–7. Studies of the effects of the outcry over the loss of Minorca in 1756, the impact of the brief Devonshire–Pitt administration of 1756–7, and the 'rain' of gold boxes for Pitt and his colleague Legge in 1757, have given more precision to its nature and influence. They have cut the popularity down to size by pointing out its very recent origin and by showing the limited reality behind the magnified appearance. Yet they confirm the value of that appearance to Pitt's political strength in 1756–7 and draw attention to his unique attempt to use popularity in office as well as in opposition.[1]

It is, however, not usually recognized how important Pitt's popular base and patriot reputation were to him in the years of waiting for victories between 1757 and 1759, and how carefully and by what methods he worked to preserve these assets against considerable difficulties. Nor is it realized how brief the popularity was. Even from the year of victories in 1759 it was far from being steady and reliable, and challenges to it so weakened Pitt's position in the new reign that his resignation in October 1761 was perhaps in part a gamble to recover it. There is, therefore, much to be explored about such a highly unusual basis for political strength in the eighteenth century, much that raises important questions about the wider political nation and its perception of and influence on the heart of politics in Court, Cabinet, and Parliament.

Such an exploration requires two approaches: on the one hand a study of the nature of Pitt's popular reputation, on the other an assessment of how he used it and how effective it was as a political support. For the latter, the activities, comments, and calculations of politicians as preserved in their correspondence and memoirs and in

---

[1] Lucy S. Sutherland, 'The City [of London and the Devonshire–Pitt Administration,] 1756–7', *Proceedings of the British Academy*, xlvi (1960), 147–93; Paul Langford, 'William Pitt and public opinion, 1757', *English Historical Review*, lxxxviii (Jan. 1973), 54–80. John Brewer, *Party Ideology [and Popular Politics at the Accession of George III]*, Cambridge, 1976, appeared while this book was being written. Ch. 6 gives a most interesting outline of the nature and effects of Pitt's popular reputation, especially in the 1760s.

accounts of parliamentary debates provide much of the answer.[2] Yet the hints they give do not carry their proper weight, nor will the true nature of Pitt's popular reputation be properly understood, unless such sources are set in the context of 'public opinion'. This will never be amenable to exact description and measurement. Even today, when opinion polls are legion, events often belie their findings. Public opinion was, nevertheless, a very real part of eighteenth-century politics. It was not dismissed lightly by contemporary politicians, even by those, like Fox and Newcastle, most adept and experienced in court and cabinet politics, and nor can it be ignored by historians. And although it cannot be depicted in exact dimensions, its major preoccupations can be described, the influences working on it assessed, and some estimate made of its component parts and fluctuating strength.

* * * * * *

To some extent the movement of opinion in the political nation can be judged from the behaviour of the large number of independents in Parliament. Outnumbering both committed politicians and placemen, they were of their very nature a varied group, usually reacting to politics in contradictory ways. Any clear response from them to controversial issues was likely to be an indication of interest outside, in the shires particularly.[3] Further indications come from the various well-established modes whereby outside opinion became known to parliament or king. The right to petition was the longest established. It was reaffirmed in the Bill of Rights but was still subject to the limitations of the 1662 Act against Tumultuous Petitioning and of the convention that petitioners must have a direct and specific interest in the subject of their petition.[4] Formal

---

[2] Regrettably few letters from Pitt survive. The detailed political history of the Seven Years' War period has still to be written. E. J. S. Fraser, 'The Pitt–Newcastle Coalition [and the Conduct of the Seven Years' War, 1757–60]', unpublished D.Phil. thesis, Oxford, 1976, is invaluable. I am very grateful to the author for allowing me to see his nearly-completed work in 1973.

[3] Unfortunately the evidence on their voting behaviour is slight because so few parliamentary division lists survive for this period. Sir Lewis Namier and John Brooke, *The History of Parliament. The House of Commons 1754–1790*, 3 vols., London, 1964, i, pp. 524–5.

[4] Peter Fraser, 'Public Petitioning and Parliament before 1832', *History*, xlvi (Oct. 1961), 200–1; T. W. Perry, *Public Opinion, Propaganda, and Politics in Eighteenth-Century England: A Study of the Jew Bill of 1753*, Cambridge, Mass., 1962, p. 64, quoting Henry Pelham. The presentation of petitions, but not usually their text, is recorded in the Journals of the Commons or Lords.

addresses of congratulation on royal or national events could be used to make political points and could even become remonstrances.[5] Less formal and less universally accepted were instructions from constituents to their members of Parliament, first used in the excitements of the seventeenth century. The right to offer them was not generally disputed but the obligation of a member to listen to them was questioned. Was a member the delegate of his constituents, bound to follow their views or, after election, a representative of the nation at large, free to make his own judgements? The latter was the view most generally accepted.[6] Fortunately the debates on this issue do not affect the value of instructions as evidence. Usually these expressions of opinion came from legally recognized bodies, the corporations of boroughs, the county assembled at quarter sessions or assizes or in a county meeting called by the lord lieutenant or sheriff. They were occasional and sporadic, not evidence of any continuous pressure of opinion. Further, as with all so-called manifestations of opinion, questions arise concerning their spontaneity. They required organization and could be stimulated by politicians and others for their own purposes. Nevertheless, if used critically, they provide some useful evidence of public opinion. Interested groups and the support they can arouse are, after all, a part of public opinion.

Because it was difficult to arouse such expressions of opinion in the country as a whole, eighteenth-century politicians, when they looked out-of-doors for support, often turned first to the City of London—the City in the corporate rather than moneyed sense. Its corporate bodies had not, like many others, become ossified oligarchies. They provided, particularly in the Courts of Common Council and Common Hall, some scope for activity on the part of the middling sort of commercial people, lesser merchants, tradesmen, shopkeepers, craftsmen, professional men. These bodies were primarily concerned with the administration of City affairs, the management of its lands, the widening of its streets, the care of the

[5] Most are recorded in the *London Gazette*, as also are petitions to the Crown, but as the decision to print lay with the Secretary of State's Office, hostile ones were sometimes ignored. A complaint about this practice appeared in *PA*, 11 Nov. 1756.

[6] On this debate see Betty Kemp, *King and Commons 1660–1832*, London, 1965, pp. 43–5; Isaac Kramnick, *Bolingbroke and his Circle*, Cambridge, Mass., 1968, pp. 172–7.

old London Bridge and the building of the new one at Blackfriars. Yet they had a well-established habit of corporate action not only on these matters but also in national politics when issues of financial or commercial policy were at stake. Further, the City had a tradition, extending well back into the seventeenth century, of lively if sporadic interest in general national questions. The atmosphere of a thriving metropolis, close to Court, administration and Parliament at Westminster, broke down habits of deference and encouraged an interest in politics which could be expressed in instructions, petitions or addresses. The City Sheriffs were entitled to present petitions in person at the bar of the House of Commons and to be heard there; the Lord Mayor had the right of access to the King. They exercised these rights actively in the troubled and exciting years from 1756.

Altogether, then, the City's corporate bodies provided the most organized and easily stimulated forum of expression of public opinion. They were not as influential as the shires but the shires could not be mobilized nearly so easily. The City could focus with particular intensity the hopes and fears of the political nation and give a lead to others. On the other hand, it sometimes had strong views which were peculiarly its own. Although the attitudes of Common Council often differed sharply from those of the moneyed interest which was so important to the regular financial operations of the Government, no minister felt easy when a 'clamour' threatened in the City. If nothing worse, this might suggest to independents in the House of Commons or foreign representatives to the Court of St. James that the Government was not entirely in control, and confidence, so vital to credit, could be undermined. Like eighteenth-century politicians looking for support, the historian looking for his evidence of opinion out-of-doors can well begin with the City's corporate bodies.

Yet the City was far from united in its attitudes. It was not the monolithic entity which undefined references to 'the City' often suggest. The broad contrast between the outlook of the plutocracy of financiers and overseas merchants and the middling sort was cut across by differing commercial and financial interests and party stances and complicated by the interaction of divisions on local and national matters. There was no set pattern of interests and loyalties but rather a kaleidoscope illuminated by diverse and fragmentary evidence which needs the analysis of a Namier to be properly understood.[7] If the response of the City to Pitt is to be adequately described, some account must be taken of these complexities behind the formal expressions of City opinion to be found in its official records. It is possible to do so in the first instance through a study of the career of Alderman William Beckford, who became Pitt's chief link with the City and one of his most devoted disciples.

William Beckford was a comparative outsider to City politics. He was West Indian in origin, the second son and eventual heir of a large and very wealthy sugar-planting family, educated like the rest of his brothers in England. In 1747 at the age of thirty-eight he began his political career by being returned to parliament for Shaftesbury, in Dorset, on the interest of the fourth Earl. Shaftesbury was close to Beckford's considerable estates at Fonthill in Wiltshire. He further secured his standing by a large-scale election campaign in 1754 which returned family and friends for four seats. He won a City seat and his brother Richard came in for Bristol. By the mid-1750s Beckford had established himself in national politics. He was an independent member of Parliament of some prominence, an indefatigable speaker in the House of Commons, if not a very effective one. He spoke out passionately for the shibboleths of the independents (notably against the army), and on occasion acted as their acknowledged spokesman.[8] From the beginning he was a committed Tory. Some of those associated with him in his election campaign, Sir John Philipps and another West Indian, James Dawkins, were well-known Tories of proven Jacobite inclination, although there is no suggestion of Jacobitism in Beckford.[9] In the early 1750s he had some association with the Duke of Bedford and perhaps with Bedford's patron, the Duke of Cumberland. Out of the

[7] Nicholas Rogers, 'London Politics [from Walpole to Pitt: Patriotism and Independency in an Era of Commercial Imperialism 1738–63]', unpublished Ph.D. thesis, Toronto, 1975, makes a substantial contribution to such an analysis. Some of his findings have been published in Nicholas Rogers, ['Resistance to Oligarchy:] The City Opposition [to Walpole and his Successors,] 1725–47', *London in the Age of Reform*, ed. John Stevenson, Oxford, 1977, pp. 1–29.

[8] Namier and Brooke, ii, p. 75; Horace Walpole, [*Memoires of the Last Ten Years of the Reign of*] *George the Second*, 2 vols., London, 1822, i, pp. 355–7, 486; P. D. G. Thomas, *The House of Commons on the Eighteenth Century*, Oxford, 1971, pp. 231, 240; Sir Lewis Namier, 'Country Gentlemen in Parliament, [1750–84]', *Crossroads of Power*, London, 1962, p.35; [*The Political Journal of George Bubb*] *Dodington*, ed. John Carswell and Lewis Arnold Drallé, Oxford, 1965, p. 106, 21, 22 [Mar. 1751].

[9] Namier and Brooke, i, p. 283; iii, p. 274; ii, pp. 304–5.

flirtation with Bedford came, probably, an admiration for his protégé, Henry Fox, which still persisted in 1755. Beckford seemed to be looking for a leader who would carry out the independents' programme in which he passionately if naïvely believed. But as yet he was committed to none.[10]

His energetic activity made him more than a typical independent country gentleman. So did his West Indian origins, which linked him with perhaps twenty members of Parliament of similar connections, some related to him. Although contemporaries often exaggerated the importance of the West Indians in Parliament, they were a cohesive social group and, with the other absentee planters, merchants, and colonial agents living in London, made up the most influential of the trading interests. Since the 1730s the West Indians had exerted organized and effective pressure in matters of concern to them, for example the Sugar Act of 1739 and the duty on sugar of 1743–4. By about 1760 the merchants had formed a permanent organization, the Society of West India Merchants, which actively opposed the proposed sugar tax of 1759 and the reopening of gin distilling in 1760. More generally, the West Indian interest tended increasingly to ally itself with demands for a more aggressive foreign policy against French and Spanish competition. Beckford stood out as one of the wealthiest of the West Indians. Although certainly not united in their politics, they were an important part of his political base.[11]

Beckford's entry into City politics in the early 1750s was a further effort to widen this base. In quick succession he became Freeman of the Company of Ironmongers (1752), Alderman for Billingsgate (1752), and Sheriff (1755). His election in 1754 as one of the City members of Parliament capped this extraordinary rise. As in national politics, so in the City, he called in his brother to support his efforts. In August 1754 Richard Beckford was made a Freeman of the Goldsmiths' Company. Having been clothed as a Liveryman in January 1755 he was, with unusual haste, elected Prime Warden in May. In 1754 he became Alderman for the Ward of Farringdon Without.[12]

---

[10] Ibid. ii, p. 75; Walpole, *Geo. II*, i, p. 377.

[11] Sir Lewis Namier, *England in the Age of the American Revolution*, second edn., London, 1966, pp. 234–41; Lilian M. Penson, 'The London West India Interest in the Eighteenth Century', *English Historical Review*, xxxvi (July 1921), 373–92; Namier and Brooke, i, pp. 156–8; Rogers, 'London Politics', pp. 396–7. See below pp. 140–1, 174–6.

[12] Namier and Brooke, ii, pp. 75, 74; records of the Goldsmiths' Company, 2 Aug., 12 Dec. 1754, 8 Jan., 21 May 1755.

Such a rapid rise to the élite of the Court of Aldermen and the City members of Parliament was highly unusual for outsiders. As West Indian planters, the Beckfords had connections with City merchants. An uncle had been Alderman for Aldgate in the late seventeenth century. But more than anything else they owed their success in City politics to the support of the City Tories.

The City had a long tradition of Toryism, originating in a reaction against the post-Revolution metamorphosis of the Whigs into supporters of government, Continental wars, Protestant dissenters, and the new moneyed interest. All these were disliked by many of City's middling sort for a variety of reasons. Although party divisions weakened in the City as elsewhere after 1714, Toryism remained very much alive as the most extreme expression of that unruly opposition to government which came naturally to the City's corporate bodies below the Court of Aldermen.

Social divisions and differences of economic interest fuelled this opposition long after party political issues moderated. The gap between the close-knit oligarchy of financiers and overseas merchants and the ordinary City tradesmen, shopkeepers, and artisans widened in the eighteenth century. The financiers grew closer to the Government while the wealthy merchants had firm links with the landed classes and national politics. Even those who began in parliamentary opposition tended to gravitate towards the Court. Although the financial élite took less interest now in City politics, the Court of Aldermen was still dominated by the very wealthy merchants. On the other hand, Common Council represented those with no links outside the City and slight connections with high finance or overseas trade. Its members feared the effect of the changing attitudes of the oligarchy to the national Government on the traditional independence of the City. Many tradesmen and artisans had suffered from the breakdown of guild control over domestic trades as the London market rapidly expanded. Toryism was strongest in those wards most affected by this development, the more populous ones beyond the City walls, around St. Paul's and along the river. Not all the middling sort were Tories, or even in opposition to the Government. Support for the Court was widened well beyond the wealthy by an extensive web of government patronage. On the other hand, the Tories found leaders among those few of the oligarchy who were also not happy about recent developments: goldsmith-bankers ousted by the new financiers, some industrialists, those merchants who did not like monopoly companies or who were not satisfied with the policies of the Whig Government. Notable among the latter were those, such as West Indian and American merchants, in the newer more dynamic sectors, who wanted a more aggressive mercantilism. By the mid-eighteenth century these social and economic differences were far more fundamental to party divisions in the City than any such differences had been in the late seventeenth century. The dissatisfied could focus their diverse discontents on those they regarded as a parvenu élite too closely linked to ministerial influence, and so identify themselves as Tories.[13]

The City's Toryism was of a strident independent popular variety. It upheld in intense form the anti-executive political principles and anti-European foreign policy which the middling sort of the City generally found congenial and which could hold together its disparate supporters.[14] It was often outspokenly anti-Hanoverian and sometimes explicitly Jacobite. Men of such views were important in the broadly-based 'patriot' opposition drawn together in the City against Walpole. Later, this opposition was divided and the Tories to some extent discredited by the strains of the '45. Pelham's conciliatory moves in financial arrangements and his repeal of the provision in the City Elections Act of 1725 for an aldermanic veto on decisions of the Common Council further moderated City attitudes. He won over the City's most prominent popular leader, Sir John Barnard, up to this time an opposition Whig. Yet the uproar in the City over the Jew Bill in 1753–4 showed that the social forces making for opposition were far from dead. Tory battlecries could be revived effectively to vent them. The Tory rump still survived as the most extreme opponents of the Pelhams and their 'lackeys' in the City, the moneyed interest.[15] The hodge-podge of Tory attitudes is well illustrated by that incendiary propagandist, Dr John Shebbeare, in his *Marriage Act*, where he linked the Marriage Act, the Jew Bill, support of monopolistic trading companies and of paper money as parts of one hated system.[16]

---

[13] Rogers, 'London Politics', chs. 6, 7 (pp. 295–429), pp. 600–3; 'The City Opposition . . . 1725–47', p. 3.

[14] See below pp. 25–7.

[15] Romney Sedgwick, [*The History of Parliament. The*]*House of Commons* [*1715–1754*], 2 vols., London, 1971, i, pp. 280–3; Sutherland, 'The City . . . 1756–7', pp. 148–9; Rogers, 'The City Opposition . . . 1725–47', *passim*, 'London Politics', pp. 151–67.

[16] John Shebbeare, *The Marriage Act*, London, 1754, p. 327.

Tories still had their rendezvous at the Half Moon Tavern in Cheapside, not far from Guildhall, meetings which were sometimes referred to as the Half Moon Club. Here, hostile contemporaries claimed, the Tories caballed to direct City affairs.[17] Something of their attitudes and activities can be glimpsed in the later 1750s through the biased eyes of John Gordon, one of Newcastle's semi-literate informers. To Gordon the Tories were the 'lurking faction', Jacobites who now disguised their real beliefs, but would support anything which would weaken the power of the Crown and thus prepare for revolution. Bitter enemies of Newcastle and his associates, they would, Gordon believed, undoubtedly show their true colours when ready and were quite certainly aiming to cause great upheavals in the forthcoming reign.[18] This highly coloured talk, unreliable as it is, at least bears witness to the survival of a strident and bitter Tory faction in the City.

With the support of this group the Beckfords established themselves in the City in the early 1750s. Temperament, ideology, and their West Indian interests naturally inclined them this way. Richard's Ward, Farringdon Without, and his Company, the Goldsmiths, were both traditionally Tory; William's Company, the Ironmongers, was another of the few among the Great Twelve to have a substantial Tory element.[19] William stood for the City in the general election of 1754 under the patronage of the well-known Jacobite and former Lord Mayor, Alderman William Benn. Benn had been very active in City politics for many years and had trained a group of supporters known as the 'Bishopsgate Boys', who continued prominent in City politics through the Half Moon Club after his death in August 1755.[20] Benn's death opened up opportunities for Beckford of leadership of a Toryism purged of embarrassing Jacobitism, opportunities which Beckford actively cultivated by his

[17] See e.g. Birch to Royston, 29 Oct. 1757, 7 Oct. 1758, 18 Aug. 1759, Add. MSS 35398, f. 383, 35399, ff. 43, 80. For accusations against the Half Moon see e.g. *PA*, 18 Aug., 8, 9, 10 Sept. 1755; *A Letter To The Common-Council Of London On Their Late Very Extraordinary Address To His Majesty*, London, 1765, p. 41.

[18] Perhaps the best example of these frequent letters is that of 20 Nov. 1759, Add. MSS 32898, f. 405.

[19] Rogers, 'London Politics', pp. 374, 381.

[20] *PA*, 25 Apr. 1754; Alfred B. Beaven, *The Aldermen of the City of London*, 2 vols., London, 1908, 1913, i, p. 7, ii, pp. 128, 197; Birch to Royston, 29 Oct. 1757, 7 Oct. 1758, Add. MSS 35398, f. 383, 35399, f. 43. Benn had been Common Councilman for Bishopsgate from 1730 to 1740.

diatribes against corruption. At the same time, with the increasing age of Sir John Barnard, for so long the unquestioned popular leader, there was some hope that the Tories could re-establish their dominance among popular opinion.

By the mid-1750s, then, William Beckford's energetic efforts had established the basis for some political influence both in the City and in national politics. In October 1755, on the eve of the opening of Parliament, he was reported to be ready for action there and 'very sanguine of the success of the approaching session against the Ministry'.[21] But how he intended to use this influence and whether he was looking to the City or to wider Tory support was not yet clear.

In Parliament there were still more than a hundred Tory members, the politically unambitious remnant of the vigorous pre-1714 Tory party and the largest identifiable group among the independent members. They were distinguished from other independent country gentlemen partly by Tory heredity or tradition but also by some hankerings after old high Toryism. All, when opportunity arose, upheld the privileges of the Church and had no sympathy for dissenters; many had a deep respect for monarchy and the royal prerogative, much as they might dislike the Hanoverians; some had only recently disavowed Jacobitism. Above all, they bitterly disliked all things Whig and the leaders of the Old Corps of the Whigs who had proscribed them for so long. Indeed they distrusted all politicians. They represented a diffused Tory sentiment in the country ranging from reactionary high Toryism, strongest in the Midlands, through the independent gentry of the South West to the radical populism of the City and a few other large constituencies like Middlesex.[22] There were traditional Tory constituencies, boroughs, like Chester, Salisbury, and Exeter, and counties, like Cheshire, Devon, Cornwall, and Somerset. In addition there were boroughs where the corporation was firmly Tory but could not control the whole electorate, like York, Bedford, and Liverpool. Because Tory members of Parliament lacked political ambition they seldom acted as a disciplined group. Yet they offered some opportunities to Beckford. In the 1750s they had no one acknowledged leader. Sir

[21] Birch to Royston, 25 Oct. 1755, Add. MSS 35398, ff. 302–3.
[22] Sedgwick, *House of Commons*, i, pp. 62–78; John B. Owen, *The Rise of the Pelhams*, London, 1957, pp. 68–70; Namier, *England*, pp. 182–4, 200–2; Namier and Brooke, i, pp. 184–8.

John Philipps, formerly prominent among them, had been out of
Parliament from 1747 to 1754 and was then returned virtually as
Beckford's protégé. Beckford could reasonably hope to take his place
as a Tory leader.

In the City there seemed less chance of success. Citizens distrusted those who sought to use their support to further a parliamentary career; City members usually put City interests first.
Even one so closely identified with the City as Sir John Barnard
could not easily manage its complex interests coherently for some
national cause. In comparison with Barnard Beckford was an
outsider. Over the next ten years he did not become as fully involved
as other leading aldermen, including the other City members of
Parliament, in the routine administration of the City, and his
influence there suffered accordingly. At the general elections of 1754
and 1761 he faced opposition for his casual attendance on his City
duties.[23] In the mid-1750s it was far from certain, then, that he
could turn his growing interest in the City to effect in national
politics. Moreover, his loyalties in national politics, apart from a
commitment to opposition, were still undetermined—and he was
scarcely of leadership calibre himself.

The unsettled circumstances of 1755–6 were to resolve some of
these uncertainties. In November 1756 Beckford committed himself
to Pitt and Pitt won one of his most stalwart allies. Beckford had at
last found his role. The relationship grew steadily in warmth and
respect on both sides until Beckford's death in 1770 and was much
noticed by contemporaries. Beckford was consulted, or at least
informed, as one of Pitt's closer allies, about major decisions. He
gave advice on matters of war policy, in one case decisively.[24]
Beckford could offer Pitt links to the City, the West Indian interest,
and the country gentlemen, especially the Tories. Yet there seems to
have been more than this, a strange compatibility between two very
unusual personalities, Pitt aloof and arrogant, awkward in personal
relationships especially with those who could claim to be his equals,
Beckford impetuous and ostentatious, neither his behaviour nor his
'heap of confused knowledge'[25] controlled by much intelligence or

---

[23] *PA*, 1, 8 May 1754, 5 Mar. 1761.

[24] On the Martinique expedition of 1759. Beckford to Pitt, 26 Aug. 1758, PRO
30/8/19, f. 47.

[25] Horace Walpole, [*Memoirs of the Reign of King*] *George the Third;* [*first published by
Sie Denis Le Marchant bart.*], ed. G. F. Russell-Barker, 4 vols., London, 1894, iv, p. 104.

judgement. Probably the key lies in Beckford's respectful earnest adulation which in no way challenged Pitt.[26] Although very different in character and status, Beckford seems to have enjoyed a closeness to Pitt akin to that of the scandalizing Thomas Potter, who likewise did not challenge Pitt. After Potter's premature death in 1759 Beckford certainly took his place as Pitt's henchman in the House of Commons and remained as such through the 1760s, most remarkably in the Chatham Administration from 1766 to 1768. From 1756 he worked consistently to turn his influence to Pitt's advantage and as the war progressed Beckford found the City rather than the Tories as a whole more congenial to this purpose. Not only did he foster Pitt's standing in the City; even more he rose to prominence in the City himself as Pitt's lieutenant and on the strength of Pitt's growing reputation as a war minister.

Fortunately there is more evidence to chart this process than the sparse remains of Beckford's papers, the passing references of interested contemporaries or even the bare formality of City records. In August 1755, as part of the Beckfords' thrust of activity in national and City politics, Richard Beckford founded the *Monitor*, a weekly political essay paper.[27] Richard lived only a few months to see the fruits of his patronage. He died in January 1756 in Lyons on his way to the south of France to nurse his 'declining state of health'. The paper nevertheless continued. It was, it said, sustained by 'many gentlemen of the *same* station and principles with himself'

[26] Cf. James, Earl Waldegrave, *Memoirs from 1754 to 1758*, London, 1821, p. 16.

[27] The actual foundation was the result of initiatives on the part of Jonathan Scott, the printer, and Arthur Beardmore, William Beckford's attorney and probably Richard's too, which led to a meeting between them and Dr John Shebbeare and the Revd John Entick. Thus were brought together the first publisher and major authors of the *Monitor*. The meeting agreed that Shebbeare and Entick should have £200 a year each, apparently for writing the paper, while the profits, after all charges had been paid, should go to Scott. Jonathan Scott's Information, 11 Oct. 1762, *A Complete Collection of State Trials . . .*, ed. T. B. Howell, 33 vols., T. Bagshaw etc., London, 1809–1926, xix, c. 1033. Shebbeare, a violent Tory propagandist, did not long remain connected with the *Monitor*. Beardmore, probably the paper's business manager, legal adviser and link with its patron, was well known to be connected with it by the 1760s. By this time he was active in City politics as a Common Councilman and also had connections with Earl Temple. He was Wilkes's attorney in the early stages of the *North Briton* affair, an acknowledged popular leader in the City by the later 1760s and on the whole a Wilkite over the Middlesex elections. Entick, a clergyman-schoolmaster of dubious standing who made his living mainly by hack writing for the press, was probably the main author of the paper. He also had some standing among popular elements in London (especially in Stepney and Mile End) and Middlesex. The paper had many occasional writers of whom the most interesting was Wilkes.

who were animated 'to concur in the *same* generous design, which he thought too important to be rested upon the contingency of a single life'. William Beckford's name was never mentioned by the paper in connection with its support. Only once or twice, and not very conclusively, did contemporaries associate him with it. Yet the paper closely followed his political line. On several occasions it had to defend itself against charges of favouring West Indian interests. One of its authors was refused permission to write to Beckford when taken up on a Secretary of State's warrant in 1762.[28] It seems certain that William was at least chief among the 'many gentlemen' who continued the paper, if not the only one. He already had some direct knowledge of the effectiveness of such a paper. In his days of association with the Duke of Bedford in 1753 he had helped to establish the anti-ministerial weekly paper, the *Protestor*, which was effective enough to persuade Newcastle to buy off the author, James Ralph.[29] It was not surprising that the Beckfords should turn again to such a paper only two years later at a new stage in their political careers.

The political essay was the forerunner of the modern editorial. Whether published separately, as in the *Monitor* and the *Protestor,* or in a newspaper, it was for most of the first half of the eighteenth century a major form of political comment in the press. It was a main item in the weekly journals, chronicles, and miscellanies which were probably the most important sources of sustained and regular political comment from the 1720s to the 1750s. It was often copied in monthly magazines and appeared in more frequently published newspapers. Although by 1760 the periodical essay had been largely absorbed into the newspaper, more ephemeral essay papers were set up on virtually every occasion of controversy. They were obviously effective for occasional debate, a convenient intermediary form between the pamphlet, the established vehicle of substantial debate for earlier generations, and the daily or tri-weekly newspaper which was just beginning to develop political comment of any volume or range. When essay papers did appear they were usually at the heart of the controversy of the moment, the 'heavies' in the battle. The two

[28] William Beckford to Newcastle, 9 Dec. 1755, Add. MSS 32861, f. 196; *Mon.*, collected edn., 2 vols., London, 1756, i, p. ii (the quotation); *The English Reports*, 176 vols., Edinburgh and London, 1900–30 (reprint), xcv, p. 791.

[29] Perry, pp. 106–7, 109; *Dodington*, p. 218, 7 [May 1753].

major essay paper exchanges of the years of this study, those
between the *Test* and *Con-Test* in 1756–7 and between the *Briton* and
Auditor on the one hand and the *Monitor* and *North Briton* on the other
in 1762–3, were, for their duration, the focal points of political
comment. Other essay papers appeared both at these and other
times.

These papers did not usually outlive the occasion, dying away in
months or at the most a couple of years. The *Monitor* lasted until
March 1765. Unlike its immediate predecessors or its contemporaries in the same form,[30] it outlived particular crises and served a
more sustained political objective, reflecting political interests of
some substance and permanence.

The programme announced in its opening numbers gives some
indication of what these interests were.[31] It affirmed an uncompromising anti-ministerialism and a set of maxims on constitutional
questions, foreign policy and public finance which clearly identified
the *Monitor* with the traditional concerns of eighteenth-century
opposition propaganda.[32] Although denying explicitly any suggestion of Jacobitism, it called itself Tory. The paper's Toryism is given
more specific substance by its later views on religion, particularly its
antipathy to Quakers, Methodists, and all dissenters. Its bitter
hostility to Walpole, the Pelhams, Hardwicke and all their works,
especially the Jewish Naturalization Act and the Marriage Act, both
of 1753, further distinguish it as Tory. Other characteristics identify
it more precisely with City Toryism, notably its interest in trade and
its hostility to monopolies, large-scale merchants, financiers and
capitalists, its concern for the welfare of the middling sort and its
defence of the citizens of London and their governing bodies against
disparaging attacks.

Clearly the *Monitor*, as part of the Beckfords' big political effort of
the mid-1750s, was intended at first simply to revivify Toryism, both
nationally and in the City. Then from November 1756 William
certainly wanted it to further the cause of William Pitt. Although
there is some reason to think that its lines were not always controlled
closely by its patron, in general they must have been agreeable to

---

[30] The only similar papers to rival it in length of life were the curious *Hyp-Doctor*, a
pro-Government paper published from 1730 to 1741, and the equally remarkable
Corn-Cutter's Journal (c.1733–1741).

[31] *Mon.* 1–4, 9–30 Aug. 1755.   [32] See below pp. 25–7.

him. If its evidence is viewed carefully, then, in the light of its origins and purpose and with other evidence, the *Monitor* can help to show how William Beckford's political purposes were sharpened and his base developed, especially in the City. Indeed, in the early years it, rather than any consistent activity in the City's corporate bodies, was his main means of influence. It can illuminate general Tory and specific City attitudes to national politics. More important, it can be used as an indicator of Beckford's success in directing his own growing influence in the City to support Pitt's unique attempt to make 'popularity' a major continuing foundation of his political power. It can show the methods used to influence public opinion. Further, it can also be a most useful measure of the obstacles to and the success of those methods. For to be effective and maintain its readership, the *Monitor* had to reflect as well as attempt to mould popular opinion—and especially to begin with the latter process was more difficult than the former.

So, because of its longevity and because both its patrons and its readers can be identified fairly precisely, the *Monitor* is a most important piece of evidence of Pitt's standing with 'public opinion'. It does not, however, tell the whole story; it needs to be considered with other pieces of political commentary which cannot be so precisely identified in origins and readership but which can still be useful evidence.

* * * * * *

There was, of course, by the middle of the eighteenth century, a great wealth and variety of forms of political information and propaganda, both occasional and periodical. The oldest established form of substantial controversy, the occasional pamphlet, still flourished, as notices in the monthly reviews and advertisements in newspapers bear witness. Pamphlets appeared on a wide range of political questions, from large issues of policy to personal attack and justification, although relatively few commented directly on political manœuvres and alliances. Like all forms of eighteenth-century political comment, they are far from providing a comprehensive cover of all matters of political interest. The reappearance of old pamphlets under new titles and references of reviewers to the works of hack writers produced to meet the interests of the moment bear some witness to their profitability. Like their subjects, their origins and authorship were varied. Most appeared anonymously. Some were clearly subsidized or even written by leading politicians and were recognized as political manifestos.[33] Others came from outsiders with no apparent political connections.[34] It is often not possible to identify either origins or author even tentatively and the snap attributions of contemporaries, the most useful of whom for this purpose is Horace Walpole, are not always reliable. Nor is detailed information on the sizes of editions readily available, although the normal edition was probably 500.[35] Even if figures were more certain, they would not be an accurate indication of readership which, for all forms of political comment in the eighteenth century, always considerably exceeded the number of copies published. The impact of individual pamphlets can, however, be roughly gauged from such things as the way they were advertised[36] and the notices given them in other publications, the reviews, newspapers and magazines, notices which at the same time extended their influence.

Especially in the monthly reviews, these notices were in themselves pieces of political comment. Of the eighteenth-century reviews the *Monthly Review*, founded in 1749, and the *Critical Review*, founded in 1756, were by far the most important, both because of the length of their careers which outlasted the century and because of the quality and comprehensiveness of their contributions on a wide variety of literature. The *Monthly*'s circulation rose above 3,000 and it was widely distributed in the country. Its rival's circulation was probably similar.[37] Political pamphlets were usually noted briefly in their 'Monthly Catalogue', rather than in main reviews.

---

[33] e.g. [John Douglas], *Seasonable Hints From An Honest Man*, London, 1761, and [Philip Francis], *A Letter From The Cocoa-Tree To The Country Gentlemen*, London, 1762, both widely regarded as Court or Government manifestos.

[34] Perhaps the most striking example is [Alexander Carlyle], *Plain Reasons For Removing A certain Great Man From His M[ajest]y's Presence and Councils for ever*, London, 1759, which had a considerable impact but which came apparently spontaneously from the pen of a Scottish divine. See below pp. 130–1.

[35] Brewer, *Party Ideology*, p. 146, gives information for the 1760s which suggests a standard edition of 500, rising to 1,500–3,000 and very occasionally 5,000 for more successful works.

[36] Pamphlets were usually advertised for about two weeks. If, after that, a title is added to the advertisement of another pamphlet as 'Where also may be had', lagging sales may be suspected.

[37] Walter Graham, *English Literary Periodicals*, New York, 1930, pp. 211–14; Brewer, *Party Ideology*, p. 147.

Brevity did not compromise comprehensiveness, however; the two reviews include between them notices of all political works which made any kind of contemporary impression.[38] The notices give some indication of the content of the works (useful when the works themselves cannot be located) and can suggest indirectly their relative importance. They also reflect among other things the subtle distinctions which defined 'Whig' or 'Tory' attitudes. Writers in the *Monthly Review* generally shared the Whig and dissenting views of its editor, Ralph Griffiths, while the *Critical Review* was founded as a Tory riposte to it.[39] Although politics was far from being their main purpose, undoubtedly both reviews helped to extend the range of political comment.

Of other periodical publications, the monthly magazines were the most substantial. The pattern was set by the *Gentleman's Magazine* founded in 1731. Of a number of other examples its most important rival was the *London Magazine* begun the next year. They were compendia of news and the wide-ranging information considered necessary to well-informed gentlemen, providing vivid evidence of the omnivorous yet naïve curiosity of the ordinary educated man of the Enlightenment. Although accounts of debates in Parliament (published after the session) were a fairly regular feature, the magazines, like the reviews, were not primarily political. Yet they took notice of political and foreign events of importance and at times of excitement included comment in the form of extracts from pamphlets and papers, letters, and even verse. There is little to suggest that controversial material was written specifically for them and only occasionally did they review works. They are important for their circulation if nothing else. Dr Johnson estimated that the

[38] A check against newspaper advertisements shows few gaps. Cf. Thomas R. Adams, 'The British Pamphlets of the American Revolution for 1774: A Progress Report', *Proceedings of the Massachusetts Historical Society*, lxxxi (1969), p. 40.

[39] Benjamin C. Nangle, *The Monthly Review First Series 1749–1789. Indexes of Contributors and Articles*, Oxford, 1934, pp. v–xi; Claude E. Jones, 'Contributors to the *Critical Review* 1756–1785', *Modern Language Notes*, lxi, 7 (Nov. 1946), 433–41. From 1756 to 1763, most of the *Monthly Review*'s political notices were written by Owen Ruffhead, a lawyer and pamphleteer of prodigious industry, and a few in 1756–7 by James Ralph, dramatist, political writer, and author of the essay paper, the *Protestor*. Nangle, pp. 35, 39. The *Critical Review*, according to Tobias Smollett who helped in its foundation and wrote at least some of its political reviews, was conducted by four men of 'proved abilities' (possibly Dr Thomas Francklin, David Mallet, Griffith Jones, and Joseph Robertson). Graham, p. 213.

Gentleman's Magazine sold 10,000 copies per issue.[40] Of a roughly similar nature on a yearly rather than a monthly basis was the *Annual Register*. From its foundation in 1757 it gives an invaluable indication of what was thought worthy of record from the previous year, in political debate and controversy as well as events and general literature. Its circulation has been estimated at more than 3,000.[41]

The most frequent of the regular vehicles of political reporting and comment were, of course, the newspapers and allied forms like the political essay paper. From tenuous and evanescent beginnings in the upheavals of the seventeenth century they had grown and developed, especially after the lapsing of the Licensing Act in 1695 which removed official pre-publication control. By the middle of the eighteenth century they had reached some maturity. The development of revenue from advertising especially from the 1730s, together with joint-stock ownership (usually by booksellers) rather than individual ownership by printers, had given them some commercial viability and a degree of financial independence from political subsidy.[42] The circulation of individual papers was still limited, partly by technical considerations, to an average of not much over 2,000,[43] but the number of papers was growing.

All of course contained news, but they varied widely in their interest in politics. This could be conveyed as desired through selected and slanted news reports, or in different forms of comment such as paragraphs in embryonic editorial style, essays and letters, and extracts from pamphlets and other works. Three main types of paper were produced in London. The morning dailies were for metropolitan circulation and contained mainly news and advertisements but sometimes some letters or an essay. Led by the *Gazetteer* from the late 1750s, they were to develop their correspondence columns as forums of politcal debate. The *Public Advertiser*

[40] Brewer, *Party Ideology*, p. 147.   [41] Ibid.

[42] The survival of Walpole's propaganda organ, the *Gazetteer*, after it lost its Government subsidies with his fall, is the best example of the importance of these developments. Robert L. Haig, *The Gazetteer 1735—1797*, Carbondale. Ill., 1960, ch. II *passim*, p. 33.

[43] D. Nichol Smith, 'The Newspaper', *Johnson's England*, ed. A. S. Turberville, 2 vols., Oxford, 1933, ii, pp. 332, 334. The evidence Brewer has gathered (*Party Ideology*, p. 143) shows that the circulation of a major daily like the *Public Advertiser*, having steadily risen in the later 1760s, had reached a minimum of 3,000 by 1770, but the *Public Advertiser* was a paper of exceptional reputation rivalled only by the *Gazetteer*.

followed the trend in the early 1760s as did the *Public Ledger* from its
foundation in 1760. The first two were to be the most influential
dailies of the 1760s. The tri-weekly evening papers were brought out
on the post days and circulated in the country as well as London.
The older Posts, like the *Whitehall Evening Post,* were largely news
and advertisements; the newer Chronicles like the *London Chronicle,*
begun in 1757, were generally more varied in content than the
dailies, attempting to offer a rounded coverage to country readers
without ready access to other publications. The *London Evening Post,*
the most popular of the evening papers, was extraordinary amongst
them for its long-standing and vigorous opposition to government.[44]
It reflected the views of the City middling sort but was widely copied
in provincial papers. The weeklies also included papers that were
amalgams of news and advertisements for country readers, like
Read's Weekly Journal and others more varied in content, like *Owen's
Weekly Chronicle.* By 1760 London had four dailies, five or six
tri-weeklies, and about four weeklies including news. In all there
were eighty-nine papers paying advertisement duties in the metropolis.[45] Provincial papers, generally weeklies, had also developed
greatly in the first part of the century and by 1760 numbered about
thirty-five.[46] Total annual sales of all papers may have been ten
million.[47] Again it must be remembered that readership, bolstered
particularly in the coffee-houses which were such a vital part of
urban social intercourse, far exceeded circulation. Contemporaries
variously estimated it as between twenty and fifty readers per
copy.[48]

There is much still to be pieced together from diverse sources
about the financing, management, and authorship of papers in this
period which would elucidate their involvement in politics. There is,
however, no doubt that by the 1750s newpapers were well-

[44] G. A. Cranfield, 'The *London Evening Post,* 1727–44: A study in the Development
of the Political Press', *Historical Journal,* vi, 1 (1963), 20–37; 'The *London Evening Post*
and the Jew Bill of 1753', *Historical Journal,* viii, 1 (1965), 16–30.

[45] Ian R. Christie, 'British Newspapers in the Later Georgian Age', *Myth and
Reality* [*in Late-Eighteenth-Century British Politics and other Papers*], London, 1970, p. 314;
Brewer, *Party Ideology,* p. 142.

[46] G. A. Cranfield, *The Development of the Provincial Newspaper 1700–1760,* Oxford,
1962, p. 21.

[47] *Politics and Literature* [*in the Eighteenth Century*], ed. H. T. Dickinson, London,
1974, p. xx.

[48] Brewer, *Party Ideology,* p. 148.

established and vigorous. And the next ten to fifteen years were to be another important growing point. Encouraged by the exciting events of the Seven Years' War and the unsettled politics and controversy of the 1760s, this growth showed itself in both the appearance of new papers and the development of the political and other content of those already established.

In the late 1750s and early 1760s political debate in the press was still initiated and shaped by pamphlets and the political essay papers. Comment in newspapers usually followed and often directly copied the lines thus established.[49] It was as yet, by force of circumstances, more repetitive and less weighty; only in the later 1760s did newspapers learn to use the advantages of regular appearance. The pamphlets and essay papers also showed more variety of argument and marked differences of loyalty, especially obvious in the period following Pitt's resignation in 1761 when newspapers on the whole remained faithful to him. So pamphlets and essays provide the stuff of debate, the varying impact of which can be tested from time to time by its reverberations in newspapers.[50]

Beyond the pamphlet and newspaper, a wide range of ephemera was published: *affiches* stuck up in public places, broadsides and handbills passed from hand to hand, ballads sung noisily in the streets and published in handbills, and political prints. It would be very difficult to make a reliable estimate of the numbers and character of the first three: no readily accessible collections exist, random survivals only are known, and no work has been done on them comparable to that on the ballads of Walpole's period.[51] Yet the comments of contemporaries leave no doubt that such productions had some influence. Political prints have been much better served. A printed catalogue exists of the major collection and a most valuable recent study of them has been made.[52]

[49] The evening papers, especially *LC*, *UC* and *Lloyd's EP* in the 1750s, used *Mon.* as a substantial part of their political comment. The statement of intent in the opening number of *OWC*, 8 Apr. 1758, suggests that readers expected news and extracts, not original comment, from such papers.

[50] A list of the newspapers used in this study to test the trends of debate at significant times is given in Appendix I.

[51] *Political Ballads Illustrating the Administration of Sir Robert Walpole*, ed. Milton Percival, Oxford, 1916.

[52] *Cat[alogue of] Prints and Drawings [in the British Museum. Division I. Political and Personal Satires]*, ed. Frederick George Stephens and Mary Dorothy George, 11 vols., London, 1870–1954. Herbert M. Atherton, *Political Prints in the Age of Hogarth. A Study of the Ideographic Representation of Politics*, Oxford, 1974.

The English political print was born of Dutch parentage in the 1720s, and rapidly grew to maturity, reaching an early peak of production in the 1730s in the excitement of opposition to Walpole and yet another in the period of the Seven Years' War. Prints were produced in small editions and although comparatively cheap were not intended for a mass market. Yet, because they were displayed profusely in the windows of the numerous print shops which spread right along the main route from London to Westminster and into many of its byways, they must have had an impact on contemporaries not far short of modern advertising.[53] They were an integral part of the visual world of eighteenth-century London, just as they captured much of its variety and detail in their cluttered frames. Seldom produced explicitly for partisan political purposes or supported by politicians, they do not provide a close commentary on politics and only occasionally do they become 'important weapons in the arena of political strife', for example over the Treaty of Paris in 1762–3. They describe general attitudes more than particular responses. Yet their account of these general attitudes as purveyed to the ordinary man is 'continuous and incisive'. As a means of roughly testing the political temperature they are invaluable.[54]

All in all, in the mid-eighteenth century, there was a wide range of political commentary catering for a variety of audiences extending well down among the 'lesser sort'. Institutions like coffee houses carried the comment to those who could not or would not pay for their own papers and pamphlets and provided a milieu for discussion of their contents and of politics generally. 'Bridging' devices like ballads and prints carried the message to the semi-literate and non-literate.[55] This rich variety of comment would not have been produced unless it found a market. Its very existence indicates the presence of a broad political nation, well informed and actively interested, around and beyond the world of Whitehall, Westminster, and the local fiefs of oligarchs, or the comfortable constituencies of country gentlemen and city merchants.

There remain, however, substantial questions about how far this varied political comment can be said to reflect the opinions of the nation and thus to be a measure of Pitt's popular reputation. The comment cannot be taken at face value, because all its modes of

---

[53] Atherton, ch. I *passim*, pp. 63–4, 81.

[54] Ibid., pp. vi, 1 (second quotation), 67, 68, 83 (first quotation), 188–9, 260–3.

[55] Brewer, *Party Ideology*, p. 155; Rogers, 'London Politics', pp. 511–21.

expression were devices for influencing more than spontaneously expressing public opinion. Few of them, from pamphlets to prints, came into existence without financial support of some kind apart from sales and advertising, whether or not such support was overtly political. The more established of the newspapers may have been striving for independence from direct subsidies and boasting of impartiality in their views. None, however, was large enough in sales or organization to be immune from the various more subtle advantages governments could offer, such as official advertisements or priority in receiving news. Comment was written more for, than by, public opinion. It shows not the spontaneous concerns of the political nation but rather what various interested parties thought they could excite opinion about. And those interested parties so often cannot be precisely identified.

This problem is not unique to the eighteenth century. Political comment by journalists, cartoonists, and pamphleteers in any period always both reflects and manipulates public opinion. The degree to which it succeeds in either is virtually impossible to distinguish. Even in the days of opinion polls it is legitimate to question how far public opinion exists in measurable and influential form apart from the instruments which mould it and the interest groups which help to compose it. Assessing opinion by means of political comment is always working at one remove, from reflection in a possibly distorting mirror.

Yet it would be ridiculously fastidious to reject the comment altogether as evidence of opinion, in the eighteenth century or any other period, just as it would be to reject the formal modes of expression of public opinion, such as petitions and addresses, simply because both were often not spontaneous. Opinion cannot be wholly created out of nothing, where no predisposition to interest exists. Indeed the readiness with which outbursts could arise in the eighteenth century, for example over Walpole's excise scheme in 1733, the Jew Bill in 1753, the fall of Minorca in 1756 and the East India Bill in 1783, suggests a body of interested opinion ready to react. Nor can opinion be manipulated effectively unless the propaganda is acceptable to its audience. Its influence will be the more effective the closer the means used are to the ways of thought of the audience, the nearer they touch the nerves of its political awareness. So, even when there is still much more to discover about the patronage and authorship of the organs of propaganda which would clarify their political purpose, much can be deduced from their content alone. The fluctuating volume of report and comment gives some indication of the degree of public interest and the subjects which aroused it. More important, the arguments used and the objections it was felt necessary to answer can reveal how the readers saw politics. Used in this way, the comment is rich evidence of a past culture and of the political perceptions of ordinary men. Propaganda will always be a very imprecise measure of the extent and degree of Pitt's popularity; but it is invaluable on the even more important questions of why he was praised and defended, where he was vulnerable, how he was attacked. It demonstrates the public image on which his popularity was based.

* * * * * *

The more one delves into the political comment of the eighteenth century the more striking does its most outstanding characteristic become. The great outbursts of controversy and the continuing themes of discussion alike dwell on a limited number of subjects. Considerable areas which concerned politicians were simply ignored. In the 1750s and 1760s the most obvious example is Ireland, which constantly featured in the correspondence of politicians but hardly appeared in propaganda. Almost as striking is the very partial cover given to the Seven Years' War. Operations in India were scarcely mentioned. The 'Black Hole of Calcutta' hardly raised an eyebrow. Instead of discussing the events of the war as they actually unfolded, debate was concentrated on a few issues, especially the Continental war. In all, in domestic and foreign affairs, there is a stereotyped inelasticity of response which seems to call in question the nature of public interest. Interest was undoubtedly there but it was peculiarly susceptible to manipulation according to set prejudices. As yet, there was not the continuous and close involvement in politics that could produce a more informed and specific response.

This outstanding characteristic of eighteenth-century political discussion is particularly important in assessing the nature of Pitt's popularity. It has been generally assumed that popularity came in response to the promise and realization of success in war and meant the good opinion of 'the people', the political nation in general. In fact in eighteenth-century terminology popularity was something more precise. It was won by the advocacy of a particular set of attitudes and policies which brought the support of specific political groups. These attitudes and policies are the dominant stereotype that shaped public responses to politics.

This stereotype view is best described by the term 'country'. Rooted in seventeenth-century experience and argument, especially that of the early Whigs of the Exclusion crisis, and adopted and shaped by eighteenth-century polemicists in opposition to government, it was the typical reaction of those not close to the heart of high politics.[56] They believed their views reflected the true interests of the nation at large, the country, against a small corrupt faction, the Court and its minions. In this sense, the precise eighteenth-century sense of the word, they were 'patriots', devoted to the true interests of their country (constitutional as much as foreign) above any selfish ambition for place.[57]

In domestic affairs the major stimulus shaping country attitudes was a revulsion against the arts of political management made necessary by the uncertain constitutional balance emerging from the seventeenth-century turmoil and so deftly practised by Walpole. Closely connected was the smaller man's distrust of modern public finance and the bureaucratic state, a distrust which grew with these developments themselves from the later seventeenth century, and arose from the fear of absolutist tyranny which might be based on administrative and financial efficiency. This revulsion and distrust showed themselves in a deep suspicion of the executive and in calls for constitutional reforms, such as shorter parliaments and the exclusion of placemen and pensioners from the House of Commons, designed to keep the constitution true to its 'first principles'.

With these political and constitutional concerns went a set of attitudes to foreign policy equally well established in political debate. They had developed first in reaction to the decisive new bent towards full involvement in Europe given to English foreign policy by William III. In response to the consequent strategy of full-scale participation in military campaigns on the Continent two divergent views crystallized. One accepted that such involvement and parti-

[56] For some account of the origins and development of these ideas, with bibliographical references, see Marie Peters, 'The *Monitor* on the constitution, 1755–1765: new light on the ideological origins of English radicalism', *English Historical Review*, lxxxvi (Oct. 1971), esp. pp. 719–23.

[57] Examples in the *Oxford English Dictionary* make it clear that this usage of the word became established in the seventeenth-century constitutional struggles, especially from *c*.1680.

cipation were in accordance with English interests and security. The other, strongly tinged with xenophobia, maintained rather that English concerns were being subordinated to those of the foreign dominions of her new King, and English resources wastefully frittered away in expensive Continental campaigns and subsidies to foreign allies. Concentration on the navy and the colonies would better promote the true English interests of trade and security and serve the common cause of resistance to the ambitions of France. England should not be involved as a principal in the struggle to preserve the balance of power in Europe. Rather she should take a narrower view of her national security. Fears of the constitutional threat of a standing army and advocacy of a militia in its stead were associated with these views from their first development in the 1690s. When England's involvement in European affairs was given a new twist by the accession of the Hanoverians and their devotion to Hanover, the tradition of opposition was adapted to the new circumstances. Protests against the subordination of English interests to Hanover and against the expense of subsidies and Continental war continued to be heard in foreign policy debates throughout the first part of the century, particularly in Pitt's vehement speeches of the early 1740s.

This complex of political, constitutional, and foreign policy attitudes became the traditional substance of eighteenth-century opposition propaganda, habitually invoked to mobilize opinion and powerfully shaping responses to politics, especially in crises. The attitudes appeared in their most stereotyped and crudely simplified form in the prints.[58] But they were pervasive in all forms of comment, because they met the needs of those excluded, for one reason or another, from close participation in government and expressed the manifold dissatisfactions masked by apparent Hanoverian stability. So country views were held with varying degrees of sincerity and intensity by ambitious politicians out of office, country gentlemen innocent of politics and bewildered by changing times, Tories reduced to a country rump by long proscription by the Whigs, and the middling sort of the City of London, increasingly aggrieved at their exclusion from adequate political influence and at odds with the landed class who had such influence. The *Monitor* blared out the country programme in its opening

[58] Atherton, ch. V *passim*, pp. 262–4.

maxims and defended it all its life.

Thus patriotism became virtually synonymous with high-minded opposition to government (although the identification was not allowed to pass without challenge[59]). 'Popularity' was won by a patriotic stand, that is by adoption of the country programme. It meant specifically the support of those to whom that programme particularly appealed. In Parliament the most readily identifiable and useful were the Tories, all of whom, whether reactionary or populist, held country ideas to some degree. Out of doors Tory support was diffused. There the most useful support popularity could bring came from the middling sort of the City of London, Tory or otherwise, who dominated its corporate bodies.

* * * * * *

Such support came to Pitt in strength more or less by chance in the later 1750s but cultivation of it by means of a patriotic stance was peculiarly well suited to his unusual character and political situation. Birth had not given him wide acres or the influence that went with them; the imperious aloof arrogance of his personality and his distaste for normal social intercourse[60] made him incapable of being a party man. He could or would not practise the arts which, with his ability, could have carried him to high office by more normal means. Even his relations with the Grenvilles were erratic, to say the least. Given his universally acknowledged powers of oratory combined with this personality, he was much better suited to appeal from above to the adulation of the people than to co-operate with colleagues in the normal workings of political connections.

If Pitt's personality made such a lofty appeal to the people a feasible political strategy for him, so too it aided him in making the appeal successful. His contempt for the aristocratic battalions, his ostentatious independence (part of the patriot ideal), his aggressive challenges to all who questioned or opposed, his matchless political courage and spirit in the conduct of the war, his magnificent plans that would brook no odds whether well or ill considered, all these

[59] The *Oxford English Dictionary* gives examples of derogatory uses of the term. See also Betty Kemp, 'Patriotism, Pledges and the People', *A Century of Conflict 1850–1950*, ed. Martin Gilbert, London, 1966, p. 39.

[60] Waldegrave, p. 16; Lord Edmond Fitzmaurice, [*Life of William, Earl of*] *Shelburne*, [*afterwards First Marquess of Lansdowne with Extracts from his Papers and Correspondence*], 3 vols., London, 1875–6, i, p. 77.

struck chords in the hearts of lesser men and gave them vicarious satisfaction. His abstemious personal life contrasted vividly with what they expected of high politics. He was an 'outsider in politics who scorned to play the game according to the accepted rules',[61] and others outside relished it.

The appeal was further enhanced by the artifice which was so large a part of his public image and even of his character.[62] His affected disdain for the bread and butter of political patronage and the normal cultivation of political power while he ostentatiously concentrated on great plans for national glory made a profound impression on contemporaries. Most of them took him at his face value. For them, despite minor setbacks, 'he still and will ever maintain credit, in that disinterestedness which makes him neglect the disposal of Places . . . and retain nothing but that active Power, which is to determine the weight and Interest of Great Britain throughout the World'.[63]

Although, as both Waldegrave and Walpole perceived, the appeal to popularity was 'contrary to his temper',[64] the real and the artificial combined eventually to make Pitt's personality his biggest asset in that appeal. The grip it exercised over the imagination of contemporaries made it possible for them to believe that he conformed to the patriot image long after he had broken most of the promises that won his reputation. It helped him to use popularity as no other politician before him had, not only to push into high office but also, with some success, as his major political strength in office. The difficulty of this task was emphasized indirectly by the prints; they were much more at ease with him as a model patriot when he was in opposition than when in office, a situation much less congenial to the patriot picture.[65] The appeal of Pitt's personality, materially aided by the background of national crisis and war, made success possible.

Pitt's success in keeping popularity in office gave him that independent political strength which was essential to an outsider who had broken through 'the chains of government by connexion'.[66]

[61] John B. Owen, *The Eighteenth Century [1714–1815]*, London, 1974, p. 93.

[62] Fitzmaurice, *Shelburne,* i. pp. 75–7.

[63] Lady Anne Egerton to Bentinck, 23 Mar. [1759], cf. same to same, 27 Apr. 1761, Eg. 1719, ff. 34, 240.

[64] Waldegrave, pp. 15–16; Walpole, *Geo. III,* ii, p. 67.

[65] Atherton, p. 255.

[66] L. S. Sutherland, 'The City [of London] in Eighteenth-Century Politics', *Essays presented to Sir Lewis Namier,* ed. Richard Pares and A. J. P. Taylor, London, 1956, p. 64.

His reputation was also of vital importance to his strength as a war minister. It is not easy to analyse precisely where that strength lay. It came not so much from any originality of strategy or administrative breakthrough,[67] although undoubtedly he had breadth and confidence of vision and energy and grasp of detail.[68] His strength came rather from the psychological impact of his personality, his ability to dominate his Cabinet colleagues, to inspire the confidence—or fear—of individuals and the devotion of the nation.[69] In so far as he made a decisive contribution to victory—and contemporaries certainly believed he did—this was where it lay. It is doubly important, therefore, to understand how and to what extent he kept his reputation untarnished and so prevented policy from being diverted by a need to fight for political survival.

There is little to suggest that the foundations of popularity laid in Pitt's early career contributed much to his political strength and, after the quietude of his years in office under the Pelhams, they might well have crumbled entirely had they not been strengthened and built on in the 1750s. Then, however, the most striking feature of the public discussion of his reputation became the universal admission, by friend and foe alike,[70] of the claim that he had won power by unusual means through popularity and appeal as a patriot. This was often established by contrast with Newcastle and especially Fox, the very antitheses of patriots.[71] With scant regard for reality, admirers obstinately interpreted the 'achievements' of his

---

[67] Richard Pares, 'American versus Continental Warfare, 1739–63', *English Historical Review*, li (July 1936), 460; Paul Langford, *The Eighteenth Century*, London, 1976, pp. 141–2; Richard Middleton, 'Pitt, Anson and the Admiralty, 1756–1761', *History*, lv (June 1970), 189–98, esp. 197–8.

[68] 'I know nobody who can plan or push the execution of any plan agreed upon in the manner Mr Pitt did.' Newcastle to Hardwicke, 15 Nov. 1761, Philip C. Yorke, *The Life and Correspondence of Philip Yorke, Earl of Hardwicke, Lord High Chancellor of Great Britain*, 3 vols., Cambridge, 1913, iii, p. 339 and cf. footnote.

[69] Namier and Brooke, iii, p. 294; Owen, *The Eighteenth Century*, pp. 92–3.

[70] e.g. by friends in *A Vindication of Mr Pitt*, London, 1758, pp. 3, 44, 45; [Alexander Carlyle], *Plain Reasons* (see above fn. 34), p. 7; and by foes in *Considerations on the Proceedings of a General Court-Martial*, London, 1758, pp. 4–5, 34–5, 37; [John Perceval, Earl of Egmont], *Things As They Are*, London, 1758, pp. 25–7; [George Bubb Dodington], *An Examination of a Letter Published under the name of L[ieutenan]t G[enera]l B[lig]h*, London, 1758, pp. 39–42.

[71] e.g. *A Letter To His Grace the D[uke] of N[ewcastl]e, on The Duty he owes himself, his King, his Country and his God, At This Important Moment*, London, 1757, pp. 24 to end. See also Atherton, ch. VIII, esp. p. 252.

first Ministry of 1756–7 and his role in the Coalition from 1757 in accordance with the patriot creed, exaggerating or even inventing what conformed to it, excusing or omitting all that did not, and dismissing all criticism as 'faction'.[72] Opponents did not deny the claims to popularity and patriotism. Rather they sought to discredit them by suggesting that the popularity was unsoundly based, won by artifice from the giddy multitude who had no judgement in political affairs, that Pitt used it unscrupulously, and that the patriotic stands were insincere and inconsistent with previous or current actions.[73] His earlier career was now assessed and reassessed in the glow of his current reputation, again by admirers and detractors alike.[74] There was enough in his past to support the dominant theme of patriotic virtue; yet its dramatic volte-faces and excesses now assumed a new significance because they could throw corrosive doubt on his sincerity and give volume to the counter-pointing theme that he was only a mock or renegade patriot. This theme had first been announced in reaction to Pulteney's behaviour after the fall of Walpole. It was sounded briefly about Pitt in the 1740s.[75] Now in the late 50s it was established as a secondary theme,[76] to rise to shrill heights in the 1760s. To a politician depending on the normal supports of connection and royal favour such public discussion of his reputation, had it occurred, would have mattered little. To Pitt, having deliberately made his appeal to reputation, it was crucial that he could protect himself against the charges of inconsistency for which the normal course of politics and policy-making was likely to give many openings.

Historians can hardly ignore this almost universal contemporary stereotype of Pitt. An assessment of it is the object of this study. The assessment is focused on the City of London, where the evidence is rich and can be attributed with some precision, and on the

---

[72] e.g. [Alexander Carlyle], *Plain Reasons*.

[73] e.g. the *Test*, 1756–7, *passim*; the *Constitution* 1 and 2, 1757; *A Letter From The Duchess of M[a]r[lborou]gh, In The Shades, To The Great Man*, London, 1759, *passim; A Defence Of The Letter from the Dutchess of M[arlboroug]h*, London, 1759, pp. 32–3, 59–61.

[74] e.g. [John Douglas], *A Letter Addressed To Two Great Men*, second edn., London, 1760, p. 50, an ironical reflection of the by then accepted view.

[75] [Richard Glover], *Memoirs [by a Celebrated Literary and Political Character from . . . 1742 to . . . 1757]*, second edn., London, 1814, p. 43; Atherton, pp. 255–6.

[76] A very early example of a hostile reassessment emphasizing Pitt's inconsistencies is *A New System of Patriot Policy Containing The Genuine Recantations of The British Cicero*, London, 1756.

metropolitan press, less easily attributed but even more rich in comment. Provincial opinion can at present be sketched only occasionally to give some comparison and contrast, from such evidence as instructions and addresses. Yet such an assessment can show the substance behind Pitt's reputation and its significance, in both strengthening and limiting his political options. It can illustrate contemporary perceptions of politics. It may also illuminate something of the complex connection between ideology and political action, by showing that what polemicists thundered and ordinary men thought not only rationalized the actions of politicians after the event but also could powerfully influence what they were able to do.

I

Pitt in Search of a Strategy 1754–1756

In 1754, at the age of forty-five and after nearly twenty years in politics, Pitt had reached office of only middle rank as Paymaster General of the Forces. Of modest although not negligible family background, he owed something in his early political career to his connection with the 'cousinhood', George Lyttelton and the Grenvilles, begun at Eton and continued in Parliament under the initial patronage of Lord Cobham. Under the nicknames of the Boy Patriots or Cobham's Cubs they had achieved some notoriety in opposition to Walpole. Pitt owed even more to his forceful and aggressive oratory which had encouraged the Pelhams to accept him as an ally in 1744. By the 1750s it had given him a mastery of debate in the House of Commons rivalled only by William Murray, later Lord Mansfield.[1]

He was seriously hampered, however, by the intense dislike of the King. This had been first aroused by his connection in opposition in the late 1730s with the Prince of Wales. Even worse was his outspoken anti-Hanoverianism in the early 1740s, when, with his patron, he broke with the Prince and remained in opposition. This dislike had not been at all mitigated by his marked change of front since the Pelhams demanded office for him in 1746, as Vice-Treasurer for Ireland and then as Paymaster General. After that, for eight years, his career had stagnated, his youthful fire apparently quenched. He served the Pelhams well. They valued him, but as a colleague of second rank whose claims to higher office they had no need to press against a hostile King. Now, in 1754, Pitt was of the same age as Walpole when he seized the great opening of his career.

---

[1] Sedgwick, *House of Commons*, ii, p. 356.

Yet Pitt's previous attainments and present situation seemed to offer little hope of emulation.

Then in March 1754 the death of Henry Pelham unexpectedly opened possibilities. In the arrangements that would have to be made for leadership of the House of Commons when the Duke of Newcastle succeeded his brother at the Treasury, Pitt had some hope of promotion. Yet the opportunity would have to be fought for against substantial difficulties. The claims of the chief contestant for promotion, Henry Fox, Secretary at War, were much more obvious. Fox was a close associate of the Pelhams and protégé of the Duke of Cumberland, the King's favourite son. Newcastle was jealous of any serious rival, whether Pitt or Fox, neither he nor Hardwicke was convinced that Pitt's claims had to be pressed, and the King was unremittingly hostile to Pitt. In the ensuing struggle, not finally settled until June 1757, Pitt's political skill in developing his resources against these considerable odds was fully demonstrated.

The initial opportunity found Pitt in Bath, incapacitated by his already chronic gout. In an unusually full series of letters to his friends[2] he outlined the tactics he thought appropriate. He advocated no threatening assertion of their claims. Indeed the Lyttelton–Grenville connection was hardly strong enough for that.[3] Instead, a skilful exploitation from within of the difficulties of the Administration might persuade Newcastle to greater efforts to win for Pitt those marks of royal favour which could give 'consideration and weight in the House of Commons'. Despite his recognition that Newcastle's and Hardwicke's 'own fears and resentments' were 'the only friends we shall ever have at Court', his letters suggest a genuine disposition to moderation and co-operation. Negotiation from within was clearly his favoured tactic. Yet he was determined not to wait much longer for greater recognition of his 'long-depressed' group (to say nothing of his own ambitions), and he had other lines of action in consideration. The Court-to-be at Leicester House was much in his mind. Its support was not an immediate alternative to royal favour for there was as yet no overt breach in the Royal Family. But in view of the King's age, Leicester House was likely soon to be of the greatest importance. A good reputation there could even now be

---

[2] The locations of these letters, most of them printed, are given in Basil Williams, *The Life of William Pitt Earl of Chatham*, 2 vols., London, 1915, i, p. 249.

[3] Waldegrave, p. 25.

valuable as a means of pressure on Newcastle. Further still, Pitt remembered that, if all else failed, 'consideration and weight in the House of Commons' could also come from 'weight in the Country, sometimes arising from opposition to the public measures'. He expressed satisfaction that he had renounced his earlier opposition. Yet if Newcastle would not fight for the essential royal favour Pitt might try to force it himself this way.[4]

So were foreshadowed, in hints rather than as a fully worked-out strategy, the ways Pitt was to respond to changing circumstances in the prolonged struggle of the next three years. None was new. In fact there were precedents for all in Pitt's earlier career, except for the finesse of his first approaches designed to overcome royal disfavour from within. Opposition to create a nuisance and increase negotiating strength had been a recognized and successful if not entirely respectable tactic as least since Walpole and Townshend had resorted to it in 1717–20. Pitt himself had exploited it in the early 1740s. The opposition to Walpole, to which Pitt had contributed, had learnt to marshall 'weight in the Country' through the varied means of propaganda and through expressions of public opinion from the counties, the City of London, and other corporations. Public opinion so marshalled could potently affect independent members in the House and even, in critical circumstances, could sway the votes of ministerial supporters.[5] It had certainly embarrassed Walpole and even more certainly would alarm Newcastle, especially in a disturbed situation. If such tactics were decided on, Pitt could turn again to the ready-made 'patriot' rhetoric on both domestic and foreign issues.

After his alliance with the Pelhams he had turned his back very firmly on the beginnings of a popular reputation and of links with the City of London, arising from his earlier opposition and his consequent dismissal, in 1736, from his commission in the Army.[6] Yet his refusal of the normal valuable perquisites of his office as

[4] Pitt to Lyttelton and the Grenvilles, 7 Mar. 1754, Pitt to Temple, 11, 24 Mar. 1754, [*The*] *Grenville Papers*, ed. William James Smith , 4 vols., London, 1852–3, i, pp. 106–10, 112–14 (second and third quotations), 115–17; Pitt to Lyttelton, 10 Mar. 1754 (2 letters), Yorke, *Hardwicke*, ii, pp. 201–4 (first and last quotations).

[5] See e.g. Paul Langford, [*The*] *Excise Crisis. [Society and Politics in the Age of Walpole]*, Oxford, 1975, pp. 66–71, 80–1.

[6] On links with Glover and Glover's standing in the City see Glover, *Mems.*, pp. viii, 12, 86–7; Namier and Brooke, ii, p. 504.

Paymaster, following Pelham's example, was some further investment in reputation for future use. He could perhaps now revert to opposition with advantage and without too much embarrassment from charges of inconsistency. As the precedents of 1717–20 and 1737–42 showed, opposition could be potently strengthened by the support of Leicester House if a breach occurred in the Royal Family. Patriot opposition rhetoric, particularly its anti-Hanoverianism, was most congenial to the Leicester House of the mid-1750s.[7] Yet both opposition and alliance with Leicester House needed a suitable major issue to be effective. It remained to be seen what use Pitt could make of either if subtler tactics failed.

In the arrangements of March 1754 by which Newcastle became First Lord of the Treasury, the Grenvilles and their friends received some crumbs of satisfaction. But Pitt himself remained absolutely barred from promotion by the royal veto.[8] His apparently resigned acceptance and talk of retirement, expressed at great length to Hardwicke, proved less lasting than his indignation and hints of a refusal to co-operate in the Commons, expressed to Newcastle.[9] Fox, too, had been disappointed by Newcastle's limited offers. Soon both Fox and Pitt made their weight felt. In the parliamentary session of 1754–5, they joined in devastating harassment of those to whom Newcastle committed government business in the House, chiefly Sir Thomas Robinson and William Murray. Newcastle—and others—were potently reminded that Pitt's youthful fires of oratory would not necessarily remain quenched. However, this alliance began to fall apart almost immediately. As difficulties grew, Newcastle made further approaches to Fox, who was admitted to the Cabinet in December. Then in March 1755 he and his patron, the Duke of Cumberland, were made Lords Justices in the Council of Regency appointed when the King left for Hanover.[10] Pitt, again thwarted, angry and genuinely puzzled at the way his abilities were passed over, was increasingly disillusioned of any hopes of

[7] John Brooke, [*King*] *George III*, London, 1972, pp. 20, 56–8.

[8] Mr Grenville's Narrative, *Grenville Papers*, i, p. 430.

[9] Pitt to Hardwicke, 4 Apr. 1754, Yorke, *Hardwicke*, ii, pp. 214–16; Pitt to Newcastle, 24 Mar., 4 Apr. 1754, Lord Rosebery, *Chatham, His Early Life and Connections*, London, 1910, pp. 329–32, 335–7.

[10] Waldegrave, pp. 31–5.

advancement through Newcastle or Fox.[11] He abandoned alliance with Fox for different courses.

Others, too, had been alarmed at Cumberland's unexpected inclusion in the Regency. The Dowager Princess of Wales, uncertain of her position in unsettled circumstances, was thrown into a panic by it. Cumberland was popularly suspected of ambitions towards military dictatorship and, at the very least, of designs on the Regency and influence over the new King in the event of the early death of George II.[12] Remembering the urgings of George Bubb Dodington and advised by the Earl of Bute (newly returned to favour at Leicester House), the Princess authorized approaches to Pitt. In the early days of May agreement was reached on what was in essence a 'defensive treaty', designed 'to connect people together' to protect the interests of both Pitt and the Princess against the ambitions of Cumberland and Fox. Although the existence of the agreement was not publicly known for some time, the Princess immediately made clear her coolness towards Newcastle, while Pitt broke with Fox.[13]

So, seizing the opportunity unexpectedly offered just as the alliance with Fox was proving useless, and 'finding himself desperate at St. James's,' Pitt 'endeavoured at the reversion'.[14] But it was not clear what immediate advantage this new alliance would bring or how Pitt thought it could be used. The agreement was limited and private. The parties, like those in all Leicester House alliances, were united not in their positive aims but in their negative opposition, in this case to Cumberland and Fox. There was no commitment to political opposition, however obvious such opposition might have been as a means of enforcing the various claims of the participants. Leicester House had not been active in politics, let

---

[11] *Corr[espondence of William Pitt, Earl of] Chatham*, ed. William Stanhope Taylor and John Henry Pringle, 4 vols., London, 1838–40, i, pp. 134–7 (Pitt's undated remarks on his correspondence with Fox before the latter's admission to the Cabinet. The correspondence is wrongly dated Apr. 1755 rather than Nov.–Dec. 1754 but the remarks probably were written at the later date. See Williams, i, pp. 259–60 and fn. 2).

[12] James Lee McKelvey, *George III and Lord Bute. The Leicester House Years*, Durham, N.C., 1973, p. 16; *Letters from George III to Lord Bute [1756–1766]*, ed. Romney Sedgwick, London, 1939, pp. xlviii–xlix. Under the Regency Act of 1751 the Princess Dowager would become Regent if her son was not of age when George II died.

[13] McKelvey, pp. 18–21; *Letters from George III to Lord Bute*, pp. xlv–xlviii.

[14] Fox to Hartington, 16 July 1755, quoted Waldegrave, p. 161.

alone opposition, since Prince Frederick's death in 1751. The Princess, although now very cool towards Newcastle, was not anxious for an open breach with the King's Ministers, remembering the consequences of such a breach for her husband.[15] Yet without open avowal and determination on opposition in Parliament, the alliance could achieve little for Pitt. At most, as its existence became suspected, it might perhaps increase Newcastle's wish to satisfy him because of Newcastle's own hopes for the future and fears of the immediate consequences of a breach in the Royal Family. Even if the alliance did lead to open opposition, Leicester House could offer little in weight of numbers. It could only marginally increase the size of Pitt's tiny connection and would be unlikely, in ordinary circumstances, to shake Newcastle's majority.[16] When originally made, and even as it gradually became known, it could hardly be said to have 'transformed the whole political situation'.[17]

However, circumstances were not ordinary. Domestic political difficulties were not the only ones Newcastle's Administration was facing. Abroad, Britain was slowly slipping into renewed conflict with France over issues arising out of the expansion of trade and settlement in North America, which the Peace of Aix-la-Chapelle in 1748 and subsequent negotiations had failed to settle. French plans for a chain of forts from Montreal to New Orleans threatened to restrict the British colonies to the eastern seaboard. Hostilities were already beginning. British Ministers recognized the importance of the conflict with France in North America. Yet their response to the French was complicated by the very uncertain European situation, and above all by the threat of French reprisals against Hanover. For strategic reasons as much as out of consideration for the feelings of George II, Hanover had to be protected before Britain went to war with France. Britain's traditional allies, Austria and the Dutch, were unwilling to help on reasonable terms. In the summer of 1755, however, Hanover's security appeared to have been achieved by subsidy treaties negotiated with Russia and Hesse-Cassel.

Yet these were to bring uncomfortable consequences. Such trea-

[15] Waldegrave, p. 39; McKelvey, pp. 14–16, 20.

[16] After the 1754 election, Dupplin listed 34 supporters of the Prince of Wales in the House of Commons. Namier and Brooke, i, p. 62. Even in 1751, after a period of considerable opposition activity, Frederick's party was estimated at only 60. Sedgwick, *House of Commons*, i, p. 57.

[17] McKelvey, pp. 29–30; *Letters from George III to Lord Bute*, p. xlv (quotation).

ties, with their controversial implications of expensive involvement on the Continent, were traditionally the object of patriot rhetoric against the supposed sacrifice of British and colonial interests to those of Hanover. They were widely disliked by independent members of Parliament and even by many leading politicians. Newcastle was served with notice of trouble in August, when Legge, the Chancellor of the Exchequer, refused to sign a warrant for payments under the Hessian treaty until it had been approved by Parliament, a refusal repeated in October over the Russian treaty. Immediate signs of popular favour for this minor politician demonstrated the potential of the issue.[18]

At exactly the same time, Leicester House was being prompted to sanction more overt opposition by the King's proposal that the elder daughter of the Duchess of Brunswick Wolfenbüttel should be considered as a wife for the Prince of Wales. For various reasons the proposal was highly distasteful to the Dowager Princess. By mid-August, her links with Pitt were openly acknowledged by his warm reception at Leicester House and Kew. Pitt began exploring the possibilities created by this now-avowed connection combined with the issue of the subsidy treaties.[19]

Newcastle, too, was prompted to action by the prospect of a difficult parliamentary passage for the subsidy treaties. From April 1756 onwards various approaches were made to Pitt for his support. Although initially reasonable, Pitt became steadily more intransigent and demanding. He took a firm stand on the subsidy treaties and was determined not to be satisfied without a major role in policy-making and patronage.[20] Clearly he calculated that he could now best improve his opportunities not by bargaining but by keeping clear of the Ministry as its difficulties mounted and exploiting the subsidies issue and his Leicester House connection. A stand on the subsidies would not be inconsistent with at least part of

18 Rigby to Bedford, 21 Aug. 1755, *Corr[espondence of John, fourth Duke of] Bedford . . . [with an introduction by Lord John Russell]*, 3 vols., London, 1842–6, ii, pp. 166–7; *Anecdotes of [the life of the Right Honourable William Pitt, Earl of] Chatham . . . [from the year 1736 to the year 1778]*, [John Almon], third edn., 3 vols., London, 1793, i, pp. 273–4; Newcastle to Hardwicke, 22 Aug. 1755, Yorke, *Hardwicke*, ii, p. 235.

19 McKelvey, pp. 22–3, 24.

20 Yorke, *Hardwicke*, ii, pp. 196–7, 227–49, esp. Hardwicke to Newcastle, 9 Aug. 1755, pp. 230–3, Newcastle to Hardwicke, 3 Sept. 1755, pp. 237–44; *Dodington*, pp. 322–7, 2, 3 [Sept. 1755]. Cf. Reed Browning, *The Duke of Newcastle*, New Haven, Conn., 1975, pp. 223–5.

his earlier conduct. It would certainly be congenial to the anti-Hanoverian views of Leicester House, and could be expected to attract independent and Tory support. Even if he were forced out of office in the process, the issue seemed an excellent one on which to raise a storm and stand forth as the spokesman of the nation.

So, if Pitt's initial tactics of 1754 had failed, success in his contingency plans now seemed possible. He continued to work on those opposed to the treaties in an attempt to build up a party against Newcastle which could either frighten him into submission to Pitt's demands or oppose him effectively when Parliament assembled.[21] Leicester House was more open than ever in avowing its alliance with Pitt, while Bute himself was using contacts in the City to 'stir up a clamour' against the subsidies. Now indeed the alliance began to have some political impact.[22] Newcastle had no alternative but to turn even more to Fox, who had kept free of the growing opposition and had given indications of his readiness to treat. By late September it was agreed that he should be Leader of the House of Commons with full authority, and, after he had faced the opening of Parliament, also Secretary of State.[23]

In the parliamentary session which opened on 13 November 1755 the long political calm which had been Henry Pelham's great achievement was decisively disrupted. Pitt stood forth clearly as the champion of a new Opposition based on Leicester House and also on the 'popular' issue of the subsidy treaties. The debate on the Address in Reply was one of the great occasions of the century, lasting until five in the morning. It turned almost entirely on the references to Hanover and the treaties in the King's Speech. Its high point came after midnight when the debate had been in progress ten hours. Then Pitt brought together all the attacks on the treaties in a great outpouring of one and a half hours 'like a torrent long obstructed'. At last, he said, a war was undertaken 'for the long-injured, long-neglected, long-forgotten people of America', a war in British interests to be fought by the British Navy. But now 'incoherent *un–British* measures are what are adopted instead of our

[21] Namier and Brooke, iii, p. 292.

[22] John Yorke to Royston, 28 Oct. 1755, Yorke, *Hardwicke*, ii, p. 252 (quotation); Fox to Hartington, 28 Oct. 1755, Hartington to Devonshire, 8 Nov. 1755, quoted W. M. Torrens, *History of Cabinets: from the Union with Scotland to the Acquisition of Canada and Bengal*, 2 vols., London, 1894, ii, pp. 238–40.

[23] Yorke, *Hardwicke*, ii, p. 198; Walpole, *Geo. II*, i, pp. 418, 419.

proper force.' These would lead irresistibly to a general war on the Continent and the wasting away of British resources, so that 'within two years his Majesty would not be able to sleep in St. James's for the cries of a bankrupt people.'[24] In the House of Lords, Lord Temple, now Pitt's brother-in-law as well as his closest political associate, was 'the incendiary of the new opposition', supported by Lord Halifax.[25] Pitt had unmistakably launched a new offensive in his bid for power. He, with George Grenville and Legge, reaped his reward in summary dismissal from office.

As yet, however, Pitt had shaken the Ministry only with the hot winds of oratory. Despite the debates, the treaties easily passed both Houses, although on the Russian treaty the Opposition had one of their highest votes of the session, 126 in a very large House.[26] The rest of the parliamentary session proved no more encouraging to Pitt's 'popular' opposition. In an unusually sustained effort he seized every opportunity to try to stimulate dissatisfaction with the Ministers and to stir up popular issues, to little avail in voting support or even the sympathy of the House.[27] After Christmas there was a marked slackening of the new mood of controversy. In the Opposition's most prolonged effort, against a Bill to allow the recruitment of foreign protestant officers for service in America, their highest vote was eighty-two and they could usually muster only about sixty.[28] Even proposals in March to bring over Hanoverian and Hessian troops to meet fears of invasion raised no great storm. Although there were 'some murmurs' over the King's message about the Hessians, and Pitt and Temple were eloquent in opposition to Lord George Sackville's motion to ask for Hanoverians, there was no serious opposition in either case. Both Hessians and Hanoverians duly arrived in April.[29] Arguments against German treaties and expensive misdirected measures were revived when the estimates for the troops were laid before the House in late

[24] Walpole, *Geo. II*, i, pp. 407–18 (quotations pp. 412, 413, 414, 416).

[25] Ibid., pp. 406–7.

[26] Ibid., pp. 453–4; *Commons' Journal*, xxvii, pp. 298, 333.

[27] Fox to Devonshire, 31 Jan. 1756, quoted Torrens, ii, pp. 273–4.

[28] Walpole, *Geo. II*, ii, pp. 6–23; *Commons' Journal*, xxvii, pp. 443, 458, 463, 466, 481.

[29] Walpole, *Geo. II*, ii, pp. 30–1; Sir George to W. H. Lyttelton, 28 Apr. 1756, *Memoirs [and Correspondence of George, Lord] Lyttelton, [from 1734 to 1773]*, ed. Robert J. Phillimore, 2 vols., London, 1845, ii, p. 507.

April and early May, and in the debates which followed on the request for a vote of credit of £1,000,000 to meet emergencies and fulfil the provisions of the Convention of Westminster signed with Prussia in January. This, made possible by Prussia's alarm at Britain's treaty with Russia, seemed to secure Hanover even more effectively by guaranteeing the neutrality of Germany. It required, however, a British subsidy. Yet neither opposition to it nor to the Hanoverian and Hessian troops aroused much enthusiasm.[30]

On the domestic front, opposition to proposals for new taxes, especially on plate, proved more fruitful. The Government survived one division by a majority of only two and the second reading was passed by only nine in a relatively small House. When, however, both sides had rallied their strength for the committal, the Government vote rose far more than the Opposition's, to give them a majority of 103.[31] Only on the question of reform of the Militia did the Opposition have support from independent opinion. The ideological grounds for such a reform as an alternative to the Army had been reinforced since 1745 by a practical interest in an efficient Militia for home defence.[32] Now at the end of 1755, in face of a threat of a French invasion, George Townshend raised the question. Pitt presented a detailed scheme with a mastery which won admiration. He presented a reformed Militia as an alternative to the ignominy of paying others for Britain's defence and as a valuable supplement to the Army, giving additional stability to the Constitution. He made a special appeal for the support of the country gentlemen. The Bill passed through its various stages in the Commons from January to May. The debate, especially in committee, was detailed and often tedious, but there was wide support for the measure. So the Government held its fire until the Bill reached the House of Lords, where Hardwicke made one of his most famous speeches against it. Although the Bill was easily rejected, he was constrained by its obvious popularity to express support in principle for the Militia and readiness to accept a suitably revised Bill in the next session.[33]

[30] Walpole, *Geo. II*, ii, pp. 33–4, 36–41.

[31] Ibid., pp. 24–8; *Dodington*, p. 339, 17 [Mar. 1756]; *Commons' Journal*, xxvii, pp. 494, 530, 538, 550.

[32] J. R. Western, *The English Militia in the Eighteenth Century*, London, 1965, ch. V.

[33] Ibid., pp. 127–33; Walpole, *Geo. II*, i, pp. 447–51; Yorke, *Hardwicke*, ii, pp. 262–5; Gilbert Elliott to George Grenville, 25 May 1756, *Grenville Papers*, i, pp. 160–1.

In all, the parliamentary session gave little promise of increased support for Pitt. Fox had every reason for satisfaction. Without a crisis or marked exertions by Leicester House, support for opposition could come only from the independents and would by nature be unreliable. The avowed Tories demonstrated in this session the hazards of an appeal to such support. 'The Tories hate both him [Fox] and Pitt so much, that they sit still to see them worry one another,' said Walpole at its beginning.[34] Pitt, indeed, was not in a particularly strong position to appeal to them. He was as yet in his own estimation and that of others an avowed Whig. In the uncertainties of 1754 he had talked the Old Corps language of the days of Walpole and Pelham, stressing the importance of a union of the Whigs in unsettled circumstances. One of his most memorable outbursts of oratory in the previous session had been against Oxford Toryism. Later still, on the very eve of launching his opposition, he had expressed his determination to act 'upon plain Whig principles'.[35] He was only just coming to see any point in courting the Tories. On the other hand, it is true that the Tories were likely to respond to Pitt's patriot campaign. But as yet the response was very uneven. They voted against the subsidy treaties in considerable numbers—West commented that of the minority of 105, 76 were Tories—but they remained unmoved by further courting.[36] Pitt was called to come reluctantly from his sickbed to oppose Lord George Sackville's motion on Hanoverian troops because it was thought, mistakenly, that they could be won to opposition. Instead they 'owned they preferred Hanoverians to Hessians'.[37] Not all of them were even for Pitt's fine Militia plan, which some independents suspected to be a mere expedient to embarrass the Government.[38]

[34] Walpole to Mann, 16 Nov. 1755, [*The Yale Edition of Horace*] *Walpole's Corr[espondence*], ed. W. S. Lewis, 39 vols., in progress, New Haven, Conn., 1937–[74], xx, p. 510.

[35] Pitt to Lyttelton and the Grenvilles, 7 Mar. 1754, to Temple, 11 Mar. 1754, *Grenville Papers*, i, pp. 106–7, 112; Pitt to Lyttelton, 24 Mar. 1754, *Mems. Lyttelton*, ii, pp. 461–2; Walpole, *Geo. II*, i, pp. 357–8; *Dodington*, p. 326, 3 [Sept. 1755] (quotation).

[36] Walpole, *Geo. II*, i, p. 477; West to Newcastle, 13 Nov. 1755, Add. MSS 32860, f. 471.

[37] Sir George to W. H. Lyttelton, 28 Apr. 1756, *Mems. Lyttelton*, ii, p. 507; Walpole, *Geo. II*, ii, p. 30 (quotation).

[38] Walpole, *Geo. II*, i, p. 448; Lord Walpole to Hardwicke, 4 Apr. 17[5]6, Add. MSS 35594, f. 40.

In any case many had practical reasons—fear of armed rioters, of the growth of a military spirit among Militia men, of further strengthening local Whig interests— which moderated their ideological commitment to the Militia. Without any strong Whig connection to follow him, Pitt needed much more reliable Tory support if his opposition was to be effective. There were no insuperable barriers to such an alliance but as yet the pressure of events was not sufficient on either side to overcome habitual attitudes.

The mood of the country was likewise discouraging to opposition. There was little evidence of dissatisfaction with the Government in its handling of the foreign situation. The *Monitor* might argue the inevitability and desirability of war with France and urge that it should be energetically fought by naval means alone for Britain's true interests in America.[39] Yet even City opinion seemed well satisfied with the measures of the Ministry, in spite of such misfortunes as Boscawen's missing the French fleet that he was sent to American waters to intercept. The merchants were flattered by attentions such as messages about the departure of naval ships to various ports, so that their ships could go under protection. They were delighted by the great number of prizes seized in the unlimited attacks on French shipping authorized in August 1755. The moneyed men were as co-operative as ever in the usual business of raising the year's supplies.[40]

There were differences of opinion in the City over the question of peace or war, Sir John Barnard being for peace while hopes of destroying the French marine inclined others to war.[41] On the question of subsidies there were reports of some concern and Sir John was reticent on the subject with his ministerial friends. However, despite Bute's reported efforts to stir up trouble, the expected petition against the subsidy treaties did not materialize and it seemed that the argument that they were intended only for the defence of Hanover and not for general war had calmed fears.[42] The general mood was well reflected in the Address presented by the

[39] e.g. *Mon.* 5, 6 Sept., 16, 22 Nov., 18, 6 Dec. 1755, 42, 22 May 1756.

[40] Birch to Royston, 23 Aug. 1755, Add. MSS 35398, f. 278; West to Newcastle, 20 Sept., Watkins to Newcastle, 26, 29 Sept. 1755, Add. MSS 32859, ff. 168, 226, 269.

[41] Hardwicke to Newcastle, 29 Dec. 1755, Add. MSS 32861, f. 495.

[42] Watkins to Newcastle, 26, 29 Sept., West to Newcastle, 20 Sept. 1755, Add. MSS 32859, ff. 226, 269, 168; John Yorke to Royston, 28 Oct. 1755, Add. MSS 35374, f. 126.

City to the King on his return from Germany in September. Expressing satisfaction at the steps taken to protect commerce and the colonies, it promised the City's 'cheerful contribution' to measures of defence.[43] In the *Monitor's* approving comment on this Address, the paper was forced to resort to deliberate misrepresentation: it implied that the City shared its eagerness for a naval war and its strong demands for a change of ministers. It tried to whip up a national campaign by adjuring other places to follow the City's supposed example. Indeed it virtually admitted disappointment by bitterly castigating supposed pro-ministerial opposition to the Address, for which there is no other evidence.[44] Even in the new year, the City as a whole certainly did not share the *Monitor's* dissatisfaction with the Adminstration's 'languid measures'. In April the City again addressed the King on the continuing invasion threat, expressing similar sentiments of satisfaction and promises of support. At the same time, a group of influential merchants presented a loyal Address.[45]

Even the Militia issue failed to stir the City significantly. The Common Council twice refused to petition in support of the measure, although on the second occasion, in April 1756, it is clear that its refusal was due less to opposition to the Militia than to attachment to City privileges. The Common Council wished to retain the exemption of the City Militia from any general regulation. The Bill provided for exemption but the proposed petition specifically asked for inclusion.[46] Only on the plate tax was the City so aroused that it not only petitioned against the tax but also instructed its representatives to oppose it on all the old grounds advanced against excise duties. The *Monitor* chorused vociferous support.[47]

By the end of the parliamentary session in May, then, Pitt's opposition, measured by either parliamentary or popular support,

---

[43] William Maitland, *The History of London from its Foundation to the Present Time . . . Continued to the year 1772 by the Rev. John Entick M.A. . . .*, 2 vols., London, 1772, ii, pp. 7–8. Walpole commented to Mann in August that in the City 'nothing is so popular as the Duke of Newcastle', 21 Aug. 1755, *Walpole's Corr.* xx, p. 493.

[44] *Mon.* 8, 27 Sept. 1755.

[45] *Mon.* 26, 31 Jan. 1756; Maitland, ii, p. 10; *PA*, 3, 7, 9 Apr. 1756.

[46] Reginald R. Sharpe, *London and the Kingdom*, 3 vols., London, 1895, iii, pp. 57–8; Maitland, ii, p. 8; Corporation of London Record Office, Jour[nals of the Court of] Common Council, 61, ff. 23–5, 57; *PA*, 26 Nov. 1755, 5 Apr. 1756.

[47] Maitland, ii, p. 10; Sharpe, iii, p. 58; Jour. Common Council, 61, ff. 49–52; *Mon.* 34, 27 Mar. 1756.

was far from prospering. Neither Leicester House nor an appeal to the country had achieved much yet. Lyttelton wrote in April, about his struggles with Legge over the plate tax, 'I flatter myself the opposition to the Plate Tax will not be more popular than that to the Prussian and Hessian Treaties.' In June Thomas Potter reported to Pitt 'Hanover treaties and Hanover troops are popular throughout every country. The almost universal language is, opposition must be wrong, when we are ready to be eat up by the French.' It seemed that Walpole's assessment, made the previous August when the subsidy issue first arose, was indeed correct:

there is not a mob in England now capable of being the dupe of patriotism; the late body of that denomination have really so discredited it, that a minister must go great lengths indeed before the people would dread him half so much as a patriot!

A pamphlet of early 1756, mocking Pitt's renewed patriot pretensions as inconsistent with his behaviour in office, apparently proved Walpole's point.[48]

William Beckford was an excellent example of Pitt's failure to win support from obvious sources. He certainly was more active in opposition than other Tories. Surely his heart must have warmed to Pitt's oratory. Pitt, moreover, was paying some court to Beckford by supporting him in the House. Yet Beckford 'till now, had appeared to prefer Mr Fox' and in November openly declared his respect for him alone among the Ministers. Although a little later there was some suggestion of disillusionment, there was no clear breach and Beckford certainly did not commit himself to Pitt. By the middle of 1756 Pitt, through his friend, Thomas Potter, was winning support from some of the City Tories. Beckford, however, was not among them and there were no visible results of the support.[49]

The *Monitor's* political loyalties were similarly undecided. It too had taken a strong opposition line on all major issues. It argued for the direction of foreign policy towards the colonies and away from Europe. It opposed subsidy treaties,[50] the use of foreign troops in

[48] Sir George to W. H. Lyttelton, 28 Apr. 1756, *Mems. Lyttelton*, ii, p. 508; Potter to Pitt, 4 June 1756, *Corr. Chatham*, i, p. 161; Walpole to Mann, 21 Aug. 1755, *Walpole's Corr.* xx, p. 493; *A New System of Patriot Policy Containing The Genuine Recantation of The British Cicero*, London, 1756.

[49] Walpole, *Geo. II*, ii, p. 3 (quotation), i, p. 422; Rigby to Bedford, 3 Dec. 1755, *Corr. Bedford*, ii, p. 174; Potter to Pitt, 4 June 1756, *Corr. Chatham*, i, p. 162.

[50] *Mon.* 11, 18 Oct., 14, 8 Nov., 16, 22 Nov. 1755.

England and, in line with the attack in Parliament, of foreign officers in America.[51] It strongly supported the proposals to reform the Militia.[52] The new taxes, particularly that on plate, were bitterly attacked.[53] Through all this the paper showed persistent, if fluctuating, hostility to the Ministers. But as yet it had no clear loyalties. It still fixed its hopes generally on the efforts of a few honest, disinterested men, although on one occasion while denigrating Newcastle, it lavishly praised Pitt for his courageous opposition to Continental connections which had lost him his place.[54] Nor was it clear for whom the *Monitor* spoke. So far, like the Beckfords, it was usually more extreme than general Tory opinion. On the plate tax it had courted City opinion and set itself up as its spokesman. Yet on the major question of confidence in the Ministers, it was clearly out of tune with official City opinion. Similarly its patrons had been quite active in the City on particular issues but had found no major opening for leadership.[55] Beckford and the *Monitor*, like Pitt, had not yet got wind in the sails of their opposition, while their lack of a clear sense of direction in national politics is a measure of Pitt's failure.

* * * * * *

From the last days of the parliamentary session, however, developments began that would decisively change the situation. On 6 May news was received in London of the landing of a French force in Minorca, a British possession much valued as a naval base and for the defence of trade in the Mediterranean. Until now, in face of apparent French plans for an invasion of Britain, neither politicians nor public had shown much interest in reports of a possible threat to Minorca, although when the reports were confirmed in February and March Admiral Byng had been dispatched to the Mediterranean with ten ships of the line. Now, a month after he had sailed on 6 April, the two expeditions became, suddenly, the focus of

[51] *Mon.* 30, 28 Feb., 32, 13 Mar., 36, 10 Apr., 40, 8 May 1756.

[52] Ibid. 19, 13 Dec. 1755, 36, 10 Apr., 38, 24 Apr., 43, 29 May 1756.

[53] Ibid. 31, 6 Mar., 34, 27 Mar. 1756.

[54] Ibid. 10, 11 Oct. 1755, 27, 7 Feb. 1756 (on Pitt).

[55] Both Beckfords were present for the first Militia petition. On the occasion of the second, William took the opportunity to stand out for City privileges against at least one spokesman with Government contacts (Calvert). See fn. 46. Neither Beckford was present when the City decided to address the King on his return from Hanover in Sept. (Jour. Common Council, 61, ff. 1–2), but William did attend when the plate tax petition was agreed (ibid., ff. 49–52).

British attention. On 18 May war was at last declared. Three days later Byng fought an indecisive engagement with the French fleet off Minorca. Afterwards, convinced he could do nothing more, he retired to Gibraltar to await reinforcements. At the end of June, Minorca fell to the French. The crisis that was to grow out of these events over the next six months brought to a head the instability of the political situation and at last gave Pitt the opportunity that led to success.

Immediately after news of the French landing was received, Pitt seized on it as yet another chance to parade his opposition in Parliament. Newcastle, typically, was thrown into a panic.[56] Fortunately for him, the parliamentary session was drawing to a close and Pitt was robbed of a platform from which to push home his attack as events developed. The first news of Byng's engagement reached London on 3 June from French sources through the Spanish Ambassador. The Ministers did not wait for Byng's report; his recall and that of his Rear-Admiral, Temple West, were ordered and announced immediately. When Byng's despatch arrived on 23 June it was published in a censored form in what can only be regarded as an attempt to divert public indignation on to Byng. On 14 July, again through the Spanish Ambassador, the news was received of the fall of Minorca.[57] When Byng arrived in England at the end of July he was put under close arrest to await court martial.

Hitherto public reaction to these events had been confused. Now a swell of indignation arose. In the extraordinary circumstances of a defeat abroad and ministerial division at home, this was to grow into one of those occasional eighteenth-century outbursts of 'public opinion' which could alter the political situation decisively. In this way the disturbance of political calm which Pitt's opposition had begun in Parliament was spread outwards and greatly magnified in effect. It quickly became clear that the Ministers' attempts to deflect resentment away from themselves would not easily prevail. Soon all forms of propaganda were working against them.

The newspapers reacted most quickly. Among them, the *London Evening Post* had already stimulated some interest by articles of information about Minorca, with some comment on the 'bungling'

[56] Walpole, *Geo. II*, ii, pp. 34–5, 37–9. Newcastle to Hardwicke, 8 May, Hardwicke to Newcastle, 9 May, John Yorke to Royston, 13 May 1756, Yorke, *Hardwicke*, ii, pp. 289–91.

[57] Walpole, *Geo. II*, ii, pp. 57–8, 65–7.

response to the French threat. Its reaction to the fall was immediate and strong. At the end of June after news of Byng's engagement but before the loss of Minorca was known in London, the *Post* began to voice suspicions of a ministerial 'cloak' and to demand an inquiry, although its columns were also full of attacks on Byng. The *Gazetteer*, too, became vehemently hostile to the Ministry. By the end of July each was reinforcing the other in exhortations to 'the people' to demand an inquiry, urging the City to give the lead.[58] More indicative of the general strength of feeling was the unusual political turn taken by the *Public Advertiser* and *Read's Weekly Journal*, which not only reported the fall of Minorca but also included hostile comment.[59] They did not long sustain this trend but the *London Evening Post* and the *Gazetteer* kept up the attack. The controversy was noticed, too, in the weightier monthlies, the *Gentleman's Magazine* and *London Magazine*. They gave both reports and background on Mediterranean developments from June onwards, and more unusually, from July, some account of and even contributions to the controversy.[60]

The *Monitor*, too, exploited the issue and in the process had its own politics sharpened. Its intermittent criticism of the Ministers immediately became much more vigorous and continuous, every paper being concerned in one way or another with their deficiencies and malign intentions and the need for a change. When it first took up the Minorca issue in detail, on 10 and 17 July, in papers written before news of the fall, the blame for Byng's inadequacies was fastened chiefly on the Ministers and especially on Newcastle. On 31 July, after news of the fall, this criticism reached its first climax in a paper which ended by urging the people to 'exert that liberty, which is our birthright', to prevent monarchy being again subverted and the people reduced to slaves by ministers. Through grand juries and corporations they could speak even when Parliament was not in session.[61] Over the next three months, the iniquities of the Ministers were frequently recapitulated while increasing demands were made for inquiry into and punishment of their shortcomings as well as those of Byng.

[58] *LEP*, 29 May–1 June, 10–12 June, 29 June–1 July, 22–4, 24–7, 27–9, 29–31 July 1756; *Gaz.*, 21, 24, 28, 29, 30 July 1756.
[59] e.g. *RWJ*, 17, 24 July 1756; *PA*, 23 July 1756.
[60] e.g. *GM*, xxvi, July 1756, pp. 346, 351–2, 356, Aug., pp. 394, 398, Sept., pp. 412, 424–7.
[61] *Mon.* 49, 10 July, 50, 17 July, 52, 31 July 1756.

Meanwhile the number of pamphlets on political subjects increased noticeably.[62] At first, they were directed against Byng and were trivial in content and unprofessional in style. By September and October, however, the pamphlet debate widened and the Ministry became their major preoccupation. Comments in the *Monthly Review* on these pamphlets bear witness to the degree and fury of revived controversy.

After a deep sleep, and dead silence, for a considerable interval, the groans of the press are heard from every quarter, and the pamphlet-shops filled with the products of its labours: every measure, and every miscarriage is publicly arraigned . . . and . . . the friends and followers of the Administration, condescend, at length, to reply.

Comments hinted, too, at the way the discussion was being turned to political purposes by being fuelled with information from 'persons who stood higher'. Likewise the *Critical Review*, although it gave the whole debate less attention, had no doubt that popular sentiments against Byng had been whipped up and kept alive by the Ministers and their advocates.[63] The controversy continued in full force in November. By this time reviews suggested some satiety as well as concern at the manner in which Byng was being prejudged in propaganda before his trial. But they also clearly showed how the original issues of the loss of Minorca and demands for an inquiry were being widened to include calls for a reformed Militia, public economy and even annual parliaments. The patriot programme was again being refurbished.[64] More generally there was a reaction against attempts to concentrate anger on Byng and a frequently expressed desire for parliamentary inquiries.[65]

In these months, too, the more ephemeral forms of propaganda sprang to renewed life. Prints multiplied, almost all of them hostile to the Ministers, showing an intensity of anger deeper even than that displayed against Walpole. From the beginning Newcastle bore the brunt; by October, Fox was sharing the blame. The failure of the

[62] In July *MR* and *CR* contained no reviews of works of immediate political interest. Over the next four months they reviewed thirty and thirteen works respectively on the Minorca question.

[63] *MR*, xv, Oct. 1756, p. 408, Sept., p. 305; *CR*, ii, Oct. 1756, pp. 252, 257, 286.

[64] e.g. *MR*, xv, Nov. 1756, pp. 517–18, 521–2.

[65] e.g. *MR*, xv, Nov. 1756, pp. 517–18, 520–1; *CR*, ii, Aug. 1756, p. 35, Oct., p. 281, Nov., p. 376.

attempt to direct anger against Byng is particularly clear in this form of publication; of the fifty or more prints attacking him, almost all include the Ministers as well, especially as the protest grew. Ballads, whether chanted in the streets of Westminster or issued in collected editions, made a prominent contribution to the outcry. George Townshend's skill in caricature added to the impact. First used for prints in support of his Militia Bill, it was now displayed on small cards suitable to be sent by post. His first venture in the new form was a pointed attack on Fox and Newcastle.[66]

The outcry in these varied forms of publicity was accompanied by more direct action, some violent, such as the burning of effigies, attacks on Byng's property in Hertfordshire and mobbing of Newcastle,[67] some in the shape of formal expressions of dissatisfaction. In August and early September, at least nine sets of instructions to members of Parliament and five addresses to the Crown showed the extent of criticism of ministerial mismanagement of the war and called for inquiry and punishment.[68] At the end of August, Sir John Willes, on circuit for the assizes, reported to Newcastle from Warwick that 'I never found all sorts of people so uneasy, and so dispirited, as they are at present. The loss of Fort St. Philip [the main fortification on Minorca] is looked upon by everyone in a most melancholy light'.[69] Other issues heightened public uneasiness. There were widespread disturbances in reaction to the critically high price of corn. Of more immediate political interest was the minor furore caused in September by the affair of the Hanoverian soldier, arrested for the theft of two handkerchiefs but then released to the Hanoverian authorities on the order of the Secretary of State and thus exempted from the ordinary process of law.[70]

---

[66] Walpole, *Geo. II*, ii, pp. 59, 68; *Cat. Prints and Drawings*, iii, pt. ii, pp. 992–1030; M. Dorothy George, *English Political Caricature to 1792. A Study of Opinion and Propaganda*, Oxford, 1959, pp. 101–4, 115–17; Potter to Grenville, 11 Sept. 1756, *Grenville Papers*, i, p. 173. Examples of ballads survive in *The Wonder of Surry! The Wonder of Surry! or the genuine Speech of an old British oak*, and a mock reply to it, *Wonder upon Wonder: Or The Cocoa Tree's Answer to the Surrey Oak . . .*, both anti-Newcastle and Fox.

[67] e.g. *GM*, xxvi, Aug. 1756, p. 409 (26 Aug.); Potter to Grenville, 11 Sept. 1756, *Grenville Papers*, i, p. 172; Browning, p. 241.

[68] Walpole, *Geo. II*, ii, pp. 69–70; Sutherland, 'The City . . . 1756–7', p. 153 and fn. 5.

[69] Quoted by Dudley Pope, *At 12 Mr Byng was shot . . .*, London, 1962, p. 183.

[70] Walpole, *Geo. II*, ii, p. 85.

Yet, as the continuing swell of propaganda showed, the loss of Minorca and its ramifications remained the chief issue. In mid-October, John Wilkes told Grenville that 'public indignation is rising very strong against Lord A[nson], and Byng has everywhere some warm advocates. . . . *Poor Byng* is the phrase in every mouth, and then comes the hackneyed simile of the *Scapegoat*.'[71] The autumn quarter sessions and the approach of the opening of Parliament brought further instructions and addresses from October to December, 'all of them breathing a true patriotic and loyal Spirit'. As in earlier times of public excitement and as in the pamphlets, the demands now widened to include the major tenets of the traditional opposition programme: the Militia, limitation of the numbers of placemen and pensioners in Parliament, and the restoration of triennial parliaments.[72]

Propaganda and direct action interacted to sustain this outburst of public opinion for over four months. There is little reason to suppose that the vehemence of the *London Evening Post*, the *Monitor* and the *Gazetteer* persuaded country gentlemen assembled at the assizes in August to protest unless they were already so inclined. But their instructions and addresses certainly boosted newspaper comment just when it was beginning to flag, even in the most interested papers. All of them, including the *Public Advertiser* and *Read's Weekly Journal*, reported the stream of instructions and addresses as they came in from mid-August to the end of the year. By reporting alone the *Public Advertiser* and *Read's* kept the Minorca issue before their readers while, for the other papers, the protests fuelled their own complaints and encouraged renewed exhortations to action. Such publicity, with or without exhortation, must have encouraged the later protests which in their turn fired newspaper comment. After some easing in September there was a crescendo of criticism in October, with greater emphasis than ever on the 'unanimous' call of the people for full inquiries into the reasons for Britain's misfortunes. By a variety of devices—letters, paragraphs of comment, full reporting of all moves to instruct or address and constant assertions

---

[71] Wilkes to Grenville, 16 Oct. 1756, *Grenville Papers*, i, p. 176.
[72] Sutherland, 'The City . . . 1756–7', p. 154 and fnn. 2, 3; Maitland, ii, p. 16 (quotation). It is difficult to be certain of the precise number of instructions and addresses from Aug. onwards. Sutherland lists thirty-three. Rogers, 'London Opinion', p. 657, lists forty. The number reported in the newspapers supports the higher figure.

of the right of the people to speak out—the *London Evening Post* kept
up its campaign, with warm support from the *Gazetteer* and
Monitor.[73] Everything possible was done to magnify the protests,
even by reporting instructions and addresses that failed, and all
opposition to them was castigated.[74] As time passed the emphasis
was less and less on Byng's faults and by the end of October there
was even a distinct turn towards sympathy for him.[75] So most of the
propaganda worked in unison against the Ministers, and undoubtedly did much to prolong and intensify the crisis. In this outburst of
opinion, the one-sided fury of prints and newspapers was for once
more important than the more varied and less regular debate of the
pamphlets.[76]

The foundation for this outcry was undoubtedly genuine indignation at a humiliating defeat by the national enemy. Blame was laid
squarely on the lethargy of Ministers and Admiral alike. However,
the opportunity was seized by interested parties. The sentiment was
sharpened and manipulated for political purposes, first by the
Ministers to divert attention from themselves and then by those
opposed to them. That the Tories were prominent in propaganda is
demonstrated by the activities of that ultra-Tory and arch-
incendiary, Dr John Shebbeare, whose *Fourth Letter To The People of
England* appeared late in August,[77] by the *Monitor* and the *London
Evening Post,* and by comments in the *Monthly Review* which warmly
welcomed a pamphlet in November because, in contrast to other
opposition pieces, it was 'founded on unadulterated Whigish principles'.[78] There is evidence that some of the instructions and addresses
of August were promoted by Tories on the grand juries. The
ignominious failure of the Address in Surrey, the only one to be
circulated for signatures, certainly suggests that not all were spontaneous representations of county opinion. The indignant comments
of the *Monitor* on obstruction in Surrey and 'a *lying spirit*' in Bristol

[73] e.g. *LEP*, 9–12, 12–14, 14–16, 16–19 Oct. 1756; *Mon.* 56, 21 Aug., 58, 4 Sept., 60,
18 Sept., 63, 9 Oct. 1756.
[74] *LEP*, 28–30 Oct., 30 Oct.–2 Nov. 1756; *Mon.* 63, 9 Oct. 1756.
[75] *LEP*, 4–7, 21–3 Sept., 23–6, 28–30 Oct. 1756; *Gaz.,* 19 Oct. 1756.
[76] *LEP*, 9–11 Nov. 1756 praised the liberty of the press as the true cause of the
awakening of the people. Cf. Jas. Weaver to Newcastle, 9 Oct. 1756, Add. MSS
32868, ff. 159–60.
[77] *CR,* ii, Aug. 1756, pp. 35–43; *MR,* xv, Sept. 1756, pp. 292–3.
[78] *MR,* xv, Nov. 1756, p. 518.

likewise suggests, in a typically indirect and reluctant fashion, a strength of opposition to those who took it upon themselves to speak for 'the people'. Lyttelton wrote later of the 'Jacobite spirit' in the addresses for inquiries, which had 'mixed itself very strongly with the discontent infused or encouraged by the late opposition'.[79] Later in August George Townshend stirred up considerable criticism by a circular letter to boroughs and corporations urging support for another Militia Bill. His letter may well have had some influence over the second round of addresses and instructions in October and November.[80] So the Tories and others helped to keep the issues alive. But the spontaneous indignation, wider than anything merely manipulated by interested groups, remained. There was a tension between its demands for vengeance on Byng and the political objectives of those who wanted attention concentrated on the Ministers, a tension which was to become more obvious and embarrassing when political circumstances changed.

The complex nature of the outburst is well illustrated in London. Now general opinion in the City was more in accord with the *Monitor*. Mediterranean trading interests were directly affected and others were alarmed. Soon after the news of the French landing, Newcastle was told by Fox that 'the City was extreamly displeased with the leaving Minorca exposed'. Newcastle and his various informants anxiously watched the situation. In mid-June Pitt remarked to Grenville, perhaps prematurely, that 'the Passengers, the City of all denominations, are in alarm, and think the ship sinking'.[81] Yet, despite urgings by the *London Evening Post* and the *Gazetteer* from the end of July,[82] moves for a formal expression of City opinion were delayed until after action elsewhere. When they came quite suddenly in mid-August they arose out of a more precise political motivation. They were attributed to the City Tories,

[79] Sutherland, 'The City . . . 1756–7', pp. 156–7; Langford, 'William Pitt and public opinion, 1757', p. 71; *Mon.* 63, 9 Oct. 1756; Lyttelton to W. H. Lyttelton, 25 Nov. 1756, *Mems. Lyttelton*, ii, p. 536. Rogers, 'London Politics', pp. 193–4, suggests that Tories were active in 6 out of 20 boroughs and 9 out of 17 counties.

[80] Walpole, *Geo. II*, ii, p. 82; Sutherland, 'The City . . . 1756–7', p. 156 and fn. 5; Western, p. 134.

[81] *Dodington*, p. 341, 18 [May 1756] (quotation); West to Newcastle, 8 May, 24 July, Newcastle to Hardwicke, 26 July, S. Squire to Newcastle, 19 Aug. 1756, Add. MSS 32864, f. 499, 32866, ff. 268–9, 275, 488–9; Pitt to Grenville, 16 June 1756, *Grenville Papers*, i, p. 168.

[82] *LEP*, 29–31 July 1756; *Gaz.* 29 July, 2 Aug. 1756.

especially by those sympathetic to the Government, who were taken by surprise.[83] The attribution is supported by the accounts of the Common Council on 18 August which adopted an outspoken Address to the King. The Address was moved by Deputy Hodges, 'one of the city demagogues',[84] and seconded by 'Mr Turner, a West Indian merchant'. William Beckford was prominent in defending the proposal, citing precedents of 1641. He was appointed to the committee to draw it up, and, when the suggested Address was reported back to the meeting, he answered the further objections of Sir John Barnard.[85] The Address was obviously designed not simply to express the indignation of the City or even to embarrass the Ministers but also to seize the opportunity created by success elsewhere to challenge the leadership of Sir John Barnard in City politics. This is borne out by the *Monitor's* part. Although it had long been urging the people to action, it made no reference to the City until 14 and 16 August, only a few days before the Address, when the *London Evening Post* was again urging the City to action. Then on 28 August the Address was praised by the *Monitor* and opposition to it deplored, with regrets that the 'capital ship, *the St. John,*' should have been 'most confoundly eaten by ministerial worms,' and perhaps become 'so rotten and crasy as not to be trusted on any service'.[86] Despite signs of divisions among the supporters of the Address between those who met at the Half Moon Tavern and its less moderate protagonists at the Black Swan (with whom the *Monitor* and Beckford were probably connected),[87] events had opened opportunities for Beckford and the Tories.

[83] Hardwicke to Newcastle, 20 Aug., West to Newcastle, 20 Aug., Lord Walpole to [unknown], 1 Sept. 1756, Add. MSS 32866, ff. 492, 496–7, 32867, ff. 166–7; Walpole to Mann, 29 Aug. 1756, *Walpole's Corr.* xx, p. 585.

[84] Birch to Royston, 14 Sept. 1754, Yorke, *Hardwicke,* ii, p. 63 fn. 1. James Hodges, a bookseller on London Bridge, Common Councilman and Deputy; active in Tory-patriot City politics from the 1740s; Town Clerk 1757–74; knighted 1759; became one of Pitt's warm supporters at least until 1762.

[85] *PA,* 19 Aug. 1756; Birch to Royston, 20 Aug. 1756, Add. MSS 35398, ff. 317–18 (quotation).

[86] *Mon.* 54, 14 Aug., 55, 16 Aug., 57, 28 Aug. 1756; *LEP,* 14–17 Aug. (also critical of Barnard), 24–6 Aug. 1756.

[87] Birch to Royston, 20 Aug. 1756, Add. MSS 35398, ff. 317–18; Hardwicke to Newcastle, 14 Aug. 1756, Add. MSS 32866, f. 445. *Mon.* 52 and 53 (powerful attacks on the Ministers) were bound with the sixth edn. of Shebbeare's *Fourth Letter,* published at this time, together with an inflammatory broadside entitled *A Serious Call to the Corporation of London, to address his M[ajest]y to remove from his Councils and Person for ever, Weak, and Wicked M[inister]s, etc.,* dated 18 Aug. 1756.

Yet once the Address was initiated there was support for it that went well beyond what could be raised by one group. Despite the strenuous efforts of minsterial supporters—Barnard advised the Lord Mayor against calling the Common Council—nothing could stop it.[88] The Common Council was said to have been earnestly desired 'by the General Voice of the Citizens of London', and certainly it was very well attended, particularly by the Aldermen. The Address was adopted after considerable debate with only three or four dissentients. It was outspoken in its expression of disgust at the mismanagement which had led to the loss of Minorca and aroused fears about the American colonies. It lamented the 'want of a constitutional and well regulated militia'.[89] So strong was the feeling behind the Address that the suggestion of launching a loyal address among merchants more sympathetic to the Government was dropped. Sir John Barnard's position in the City was virtually destroyed by his efforts to stem what he called 'the Impetuosity and Madness of people'; Walpole reported to Mann that he had grown 'almost as unpopular as Byng'. His continued urgings of peace merely emphasized his isolation. As West had remarked earlier, 'perhaps He has not always that Attention to Publick Clamour which a wise Man should have'.[90]

It was as yet by no means clear who would replace him as leader of the City's popular elements. The continuing evidence of anti-ministerial sentiment in the City is criss-crossed with signs of connections with an obscure struggle for power. In September the strength of feeling was shown in a most unusual attempt to challenge the nomination of the senior Alderman 'below the chair', Marshe Dickinson, for election as Lord Mayor simply because he had voted for the Address to the King to bring over Hanoverian troops. The rival candidate, Sir Richard Glyn, was first declared chosen, but when a poll was demanded he was decisively defeated.[91]

---

[88] West to Newcastle, 14, 20 Aug., Hardwicke to Newcastle, 14 Aug. 1756, Add. MSS 32864, ff. 448–9, 496, 445; Birch to Royston, 20 Aug. 1756, Add. MSS 35398, ff. 317–18; *Gaz.*, 16, 18 Aug. 1756.

[89] *PA*, 12 Aug. 1756 (first quotation); Birch to Royston, 20 Aug. 1756, Add. MSS 35398, ff. 317–18; *GM*, xxvi, Aug. 1756, p. 408 (second quotation).

[90] West to Newcastle, 16 July (third quotation), 20 Aug. (first quotation), 24 Sept., Watkins to Newcastle, 2 Sept. 1756, Add. MSS 32866, ff. 191, 496, 32867, ff. 411–12, 209; Walpole to Mann, 29 Aug. 1756, *Walpole's Corr.* xx, p. 586.

[91] *PA*, 30 Sept.–8 Oct. 1756; *GM*, xxvi, Oct. 1756, p. 475. Sir Richard Glyn, banker, Salters' Company, Alderman for Dowgate 1750–73, Sheriff 1752–3, Lord

At the end of October the Common Council agreed unanimously to instruct its members of Parliament. A most outspoken set of instructions was produced which, alongside the other traditional demands, required the City members to refuse supply until a Militia had been established.[92] Beckford, however, took no part in these events. He did not vote in the mayoral election and was not present at the Common Council which agreed to the Instructions. The *Monitor* was similarly reticent. It gave some support to the opposition to Dickinson (and was followed by the *London Evening Post*) but made no reference, direct or oblique, to the Instructions, despite its continuing concern for constitutional issues.[93] Instead of Beckford, the leader in these moves was another Tory, Alderman Blachford. He was the only Alderman to vote for Glyn for Lord Mayor after the poll of the Livery, and West reported to Newcastle that he was 'at the head' of the move to vote 'Violent Instructions'.[94] In the divisions in anti-ministerial opinion in the City, Beckford, it would seem, was in danger of being worsted as that opinion grew stronger.

In the City, even more than elsewhere, 'the warmth on the loss of Minorca' undoubtedly 'opened every sluice of opposition, that have been so long dammed up'.[95] In early October, however, it was still far from clear what the effects would be, in either City or national politics. Pitt's name was scarcely mentioned in the public controversy before the autumn. Not until late in September did the *London Evening Post* make a brief but favourable reference to his opposition of the last year. The *Monitor* concentrated on attacking Newcastle, Anson, and Hardwicke, only mildly jibing at Fox and showing no

Mayor 1758–9, knighted 1752, baronet 1759 (see below p. 174), City M.P. 1758–68, defeated 1754, 1768, M.P. for Coventry 1768–73, died 1773; a Tory-patriot associated with Benn and the Half Moon Club, certainly a Pittite by 1759. Marshe Dickinson, attorney and financier, Grocers' Company, Alderman for Queenhithe 1749–65, Sheriff 1751–2, Lord Mayor 1756–7, M.P. for Brackley 1754–65, Chairman of Committees, House of Commons, 1761–5, died 1765; sometimes reckoned a Tory (Namier, *England*, p. 194), he was in fact a Court sympathizer and had connections with Newcastle and Hardwicke through Lord Mansfield (see below p. 190 fn. 53).

[92] Jour. Common Council, 61, ff. 113–15.

[93] *Mon.* 61, 25 Sept. 1756; *LEP*, 28–30 Sept., 30 Sept.–2 Oct. 1756.

[94] *PA*, 8 Oct. 1756; West to Newcastle, 28 Oct. 1756, Add. MSS 32868, f. 451. John Blachford, sugar refiner, Goldsmiths' Company, Alderman for Cripplegate 1743–59, Sheriff 1745–6, Lord Mayor 1750–1, died 1759; a long-standing Tory, reputedly Jacobite.

[95] Walpole to Mann, 29 Aug. 1756, *Walpole's Corr.* xx, p. 585.

positive loyalties.[96] Similarly, with only one early exception in July favourably comparing Opposition leaders, including Pitt, with the Ministers, the campaign in the prints was against Newcastle and Fox. Otherwise the only attention Pitt received in the summer was in the pamphlet in August which urged a coalition between him and Fox and was favourably noticed by the *Public Advertiser*.[97]

The *London Evening Post* might look to 'genuine Patriots' to save the situation but Pitt certainly did not immediately reap a harvest from the seeds of the patriot opposition he had already so industriously cultivated. Indeed there were signs that those more extreme in indignation, learning from past betrayals, might react against all politicians. As late as the end of October Newcastle was told 'It begins to be talked publickly in the City coffee houses, that Both Sides at Court are doing the business and answer the wishes of France.'[98] It remained to be seen who could profit from the crisis.

[96] *LEP*, 21–3 Sept. 1756; *Mon.* 48, 3 July, 57, 28 Aug., 65, 23 Oct. 1756.

[97] *Byng Returned; or the Council of Expedients, Cat. Prints and Drawings*, iii, pt. ii, p. 993; *A Letter to the Gentlemen of the Common Council By a Citizen and Watchmaker*, London, 1756; *PA*, 19 Aug. 1756. This pamphlet was attributed by Newcastle to Beckford (to Hardwicke, 28 Aug. 1756, Add. MSS 35415, f. 259). There is nothing to confirm this but the pamphlet may well reflect Beckford's views at this time.

[98] West to Newcastle, 28 Oct. 1756, Add. MSS 32868, f. 451. Cf. Britannicus in *LEP*, 2–4 Nov. 1756.

II

Popularity Won, Tested, and Confirmed
1756–1757

Despite the strong public reaction to the loss of Minorca, the situation of the Administration was initially far from hopeless. It had a very large majority in Parliament and good connections in the City. Both were likely to respond to a firm lead, for which there was plenty of time before Parliament met.[1] Even the anger of the City Address could have been mitigated by its conciliatory reception[2] and diverted to Barnard for his opposition. Popular forces in the City were divided.

As problems abroad and at home multiplied there was little scope for a lead. In Europe, the implications of the British agreement with Prussia in January 1756 had alarmed not only Prussia's enemies, Russia and Austria, but also her friend, France. It thus set in train the dramatic reversal of alliances of 1756–7, begun in May 1756 by the Treaty of Versailles between France and Austria. At the end of August, Frederick of Prussia pushed matters further by attacking Saxony, against British advice and on the flimsiest of pretexts. Britain's new ally looked like becoming a liability. The situation was no better in America. In early October news arrived that Fort Oswego on Lake Ontario had fallen to the French.

At home, besides the corn riots and the affair of the Hanoverian soldier, the Ministry had been harassed all summer by the delicate question of arrangements for the Prince of Wales now that he was of

[1] When fully reporting the City's immediate concern at the loss of Minorca, West was sure that a timely display of spirit by the Government would dissipate any clamour. West to Newcastle, 16 July 1756, Add. MSS 32866, f. 194.

[2] *GM*, xxvi, Aug. 1756, p. 408; Hardwicke to Newcastle, 20 Aug. 1756, Add. MSS 32866, f. 492.

age. On this there were deep differences between the King and the Prince and his mother. An overt breach in the Royal Family, with all the consequent political embarrassments, seemed imminent. At length it was averted by an agreement patched up early in October. But it was delayed so long and was reached in such a way as to bring no reconciliation between Leicester House and Newcastle nor real promises of political quiescence from Leicester House. A chance to strengthen the Ministry's position was lost by Newcastle's ineptitude.[3]

The Ministry lost all coherence as Newcastle sought vainly for support.[4] When formal expressions of opinion to members of Parliament revived in October and November it was clear that the parliamentary session would be difficult. By late October Sir John Barnard was convinced by what he saw in the City that Newcastle had no option but to resign.[5] Then came the violent City Instructions. The opportunity to quell the storm by decisive leadership had clearly gone.

It was Fox who pushed the effects of the loss of Minorca into the heart of politics. Never wholly satisfied with Newcastle's treatment, Fox now feared that he would be used as a scapegoat while bearing the full brunt of the attack on the Ministry in the House of Commons. On 15 October his decision to resign was conveyed to the King. Another spokesman for the Ministry was lost when William Murray demanded fulfilment of a promise of the vacant position of Chief Justice, with a peerage, and would take neither refusal nor delay. Newcastle was now faced with a leaderless House of Commons and the prospect that Fox might reach agreement with Leicester House and Pitt. With Hardwicke's support, Newcastle now insisted that the King allow another approach to Pitt.[6]

Already there had been rumours of resignations and of office for Pitt and Charles Townshend. Now public opinion began to turn to Pitt. Early in October the *Monitor* grew warmer. The prints changed from attacking Fox and Newcastle to supporting the patriot Pitt.[7]

[3] McKelvey, pp. 33–47.   [4] Browning, pp. 240–3.
[5] West to Newcastle, 23 Oct. 1756, Add. MSS 32868, f. 390.
[6] Walpole, *Geo. II*, ii, pp. 86–9; Waldegrave, pp. 59, 80–3; Newcastle to Hardwicke, 13, 14, 15 Oct., Hardwicke to Newcastle, 14 Oct. 1756, Yorke, *Hardwicke*, ii, pp. 318–24.
[7] *LEP* 7–9 Oct., *PA*, 7 Oct. 1756; *Mon.* 62, 2 Oct. 1756; *Cat. Prints and Drawings*, iii, pt. ii, pp. 1013–30.

The turn was not overwhelming. One of the few pamphlets commenting on the situation in October was strongly against Fox and in favour of inquiries but not particularly for Pitt. A broadsheet on similar lines, circulated in London in late October, did not even mention him. The *London Evening Post* had relatively little to say except to insist that there must be a change of measures as well as men. Still, as Newcastle's nerve collapsed, it began to look as though Pitt might at last win popularity from Newcastle's unpopularity and inability to give a lead in the crisis.[8]

On 19 October Pitt had a long interview with Hardwicke. Acting without any consultation with Leicester House, he set his terms very high. He was now offered what he had set out for in 1754—the Secretary's Seals and a good reception from the King. Yet not only did he refuse again, as he had already done in June, to have any part in an administration which included Newcastle; he also stipulated a programme which included the main demands of the popular outcry. Immediately after the interview, he set about establishing for the first time his own lines of communication to the King through Lady Yarmouth.[9] He did not immediately succeed in his demands. The negotiation had, after all, been initiated to strengthen the existing Ministry. Yet his intransigence and the impossibility of finding any alternative leader of the House very quickly brought about a declaration from Newcastle and Hardwicke to the King on 26 October that they could no longer continue.[10]

In the negotiations which followed,[11] the King made desperate efforts to avoid having to succumb to Pitt, and Fox tried hard to secure some major part in the outcome. Pitt had to play the politician to protect his position. Having begun independently, he found it advisable to restore good relations with Leicester House. These had been somewhat interrupted by the long-drawn-out negotiations over the Prince's Household in which Pitt had no

[8] *The Resignation: Or, The Fox Out of the Pit, And The Geese In, with B[yn]g at the Bottom,* London, [Oct.] 1756; *Admiral B[yn]g's Answer to the Friendly Advice, Or The Fox out of the Pit And The Geese In,* London, [1756]; *LEP,* e.g. 24–6 Oct. 1756; Glover, *Mems.,* p. 96.

[9] Browning, p. 240; Hardwicke, Relation of my Conference with Mr Pitt, 24 Oct., Harwicke to Royston, 21 Oct. 1756, Yorke, *Hardwicke,* ii, pp. 277–9, 328–9; Pitt to Grenville, 17 Oct. 1756, *Grenville Papers,* i, p. 178.

[10] Walpole, *Geo. II,* ii, p. 97.

[11] For brief accounts see Hardwicke to Joseph Yorke, 31 Oct. 1756, Yorke, *Hardwicke,* ii, pp. 332–4; Walpole to Mann, 4 Nov. 1756, *Walpole's Corr.* xxi, pp. 10–13; Walpole, *Geo. II,* ii, pp. 97–103.

pressing interest and played no part. On their side the Princess and Bute were alarmed by the activities of Fox and the King's obvious preference for him. By early November warm relations were restored.[12] Pitt had also to modify some of his original demands, including the active pressing of inquiries into the misfortunes of war and the dropping of Holdernesse, held responsible for the Hanoverian soldier affair.[13] But he maintained his adamant negatives on any co-operation with Newcastle and any Cabinet office for Fox. On 11 November Newcastle formally resigned and four days later the new Ministry took office with the Duke of Devonshire, an independent Whig of considerable standing but little political experience, as first Lord of the Treasury. Pitt became Secretary of State. So, flying in the face of all calculations, Pitt stood out against alliance with either Newcastle or Fox, his mood well reflected in his famous remark to Devonshire, 'I am sure I can save this country, and nobody else can.'[14] His self-confidence had greatly increased since 1754, when he had planned such careful manoeuvres and assured Newcastle and Hardwicke of his respect. Yet why now could he and his associates, '15 or 16 persons', as Walpole put it,[15] have such influence, when over the last two years they had not been able to put enough pressure on Newcastle to force the King to accept them?

The support of Leicester House was an important consideration in everyone's minds, in Newcastle's and Hardwicke's in insisting on the approach to Pitt, in Fox's in deciding to resign and even attempting to make his own court there later. But, with the Prince's Household decided just as the political crisis began to develop, the major reason for fearing that Bute and the Princess might support active opposition was removed. Although they were not reconciled to Newcastle they did not seem inclined to positive measures.[16] Their role in the negotiation was passive. Although Bute declared he would approve whatever Pitt decided, his intervention was restricted to ironing out some difficulties over appointments with Devonshire and Charles Townshend.[17] In these circumstances the

[12] McKelvey, pp. 43, 49–50.

[13] Walpole, *Geo. II*, ii, pp. 98–9, 100–1, 104; Etough to Birch, 1 June 1[7]57, Add. MSS 9201, f. 128.

[14] Walpole, *Geo. II*, ii, p. 271.

[15] Walpole to Mann, 4 Nov. 1756, *Walpole's Corr.* xxi, p. 12.

[16] Ibid., p. 13.

[17] McKelvey, pp. 191–2; Temple to Pitt, [11 Nov. 1756], *Corr. Chatham*, i, pp. 192, 193.

continued support of Leicester House for Pitt would not of itself have driven Newcastle to resignation and the King to acceptance of Pitt.

It was the situation in the House of Commons that was crucial, as it had been since 1754. What seemed now decisively to threaten Newcastle's control there was not any subtle politickings by Leicester House but the storm arising out of the loss of Minorca and kept alive by a mixture of ineptitude, manipulation, and continued misfortunes. Fear of being left to face the storm alone was the major calculation in Fox's moves which precipitated the immediate crisis.[18] Negotiations took place against the background of the second round of instructions and addresses. Pitt may not have immediately benefited from the public outcry. But, once the removal of Fox and Murray made him the only possible support for the Ministry in the House of Commons and he was singled out by negotiations, he began at last to reap the rewards of having the previous autumn turned from negotiation to opposition to enforce his claims to office. Now, belatedly and by chance, wind filled the sails of his patriotic opposition. This bolstered his confidence. It made realistic his determination not to serve with Newcastle and to stand on popular issues. It also affected the details of negotiation. Pitt's popularity and Fox's unpopularity inclined the Duke of Devonshire to him at last rather than to his old friend, Fox.[19] Popular outcry so enhanced Pitt's already demonstrated influence over the House of Commons that no leading politician was ready to face the situation without him. Of course, without the internal weaknesses of the Newcastle Administration and the weight of Leicester House the situation might well have been resolved differently. Equally these alone might have brought Pitt in with Newcastle. Popular clamour added the weight to bring Newcastle down and thus decisively shaped the outcome. It was immaterial that Pitt's popularity came belatedly from Newcastle's default in a time of national crisis. Many contemporaries soon had no doubt that it was 'prodigious popularity, which supplied every other defect'.[20]

[18] See e.g. Fox to Devonshire, 16 Oct. 1756, quoted Torrens, ii, p. 314.

[19] Waldegrave, p. 88; Walpole, *Geo. II,* ii, p. 103.

[20] *AR*, i, 1758, p. 11. For a different view see McKelvey, p. 51, but note that Walpole to Mann, 4 Nov. 1756 (*Walpole's Corr.* xxi, pp. 12–13), cited there, lists Leicester House as only the last of three linked reasons for Pitt's success. On Newcastle's fall see Browning, pp. 245–53.

The swell of popularity which began during the negotiations grew to greet the appointment of the new Ministry with a wave of enthusiasm. The *Public Advertiser* reacted warmly to Pitt's declaration while ballads captured the mood of patriot expectations. The *London Magazine* explained its frontispiece for the year's collected edition as showing Pitt in the form of Perseus flying to the relief of Britannia, to deliver her from her bonds to the Continent and from the 'fell Monster', corruption.[21]

The country gentlemen 'deserted their hounds and their horses, preferring for once their parliamentary duty; and under their new Whig leader, the gallant George Townshend, displayed their banner for Pitt', one contemporary enthusiastically exulted. George Townshend, although not prepared to take office, was a valuable acquisition for his links with the country gentlemen, forged in part by his concern for the Militia, but also for his skill in manipulating public opinion by his gift for caricature. And at last Beckford committed himself, offering his services as 'one of your private soldiers without commission' in 'the cause of liberty'. Other respected independents, Tory and Whig, also declared their support.[22] More important, early parliamentary debates made it clear that not only individuals but the main body of the Tories, seeing the Old Corps out of office at last, was responding to Pitt's year-long courtship. A group of fifteen or so leading Tory Lords and Commoners wrote a letter inviting their friends to town to support the new Minister, and Potter was co-ordinating their support—although Beckford was not certain that all the Tories would see where their true interests lay.[23]

So, whatever the exact role of popularity in getting Pitt into office, his reputation had been decisively shaped. He was now not only a patriot but a patriot minister, committed in the eyes of his enthusiastic new supporters to the patriot line in foreign and domestic affairs. For Pitt this new status had advantages and disadvantages. The Tories could give him over a hundred votes in the Commons

---

[21] *PA*, 4 Dec. 1756; *The Ministry Changed: Or, The clean contrary Way. A New Song, To an Old Tune*, [London, 1756]; *LM*, xxv, 1756.

[22] Glover, *Mems.*, pp. 96–7 (quotation), 99–100; Beckford to Pitt, 6 Nov. 1756, *Corr. Chatham*, i, pp. 185–6.

[23] Newcastle to Holdernesse, 10 Dec. 1756, Add. MSS 32869, f. 316; H. Digby to Lord Digby, 14 Dec. 1756, HMC, *Eighth Report*, pt. i, 223a; Fox to Lady Caroline Fox, 14 Dec. 1756, Add. MSS 51416, f. 9; Potter to Temple, [late 1756], Beckford to Cole, 13 Dec. 1756, PRO 30/8/53, ff. 92–3, 30/8/19, f. 40.

compared with sixty at most from a revived Leicester House party.[24] Only with such support did Pitt have any immediate hope of independence of Newcastle's majority which, despite his abdication, was still holding. Yet early debates showed that obvious Tory support could draw embarrassing Whig comment and might offend other possible allies.[25] More important, it would not be easy to keep independent and popular support. It came with high expectations that Pitt would fulfil the demands of the addresses and instructions not only for strict inquiries into recent misfortunes and the expenditure of public money and the righting of immediate grievances about foreign troops and the Hanoverian soldier, but also for the traditional reforms, triennial parliaments, measures to exclude placemen and pensioners from the Commons, and an effective Militia. Such high expectations were emphatically reiterated by the *Monitor* and the *London Evening Post*. There had to be, they insisted, no coalition with past ministers and a change of measures as well as of men. Unlike previous Oppositions, the new Ministers should not forget in office the principles of opposition. The 'patriotic system, to cleanse the Augean stable' should be put into practice in full, and proper measures for the country's defence should be taken, without paying lavish subsidies. Should the new Ministry forget all this, 'let them remember, that the MONITOR will not fail to tell them in plain English of their doings'; nor would the people forget their rights.[26] These expectations were not merely propaganda. Beckford, too, wanted a new system, a virtually complete change of men and measures, and saw Pitt as 'the instrument of our deliverance'. Richard Glover, an old admirer once before bitterly disillusioned with Pitt, now renewed his friendship and expressed his hopes in similar terms.[27] He, too, spoke for opinion in the City.

Yet there were already gaps between the popular and independent expectations of Pitt and the stand he had taken on popular demands. His stipulations were further modified in the course of

[24] Namier and Brooke, i, p. 106; cf. above p. 37 and fn. 16.

[25] Walpole, *Geo. II*, ii, p. 109 and e.g. Newcastle to Holdernesse, 10 Dec. 1756, Add. MSS 32869, f. 316; Fox to Lord Digby, 14 Dec. 1756, HMC, *Eighth Report*, pt. i, 221b; Lyttelton to W. H. Lyttelton, 30 Jan. 1757, *Mems. Lyttelton*, ii, p. 584.

[26] *Mon.* 68, 13 Nov. (quotations)—74, 25 Dec. 1756; *LEP*, 13–16, 16–18, 18–20, 20–3 Nov., 9–11 Dec. 1756.

[27] Beckford to Pitt, 6 Nov. 1756, *Corr. Chatham*, i, p. 185; Glover, *Mems.*, pp. 86–92.

negotiations. His more enthusiastic supporters certainly thought he had promised more than he had.[28]

These gaps were likely to widen even further out of practical necessity. The new Ministry was a very weak one. Pitt had few personal supporters; the Duke of Devonshire was not completely committed to him; the King's heart was obviously not in the changes and Fox's credit was still high with him. Pitt would have to modify his resistance to involvement in Germany if he was to have any hope of winning the King, quite apart from what the realities of war might require; several former ministers remained in important places; and, scarcely surprising in the circumstances, Newcastle kept his majority in the House of Commons and his levées were as well attended as ever.[29] In these circumstances 'prodigious popularity', so recently won by the default of Newcastle, could hardly 'supply every other defect'. The Ministry's hold on power would probably be tenuous and its immediate achievements limited. Pitt gave all his energy to planning an expedition to check the French in America by attacking Louisbourg, the gateway to French Canada and key to French naval power in American waters. But this would not bring rapid results. At home there was little hope of relief from high corn prices. The patriot Minister was likely to prove a sham. In the disillusionment there was every likelihood that Pitt would lose his newly-won popularity in the floods of obloquy reserved for turncoat patriots by those who still remembered Pulteney.

To aggravate Pitt's difficulties he now had public critics much less sympathetic than the *Monitor* and the *London Evening Post*. On 6 November, just as the *Monitor* was boasting that its attack on the falling Ministry had called forth no defending champion, the first issue of a rival weekly essay paper appeared. This was the *Test*, launched to support Fox. Very ably written,[30] more pungent and incisive than the *Monitor*, it called ostensibly for a coalition between Fox and Pitt. But soon it was doing all it could to discredit Pitt's

[28] Lyttelton to W. H. Lyttelton, 25 Nov. 1756, *Mems. Lyttelton*, ii, p. 536, says Pitt was thought to have promised inquiries, a new parliament, measures against corruption, perhaps a triennial bill, and no subsidies to any foreign prince; Glover, *Mems.*, pp. 90–2. Cf. above p. 61 and fn. 13.

[29] Walpole, *Geo. II*, ii, pp. 107–9; Waldegrave, pp. 95–6; Lyttelton to W. H. Lyttelton, 25 Nov. 1756, *Mems. Lyttelton,* ii, p. 535.

[30] Probably mostly by Dr Philip Francis and Arthur Murphy. Sutherland, 'The City . . . 1756–7', p. 163 fn. 3.

patriot professions. It showed the inconsistencies between them and his past political conduct, attacked his arrogance, ambition and alleged nepotism, and questioned whether he could achieve anything in the present circumstances. Vitriolic personal attacks on 'William IV' and the 'Man-mountain' were its hallmark. It was immediately countered by the *Con-Test* in overt defence of Pitt[31] and the battle was joined briefly by other more transient publications.[32] But at first the *Con-Test* proved little better than a tame answering echo, the *Monitor* was an equivocal ally and the pace was set by the *Test*. These weekly exchanges provided the substance of public discussion, echoed and carried into the country in the newspapers, and simplified in visual form in the prints.[33] Against the background of this weekly barrage Pitt had to make his way. Could he, in spite of all difficulties, 'direct the storm' he had raised and fix the fluctuating tide of popularity on the side of the Ministry, the only way one observer saw of ensuring its survival? Walpole succinctly put his dilemma: 'If he Hanoverizes, or checks any inquiries, he loses popularity, and falls that way: if he humours the present rage of the people, he provokes two powerful factions' (Fox and Newcastle).[34]

The King's Speech was deliberately made 'captivating to the people'. It, with the Commons' Address in Reply, set out at least some of the issues on which Pitt had made his popular stand.[35] Pitt and Temple made the most of the sending home of the Hanoverian troops, in fact ordered by the outgoing Administration, by dramatic stands against any clause of thanks to the King for their services in the Addresses in Reply.[36] Yet Pitt's speech on the Address was

[31] Attributed to Arthur Ruffhead, Sutherland, 'The City . . . 1756–7', p. 163, fn. 4.

[32] e.g. the *Reformer* 1, 19 Nov.–3, 3 Dec. 1756; and the *Constitution* 1–3 (pro-Fox) and the *Aequipoise, or the Constitution Balanced* (pro-Pitt), 1757(occasional pamphlets rather than regular papers).

[33] *LC* regularly carried extracts from the essay papers from its first issue, 1 Jan. 1757; *Cat. Prints and Drawings*, iii, pt. ii, pp. 1030–1132 (esp. Nov.–Dec.).

[34] Lyttelton to W. H. Lyttelton, 25 Nov. 1756, *Mems. Lyttelton*, ii, p. 536 (first quotation); Symmer to Mitchell, 17 Dec. 1756, Add. MSS 6839, f. 29; Walpole to Mann, 13 Nov. 1756, *Walpole's Corr.* xxi, p. 17.

[35] Pitt to Devonshire, 15 Nov. 1757, quoted Torrens, ii, p. 342; [*The*] *Parliamentary History* [*of England from the Earliest Period to the Year 1803*], ed. William Cobbett, 36 vols., London, 1806–20, xv, cc. 771–5, 777–8.

[36] Pitt to Bute, 1, 4 Dec. 1756, Romney Sedgwick, 'Letters from [William] Pitt to [Lord] Bute: [1755–1758]', *Essays presented to Sir Lewis Namier*, ed. Richard Pares and A. J. P. Taylor, London, 1956, pp. 116–17; Temple to Devonshire, 1 Dec., Mrs Grenville to Grenville, 4 Dec. 1756, *Grenville Papers*, i, pp. 182–4, 185–6; Lyttelton to W. H. Lyttelton, 9 Dec. 1756, *Mems. Lyttelton*, ii. pp. 539–43.

studiously moderate and deliberately dampening to the high spirits of Beckford; 'in short, he spoke like a minister, and unsaid almost all he had said in opposition.'[37] Soon he was incapacitated by gout from taking an active part in business or speaking in Parliament. A lassitude fell over the outlined programme and measures proceeded only at a snail's pace.

Of the main issues, although the Hanoverians departed the Hessians had to be kept for some months and winter quarters provided for them. Pitt was anxious to make clear that this meant no permanent withdrawal from his undertakings but in the event attention was diverted by an attack from Fox on the sending away of any troops, and the Tories clearly demonstrated their support for Pitt against the sympathies of the rest of the House.[38] The question seems to have attracted little further attention outside.

A new Militia Bill was ordered on 4 October and first presented and read on 26 January. The strength of Newcastle's friends in the House ensured a lengthy and harassed passage and the Bill did not receive its third reading until 25 March on the eve of the Ministry's collapse. Despite an urgent plea from George Townshend in February, there is no record that Pitt played any part in promoting the Bill, and his illness is not a full explanation of his inaction. The Bill went on to be much amended by the Lords. Before it received the Royal Assent on 28 June the Commons had to accept some important changes which modified its ideological character if not its military usefulness.[39] There were to be yet further disappointments in the process of attempts to implement it.

The most pressing of the demands in the addresses and instruction, and a major Tory point, was for an inquiry into the disasters abroad and the misdeeds of past ministers. The *Monitor* and the *London Evening Post* continued to press this through February into March.[40] Yet this commitment was the most embarrassing for Pitt. Very early he began to draw back from it, in face of the danger of cementing a Newcastle–Fox coalition or giving Fox a chance to distinguish himself from other former ministers. The imminence of

---

[37] Lyttelton to W. H. Lyttelton, 9 Dec. 1756, *Mems. Lyttelton*, ii, p. 543 (quotation); Digby to Lord Digby, 7 Dec. 1756, HMC, *Eighth Report*, pt. i, 222b–223a.

[38] Pitt to Grenville, [12], 15 Dec. 1756, *Grenville Papers*, i, pp. 187, 188.

[39] Western, pp. 135–40; George Townshend to Pitt, 14 Feb. 1757, *Corr. Chatham*, i, p. 222.

[40] *Mon.* 83, 19 Feb., 85, 5 Mar., 88, 26 Mar. 1757; *LEP*, 19–22 Feb., 19–22 Mar. 1757.

Byng's trial, with the facts it was expected to reveal, together with Pitt's gout and the impossibility of proceeding without him, provided convenient excuses for delay.[41] Early in 1757 George Townshend took a lead, consulted with the Tories and made the first moves in the House. But these were very lethargically pressed. They came to a point only when rumours of impending changes in the Ministry began to thicken in March and then on the motion of Fox, who wanted this obstacle to a return to office out of the way. Even then, in a meeting with the Tories, Pitt continued wary; he 'promised his support, but feared he should not be able to speak five minutes for his cough'. When at last after the Easter recess and the fall of the Administration, the inquiry was held, Pitt did make a theatrical appearance and a fairly severe speech. But the final result, with every help from Pitt, vindicated the policies of the Newcastle Administration. So much for the fury of the addresses.[42]

The measures on which the Administration did take positive steps were almost equally disappointing. It introduced through Legge, the Chancellor of the Exchequer, financial policies in tune with the strong popular distrust of the moneyed interest, the National Debt, and the raising of money by private arrangements. These were worked out in co-operation with Sir John Barnard, who had not abandoned his hostility to Pitt but could not resist the chance to implement his long-advocated reforms. Yet Legge's two chief money-raising schemes, a lottery and an issue of annuities, both unconventional in form, were miserable failures and after his resignation a conventional loan had to be raised.[43] The *Test* was able to make capital out of mocking these measures as mere pretended reforms, and they were equally bitterly mocked in the third issue of the occasional pamphlet, the *Constitution*.[44] In his financial endeavours, Legge made only one small effort, in the Wine Licences Office, towards the achievement of another popular demand, reduction of the numbers of unnecessary places.[45]

[41] Hardwicke to Newcastle, 6 Dec. 1756, Yorke, *Hardwicke,* ii, pp. 376–7; Rigby to Bedford, 20 Jan., 3 Feb. 1757, *Corr. Bedford*, ii, pp. 223, 230; Glover, *Mems.*, p. 116.

[42] Walpole, *Geo. II*, ii, pp. 133–5, 198, 201 (the quotation)— 2, 205–7; Namier, 'Country Gentlemen in Parliament', pp. 39–40; Glover, *Mems.*, pp. 130–4.

[43] Sutherland, 'The City . . . 1756–7', pp. 164–8.

[44] The *Test* 14, 12 Feb., 18, 12 Mar., 20, 26 Mar., 21, 2 Apr. 1757; the *Constitution*, iii, pp. 31–2, 36–7.

[45] Walpole, *Geo. III*, ii, pp. 194–5.

Worse still, on the question of Britain's part in the war on the Continent the Ministry seemed clearly to deviate from the patriot line. Here the gap between Pitt's stand in negotiation and what his supporters thought he had promised was widest. In the previous session he had declared that he would not have signed the Prussian Treaty 'for the five great places of those who had signed it'. Yet now, in his speech in the debate on the Address in Reply he spoke of help to the Continent when everything had been done 'for yourselves', for 'you must go as far as the interests of this country were combined with those of the Powers on the continent, for combined they were'. The King's Speech was held by those sympathetic to the former Ministers to have 'enough of *Germany* in it'. There is even evidence that at this time, right at the beginning of the Administration, Pitt considered measures to help Hanover and the Continental war.[46] In any case, on 17 February Pitt made his first appearance in the House since his re-election to present a message from the King asking for money to support an army of observation for Hanover and to enable him to fulfil his engagements to Prussia. The next day Pitt moved, successfully, for a grant of £200,000, despite the gibes of Fox and a lengthy debate.[47]

Most damaging of all to the Ministry's reputation, because it keenly interested a much wider range of opinion than these ideological issues, was their attitude to the fate of Byng. This issue still dominated pamphlets, newspaper, and magazine discussion, especially when accounts of his trial were available. The pamphlets and their reviewers, notably in the *Critical Review*, were not uniformly anti-Byng, but the reviews make it clear that public clamour was still hostile.[48] Without some change in the gloomy war situation to create a diversion, it was likely to remain so. Pitt was inclined to mercy or at least fairness to Byng. It was not in his interest to allow popular anger at the early misfortunes of the war to be entirely satisfied by vengeance on Byng. The former ministers ought to bear at least some of the discredit. However, Byng's court martial went

[46] Ibid., p. 38; H. Digby to Lord Digby, 7 Dec. 1756, HMC, *Eighth Report*, pt. i, 223a (first quotation); Lyttelton to W. H. Lyttelton, 9 Dec. 1756, *Mems. Lyttelton*, ii, p. 543 (second quotation); Newcastle to Hardwicke, 11 Dec., to Holdernesse, 12 Dec. 1756, Add. MSS 35416, f. 148, 32869, f. 351.

[47] *Parl. Hist.* xv, cc. 782–803; Walpole, *Geo. II*, ii, pp. 140–2.

[48] e.g. *CR*, iii, Mar. 1757, pp. 231, 238. Of the newspapers only *PA* gave the trial little attention.

ahead as planned and on 27 January produced its verdict, a sentence of death coupled with a strong recommendation to mercy. This curious result led to a complicated series of efforts to save Byng in which the Ministers played some part.[49] Right from the beginning they were suspected of 'tenderness to Byng'. Now in the House of Commons on two occasions Pitt spoke slightingly of the court martial and in favour of mercy. Both he and Temple made representation to the King in Byng's favour. All the efforts were to no avail. After one reprieve of a fortnight, Byng was executed on the quarter-deck of the *Monarch* on 14 March 1757.[50]

There is no doubt that this outcome was in tune with the continuing general indignation of public opinion. Any reaction in Byng's favour appeared reversed by the sentence. (Not until his brave death was there another sympathetic reaction.)[51] Pitt's and Temple's efforts to avert the execution brought retribution on them. They were attacked in papers, pamphlets, and broadsides. The *Con-Test*, tentatively taking up the issue, admitted that the Administration depended on popularity yet popularity was not on its side in this issue. The paper tried to defend the Ministers for attempting to do what was right and condemned unthinking clamour which interfered with the royal prerogative of mercy. This merely provoked the *Test* to charge them with flaunting the wishes of 'an whole people' and denying the voice and majesty of the people.[52] Pitt himself said he received threatening letters. All observers agreed that his popularity was seriously challenged. One even thought it totally ruined.[53] In the City feeling ran particularly high. The Lord Mayor told Rigby that 'there never was any thing in the City like the unpopularity of the House of Commons and Mr Pitt. . . . He is not apt to be warm in his expressions, but he was so today.' The issue was regarded there as 'a Tyral of the Strength of the Old and New

[49] Walpole, *Geo. II*, ii, pp. 116–24, 135–40, 144–88; Pope, pp. 263–83.

[50] Walpole to Mann, 29 Nov. 1756, *Walpole's Corr.* xxi, p. 23; Walpole, *Geo. II*, ii, pp. 108, 139, 140, 149–50, 152, 157, 163, 189–90.

[51] Walpole, *Geo. II*, ii, p. 145; Symmer to Mitchell, 1, 8 Feb., 11 Mar. 1757, Add. MSS 6839, ff. 36, 38, 43; cf. *A too hasty censure, Feb. 15, 1757. And a too necessary retraction, Mar. 20 1757. Verses relative to the late unhappy A[dmira]l*, reviewed *CR*, iii, Apr. 1757, p. 377; *GM*, xxvii, Apr. 1757, pp. 173–6.

[52] The *Con-Test* 16, 5 Mar., 18, 19 Mar. 1757; the *Test* 17, 5 Mar. (quotation), 18, 12 Mar. 1757.

[53] Walpole, *Geo. II*, ii, pp. 138, 140; Symmer to Mitchell, 4 Mar. 1757, Add. MSS 6839, f. 41; Calcraft to Abercrombie, 5 Mar. 1757, Add. MSS 17493, f. 51.

Ministry, in which the latter have greatly lost themselves, and exposed their Weakness'. City financiers were said to be strengthened in their determination not to lend money to the Government. The fall of the Ministry seemed imminent. 'The Dyke of Popularity being broke down they ly open to Inundation.'[54]

Yet, ironically, neither the Tories, nor Richard Glover as spokesman for popular elements in the City, joined this particular hue and cry. The Tories even more than Pitt (because they did not share his interest in a possible coalition) wanted the former Ministers rather then Byng to be the scapegoat for the nation's misfortunes. Beckford, although he acknowledged the unpopularity of any attempt to save Byng, declared the sentence 'cruel' in the House of Commons and supported the Bill to release members of the court martial from their oaths so they could explain their verdict. In the City, despite the height of feeling there, the Tories even made a last-minute effort, led by Aldermen Blakiston and Scott, to call a Common Council to address the King for mercy, only to have their hesitant moves stalled by the Lord Mayor.[55] The attitude of the Tories helps to explain why the *Monitor* was strangely silent on such a potent subject through all the period of Byng's court martial and its aftermath, until 12 March, on the very eve of his execution. It did not dare earlier to try to counter the dominant demand for vengeance. Then, when all hope of mercy was past, it was not above making some capital out of the situation by declaring strongly for the harshest punishment. The *London Evening Post* was also silent at first, but came out for Byng early in March, and Shebbeare was furious against the court martial and those in the City ('blood-thirsty hypocrites') who had opposed mercy.[56]

[54] Rigby to Bedford, 3 Mar. 1757, *Corr. Bedford*, ii, p. 239 (first quotation); Edward Owen to Edward Weston, 5 Mar. 1757, HMC, *Tenth Report*, pt. i, p. 312 (second quotation); Calcraft to Abercrombie, 5 Mar. 1757, Add MSS 17493, f. 51; Symmer to Mitchell, 11 Mar. 1757, Add. MSS 6839, f. 43 (third quotation).

[55] Glover, *Mems.*, pp. 118–21; Walpole, *Geo. II,* ii, pp. 149, 188–9; Sir Thomas Robinson to Newcastle, 26 Feb., memorandum of West, 11 Mar., Hardwicke to Newcastle, 11 Mar. 1757, Add. MSS 32870, ff. 121, 254, 260. For further details see Rogers, 'London Politics', pp. 199–200. Sir Matthew Blakiston, wholesale grocer, Grocers' Company, Alderman for Bishopsgate 1750–69, Sheriff 1753–4, Lord Mayor 1760–1 (see below pp. 173, 191), knighted 1759, baronet 1763, died 1774; a Tory, prominent in opposition to the East India Company monopoly (see below p. 151). Robert Scott, West India merchant, Coopers' Company, Alderman for Aldergate 1752–60, Sheriff 1750–1.

[56] *Mon.* 86, 12 Mar. 1757; *LEP*, 5–8, 8–10, 10–12 Mar. 1757; *An Appeal To The People: Part the Second*, London, 1757, attributed by *MR*, xvi, May 1757, p. 469, to Shebbeare. See also *CR*, iii, May 1757, pp. 478–9 (quotation).

Indeed, despite the mocking commentary of the *Test*, there is little evidence of disillusionment among Pitt's particular supporters in the City, or among the Tories, even on the other issues on which there had been delays, disappointments and apparent reversals. True, Richard Glover commented caustically that the measures of the parliamentary session were

all within the old narrow circle, trite, trifling, and iniquitous, except one absurd deviation from the plain track of borrowing money for the annual supplies, where an affectation of doing better than well, ended in disappointment and disgrace.

With equal sharpness he questioned the sincerity of Pitt's support for the Militia and the inquiries. He also commented on the effects of Pitt's illness and consequent inaccessibility, peevishness and pride, by which 'he rather lost than gained adherents'.[57] But on the Militia the *Monitor* showed no signs of disappointment with Pitt. It supported the measure during its passage and answered objections without any complaints of delay. Only much later, a month or so after the Royal Assent was given, did it protest in detail and then over the amendments made in the Lords.[58] Nor were there other signs of Tory or independent dissatisfaction. The number of pamphlets still appearing on the Militia bore some witness to a continuing public interest, with a general consensus in favour of some scheme, but this discussion was not turned to any political point. The *Test* made no use of the issue in its general criticism of Pitt.

The *Test* did constantly harp on the delay of the inquiries while the *Con-Test* on the whole avoided the subject.[59] On this question the Tories showed some sympathy with Pitt's political dilemma. They, too, had no wish to unite his opponents and the delays in pressing the inquiries seem to have arisen at least in part from this sympathy.[60] Outside, the *London Evening Post* and the *Monitor* continued their exhortations and the *Monitor* reacted to the final outcome by publishing its own pamphlet refuting the mild resolu-

[57] Glover, *Mems.*, pp. 104 (first quotation), 107, 112 (second quotation), 124–5.

[58] *Mon.* 76, 8 Jan., 84, 26 Feb., 85, 5 Mar., 105, 23 July 1757.

[59] The *Test* 3, 27 Nov. 1757, 14, 12 Feb., 17, 5 Mar., 19, 19 Mar., 21, 2 Apr. 1757; the *Con-Test* 19, 26 Mar. 1757.

[60] Potter to Temple [late 1756], PRO 30/8/53, f. 92; Rigby to Bedford, 20 Jan, 1757, *Corr. Bedford*, ii, p. 223; Walpole to Mann, 13 Feb. 1757, *Walpole's Corr.* xxi, pp. 55–6.

tions passed by the Commons. Yet again Pitt was not blamed. While his Ministry was still in office the *Monitor* found sufficient excuse for delay in the need first to pass supplies. Later, the fall of the Ministry was held to have denied the people the fulfilment of their expectations of seeing the guilty punished.[61]

Even on the question of help to the Continent the Tories supported Pitt in the House of Commons, while Beckford declared his agreement in the name of the City.[62] Undoubtedly this issue caused considerable discomfort which the *Test* did its best to increase.[63] George Townshend was seriously offended by Pitt's move and was only with difficulty persuaded to mollify the independents. Sir John Philipps felt obliged, a few days after the vote, to defend himself and the Tories against charges of inconsistency. Pitt had to emphasize that no British troops were to be sent to Germany, and the next month he and Legge had to make explicit denials of rumours to this effect.[64] The *Monitor*, however, defended the aid to Prussia, and its arguments give some indication of those used to win over the Tories. To the *Monitor*, the small amount of the subsidy and the fact that it was being paid to secure the alliance of Prussia, no mere puny German prince or far-distant Russia, made the difference. The alliance was being made in purely British interests. Foreign interests had not been given the chief attention in British policy; nor had Britain entered as a principal in their quarrels. Pitt's measure, linking Britain with 'the idolized King of Prussia', could thus be represented as 'just the happy Medium in which we ought to steer'.[65]

As for the Administration's novel financial moves, the fact that it had tried and apparently been defeated by the moneyed interest of the City was likely to endear it to popular elements there, despite the

[61] *LEP*, 17–19 Mar., 5–7 Apr. 1757; *Mon.* 88, 26 Mar., 89, 2 Apr., 94, 7 May, 95, 14 May, 99, 11 June 1757; *An Account Of The Facts which appeared on the late Enquiry into the Loss of Minorca from Authentic Papers*, published 16 July 1757.

[62] Walpole, *Geo. II*, ii, p. 142; Jenkinson to Miller, 19 Feb. 1757, *An Eighteenth Century Correspondence*, ed. Lilian Dickins and Mary Stanton, London, 1910, pp. 353–4.

[63] The *Test* 15, 19 Feb., 17, 5 Mar., 20, 26 Mar. 1757.

[64] Glover, *Mems.*, pp. 112–15; Diary of Sir Roger Newdigate, transcript held by History of Parliament Trust, 21 Feb. 1757; Fox to Dodington, [20 Mar. 1757], *Dodington*, pp. 358, 359; Rigby to Bedford, 21 Mar. 1757, *Corr. Bedford*, ii, pp. 240–1.

[65] *Mon.* 87, 19 Mar., 92, 23 Apr. 1757; Glover, *Mems.*, p. 114 (first quotation); Jenkinson to Miller, 19 Feb. 1757, *An Eighteenth Century Corr.*, p. 354 (second quotation).

mockery of the *Test*. They would continue to concur with the claims of the *Con-Test* that the moves had been foiled by a conspiracy of opponents to the Administration. The *Monitor* gave its support not to the plans of the Administration but to Beckford's own idea, aired in the House of Commons, for new taxes on tea and salt. But this is more evidence of divisions among popular forces in the City than of disillusionment with Pitt.[66]

So the Ministry was not deserted by its friends. Even more its reputation was saved by its enemies. It was at least some use to Pitt that 'he was understood by all to be only *a nominal minister without a grain of power*' as he described himself in the House.[67] The very forcefulness of the *Test's* continuing personal attacks, especially when amplified and coarsened by the *Constitution,* provoked a reaction in his favour. Particularly damaging to its case was its scant sympathy for Pitt's illness.[68] By March at the latest its attacks were acquiring a certain repetitive monotony, while the *Con-Test* was showing more vigour and initiative, especially with the argument that the Ministry was doing everything possible against great odds.[69] The reaction against the *Test* can be seen clearly in the *Monitor*'s changing tone. From its initial high expectations of the Ministers it soon moved to defend them against criticism and to urge that too much could not be expected too soon in view of the magnitude of the task that faced them. As time passed, the *Monitor* made as much as possible of what was done as portents of more to come. Increasing emphasis was placed on the difficulties of the Ministry's situation, denied proper confidence and power and surrounded by 'enemies'. Explicitly or implicitly, delays and deficiencies were attributed to the problems inherited from, or the continuing influence of, the former Ministers, on whom the paper continued to pour scorn. Many of its most explicit defences of Pitt were direct answers to the *Test*.[70] Its growing animosity towards Fox is even clearer evidence of the *Test's* effect.[71]

[66] Sutherland, 'The City . . . 1756–7', pp. 169–71; *Mon.* 80, 29 Jan. 1757; *LEP*, 18–21 Dec. 1756, 17–19 Mar. 1757.

[67] Glover, *Mems.*, pp. 111–12.

[68] The *Test* 6, 18 Dec. 1756, 9, 8 Jan., 10, 15 Jan., 12, 29 Jan. 1757.

[69] The *Con-Test* 19, 26 Mar., 21, 9 Apr. 1757.

[70] e.g. *Mon.* 74, 25 Dec. 1756, 79, 22 Jan., 87, 19 Mar., 89, 2 Apr. 1757; cf. *LEP*, 25–7 Jan., 17–19 Mar. 1757.

[71] *Mon.* 81, 4 Feb., 92, 23 Apr. 1757.

More widely, the *Test–Con-Test* duel confirmed the now inveterate Fox–Pitt rivalry and caused others who, like Beckford, favoured both, or like Sir John Philipps, leaned to Fox,[72] to make their choice—which for the same reasons as those of the *Monitor* went to Pitt. There was a marked swing in all forms of publicity in favour of Pitt, shown for example in the *Constitution*'s irritated reference to pro-Pitt papers and in the general tone of notices in the *Critical Review*. The *Monthly Review*, in particular, observed 'how much like a wreck the Commonwealth has fallen into their hands: how difficult a task the Salvage is like to prove'. The *London Chronicle* quickly abandoned its initial impartiality to convey praise of Pitt from the *London Evening Post* and the *Gazetteer* to its readers.[73]

Even more was Pitt's standing secured by the circumstances of the fall of the Administration—as Newcastle foresaw it would be.[74] This arose out of the dissatisfaction of the King and had little to do with Pitt's popular reputation. By February and March the King was putting out constant feelers for a change and doing all he could to provoke a resignation. In the end, Cumberland's approaching departure to command the forces for the defence of Hanover precipitated matters. On 5 April Temple was dismissed; when this failed to provoke Pitt to resign, he, too, was dismissed the next day. The resignations of Legge and George and James Grenville followed. On 9 April Cumberland left for Germany.[75]

Such ill-considered action by the King gave rise to the most impressive demonstrations yet of Pitt's popularity. His dismissal enabled his supporters to represent him as the victim of 'the Remnant of the old Ministry, connected with the Patriots in his Majesty's Service and Councils', the 'old junto' who misrepresented him to the King.[76] Thus he was seen as a martyr rather than betrayer of the popular cause. To such sentiments, far more than to any particular policies, Pitt owed the apparently overwhelming wave of popular support that followed, shown in the 'clamour' after

---

[72] Potter to Temple, [late 1756], PRO 30/8/53, f. 92.

[73] The *Constitution*, ii, 1757, p. 26; *MR*, xvi, Feb. 1757, p. 167 (reviewing the *Aequipoise*, a pro-Pitt answer to the *Constitution*; *LC*, 22–4 Mar. 1757.

[74] Newcastle to Hardwicke, 26 Mar. 1757, Add. MSS 32870, ff. 339–40; cf. Symmer to Mitchell, 5 Apr. 1757, Add. MSS 6839, f. 47.

[75] Waldegrave, pp. 95–107; Walpole, *Geo. II*, ii, pp. 192, 195–9; *Dodington*, pp. 355–60.

[76] Maitland, ii, p. 17; Smollett, quoted in *Parl. Hist.* xv, c. 774 fn.

the dismissals and in the 'rain' of gold boxes containing the freedom and compliments of a dozen cities that fell on him and Legge. The ecstatic terms of these addresses bear witness not to their recipients' actual achievements but rather to the degree to which eyes which might otherwise have been opened to their shortcomings were closed by their martyr's role.[77] It did not matter that the clamour and the gold boxes were carefully manœuvred in almost all cases by Pitt's personal supporters and the Tories, who had some considerable interest in his fate. Nor did it matter that the most was made of the evidence of popularity. For example, the *Monitor* claimed that 'every city is striving, who shall first imitate the gratitude of London, with their freedom presented to the firm patriots, who have retired.'[78] Despite the sorry performance of the Devonshire Administration, which Glover at least saw clearly, Pitt had avoided the bitter denunciations still heaped on Pulteney for deserting the patriot cause some fifteen years before. Both contemporaries and historians were impressed. As Glover recognized, the essential popular basis of Pitt's political strength seemed secured.[79]

Nowhere was this more remarkably shown than in London. For the first time in the century the City was prepared to praise a government. Within a few days moves were afoot to present the freedom of the City to Pitt and Legge. The leadership came once again from popular Tory circles. Deputy Hodges proposed the motion at the meeting of the Common Council on 15 April. According to the *Test*, Beckford was the mastermind behind the move, a sign that he was coming to be recognized as Pitt's spokesman—to the *Test*, his incendiary—in the City. In fact he was not present at the Common Council and there is no other evidence about his part in the proceedings. The *Monitor* had nothing to say about the City vote either before or immediately after it took place. It was mentioned only in passing in the issue of 23 April. For the time being the *Con-Test* was left to defend the addresses, especially that of London, against the charges of the *Test* that they were unconstitutional invasions of the King's prerogative, a most telling

---

[77] See e.g. the City's Address, Maitland, ii, p. 18, and that of Chester, *GM*, xxvii, Aug. 1757, p. 387. Legge shared the glory rather than Temple because of his financial measures.

[78] Langford, 'William Pitt and public opinion, 1757', esp. pp. 54–72; *Mon.* 92, 23 Apr. 1757.

[79] Glover, *Mems.*, p. 124; cf. *AR*, i, 1758, p. 12.

point. Altogether it seems again that Beckford was far from being in control of the swing of City opinion or uppermost among the Tories there.[80] This time, however, there was none of the signs of divisions among the Tories or of Whig reluctance that there had been over the Address and Instructions in 1756 and earlier in 1757. No one spoke against the motion. Only Sir John Barnard voted against it.[81]

True, this near-unanimity was possible only because the Lord Mayor had already insisted on a moderate motion. The general alarm in the City at the political changes did not arise entirely out of devotion to Pitt. Sympathy for Newcastle, who did not look like benefiting from the changes, had strengthened in some moneyed circles. More important, much of the alarm was due to the fears of sinister designs of military government and attempts on the succession on the part of Fox and Cumberland. These fears, which Pitt was not above stimulating, occupied much of the attention of the *Test* and *Con-Test*—although not the *Monitor*—in the weeks after the dismissal.[82] All these feelings, however, with the help of the leadership of the Tories, worked for Pitt. In the City at least, the demonstration of opinion cannot be dismissed as merely the result of manipulation. The election the next month of Hodges as Town Clerk, although he did not have the usual legal training, was a clear sign of the strength of pro-Pitt popular feeling, even if it also showed that the Court faction was far from overtaken yet.[83]

Reaction to the ministerial changes was suspicious, even hostile, in almost all the newspapers and magazines. The *Public Advertiser* and *Read's Weekly Journal* made little or no comment, but the *London*

[80] *PA*, 8 Apr. 1757; Jour. Common Council, 61, ff. 155–6; *Mon.* 92, 23 Apr., the *Con-Test* 23, 23 Apr., the *Test* 23, 16 Apr., 24, 23 Apr. 1757.

[81] West to Newcastle, 15 Apr. 1757, Add. MSS 32870, f. 437; *GM*, xxvii, Apr. 1757, p. 186. A City broadsheet of early 1757 in the style of the *Test* suggests bitter Whig hostility to Tory 'Cabals'. *The Enquiry is not begun! When will it?* [London, 1757].

[82] Newcastle to Hardwicke, 8 Apr., Abercrombie to Halifax [*c.* 7 Apr.], Watkins to Newcastle, 12 Apr. 1757, Add. MSS 32870, ff. 388, 372, 409; Glover, *Mems.*, p. 127; *Letters from George III to Lord Bute*, p. xlix; the *Test* 15, 19 Feb., 28, 21 May, 32, 18 June, the *Con-Test* 25, 7 May, 30, 11 June 1757. See also Rogers, 'London Politics', p. 201.

[83] Rogers, 'London Politics', pp. 206–7. 122 Common Councilmen and 13 Aldermen voted for Hodges, 102 and 11 for his rival, John Paterson, a lawyer. The Aldermanic majority for Hodges is noteworthy. The *PA* report, 11 May 1757, makes clear the great interest in this election. Only 22 members of Common Council were absent.

Chronicle continued its recent pro-Pitt sympathies, which were also shown in different ways by the magazines.[84] Against such a background the *London Evening Post* and the *Monitor* could shape their now enthusiastic account of Pitt's supposed achievements. 'Foreign connections were not disregarded: neither were they admitted to the chief attention of the British policy. Our allies were not to be deserted: neither were we to enter as principals into their quarrels.' Prudent measures of economy and tax relief had been taken; a well-regulated Militia was being established; the Hessians and Hanoverians had been dismissed; America had been made the chief object of armaments, and France the target to which all councils and armaments were pointed; the system of placemen and pensioners was despised and abolished, so that the people were no longer burdened with taxes to pay them; a free Parliament and a disembarrassed Ministry were ready to pursue the authors of the nation's troubles to justice; Pitt had united 'all parties to the sovereign and his family'.[85] His patriot reputation, rather than being tarnished, shone the more brightly.

Although the immediate impact of the spectacular outburst following Pitt's dismissal is unquestionable, recent months had revealed some complexities about Pitt's 'popularity' which could vitally affect its reliability. Popularity could have two meanings, not necessarily coinciding. In the sense of a general reputation among 'public opinion' it was vague, fickle and transient, especially in the circumstances of continued gloom abroad, no good news from America and economic hardship at home. The violent swings of the last few months had shown its unreliability. Despite appearances now, there was little to suggest that Pitt was secure in this opinion. At the most such popularity could give a temporary stimulus to a politician's negotiating power because it could create an uneasy feeling that any government without him would not be in control of affairs. But popularity could also mean the support of specific groups such as the Tories and the popular elements in the City, which favoured particular 'popular' policies in constitutional, financial, and foreign affairs. Such support could be less fickle and transient and therefore more useful politically. Yet it was vulnerable

---

[84] *LC,* 2–5, 7–9, 12–14 Apr. 1757; *GM,* xxvii, Apr. 1757, pp. 156–8; *LM,* xxvi, May 1757, p. 251.

[85] *Mon.* 90–3, 9–30 Apr. 1757 (quoting 92 and 91); *LEP,* 5–7, 7–9, 9–12 Apr. 1757.

in other ways. It was not easy to maintain a patriot reputation by firmly following popular policies in office. The Tories had their own reasons for supporting Pitt, arising more from antipathy to other politicans of the Whig Corps and resentment at their long exclusion from influence than from warmth towards him. Although they had no one else of first rank to turn to they might well lapse into the political backwaters again.[86] In all, Pitt's 'popularity' was extremely vulnerable. It still remained to be seen whether effective use could be made of it.

[86] Walpole, *Geo. II*, ii, p. 109 fn.; Lyttelton to W. H. Lyttelton, 30 Jan. 1757, *Mems. Lyttelton*, ii, pp. 584–5.

III

The Patriot Minister in Coalition
1757–1758

Despite the apparent unanimity of public opinion in support of Pitt, in April 1757 political stability was as far away as ever. Although the King inclined to Fox, the most obvious solution was a coalition of Pitt and Newcastle. Hardwicke and Newcastle had for some time favoured this; Pitt would intrude less on Newcastle's interests in the Treasury and patronage than Fox, and the reversionary interest was much more attractive than the military interest.[1] Some of the moneyed men and others in the City were proposing a Pitt–Newcastle alliance. Temple expected it as the outcome of the situation as early as 8 April.[2] Leicester House now saw it as the only protection against the influence of Cumberland and the King's obvious preference for Fox. Bute and the Princess rejected reconciliation with Fox and quickly established cautious contact with Newcastle.[3] Even Pitt, although he might have appeared to 'fling himself upon the people, and the Tories,' and to be 'determined to have Nothing to do either with Fox, or Us', had kept open his contacts with Newcastle and especially Hardwicke.[4] Certainly the last five months had made it clear that without some alliance his political situation was very weak, and Newcastle was likely to be a more malleable ally than Fox.

 Yet, because of Pitt's weakness, he was not likely to acquiesce until he had done all he could to secure his independence in any

    [1] Hardwicke to Newcastle, 6 Dec. 1756, Yorke, *Hardwicke*, ii, pp. 375–8; Browning, pp. 256–7.
    [2] Glover, *Mems.*, pp. 124–7; Watkins to Newcastle, 10 May 1757, Add. MSS 32871, f. 53; Temple to Grenville, 8 Apr. 1757, *Grenville Papers*, i, p. 193.
    [3] Walpole, *Geo. II*, ii, p. 203; McKelvey, pp. 55–8.
    [4] Newcastle to Hardwicke, 11 Dec. 1756, Add. MSS 35416, f. 150.

arrangements. The obvious outcome was delayed for nearly three months, in the midst of an unsuccessful war, largely because of the difficulties he raised, together with the extreme reluctance of the King. The King much preferred Fox but his unpopularity and that of his patron, Cumberland, with both politicians and public made impossible a ministry under him, or even with him in a prominent position. Neither Newcastle nor others would go it alone. Eventually, both the King and Pitt were brought to modify their demands and on 29 June the Pitt–Newcastle Coalition kissed hands.[5]

So began what was to be one of the strongest and most successful ministries of the century. In it, Pitt's place at the pinnacle of political office was secured. In face of the unremitting hostility of the King, the support of Leicester House was undoubtedly important in securing this outcome. This time Bute and Pitt kept in close touch throughout the negotiations; Glover certainly thought that Pitt was acting under strong influence from Leicester House which Glover saw as 'his only foundation'. Bute was instrumental in renewing contact between Pitt and Newcastle when it had broken down, and helped to resolve last-minute difficulties with Legge.[6] Lord George Sackville (now attached to Leicester House) was not the only one to see the negotiations as a contest 'between Leicester-house and the Duke', and, in view of the King's age, the reversionary interest was the stronger. Concern for a union of the Royal Family when circumstances abroad were critical was a potent motive both for Fox in seeking a reconciliation with Leicester House at the outset and for Hardwicke in recommending the final outcome. Union would bring substantial advantage to whoever secured it; success in achieving it was regarded as a major strength of the new Administration.[7] To many people, Pitt and his friends entered it as the Prince of Wales's men, the tokens of this success.

Yet the support of Leicester House for Pitt was not as unequivocal as it might have seemed. In Bute's contacts with Newcastle, the

[5] For contemporary accounts of the negotiations see Waldegrave, pp. 109–34; Walpole, *Geo. II*, ii, pp. 203–4, 207–8, 210–11, 215–24; Lyttelton to W. H. Lyttelton, 23 Jan. 1758 [?June 1757], *Mems. Lyttelton*, ii, pp. 596–600. See also Browning, pp. 256–61.

[6] 'Letters from Pitt to Bute', pp. 121–6; Glover, *Mems.*, pp. 138, 150; Lyttelton to W. H. Lyttelton, 23 Jan. 1758 [? June 1757], *Mems. Lyttelton*, ii, p. 597; Walpole, *Geo. II*, ii, p. 224; McKelvey, p. 59.

[7] Walpole, *Geo. II*, ii, pp. 222 (quotation), 203; Lyttelton to W. H. Lyttelton, 23 Jan. 1758 [? June 1757], *Mems. Lyttelton*, ii, p. 599.

claims of Pitt were not always vigorously pressed and indeed sometimes did not feature at all.[8] As always there were differences of purpose between Leicester House and its political allies. Although it was in Leicester House's interests to have the claim of its ally recognized, without other strengths Pitt's claims to highest office might well not have seemed so unanswerable. Certainly he would have had less prospect of independence.

So Pitt's revived popularity and the effects it was likely to have on management of the House of Commons were again of major importance. There were no significant signs of abatement in the course of the negotiations. Throughout, all the newspapers kept Pitt's name to the fore by reporting the grants of freedoms while the *London Evening Post* employed its usual variety of devices to extol him. Even *Read's Weekly Journal* had an occasional verse of praise. 'The Popularity of Mr Pitt is immense', noted Charles Jenkinson of 21 April. In early June, Waldegrave, explaining to the King his inability to form a ministry, gave as one of his reasons that 'the popular cry without doors was violent in favor of Mr Pitt'.[9]

This is confirmed by the continuing public controversy which accompanied the negotiations. The rivalry of Pitt and Fox was fought out as bitterly as ever in pamphlets, prints and especially in the weekly essays of the *Test* and *Con-Test*, regularly carried in the *London Chronicle*. Through April and May the *Test* felt obliged to make repeated attempts to depreciate the expressions of popular support for Pitt, particularly those from the City and Bath. The people, it suggested, were easily misled and could quickly change their views as the fluctuations of past months showed. A pamphlet of late April in defence of Fox made a telling attack on the City's grant of its freedom to Pitt and Legge and on their patriot image reflected in the speeches and addresses accompanying the grant. The attack was reinforced by a sham reply. Another powerful pamphlet widened the criticism to accuse Pitt of attempting to use popularity to establish an 'ambitious despotism' and a virulent broadsheet put the personal and political case against his in the crudest terms. No comparable works appeared in defence. Yet the appearance of popularity was not dispelled. Although the *Test* hinted late in May

[8] McKelvey, pp. 56–8.

[9] e.g. *LEP*, 16–19, 19–21, 26–8 Apr. 1757; *RWJ*, 11 June 1757; Jenkinson to Sanderson Miller, 21 Apr. 1757, *An Eighteenth Century Corr.*, p. 365; Waldegrave, pp. 129–30.

that the people might change their views again if rumours of an impending coalition proved true, during June it was unable to seize on anything to suggest that such a change had happened.[10] In different ways , both the determined efforts to belittle Pitt's popularity and the apparent lack of success in changing opinion bear witness to the effectiveness of the expressions of support.

This continuing appearance of popularity greatly strengthened Pitt's hand. It, rather than the somewhat equivocal support of Leicester House, made all other politicians in turn afraid to serve without Pitt despite the feelings of the King. So also Fox's unpopularity and the exaggerated fears of his patron, Cumberland, made others reluctant to serve with Fox despite the urgings of the King. If Newcastle's majority in the House of Commons and the united support of the Royal Family were necessary to any stable ministry in such critical circumstances, so too, observers felt, was some popular standing outside.[11] The popular outcry, having opened the way for Pitt in 1756 in unpromising circumstances, now helped to restore him to high office in an alliance which could make his tenure more certain.

The value of popularity seemed proved. Yet Pitt accepted the new arrangements only as a 'bitter, but necessary cup'.[12] Initially the strength of the union favoured Newcastle far more than Pitt by finally solving the various problems which had harried him since the death of Pelham: leadership in the Commons, jealousy of Fox, and differences with Leicester House. Pitt on the other hand was in real danger of being swamped. His dissatisfaction arose partly from the enforced concessions over offices for his allies which left them unhappy.[13] But there was much more to it than that. The very manner of his 'victory' threatened the popularity which helped to secure it and gave him independence. He was now the ally of that 'arch-corrupter', the Duke of Newcastle, in popular eyes the source

---

[10] e.g. the *Test* 22–4, 9–23 Apr., 26–7, 7–14 May, 29, 28 May 1757; *An Essay On Political Lying*, London, 1757, esp. pp. 20–8; *A Seasonable Reply To A Scurrilous Pamphlet, Called An Essay On Political Lying*, London, 1757; *A Letter To the Right Honorable H[enry] F[ox], Esq.*, London, 1757; *The Speech of William the Fourth, to both Houses of P[arliament]*, London, [Apr. 1757].

[11] Waldegrave, pp. 129–31; Hardwicke to Lyttelton, 4 July 1757, Lyttelton to Hardwicke, 7 July 1757, Yorke, *Hardwicke*, ii, pp. 410–11.

[12] Pitt to Bute, 28 June 1757, 'Letters from Pitt to Bute', p. 124.

[13] McKelvey, p. 60.

of all misfortunes. Anson was restored to the Admiralty, and Fox returned, even if only as Paymaster. In these arrangements 'measures' had hardly been discussed, let alone insisted on. Lyttelton put his finger on the heart of the problem: 'how will he now deserve the gold boxes which were sent him for having turned out those vile ministers?'.[14] Could Pitt remain a patriot in such circumstances?

In the City, the moneyed men responded warmly enough to Newcastle's return to office[15] but general reactions were very different. Glover had consistently made clear his hostility to any coalition with Newcastle, urging Pitt to rely instead on a change of heart in the nation in response to dire calamity. Now he bitterly reflected that Newcastle had inveigled Pitt as he had seduced other 'distinguished popular leaders' before. Walpole reported that the City was especially indignant at the return of Anson, and Birch told Lord Royston on good authority that Pitt had deemed it necessary to send for James Hodges, recently elected Town Clerk, to explain to him 'the Grounds upon which himself and his Friends were induced to consent to the Coalition'.[16]

Among the independents, the reaction of George Townshend was ominous. He retired into the country disgusted with 'the ridiculous and dishonest arrangement of men'. Doubtless he was offended by the 'amnesty for Fox' as his brother Charles was at his failure to win promotion. Yet George's disgust also stemmed from 'not the least adoption of any Public System of Measures being declared or even hinted at by him', while Charles doubted whether a sincere union or a uniform system of measures could be expected 'from the present coalition of men', with their 'inveterate jealousies and confirmed mutual distrust'.[17] From Oxfordshire Charles reported that Pitt's popularity was 'strangely abated'. There were reports that 'the Body Corporate of Chester have sent an express to Sir Richard

[14] Lyttelton to W. H. Lyttelton, 23 Jan. 1758 [? June 1757], *Mems. Lyttelton*, ii, p. 599.

[15] Watkins to Newcastle, 25 June 1757, Add. MSS 32871, f. 399.

[16] Glover, *Mems.*, pp. 127–30, 137–8, 143–5, 150–3 (quotation p. 152); Walpole, *Geo. II*, ii, p. 227; Birch to Royston, 6 Aug. 1757, Add. MSS 35398, ff. 344–5.

[17] Endorsement 20 June of Pitt to Townshend, 18 June 1757, HMC, *Eleventh Report*, pt. iv, p. 393; Walpole, *Geo. II*, ii, p. 222; C. Townshend to Devonshire, 30 June 1757, quoted Sir Lewis Namier and John Brooke, *Charles Townshend*, London, 1964, pp. 54–5. See also Atherton, pp. 56–7 and plate 95 for a mocking print probably by George Townshend.

Grosvenor not to give their Gold Box and freedom to Pitt and Legge, as they began to Suspect them, many other Corporations talk of Recalling theirs too'.[18]

The *Monitor* shared such suspicions. Through the long negotiations it had never considered the possibility of any coalition.[19] Then, in the paper of 2 July, when the arrangements were already known, the author lectured the *Monitor* on what its reaction should be

should a coalition take place; should the gentlemen, so lately idolized by the nation for the rectitude of their actions, be overcome by the intrigues of a court to join with the heads of that administration, to whose misconduct all the world has placed the losses, and disgrace of Great Britain; then will be the time to convince your readers that no power, nor interest is capable of shaking your honest resolution to give the people alarm in time.

And he asked

Might not such a coalition induce a belief that he, who was adored for his upright professions, had veered about; deserted the cause of his country; adopted the German measures, was never sincere in his enquiry after the authors of our misfortunes, and only attentive to serve some private passion or interest in preference to his country?[20]

The *Monitor* was not alone in its plain speaking against Pitt. The short-lived *Crab-Tree* advertised for lost gold boxes 'supposed to have been either given away by mistake or thrown away in a hurry'. Suddenly it dropped the 'allegorical mask' which for ten weeks it had used to establish its determinedly Tory and country view of recent English history to launch an attack even stronger than the *Monitor*'s on the 'heterogeneous jumble' of the Coalition and on Pitt and Legge for making such an 'unnatural junction' without any consideration for the public good. How in such circumstances, it asked, could effective government result, whatever the assurances given by the 'two admired patriots'? The longer-lasting *Citizen* reproached Pitt for 'condescending to be a Court-hack'.[21] The

---

[18] C. Townshend to Devonshire, 30 June 1757, quoted Namier and Brooke, *Charles Townshend*, p. 55; Calcraft to Loudoun, 10 July 1757, Add. MSS 17493, f. 80.

[19] With one exception, a briefly expressed early hope that 'the lion will never couch with the fox'. *Mon.* 93, 30 Apr. 1757.

[20] *Mon.* 102, 2 July 1757. The next two papers continue very hostile to the Coalition.

[21] The *Crab-Tree* 10, 28 June (quotation), 11, 5 July 1757; Birch to Royston, 23 July 1757, Add. MSS 35398, f. 338.

London Evening Post was also shaken, if only briefly. Throughout the negotiations it had been fearful of the return of its old enemies to power. It did foreshadow a defence of the Coalition in the last week in June but, unlike other papers, it did not carry a full list of the new Ministry, and made no comment at the time of the announcements. It later relayed some of the more outspoken misgivings. So did the *London Chronicle*, which, in its excerpts of the weeklies, had tended hitherto to give more space to the supporters of Pitt. The Coalition was little noticed in pamphlets, but one defence was sceptically received by both the Reviews.[22]

The *Con-Test*, by contrast, remained committed to Pitt and accepted the Coalition as the much-desired return of the patriots to office. It was relieved of its antagonist on one front when the *Test* went down bravely on 9 July, ironically claiming to have brought its opponents to see the merits of those they reviled and accentuating in its praise the very features of the Coalition least acceptable to Pitt's supporters. The *Con-Test* now turned to counter the new attack on Pitt from the rear. At first, uneasily, it urged trust in the good faith of the 'patriots'. Then, in answer to the *Monitor*, it denied that there were any grounds to suspect that they had deserted their principles. Rather there was hope that they had convinced their enemies. As it was Pitt's duty to work with these new allies for the good of the country and in due obedience to the King's wishes, so it was the duty of those outside to wait and judge on future conduct, rather than inflaming public opinion.[23] The vehemence both of the attack and of the *Con-Test*'s expostulations against the *Monitor*, sustained over five issues well after the *Monitor* had dropped the exchange, emphasizes the depth of this crisis of reputation. It indeed justifies Glover's assessment that Pitt 'stood almost single, deserted by the country gentlemen, declining in popularity'.[24]

The seriousness of his situation can scarcely be exaggerated. Far from establishing him firmly in power where he could wait for success in war to confirm his popularity as of course, the Coalition threatened the most important of the supports which had put him

---

[22] *LEP*, 23–5 June, 9–12, 12–14 July 1757; *LC*, 5–7, 9–12 July 1757; *Considerations upon the present Coalition of Parties*, *CR*, iv, Aug. 1757, p. 181, *MR*, xvii, Aug. 1757, p. 185.

[23] The *Test* 34, 2 July, 35, 9 July 1757; the *Con-Test* 34–8, 9 July–6 Aug. 1757.

[24] Glover, *Mems.*, p. 150 (commenting on Pitt's situation just *before* the Coalition was finally negotiated).

there. The reactions against his part in the Coalition might well persuade the King and Newcastle that he could soon be safely dropped—and success in war was unlikely to come quickly enough to save him. The crisis called for all Pitt's political finesse.

There were grounds for hope. In fact his various allies had little alternative but to make the best of the *fait accompli* of the Coalition if they wished to preserve any influence over affairs and not leave their Whig enemies again dominant. It appears that Shebbeare and perhaps other Tories were prepared to accept such a coalition because they feared Fox and Cumberland more than Newcastle.[25] Certainly the *Monitor* immediately moderated its criticisms of Pitt. It never lost its distrust of the Coalition but it came to hope that honesty and integrity at the helm could still bring a change of measures and avert destruction.

> But soon again, (we'll hope,) to peerless PITT,
> And strenuous LEGG, the faction must submit.

Similarly the *Crab-Tree*, following the *Con-Test*'s advice, was soon urging its readers to wait and judge fairly by results, while the *London Chronicle* enjoined trust in Pitt. The *London Evening Post*, earliest to recover, was more effusive.

> What though discordant Principles are join'd
> Though some are Dross, whilst Thou art Gold refin'd,
> Thou, of the compound Body, art the Soul,
> To kindly guide and animate the Whole:
> Thou art the great Physician of the State;
> We on thy Skill, with Hope and Patience Wait.[26]

More concrete grounds for hope were provided in August when, despite the reaction against the Coalition in the City, Pitt and Legge were fêted by the Grocers' Company.[27] If Pitt could do something to satisfy the expectations of his friends and at the same time make use

---

[25] *A Letter To His Grace the D[uke] of N[ewcastle]*, London, 1757, attributed by *MR*, xvi, May 1757, pp. 466–7, to Shebbeare. Cf. *The Treaty or Dr Shabear's Administration*, a print of June 1757 (*Cat. Prints and Drawings*, iii, pt. ii, pp. 1149–50).

[26] *Mon.* 104, 16 July, 108, 13 Aug. 1757 (quotation). Cf. the high hopes of Pitt and Legge expressed in the dedication of the second collected edition published at this time. The *Crab-Tree* 12, 12 July 1757; *LC*, 12–14 July 1757; *LEP*, 5–7 July 1757.

[27] Sutherland, 'The City . . . 1756–7', p. 170. They were made freemen of the Company in order to be qualified for freedom of the City (*RWJ*, 23 Apr. 1757).

of the distinction, suggested by the *Monitor*, between Newcastle's 'faction' and the patriots in the Coalition, he might again be able to turn his very weakness to advantage. While in fact controlling policy through his personal dominance in the Cabinet, he could publicly attribute necessary but unpopular moves to the strength of Newcastle's friends in Parliament and the Closet. At the same time he could highlight and take full credit himself for popular measures. Thus he might still secure support and with it his independence, even while he waited for success in war and even when the war demanded considerable modification of patriot policies. His independence thus deviously protected, his control of policy, which was his chief concern, would be the stronger.

Of the success of such unusual and devious manœuvres over the next two years, votes in Parliament and public reaction in general are a measure. With City opinion particularly, there is good reason to consider the *Monitor* as both an instrument of these tactics and a measure of obstacles and success alike. For, from now onwards, if not before, Beckford lived up to the declaration of allegiance he had made in November 1756. There is no evidence of his views when the Coalition was formed but the attitudes of the *Monitor* would suggest that he did not accept it 'without some heart-burning'. Yet by late September he had certainly come to terms with it. He was closely in touch with Pitt and had 'presumed' to be his guarantee to George Townshend 'and many other very worthy Gentlemen'.[28] Soon he was recognized as one of Pitt's closest and most devoted followers. In a sense he was seen as Pitt's spokesman in the City, although the evidence for 1756–7 suggests that he was as yet far from controlling the support the City gave to Pitt. His loyalty never seriously faltered. Obviously, therefore, he would wish to use his paper to maintain Pitt's reputation with popular opinion, which had developed in the City and elsewhere over the months since the fall of Minorca. The degree to which popular opinion was amenable to such management can be illustrated in large part by the *Monitor*'s reactions to major issues.

Immediately Pitt's task was eased by the lull in political debate encouraged by the summer prorogation of Parliament. This also gave him four or five months before he would have to face effective

---

[28] Sutherland, 'The City . . . 1756–7', p. 162 fn. 1; Beckford to Pitt, 20 Sept. 1757, PRO 30/8/19, f. 42.

public opposition. There were difficulties enough. At home the situation was little short of tumultuous. There were not only continuing disturbances because of the high price of corn. More serious because more directly political, there were also widespread difficulties in the implementation of the Militia Act. Riots occurred in the late summer in opposition to the drawing up of lists of those liable to serve. Another grave if less spectacular obstacle was the lack of enthusiasm among the gentry about serving as officers, even where the lords lieutenant did their best to put the Act into effect. As a result the implementation of the Act had to be postponed until Parliament met again.[29] All this would seem to throw doubt on Pitt's ability to judge the popularity of the measure he had espoused.

Even more difficult was the foreign situation. The prospect outside Europe, especially in America, was gloomy enough but more vigorous efforts to deal with it, especially the attempt on Louisbourg planned earlier by Pitt, caused no contention. It was European policy that was controversial, as it was to be throughout the war. Indeed, by mid-1757 the situation on the Continent was alarming. Just a few days after the Coalition took office, news arrived that England's ally, the King of Prussia, had been drastically defeated at Kolin in Bohemia on 18 June. His hopes of holding Bohemia and continuing an offensive campaign were shattered. Prussia was threatened both by the Swedes and by the Russians, whose juncture with Austria had been confirmed by the Treaty of St. Petersburg in January 1757. In May, the second Treaty of Versailles transformed Austria's agreement with France into an offensive alliance to help achieve her long-standing aim to recover Silesia from Prussia. In July the French seized Emden, the only important Prussian port as well as the main communication line from England to the Duke of Cumberland. More threatening to Britain, tensions between the French and the Austrians over the direction of the war effort were resolved, the Austrian barrier towns of Ostend and Nieuport received French garrisons and the Austrian Minister in London left without taking leave. Most immediately embarrassing to the British, in the west Cumberland was unable to resist the superior strength of the French and had to retreat before them. In late July, no longer able to avoid confrontation, he was decisively defeated at Hasten-beck on the Weser. Hanover was left open to the French. Thus

29 Western, pp. 290–4, 140–1.

within the first few weeks of office the Coalition was faced with a rapidly deteriorating situation in Hanover and an ally who could give no help. Indeed he was putting out feelers for a separate peace with France. The situation seemed to make inevitable the further British help for which Frederick had been pressing all year.

Pitt was again quite prepared to accept the need for greater involvement in Europe.[30] But he was seriously hampered by his earlier statements. Not only had he firmly denied in February and March any intention of sending British troops to the Continent. In May, in debate on a vote of credit for £1,000,000, he had also taken what seemed another strong stand against subsidies, although praising the King of Prussia as worthy of help.[31] Certainly when he entered the Coalition some of his supporters believed that he was much more firmly committed against Continental measures than in fact he was. Hardwicke thought that Pitt must have given some promise not to send troops in return for support for subsidies.[32]

The sudden about-turn of the *Con-Test* on this issue in July and August suggests that Pitt was making a determined effort to modify the views of his supporters. In June it had expressed the usual fears about over-attention to Continental interests. Now it argued that properly conceived measures, including the sending of troops, might be inevitable and might even be a desirable part of a more aggressive policy.[33] In the exchanges between the *Con-Test* and the *Monitor* in reaction to the Coalition, Continental questions were the major issue. The *Monitor* had already moved a long way in support of Pitt's developing Continental policy and was prepared now to admit a positive British interest in Europe. Having made that admission, however, it defined very carefully how the interest should be secured. Britain should not intervene directly but should encourage a coalition of German Powers to which she could give monetary support. The sending of British troops might be recommended if really inevitable but such a move was not yet 'an apparent and immediate necessity'. The *Monitor* anxiously sought grounds for hope in the King's Speech at the close of the parliamentary session

[30] See above p. 69; Devonshire to Newcastle, 20 July 1757, Add. MSS 32872, ff. 269–70.

[31] See above p. 73; Walpole, *Geo. II*, ii, pp. 212–14; Glover, *Mems.*, pp. 142–3.

[32] Rigby to Bedford, 28 June 1757, *Corr. Bedford*, ii, p. 256; Glover, *Mems.*, pp. 131–2; Hardwicke to Newcastle, 29 Jan. 1758, Yorke, *Hardwicke*, iii, p. 118.

[33] The *Con-Test* 30, 11 June, 33, 2 July, 35, 16 July, 37, 30 July, 38, 6 Aug. 1757.

that Continental connections would be disavowed and attention directed to America.[34]

In reply the *Con-Test* denied that the Speech had declared against all Continental connections and mocked the restraints the *Monitor* would impose on them.[35] But it did not convert its antagonist. The *Monitor*'s arguments indicate the degree to which some of Pitt's most sympathetic supporters wished to restrain his response to Frederick's plight. The *London Evening Post* frequently expressed concern about Continental involvement and on these grounds had qualms about the Coalition. Moreover, it was not only those closest to Pitt who were interested in this question. The *London Chronicle* carried material on both sides, including the *Con-Test–Monitor* exchange, and in August the *Gentleman's Magazine* published extracts on the issue from all three essay papers. At the same time the deteriorating European situation provoked some revival of crude anti-Hanoverian propaganda.[36]

It was not surprising, then, that the first decision of the new Cabinet, going against Newcastle's inclinations, was to reject Frederick's renewed request for a Baltic squadron. Instead it was decided unanimously to explore the feasibility of another of Frederick's suggestions, first made in December 1756—an amphibious operation on the French coast, to divert French attention from Germany. Pitt pressed ahead with investigations and preparations. Formal approval of the scheme was given on 14 July and details were sent to Frederick.[37] So was conceived and set in motion the Rochefort expedition.

Yet the ever-deteriorating situation in Germany soon demanded more than this. The defeat of Cumberland at Hastenbeck in July raised the alarming prospect of a separate Hanoverian peace that would certainly offend Frederick, perhaps force him also to a peace and lead to the collapse of the whole Continental front. To avoid

[34] *Mon.* 97, 28 May, 99, 11 June, 103, 9 July, 106, 30 July (quotation), 109, 20 Aug., 111, 3 Sept., 114, 24 Sept. 1757. Its uneasiness was shared by the *Crab-Tree* 12, 12 July 1757.

[35] The *Con-Test* 35, 16 July, 37, 30 July 1757.

[36] e.g. *LEP*, 19–21, 21–3 Apr., 9–12, 12–14 July 1757; *LC*, 2–4 June, 9–12, 16–19 July 1757; *GM*, xxvii, Aug. 1757, pp. 345–6; *CR*, iv, July 1757, pp. 92–3, Aug. p. 180.

[37] Holdernesse to Mitchell, 5 July 1757, HMC, *Third Report*, app., p. 128; Julian S. Corbett, *England in the Seven Years' War: a study in combined strategy*, 2nd edn., 2 vols., London, 1918, i, pp. 153, 189–90.

this, Pitt readily accepted further Continental measures. On 3 August he suggested himself an increased grant to Prussia straight away and agreed to further subsidies to Hanover and Hesse in the following year's supply. The next week he proposed an immediate grant of £100,000 to Hanover from the vote of credit and a present of £20,000 to the Landgrave of Hesse.[38] Moreover, he undertook to secure the necessary support of Legge and James Grenville, one of the Lords of the Treasury. '[W]e must depart from the rigidness of our declarations', he said to Legge, and he carefully explained his decision to his chief political allies as a 'concession . . . upon the grounds of a fatal necessity'. Temple accepted it, albeit with some reservations. Bute alone raised serious doubts. Potter was given the task of explanation among Pitt's lesser supporters and looked forward to having 'to sustain some jokes upon our change of principles'.[39]

Paradoxically, these Continental moves brought the Rochefort expedition to the centre of public attention. It was just the kind of exercise of Britain's seapower to divert France in Europe that upholders of a colonial and naval war would readily accept. The *Monitor* promoted it as the sort of operation 'that will presently cure [the French] of marching the strength of their country . . . beyond the Rhine' and so allow Britain to concentrate her strength in America.[40] Seen in this way, the expedition could distract attention from unpalatable Continental moves. For this reason, to divert his followers rather than out of any great hopes of diverting the French, Pitt made the expedition peculiarly his own. He pressed ahead despite the scepticism of his ministerial colleagues and professional advisers. He resisted any suggestion that the expedition might be cancelled or sent to Flanders to counter a possible threat of invasion from there. From the beginning contrived leaks kept public speculation high and ensured that Pitt

[38] Newcastle to Hardwicke, 3, 9 Aug., Hardwicke to Newcastle, 4, 11 Aug. 1757, Yorke, *Hardwicke,* iii, pp. 161–2, 163, 165, 167–8.

[39] Newcastle to Hardwicke, 9 Aug. 1757, Yorke, *Hardwicke,* iii, p. 166 (first quotation), p. 121 fn. 4 (Potter's comments); Pitt to Bute, [5 Aug. 1757], 'Letters of Pitt to Bute', p. 128; Bute to Pitt [in reply, wrongly dated 11 Mar. 1758], Grenville to Pitt, 14 Aug. 1757, *Corr. Chatham,* i, pp. 301, 243–5; Pitt to Grenville, 11 Aug. 1757, *Grenville Papers,* i, p. 206 (second quotation); Temple to Pitt, 14 Aug. 1757, PRO 30/8/61, f. 23.

[40] *Mon.* 109, 20 Aug. 1757 (quotation); 111, 3 Sept. 1757.

received all the credit for supposedly preventing the troops and ships being sent to Germany.[41]

So when at last it set out on 8 September the expedition was firmly identified with Pitt. 'Whatever it is, Mr Pit will either have the glory or disgrace of it, for every one calls it his scheme.' For this reason Beckford, as he gave his guarantees of Pitt's good faith, 'never longed for our success so much as at the present moment'.[42]

The prospects of glory proved short-lived. Once on the move the expedition became a story of more delays, excessive caution, lingering councils of war, and failure of co-operation between the military and naval commands. Although the Island of Aix in the Basque Roads was easily taken, it was decided to give up the idea of an attack directly on Rochefort. All that eventuated was a botched-up attempt to land at nearby Fouras. On 29 September, with only this to show for an expedition estimated to have cost £1 million, the commanders decided to return home.[43]

Such a blow to a policy he had made his own could not have come at a worse time for Pitt. Within a week or so of the expedition's departure had come news from America that the attempt on Louisbourg had been abandoned. Even worse, on the very day the expedition sailed Cumberland had concluded the Convention of Klosterzeven with the French. This immobilized the Hanoverian troops and sent home the Hessian and Brunswick men in the army of observation. Hanover was virtually abandoned to the French and Frederick's flank was exposed.[44] In reaction Pitt committed himself even further to direct aid to the war in Germany. He took the lead in expressing the general indignation of British Ministers at Cumberland's policy. He secured the King's authority to dissociate the Ministry from the Convention and ensured that it was not ratified. He prompted almost immediate moves to break it. Afraid of embarrassment in Parliament, he pressed steadily for a decisive

---

[41] e.g. Royston to Birch, 26 July, Birch to Royston, 30 July 1757, Add. MSS 35398, ff. 340, 342; Jenkinson to Grenville, 9, 19 July, Pitt to Grenville, 11 Aug. 1757, *Grenville Papers*, i, pp. 199, 200, 206; Pitt to Bute, 5 Aug. 1757, 'Letters of Pitt to Bute', p. 128; *Dodington*, p. 368. All the newspapers carried reports and speculation about the expedition.

[42] Mrs Donnellan to Mrs Montagu, 15 Sept. 1757, *Elizabeth Montagu, [the Queen of the Bluestockings. Her Correspondence from 1720 to 1761]*, ed. Emily J. Climenson, 2 vols., London, 1906, ii, p. 116; Beckford to Pitt, 20 Sept. 1757, PRO 30/8/19, f. 42.

[43] Walpole, *Geo. II*, ii, pp. 240–5; *Dodington*, pp. 367–8; Corbett, i, pp. 200–22.

[44] Corbett, i, pp. 223–4, 225–6.

repudiation and immediate resumption of the offensive by the remnants of Cumberland's army. Early in October he persuaded the rest of the Ministers to refuse any financial help while the army remained inactive. On the other hand, an offer was made that if the convention were annulled and hostilities resumed the British Government would take the army entirely into their pay.[45] Thus on the eve of the opening of Parliament, where Pitt would have to defend his policies in the general gloom, he was more than ever committed to the war in Europe. 'I hear [Pitt] is determined to push the King of Prussia's cause to the utmost, and not to talk of what war shall cost next year,' wrote Fox to Bedford.[46] Indignation and suspicion of Klosterzeven would be acceptable enough to the Tories and country gentlemen. The accompanying commitment to Europe was unlikely to be so.

With such policies to answer for, the failure of the Rochefort expedition was doubly embarrassing. Pitt was soon facing a test at least as serious as those he had survived earlier in the year. Clamour and discontent began almost immediately. By 15 October Newcastle considered it worse than the reaction to the loss of Minorca. Thomas Potter reported to Pitt from Bristol a discontent that 'makes me tremble'.[47] In the storm, as Potter made clear, the anti-Hanoverian bogey was out again very strongly. In London as well as Bristol it was insinuated that, unknown to Pitt, instructions had been sent out to the expedition that the soldiers were not to be landed, so that better terms could be obtained for Hanover at Klosterzeven. 'It is to no purpose to talk of the misconduct of the officers concerned,' reported Potter. 'The people carry their resentments higher.'[48] Yet there was another main line of protest 'levelled directly against Mr Pitt . . . viz. that the expedition was chimerical, and impracticable, and the production of a *hotheaded minister*'. The political writers were

[45] Corbett, i, pp. 227–30; Newcastle to Hardwicke, 10, 18 Sept., 3, 8 Oct., 5 Nov. 1757, Yorke, *Hardwicke*, iii, pp. 173–5, 179, 185, 187, 194; Cabinet minute, 7 Oct. 1757, Add. MSS 32874, f. 475.

[46] Fox to Bedford, 12 Oct. 1757, *Corr. Bedford*, ii, p. 280.

[47] Devonshire to Bedford, 15 Oct. 1757, *Corr. Bedford*, ii, p. 283; *LC*, 20–2 Oct. 1757, quoting *Gaz.*; Potter to Pitt, 11 Oct. 1757, *Corr. Chatham*, i, pp. 277–8; Newcastle to Hardwicke, 15 Oct. 1757, Add. MSS 32875, f. 124.

[48] Walpole to Conway, 13 Oct. 1757, *The Letters of Horace Walpole* [*Fourth Earl of Orford*], ed. Mrs Paget Toynbee, 16 vols., London, 1903–5, iv, p. 105; Birch to Royston, 8, 15 Oct. 1757, Add. MSS 35398, ff. 374, 377; Potter to Pitt, 11 Oct. 1757, *Corr. Chatham*, i, p. 277.

reported to be ready to seize on the failure 'to make War upon their late Favourites in the Ministry'.[49]

This public alarm was directly reflected in the newspapers and weeklies. The weekly *Citizen* again turned from entertainment to politics and 'spared only the Vowel of Mr Pitt's Name' in demanding 'an Account of the late Expence and Disgrace'. A new weekly, the *Herald*, was jolted from general comment into contemporary politics with an outburst of indignant disappointment of the high expectations that had been encouraged. It demanded inquiry and satisfaction. Yet another weekly, the *Patriot*, reacted in the same strong vein of great hopes so greatly disappointed, and insisted on an inquiry to decide whether the commanders or the Ministry 'who have been so highly extolled' should now be blamed. The *British Alarmer*, a new occasional paper, was published expressly to dwell on the miscarriage.[50] The *Monitor*'s growing confidence in the ability of the new Administration to carry out the kind of policy the paper wanted was suddenly shattered. Its tone again became one of bitter complaint and despondency, with demands for a strict inquiry and ominous parallels to the just fate of Byng. It raised suggestions of Hanoverian influence and extended them to the activities of Cumberland and his army.[51]

The ire of the newspapers was compounded by their annoyance at the additional stamp duties recently laid on them, so much so that it was said to be almost impossible to get pro-Government paragraphs inserted in them.[52] The volume and unaminity of comment through October, in similar vein to that of the weeklies, certainly justified Newcastle's comparison with the outcry over Minorca. The *London Evening Post*, in virtually every issue from 8 October, dwelt on the high expectations frustrated by the shortcomings of the officers. It

---

[49] Newcastle to Hardwicke, 15 Oct. 1757, Add. MSS 32875, f. 124; Birch to Royston, 15 Oct. 1757, Add. MSS 35398, f. 380.

[50] On the *Citizen* see Birch to Royston, 22 Sept., 15 Oct. 1757 (quotation), Add. MSS 35399, ff. 363, 380, and also *LC*, 8–11, 11–13, 15–18 Oct. 1757; the *Herald; Or, Patriot Proclaimer* 6, 20 Oct. 1757; *GM*, xxvii, Oct. 1757, pp. 460–1, 468–9 extracts the *Patriot* (no surviving copies of which have been located); *MR*, xvii, Oct. 1757, p. 379.

[51] *Mon.* 117, 15 Oct., 118, 22 Oct., 120, 5 Nov., 121, 12 Nov. 1757; Birch to Royston, 15 Oct. 1757, Add. MSS 35398, f. 380.

[52] Mr G— to Newcastle, 17 Nov. 1757, Add. MSS 32876, f. 4. The Stamp Act of 1757 raised the duty on papers of one sheet (four pages) or less by $\frac{1}{2}d$ and doubled the advertisement duty to two shillings. The newspapers of the time are full of complaints about it.

also made anti-Hanoverian insinuations. The *London Chronicle* carried much comment from a wide variety of other papers. The *Gazetteer*, while suggesting that the commanders might be to blame for faulty execution, also raised serious doubts about the concept of the expedition and implied a connection between its failure and Hanoverian influence on British policy, also to be seen, it alleged, in the mismanagement of the army of observation.[53]

The first substantial comment on the expedition, *A Genuine Account of the Late Grand Expedition to the Coast of France*, was out by mid-October and quickly went throught three editions. It illustrated the generally unsettled state of opinion by initially gibing at the patriot Pitt (for which it was rebuked by the *Critical Review*), yet generally supporting the feasibility of the expedition and criticizing the conduct of the officers. It was eagerly extracted in the magazines, which further demonstrated public interest by giving excerpts from other papers and their own accounts. They, too, asked whether the officers or the Ministry should be blamed.[54] More ephemeral works, odes, ballads, farces, appeared which, even when they were not overtly hostile to Pitt, at least raised serious doubts about the wisdom of a policy which he had made his own—or exploited the potent anti-Hanoverian theme.[55]

With the anti-Hanoverian outcry especially in mind, Potter urged on Pitt the need for some action to 'obviate what may be attended with such dreadful consequences'.[56] Pitt certainly felt the blow severely. 'I feel more and more I never shall get Rochefort off my heart,' he wrote to Bute.[57] There were two possible lines of escape. At first he attempted to take advantage of the anti-Hanoverian

[53] See esp. *LEP,* 8–11, 11–13 Oct. (for anti-Hanoverian suggestions), *LC,* 8–11, 11–13, 13–15, 15–18, 20–2 Oct. 1757; *Gaz.* as in *LC,* 11–13 Oct. and *GM,* xxvii, Oct. 1757, pp. 461–3.

[54] *A Genuine Account of the Late Grand Expedition to the Coast of France*, 3rd edn., London, 1757; *CR,* iv, Oct. 1757, p. 371; Rodney to Grenville, 19 Oct. 1757, *Grenville Papers,* i, p. 219; *GM,* xxvii, Oct. 1757, pp. 441, 456–60; *LM,* xxvi, Oct. 1757, pp. 467–9, 504–5.

[55] See *MR,* xvii, Oct. 1757, pp. 378, 379, Nov. 1757, p. 470, *CR,* iv, Nov. 1757, p. 467, v, Jan. 1758, p. 75; and also *The Secret Expedition. A New Hugbug ballad,* [London, 1757]; *A New . . . Burlesque Ode, On . . . The . . . Secret Expedition,* London, 1757 (anti-Hanoverian).

[56] Potter to Pitt, 11 Oct. 1757, *Corr. Chatham,* i, p. 278.

[57] Pitt to Bute, 17 Oct. 1757, 'Letters of Pitt to Bute', p. 134; Hardwicke to Newcastle, 29 Oct. 1757, Yorke, *Hardwicke,* iii, p. 38; Walpole, *Geo. II,* ii, pp. 261–2 fn.

upsurge and the prevailing opinion that the King and Cumberland had wanted the expedition to fail in order to show that the only practical measure was direct intervention in Germany. Yet within a week, perhaps on Potter's prompting, he dropped this line. Instead he took steps to stem the current accusations by publishing in the *Gazette* of 13 October the only instructions that had been sent to the expedition after it had left, a letter countermanding earlier instructions to return by the end of September. Perhaps he had decided that anti-Hanoverianism was too dangerous a defence. It would, of course, offend the King and would also make German measures even harder to defend. More probably he was looking for a more adequate answer to the second theme in the protest, that against a '*hotheaded minister*', which 'affects him most'. He found his answer in turning the blame on to the land officers in the expedition. For once, Newcastle fathomed his motives:

He told me yesterday, that *he*, or (or and) Sir John Mordaunt must be tried; and in describing the present run upon the expedition, from *some quarters*, took plainly the whole merit of it to himself; thinking, (and he thought right) that the measure would greatly increase his popularity, when it should appear that it failed purely from the behaviour of the land officers.[58]

Pitt's moves allowed some recovery of his reputation—'mankind' again began to 'do justice to his singular merit'. The *Herald* held that the publication of the dispatch 'effectively freed his character and conduct from all insinuating doubts'. The *Monitor* was not nearly so certain, but as it continued to mull over the questions to be asked it tended to justify Pitt and blame the commanders. From the beginning the *London Evening Post* had blamed the commanders and comment in the *London Chronicle* now followed suit.[59]

But the moves did not quell the storm. In the last week of October steps were taken in the City to address the Crown on the disaster. The very elements previously most sympathetic to Pitt, the Half Moon Club, Deputy Long and others of 'Benn's Boys', initiated these steps. The *Monitor* and *London Evening Post* supported them. The moves raised the strong possibility of a campaign of addresses

[58] Newcastle to Hardwicke, 8 Oct. 1757, Yorke, *Hardwicke*, iii, p. 187; Newcastle to Hardwicke, 15 Oct. 1757, Add. MSS 32875, f. 124; Walpole, *Geo. II*, ii, pp. 260–1.

[59] Wilkes to Grenville, 22 Oct., cf. Jenkinson to Grenville, 22 Oct. 1757, *Grenville Papers*, i, pp. 223, 225–6; the *Herald* 7, 27 Oct. 1757; *Mon.* 117–18, 15–22 Oct. 1757; *LC* e.g. 13–15, 18–20 Oct. 1757.

and instructions such as had followed the Minorca débâcle. This could have brought the whole affair before Parliament and would have been a grave embarrassment, disastrously disrupting necessary war business. The Ministry chose to deflect the attack by taking the initiative in instituting an inquiry. When the highly unusual step was taken of sending a message to this effect to the Lord Mayor through one of the Privy Council clerks, the address was successfully forestalled and the danger of a concerted campaign averted.[60]

The threat to Pitt was not however ended. The patriots were now most suspicious of a Court intrigue. Whereas before the message there had been signs of some abatement of zeal for the address and distinctions were being made between the failure at Rochefort and the loss of Minorca, now some were asking 'Why Mr Pitt himself did not come to them, and give them Satisfaction?'[61] The *Monitor* (but not the *London Evening Post*) exploded in wrath that its urgings had been ignored. Was it possible, it asked, that the Common Council of the British metropolis could be swayed by unsatisfactory messages and the collusive dealings of their chief magistrate with the men who, their works being evil, loved darkness rather than light? Other corporate bodies, it hoped, would not be so easily satisfied. The *Monitor* seemed intent on stirring up another Minorca crisis with complete disregard for Pitt's interests.[62]

Yet Beckford took no part in all this. The day the *Monitor* first urged the City to take the lead, he wrote to Pitt from Fonthill where he was confined by illness. He referred regretfully but coolly to the failure of the expedition and the uneasiness of the City. He took no part in the preliminary moves there and he did not attend the Common Council of 4 November.[63] The *Monitor*'s reaction directly reflects not its patron's wishes but the strength of feelings among the

[60] *PA*, 27 Oct., 31 Oct., 5 Nov. 1757; Birch to Royston, 29 Oct., 5 Nov. 1757, Add. MSS 35398, ff. 383, 393; Jour. Common Council, 61, ff. 185–6; *Mon.* 118, 22 Oct. 1757; *LEP*, 20–2 Oct., 1–3 Nov. 1757.

[61] Birch to Royston, 3, 5 Nov. (quotation) 1757, Add. MSS 35398, ff. 391, 393; Rogers, 'London Politics', pp. 231–2. It was rumoured Pitt had intervened to mollify his friends but probably he did not do so. Cf. Royston to Hardwicke, 1 Nov. 1757, Add. MSS 35351, f. 430 with Newcastle to Hardwicke, 5 Nov. 1757, Add. MSS 35417, f. 152.

[62] *Mon.* 121, 12 Nov. 1757. This paper provoked a libel action by the Lord Mayor, Marshe Dickinson.

[63] Beckford to Pitt, 22 Oct. 1757, *Corr. Chatham*, i, pp. 278–81; Jour. Common Council, 61, f. 185.

readership it wanted to keep. Although Birch reported that on the Lord Mayor's Day, only a little later, Pitt's popularity with the crowds was still high, those who had earlier led the moves that brought Pitt support in the City were still deeply distrustful of the Ministry of which he was a part.[64] They would not easily be harnessed as reliable support for a minister in office—and as yet Beckford was far from fully involved in trying to make them such. Indeed the best thing that he and Pitt could do was to stand back.

Gradually the focus of general public debate shifted to the alleged shortcomings of the officers who led the expedition and the hubbub in most of the papers died away. This trend was helped by the appointment on 1 November of a Commission of Enquiry into the conduct of the land officers and then, in December, by the court martial of Sir John Mordaunt, Commander-in-Chief of the land forces. Pitt encouraged the trend by giving evidence at the court martial and by references in the House of Commons.[65]

He was, however, not entirely freed from embarrassment by it. The popular mood remained very dissatisfied. Remarks in the *London Evening Post* suggest that there was still criticism of Pitt, probably in the *Gazetteer*. The *Herald,* the *London Evening Post,* and the *Monitor* might tend to exculpate Pitt and blame the commanders, but they still wanted a full inquiry and explanation, as did a pamphlet addressed to him.[66] They were not alone. In mid-November it was reported that there was to be another City meeting to address the Crown.[67] Delay in acting on the report of the commission of inquiry, presented on 21 November, created further discontent. The *Monitor* delivered a stern warning to Pitt on the duty of the Minister who had advised the expedition 'to search this matter to the bottom'. Similar sentiments appeared in a pamphlet which, although exonerating Pitt, quoted the *Patriot* in support of its demands for a full parliamentary inquiry and urged constituents to insist on one to their members. Its references to Byng confirmed that

---

[64] Birch to Royston, 12 Nov. 1757, Add. MSS 35398, f. 401. Rogers, 'London Politics', p. 276 fn. 12, gives more details of those who led the moves.

[65] Walpole, *Geo. II,* ii, pp. 262–5, 275; West's account, 20 Jan. 1758, Add. MSS 32877, f. 183. Pitt's speech was noticed in *LM,* xxvii, Jan. 1758, p. 30.

[66] Walpole to Mann, 20 Nov. 1757, *Walpole's Corr.* xxi, pp. 153–4; *LEP,* 18–20 Oct., 1–3 Nov. 1757, 21–4 Jan. 1758; see above p. 97; *LM,* xxvi, Nov. 1757, pp. 547–9, *GM,* xxvii, Nov. 1757, pp. 504–6.

[67] Mr G— to Newcastle, 17 Nov. 1757, Add. MSS 32876, f. 4.

there was still a danger that 'it will be the second part of Mr Byng's story, and the city will drive [the Government] to be more violent than they would choose to be' and perhaps also force the matter to be raised in the House of Commons. Then when the court martial of 14–18 December found Mordaunt not guilty there were more calls in the City for parliamentary action.[68]

Fears about further formal City action and about disturbance of parliamentary business came to nothing. Beckford did occasion a 'little brush' over Rochefort at the beginning of the session but it subsided quite easily.[69] The debate outside lingered on well into the new year, however, and continued to raise issues embarrassing to Pitt. The inquiry and court martial prompted a major pamphlet exchange. When the *Candid Reflections on the Report . . . of the General-Officers*, published in January,[70] questioned the feasibility of the expedition and asked whether the efforts should not rather have been directed to America, Pitt's close associate, Thomas Potter, felt bound to reply. With characteristic forthrightness, he markedly increased the political overtones of the exchange. In no uncertain terms he attributed both attempts to defend the officers and the failure of the expedition to that 'faction' who, 'by their private Intrigues and Cabals, had a few Months before thrown the Affairs of the King and the Kingdom into so much Confusion'.[71] This provoked a rejoinder from the author of the *Candid Reflections*. Much more than before, he gibed at Pitt, his supposed popularity, his coalition with Newcastle and the changes in patriot policy it might bring. The reviewers were unequivocally on Potter's side against such 'invidious and untrue [insinuations], levelled at a minister

[68] *Mon.* 125, 10 Dec. 1757; *Public Injuries Require Public Justice*, London, 1757, esp. pp. 38–41, 52–3; Lady Elizabeth Waldegrave to Bedford, 26 Nov. 1757, *Corr. Bedford*, ii, p. 304 (quotation); Fox to Ilchester, 26 Nov. 1757, Add. MSS 51420, f. 81; Symmer to Mitchell, 30 Dec. 1757, 24 Jan. 1758, Add. MSS 6839, ff. 89, 91; Alexander Hume Campbell to Marchmont, 24 Dec. 1757, 3 Jan. 1758, HMC, *Polwarth*, v, pp. 337, 338.

[69] Symmer to Mitchell, 2 Dec. 1757, Add, MSS 6839, f. 85.

[70] *Candid Reflections on the Report (As Published by Authority) of the General-Officers*, London, 1758. Although the attribution to Fox is unlikely, the pamphlet is certainly in the style of the *Test* (Samuel Halkett and John Laing, *Dictionary of Anonymous and Pseudonymous English Literature*, new edn., 7 vols., Edinburgh, 1926–34). It and its sequel could be Dodington's 'one or two bitter pamphlets against Mr Pitt' (Walpole, *Geo. II*, ii, p. 265), but see also *Walpole's Corr.* xxxvii, pp. 523–4 fn. 1.

[71] [Thomas Potter], *The Expedition against Rochefort Fully Stated and Considered*, London, 1758, esp. pp. 7, 4.

whose genius every man of taste must admire, and whose heart
ought to endear him to every lover of his country'.[72] Nevertheless,
Potter's criticisms of the conduct of the expedition set off another
vigorous exchange.[73] Echoes with sour anti-Pitt notes lingered on
into March, April, and even May. One contribution condescend-
ingly attributed Pitt's mistake 'beyond the bounds of political
prudence' to his 'desire of popularity, or . . . his too sanguine
inclinations to demonstrate his patriot affections'.[74]

The *London Evening Post* relentlessly kept up its criticisms of the
military officers into 1758.[75] The *Monitor* continued pre-occupied
with the affair. It was, however, brought round at least to implicit
defence of Pitt by the pamphlet controversy over the feasibility of the
expedition. In almost direct quotation from Potter, it sharpened its
'faction' argument to explain the doubts raised and accused this
'lurking faction' of undermining the expedition from the beginning.
The *Monitor*'s importance in giving Potter's arguments wider circulation, particularly in the City, is suggested by several compliments
and direct answers to it in the pamphlets.[76] And slowly City opinion
came round to share the *Monitor*'s views of the affair and to
satisfaction with the Ministry.[77]

So Pitt was gradually extricated from the difficulties created by
the failure of the Rochefort expedition. It is not easy to assess just
how serious they were. There is little to suggest that his position in
the Coalition was put in doubt by it. Although Newcastle, with
Hardwicke's help, clearly recognized how closely the failure affected

[72] *Considerations on the Proceedings of a General Court-Martial*, London, 1758, esp. pp.
4, 13, 26, 34–8, 41; *MR*, xviii, Feb. 1758, pp. 179–80; *CR*, v, Feb,. 1758, pp. 165–6
(quotation).
[73] *MR*, xviii, Feb. 1758, pp. 180–1; Mar., pp. 263–4; Apr., p. 400; *CR*, v, Apr.
1758, pp. 355–60. For the attribution of the defence of the officers to General Conway,
second in command to Mordaunt, and of the attack to Potter, see Walpole, *Geo. II*, ii,
p. 265; Sir Richard to W. H. Lyttelton, [Mar. 1758], Maud Wyndham, *Chronicles of the
Eighteenth Century* [*Founded on the Correspondence of Sir Thomas Lyttelton and his Family*], 2
vols., London, 1924, ii, p. 257; *Walpole's Corr.* xxxvii, pp. 523–4 fn. 1.
[74] *MR*, xviii, Feb. 1758, pp. 178–9 (quotation); Mar., pp. 265–7; *CR*, v, Feb. 1758,
pp. 163–4, Apr., pp. 354–5, 360, May, pp. 438–9.
[75] *LEP*, e.g. 12–15 Nov., 29 Nov.–1 Dec., 24–7 Dec. 1757, 26–8 Jan. 1758.
[76] *Mon.* 125, 10 Dec., 128, 31 Dec. 1757, 131, 21 Jan. (quotation), 132, 28 Jan.,
133, 4 Feb. 1758; *Considerations on the Proceedings of a General Court-Martial*, p. 61; *A
Letter To The Citizens of London*, London, 1758, pp. 12–18. On the 'faction' argument cf.
A Vindication of Mr Pitt, London, 1758, esp. pp. 43–5.
[77] Watkins to Newcastle, 7 Feb. 1758, Add. MSS 32877, f. 374.

Pitt, he showed every sympathy with Pitt's efforts to get out of trouble and no disposition to take advantage of the embarrassment.[78] Despite fears, there was no disturbance of business in the House of Commons. And there are grounds for believing that the general prepossession of opinion in favour of Pitt was not seriously shaken despite all the noise.[79] Throughout the controversy, the reviewers in the *Monthly Review* and *Critical Review*, representing, perhaps, more considered and detached opinion, were sympathetic to the Administration and to Pitt, the *Critical Review* increasingly so.

Yet Pitt owed something to luck. The disgrace of Cumberland after Klosterzeven and the weakening of his protégé, Fox, removed one of the most influential proponents of the old Continental policy and altered the balance in the Coalition in Pitt's favour. He was able to secure a commander of the army, Lord Ligonier, to his own liking.[80] At the beginning of November, the European situation began to change decisively with the great victory of Frederick over the French and Imperial armies at Rossbach in Saxony. Exactly a month later he defeated the Austrians at Leuthen, thus clearing them out of Silesia. The Russians retired from Berlin and the Swedes from Prussian Pomerania. Meanwhile, the Hanoverians hastened their concentration of troops, and Prince Ferdinand of Brunswick, one of Frederick's most outstanding officers, was appointed to command them. On 28 November Ferdinand at last formally denounced the Convention and began an advance. Such successes helped to dissipate discontent with the conduct of the war and encouraged a more favourable attitude to Continental policy in the City. The *Monitor* reflected this, even in the midst of its concern over the expedition, by further lavish praise of Frederick and the wisdom of supporting him, although still rejecting direct British involvement.[81]

Without such fortuitous aids Pitt might well not have survived the crisis so unscathed. For the sour uncertain mood of the prolonged

---

[78] e.g. Newcastle to Hardwicke, 15 Oct., 5 Nov. 1757, Add. MSS 35416, f. 118, 35417, f. 152; Fox to Bedford, 12 Oct. 1757, *Corr. Bedford*, ii, p. 280.

[79] Sir Richard to W. H. Lyttelton, Dean Lyttelton to W. H. Lyttelton, [Dec. 1757], *Chronicles of the Eighteenth Century*, ii, pp. 255, 256.

[80] Pitt to Bute, 17 Oct. 1757, 'Letters of Pitt to Bute', p. 134; Hardwicke to Newcastle, 29 Oct. 1757, Yorke, *Hardwicke*, iii, p. 38;

[81] Symmer to Mitchell, 22 Nov. 1757, Add. MSS 6839, f. 81; *Mon.* 124, 3 Dec., 127, 24 Dec. 1757. Cf. the *Herald* 15, 22 Dec. 1757, 19, 19 Jan. 1758.

controversy leaves no doubt that it was a serious challenge to his reputation, especially in the City. Pitt did not need to turn Mordaunt into another Byng, but he allowed the propaganda case against the commanders to be pressed because it was from propaganda that the challenge came. It was not for that reason unreal. It put in direct question the popularity which was so important to his independence. Whatever Newcastle's reactions, the King was still unsympathetic, and had the challenge not been checked, fortuitously or otherwise, Pitt's position would surely have been weakened.

On 1 December, while the Rochefort affair was still in the forefront of attention, the new session of Parliament opened. It promised to be a testing one for Pitt, especially on the controversial issue of commitment to Europe. Not only would Parliament have to sanction the assumption of financial responsibility for the renewed activities of the Hanoverian army. A definitive convention with Prussia had to be negotiated—and Frederick wanted British troops, not more money.[82] Pitt would have to proceed very skilfully if he was to avoid offence to his supporters by the development of his European policy, a development which could look like a sudden revolution.[83] The successes of the King of Prussia which were turning him into a popular hero in Britain would help. Pitt could hope for more in the colonies eventually, as a result of his careful and energetic planning of operations from November onwards. In the meantime, tact was essential.

For this reason probably, Pitt was very reluctant to have anything to do with the pre-session circular to supporters of the Government. He wanted to be as little associated with official Government policy as possible so that he could excuse himself to his supporters on the grounds that it was 'not his Parliament, but the Duke of Newcastle's'.[84] The Speech from the Throne, which although written by Hardwicke was approved by Pitt,[85] left plenty of scope for European policy. Yet when, in the debate on the army estimates on 14 December, Lord Barrington complacently dwelt on its reference to defence of British rights in America 'and elsewhere', Pitt seized the opportunity to reinforce his earlier attitudes. In a great speech

[82] Corbett, i, pp. 240.

[83] e.g. to Almon in *Anecdotes of Chatham*, pp. 323–9; Waldegrave, p. 138.

[84] West to Newcastle, 2 Nov, 2 Nov. 1757, quoted Torrens, ii, p. 430.

[85] Pitt to Bute, 27 Nov. 1757, 'Letters of Pitt to Bute', p. 136.

'admired almost beyond any of his orations', he declared that the army to be voted was meant 'for our immediate selves. He had never been against continental measures when practicable; but would not now send a drop of our blood to the Elbe, to be lost in that ocean of gore.' This was not the only declaration that troops would not be sent to Germany.[86] In the Cabinet too, Pitt reacted strongly against the pleas coming from Frederick and Ferdinand for British troops. 'It is not the plan of our administration,' he wrote angrily to Newcastle in January, 'and the tools of another system are perpetually marring every hopeful measure of the present administration.'[87] Nevertheless, in January Pitt secured the ready support of the House for a grant of £100,000 for supplies for the Hanoverian army. Earlier, two millions had been voted for the general supply of the year without a single negative. After reassurances from Pitt, Beckford declared his support for the Hanoverian vote on what Almon called 'the new principle of politics', that the troops were now under British direction and could be used for British purposes. Clearly Pitt's vehemence as the protector of British interests had the desired effect. Attacks by him on the Convention of Klosterzeven also helped, as did the general admiration of the King of Prussia. Pitt emphasized the opportunities opened by his successes and Chesterfield commented, 'the king of Prussia has united all our parties in his support; and the Tories have declared, that they will give Mr Pitt unlimited credit for this session.' Whatever the reasons for their amenability the results were satisfactory. Symmer reported to Mitchell, 'Mr Pitt was never more popular than he is at present. They who applauded him last year for opposing, applaud him now for promoting the very same measures.'[88]

There were bigger hurdles yet to face. Pitt's refusals, against pressure from his colleagues and the King, of reiterated demands from Frederick and Ferdinand for more than money made Frederick unwilling to sign the definitive convention which British Ministers so much wanted. There were fears of a separate peace. It seems likely

---

[86] *Parl. Hist.* xv, cc. 829–30; Walpole, *Geo. II,* ii, pp. 274–5 (quotations); Calcraft to Home, 26 Feb. 1758, Add. MSS 17493, f. 148.

[87] Pitt to Newcastle, 28 Jan. 1758, Add. MSS 32877, ff. 256–7, quoted Corbett, i, p. 240.

[88] Yorke, *Hardwicke,* ii, pp. 125–6; *Dodington,* p. 370, 18 Jan. 1758; *Anecdotes of Chatham,* i. pp. 330–1 (first quotation); West's account, 20 Jan. 1758, Add. MSS 32877, f. 183; Symmer to Mitchell, 24 Jan. 1758, Add. MSS 6839, f. 91; Chesterfield to his son, 8 Feb. 1758, quoted in *Parl. Hist.* xv, c. 870 fn.

that Pitt's demand for the recall of Andrew Mitchell, the British envoy to the Prussian Court, insisted on against all his colleagues and relaxed only after the Convention of London was signed and approved in Parliament, was made to provide a scapegoat should he have to agree to Frederick's demands in order secure the convention.[89] Then in March, while negotiations were still in train, the French withdrawal from Emden created very strong strategic arguments for sending a small British garrison 'to shut the Emden door' until Frederick could secure East Friesland. Despite Pitt's declarations of only three months before, he readily recognized the opportunity. As usual, however, he took great care to disguise his acquiescence, especially by exaggerating difficulties in the way of a Prussian convention just when, in fact, Frederick was relaxing his demands.[90]

At the same time Pitt took up a suggestion made by Frederick some weeks before of another raid on the French coast. Cabinet approval of this could be represented as a recompense for his 'concession' over Emden. When the Convention of London was finally signed in April such an expedition was among the various means of British support promised. It developed into a three-stage expedition to St. Malo, Cherbourg and St. Cas, extending from June to September 1758. Like the Rochefort expedition of the previous year, it was to be the centre of attention from June onwards. From the beginning it was intended to be a much bigger undertaking, to seize and hold some point on the French coast as a continuing diversion. Pitt took the initiative throughout. Although others, both ministers and likely commanders, had doubts, Newcastle recorded that there was 'no difference of opinion' in the meeting of 19 May which approved the expedition.[91] Its political value to Pitt was obvious: if successful it would again be something of a *quid pro quo* for his supporters for growing German commitments, another distraction for British public opinion as well as of the French from Germany.

The *Monitor* shows how effective this could be. Its long preoccupation with the Rochefort affair had led it to ignore issues of the earlier

[89] D'Abreu to Wall, 3 Mar. 1758, *Corr. Chatham*, i. pp. 294–7 (D'Abreu suggests that Pitt was concerned not only for his reputation but also that Cumberland might resume his command of any troops sent); Yorke, *Hardwicke*, iii, pp. 126–7, 132–3; Andrew Bisset, *Memoirs [and Papers] of [Sir Andrew] Mitchell, K. B.*, 2 vols., London, 1850, ii, esp. pp. 5, 8; Torrens, ii, pp. 439–44.

[90] Corbett, i, pp. 251–2; Torrens, ii, pp. 445–6.   [91] Corbett, i, pp. 262–72.

part of the parliamentary session. Now, from mid-March, it returned to more positive support for a 'just' war directed against the overweening ambition of France. With this revival of spirits, however, went an insistence on the central importance of America and the necessity of directing Britain's strength against the navy and commerce of France. In March and again in April the policy of coastal expeditions was recommended. '[T]hough not crowned with the utmost advantages, as might have been expected from their force and commission,' such coastal expeditions, with other naval operations, had deprived the French

of all hopes to play off their state bugbear of an invasion upon our dominions; protected our trade and navigation; ruined their commerce from the four winds, and cut off their last efforts, for continuing the war, and favouring their usurpations on our settlements in America.

Such results were worth much more than the defence of any friend in Germany. The blockade of French ports, and the victories of Admirals Osborne and Hawke off Cartagena in late February and in the Basque Roads early in April, deserved 'a merit in our annals, prior to the emblazoned trophies of Blenheim and Ramillies'. Such policies, the *Monitor* was convinced, had now become 'the chief object of our councils', and it made its own suggestions about coastal expeditions.[92] By making further gestures to such sentiments Pitt could do much to convince popular opinion that truly British policies were indeed now 'the chief object of our councils'.

In the meantime, however, the further subsidy of £670,000 a year to Prussia and money for the continuing support of the Hanoverian army of 50,000 men agreed to in the Prussian Convention had to be approved by Parliament. To sweeten this pill for Pitt's supporters, domestic issues could be as useful as support for coastal expeditions. The serious difficulties in implementing the Militia Act raised grave doubts as to its continuing value as a patriot issue. Pitt had reacted typically by throwing the blame on others, accusing the lords lieutenant and justices of the peace of not explaining the Act properly and claiming that 'the people had been inflamed by art and management'.[93] Meanwhile, further public comment showed conti-

---

[92] *Mon.* 136, 25 Feb., 138, 11 Mar., 139, 18 Mar., 145, 29 Apr. 1758 (all quotations).

[93] Newcastle to Hardwicke, 10 Sept. 1757, Add. MSS 32873, f. 547; C. Yorke to Hardwicke, 15 Sept. 1757, Add. MSS 35353, f. 226 (quotation).

nuing interest in the Militia, although acknowledging mistakes in the Act. This may have helped Pitt to decide that the advantage lay with continuing support. Anyway he supported with disproportionate enthusiasm George Townshend's Bill to explain the Militia Act. The Bill was designed both to meet popular objections and to prevent deliberate delay. Newcastle and others were as lukewarm as ever. Townshend wanted to keep off the ideological issues and reduce contention. Pitt, however, showed more enthusiasm than he had over the original measure and more than Townshend himself. Political calculation rather than the merits of the measure seemed to lie behind his support.[94]

Another Tory issue was treated more circumspectly. Apparently even Pitt felt that the motion of Sir John Glynne on 20 February 1758, seconded by Sir John Philipps and supported by Beckford, for leave to bring in a bill shortening the duration of parliaments was too 'popular' to be given support. Potter referred to it as that 'silly Business'. Pitt was careful, however, to avoid giving offence. He was conveniently absent with the gout, but two of his close associates, Potter and George Grenville, although opposing, expressed sympathy with the aims and principles of the measure while pointing out the difficulties of reform at the present time. Grenville's opposition 'was very much managed and minced by the prevailing tenderness for country gentlemen'. Even while supporting the motion in typical ranting fashion, Beckford made his distinctions, easing the embarrassment the defeat of the measure would cause Pitt. He would, he said, have preferred a bill lessening the number of placemen and pensioners in parliament. Even so, Pitt's management did not entirely avoid embarrassment. The *London Magazine*, for example, reported that many regarded the defeat of the motion with surprise, having thought 'that the preservation of our constitution at home was now to be attended to, as well as the preservation of our rights and possessions in America'.[95] A safer measure on which to demonstrate Pitt's influence over his colleagues in patriot matters was Grenville's Bill for the better payment of seamen's wages. This had been defeated in the last session but was now passed,

[94] Western, pp. 142–5, 180–1; Royston to Hardwicke, 10 Apr. 1758, Add. MSS 35352, ff. 5–6.

[95] *Parl. Hist.* xv, cc. 870–1; Potter to Pitt, [n.d.], PRO 30/8/53, f. 99; John Yorke to Royston, 20 Feb. 1758, Add. MSS 35374, ff. 144–5 (second quotation); *LM*, quoted in Langford, 'William Pitt and public opinion, 1757', p. 76.

with Pitt's renewed support and that of other Ministers who had previously opposed it.[96]

Most contentious by far of all the measures on which Pitt sought to cultivate popular support was the Habeas Corpus Bill, passed by the Commons in this session but rejected in the Lords. The Bill arose out of the problems associated with the use of the writ of habeas corpus in cases of alleged illegal impressment. If passed, the Bill was likely to increase the difficulties of manning the Navy. Nevertheless, Pitt seized the opportunity of a refusal of the writ by Lord Mansfield to vindicate his patriotism cheaply. Without consulting other members of the Administration with legal experience, the Attorney-General, Sir Charles Pratt, one of Pitt's men, drafted a Bill 'for explaining and extending the Habeas Corpus, and ascertaining its full operation'. It passed through the House of Commons fairly easily, though not without lengthy legal argument and vehement attacks by Pitt on lawyers and judges. It certainly attracted the interest of the country gentlemen.[97]

Pitt pressed the matter very hard with Newcastle. He threatened that 'the nation would be in a flame' if the Bill were rejected. More to the point, he declared that there would be dangerous difficulties for His Majesty's servants in the House of Commons if the measure were defeated. He even carried his arguments to Lady Yarmouth.[98] Such popular stands caused serious strains in the Ministry. Newcastle was much alarmed at the popular clamour. 'Mr Pitt should certainly be spoke to by some person of great weight and consideration, and showed the consequences to government which must arise from letting the mob loose in this manner.' He was bitter, too, about the differences amongst Ministers that had appeared in the House of Commons. The King, even more offended, refused to speak to Pitt at his levées and went as far as considering ways to replace him. Newcastle, although aware that this was impracticable, was pre-

---

[96] Walpole, *Geo. II*, ii, pp. 214–15, 289–90. Pitt did not take up Sir John Philipps's bill to secure the rights of freeholders at county elections, which was passed (*Commons' Journal*, xxviii, pp. 112, 290). Nor did he support Legge's proposed tax on the salaries of placemen and pensioners, 'a poor tribute to popularity' (Walpole, *Geo. II*, ii, p. 294).

[97] Walpole, *Geo II*, ii, pp. 286–8 (quotation); Yorke, *Hardwicke*, iii, pp. 1–5; Newdigate Diary (transcript), 17 Mar. 1758.

[98] Newcastle to Hardwicke, 14 Apr., 16, 21 May 1758, Yorke *Hardwicke*, iii, pp. 44–5, 46, 49 (quotation); Pitt to Newcastle, 22 May 1758, Add. MSS 32880, ff. 180–2.

pared to threaten Pitt with being left on his own if he persisted.[99] Pitt too knew such threats were empty so long as he achieved his purpose—the approval of the Ministry's foreign policy in Parliament without the loss of his own supporters.

The Habeas Corpus Bill was in the end stopped in the Lords at the beginning of June, in response to the lead given by Hardwicke and Mansfield and the unanimous opinion of all the judges. '[E]ven Tory Lords, and those most violent in their wishes for it, declared they were convinced', although the debates brought some sharp clashes with Lord Temple who supported the Bill and attacked the lawyers.[100]

By this time, however, Pitt's careful furbishing of his patriot image had served its purpose. On 19 April the subsidy for the King of Prussia and further provision for Ferdinand's army passed the House of Commons without any serious trouble. Some leading Tories were so anxious about possible divisions among their more unruly colleagues and so keen to give an impression of wholehearted confidence in Pitt among the 'country party' that they proposed to organize a group of twelve or fifteen to make a previous declaration of their approval. Beckford was to be one. No such declaration proved necessary. No Tory spoke against the Prussian subsidy and several supported it. Opposition was left to the independent Whigs, Sir Francis Dashwood and Robert Vyner. Only in the House of Lords was there some Tory acrimony. There may have been more dissatisfaction than was expressed. Sir Roger Newdigate confided to his diary that it was 'no British measure'. But all found some way to silence their qualms.

The advice of Pitt's Tory well-wishers on how to present his arguments gives some indication of how qualms were settled. 'The *bitter Part of the Pill* is Hanover Troops, the Sugar Plumb, the K[in]g of Prussia.' So the Hanoverian troops should be presented as useful to Prussia and part of the prosecution of the war against France, making possible the employment of British troops in British interests. Pitt had already begun such an approach earlier in the year, making the Prussian alliance and British control over the Hano-

---

[99] Newcastle to Hardwicke, 27 Mar. (quotation), 16, 21 May 1758, Yorke, *Hardwicke*, iii, pp. 44, 46, 49–50; Newcastle memorandum, [Apr.] 1758, Add. MSS 32998, f. 26.

[100] Walpole, *Geo. II*, ii, pp. 294–302; Mrs Montagu to Dr Stillingfleet, 13 June 1758, *Elizabeth Montagu*, ii, p. 127 (quotation).

verian army seem compatible with what the Tories regarded as British interests. Now, in the debate, he took the line that all past reigns showed that England could not escape Continental involvement. However, he said, the Prussian alliance removed the danger that England might be weakened by the defeat of her allies in Europe and thus reduced rather than increased the possibility of her being further drawn in. His friends had warned that there was still great sensitivity over the possiblity of British troops being sent to the Continent. By such historical arguments Pitt avoided yet another commitment against such a move—indeed he said that he could not preclude the possibility—but at the same time was able to appear reassuring.[101]

One further hurdle remained. On 7 June, a vote of credit allowing a subsidy to Hesse-Cassel passed smoothly, despite Hardwicke's fears that Pitt might disavow responsibility for the benefit of his Tory friends. Pitt himself was certainly very anxious about the vote. Late in May he had offered to support the measure if the Habeas Corpus Bill were allowed to pass, presumably so that he would have it as a popular *quid pro quo*. When this failed he turned his attention to the wording of the vote and set Potter to a careful search for precedents.[102] Nothing shows more clearly the political motivation of Pitt's earlier manœuvres than the way in which, once this measure was passed, he dropped the Habeas Corpus issue.[103] After its defeat in the House of Lords on 2 June, the hubbub over the Bill subsided with surprising speed, partly because of Hardwicke's promise to ask the judges to prepare a new more acceptable measure, but largely because Pitt had lost interest. His colleagues noted a general moderation of his manner, a measure of his considerable relief over the success of his moves. True, in retribution for opposition to Habeas Corpus, he spoke against a motion in mid-June to increase judges' salaries and was supported by Grenville and Beckford. But they did not vote against the measure, which

[101] Walpole, *Geo. II*, ii, pp. 293–4; Potter to Pitt, [Feb.–Apr. 1758], PRO 30/8/53, ff. 98 (quotation)–9; Calcraft to Rigby, 20 Apr. 1758, Add. MSS 17493, ff. 153–4; Newdigate Diary (transcript), 19 Apr. 1758; [Richard Aldworth] Neville's parliamentary diary, 19 Apr. 1758, Neville (Aldworth) papers, Berkshire Record Office, D/EN 034/16.

[102] *Parl. Hist.* xv, c. 926; Newcastle to Hardwicke, 21 May 1758, Yorke, *Hardwicke*, iii, p. 49; Hardwicke to Newcastle, 2 June, Newcastle to Hardwicke, [3 June] 1758, Add. MSS 32880, f. 303, 35417, f. 224.

[103] Cf. Hardwicke to Newcastle, 17 May 1758, Yorke, *Hardwicke*, iii, p. 47, and Walpole, *Geo. II,* ii, pp. 289–90.

passed easily. Nor, despite expectations, was the Habeas Corpus agitation renewed in the next session, even though Hardwicke's promised measure from the judges never saw the light of day.[104]

Pitt had good reason to be satisfied with the outcome of the parliamentary session. Despite the crises of 1757 and the considerable modification of his European policy he had retained his patriot image and the independent support it brought. Beckford's support on all important matters was a token of this. On several occasions he made a point of distinguishing Pitt among the Ministers. Pitt showed in no uncertain terms that he valued such support, despite the difficulties that Beckford's hotheadedness could sometimes cause.[105] When, in the debate of 7 June on the subsidy to Hesse-Cassel, Lord Royston (Hardwicke's son) presumed to answer Beckford's abuse of the peers in the Administration, Pitt replied:

he set forth the great importance and dignity of Mr Beckford personally, and above all the dignity and importance of an alderman, concluding it was a title he should be more proud of than that of a Peer. This speech has enraged the Lords, offended the Commons, and the City ungratefully say was too gross.

Such warmth naturally attracted much comment.[106]

The issues of the parliamentary session attracted relatively little comment out of doors. Even over the Habeas Corpus Bill there were few signs of the uproar Pitt threatened. There was little comment at all until the Bill was before the Commons and then the *London Chronicle* and the Magazines, rather than the papers more committed to Pitt, took the lead.[107] From late March until the beginning of

---

[104] Hardwicke to Newcastle, 2 June, West to Newcastle, 16 June, Newcastle to Hardwicke, [3 June] 1758, Kinnoull to Newcastle, 25 Jan. 1759, Hardwicke to Newcastle, 31 Jan., 9 Mar. 1759, Add. MSS 32880, ff. 303, 470, 35417, f. 224, 32887, ff. 335, 432–3, 32888, f. 436; Yorke, *Hardwicke*, iii, p. 19.

[105] e.g. over the *Anti-Gallican* affair (West to Newcastle, 11 Feb. 1758, Add. MSS 32877, ff. 422–3), over Irish pensions (West to Newcastle, 28 Apr. 1758, Add. MSS 32879, f. 331); over Habeas Corpus (R. Kenyon to Lloyd Kenyon, [?] Mar. 1758, HMC, *Fourteenth Report*, pt. iv, p. 495).

[106] Mrs Montagu to Dr Stillingfleet, 13 June 1758, *Elizabeth Montagu*, ii, pp. 127–8 (quotation); Lyttelton to Sanderson Miller, June 1758, *An Eighteenth Century Corr.*, p. 391; Elliot to Grenville, 10 July 1758, *Grenville Papers*, i, p. 248.

[107] e.g. *LC*, 18–21 Mar. 1757; *GM*, xxviii, Mar. 1758, pp. 143–4; *LM*, xxvii, Mar. 1758, pp. 111–14.

June there was considerable discussion of the issue.[108] Pratt became a popular hero, linked with Pitt and Legge to complete '*The Three Monosyllables*'.[109] The *Monitor* and the *London Evening Post* now took up the question, more, it would seem, because of the political capital to be made for Pitt than because of burning public indignation.[110] True, there were rumours at the end of March of moves in the City. In mid-April an attempt was made by Deputy Long and others associated with the Half Moon to stir up 'a popular storm' against Mansfield over the original case and to get the City to apply to Parliament over the matter. But the attempt was a failure. It was said to have been instigated 'from the other Ends of the Town'.[111] There is every sign that the Habeas Corpus was indeed an issue manufactured by Pitt for political purposes. Its defeat was quietly accepted.[112]

Nevertheless, the 'popular' issues served their end outside Parliament as within. The *London Evening Post* could recommend the Seamen's, Militia and Habeas Corpus Bills as 'countenanced and approved by our present most excellent M[inistr]y, highly to their Honour'. The *London Chronicle* reassured its readers that although the Habeas Corpus Bill was lost the '*People's Minister*' still had power. It had been his measure and that of his friends and he would not disappoint.[113] The *Monitor* could now be used clearly for Pitt's political ends. Although it had not forgotten its expectations of a patriot minister, it recommended the measures he adopted, like the Seamen's Wages Act, ignoring others, like the motion for more frequent parliaments, which at other times it would have sup-

---

[108] e.g. *LC*, 1–4, 4–6 Apr. 20–3 May, 3–6 June 1758; *UC*, 8, 15–22 Apr., 20–7 May 1758; *OWC*, 29 Apr.–6 May 1758; *CR*, v, May 1758, p. 441; *MR*, xviii, June 1758, pp. 602–8.

[109] Newcastle to Hardwicke, 27 Mar. 1758 (quotation), Yorke, *Hardwicke*, iii, p. 44; *LC*, 18–21 Mar. 1758; *Mon.* 141, 1 Apr. 1758.

[110] *Mon.* 141, 1 Apr., 142, 8 Apr., 146, 6 May, 147, 13 May, 151, 10 June 1758; *LEP*, e.g. 23–5, 25–7 May, 1–3, 6–8 June 1758.

[111] Newcastle to Hardwicke, 27 Mar., Mansfield to Hardwicke, 18 Apr. 1758, Yorke, *Hardwicke*, iii, p. 44; Marshe Dickinson to Hardwicke, 14 Apr., Mansfield to Newcastle, 19 Apr. 1758 (second quotation), Add. MSS 35595, f. 169, 32879, f. 224; Lyttelton to W. H. Lyttelton, 5 May 1758, *Mems. Lyttelton*, ii, p. 609 (first quotation).

[112] West, quoted by Rogers, 'London Politics', p. 279 fn. 33; Hardwicke to Newcastle, 17 May 1758, Yorke, *Hardwicke*, iii, p. 47; *LEP*, 6–8 June 1758.

[113] *LEP*, 21–3 Mar. 1758; *LC*, 3–6 June 1758.

ported.[114] The Prussian treaty passed with only a murmur of concern from the *London Evening Post* at the burden it placed on England. It was defended by the *Monitor*, with renewed concern for Europe, as the best way to follow a proper middle course between rejection of all Continental measures and undue attention to them, and recommended by an appeal to history which echoed that of Pitt. Pitt's domestic measures created an image of him as the defender of the true interests of the nation, an image then used by the *Monitor* to put his foreign policy in a more favourable light.[115]

By the middle of 1758 Pitt's reputation out of doors as within was secure and indeed growing. Despite the failure of the obscure moves in the City over the Habeas Corpus issue, which could mean that Pitt's Tory-patriot friends were still divided and uneasy, the warmth of the *Monitor* suggests renewed enthusiasm there. The last weeks of the parliamentary session were coloured by the sailing of the new expedition on 1 June and its initial successes around St. Malo.[116] Large forces were being gathered for a renewed attack on Louisbourg. Truly British measures seemed indeed to be in hand, and praise was widely lavished on Pitt for the 'prodigious Alteration' for the better in national affairs.[117] The crises of 1757 appeared past.

Yet reputation was still Pitt's main strength and not everyone accepted it in these terms. In different ways Lord Egmont, a former Leicester House adherent who spoke forcefully against the motion for more frequent parliaments, Sir Francis Dashwood, the independent Whig who opposed the Prussian subsidy, and Lord Lyttelton, formerly Pitt's ally, who gibed at the '*fearful consistency*' of the King's measures in foreign affairs, all expressed reservations.

[114] e.g. *Mon.* 155, 8 July (constitutional expectations), 146–7, 6–13 May 1758 (on the Seamen's Wages Act). Unlike Pitt (see above fn. 96) the *Monitor* did support the Act to secure the rights of county freeholders. On the eve of the next session it raised the issue of more frequent elections (170, 21 Oct. 1758).

[115] *LEP*, 18–20 Apr. 1758; *Mon.* 138, 11 Mar., 139, 18 Mar., 144, 22 Apr., 145, 29 Apr., 147, 13 May, 149, 27 May, 156, 15 July 1758.

[116] Walpole, *Geo. II*, ii, p. 305; e.g. *LEP*, 25–7 May, 6–8 June 1758; *LC*, 8–10 June 1758; *GM*, xxviii, June 1758, pp. 253–4; *LM*, xxvii, June 1758, pp. 303–4.

[117] e.g. *LEP*, 20–3 May 1758 (quotation); *LC*, 27–30 May, 30 May–1 June, 3–6 June 1758; *RWJ*, 29 Apr., 6 May 1758; *CR*, v, May 1758, pp. 442–3; *MR*, xviii, June 1758, p. 624.

Each could be said to speak for opinion which might have been sympathetic. Furthermore, Pitt could be remarkably reckless. His extravagant courting of Beckford offended many and his popular antics severely taxed the patience of those colleagues on whom he still depended for the support of the King.[118] Had George II the nerve of his grandson he might well have used the Habeas Corpus issue to dismiss Pitt. And Pitt's as-yet resilient reputation was about to be subjected to an even greater test than those of 1757.

---

[118] John Yorke to Royston, 20 Feb. 1758, Add. MSS 35374, f. 145; Calcraft to Rigby, 20 Apr. 1758, Add. MSS 17493, f. 153; Lyttelton to W. H. Lyttelton, 5 May 1758, *Mems. Lyttelton*, ii, p. 609; Lyttelton to Sanderson Miller, June 1758, *An Eighteenth Century Corr.*, p. 391. Pitt may have been gaining 'ground in the closet'. See Chesterfield to his son, 25 Apr., 18 May 1758, quoted *Parl. Hist.* xv, c. 870 fn.

IV

Continental Connections 1758–1759

In the latter part of June 1758, after the prorogation of Parliament, Pitt proposed to his ministerial colleagues that 6,000 British troops and four regiments of cavalry should be sent to Germany.[1] His conversion to 'Continental connections', begun in February 1757 when he first asked for money for Germany, was complete. What now of his patriot image?

Pitt had, of course, been strongly urged for some time to allow such a move. Now the military situation seemed right. There was every reason to help Prince Ferdinand maintain his successful offensive on the left bank of the Rhine. He had, the day after Pitt made his proposal, won a great victory over the French at Crefeld. The enlarged British army was capable of more than expeditions to the French coast. Anyway, the season for them would soon be over and they gave no scope for cavalry. As Frederick had complained before, it seemed pointless for England to keep soldiers at home idle, especially when Anson's successful blockade of Brest had removed the fear of invasion.[2] Neither Pitt's colleagues nor the King had any reason to object to his proposal. Moreover the measure was likely to be generally welcomed. Frederick's popularity was immense and, after the victory at Crefeld, Ferdinand began to share it. Pitt had some grounds for his claim to Bute that the 'publick approbation I have no reason to doubt of'. Nevertheless the proposal was made 'at

---

[1] Newcastle to Hardwicke, [23 June], Newcastle to Rockingham, 24 June, Barrington to Newcastle, 24 June, Newcastle to Henry Campion, 15 July 1758, Add. MSS 35417, f. 238, 32881, ff. 37, 35, 335. Details given of the proposal vary and were probably altered during discussion.

[2] Corbett, i, p. 285.

the risk (and certainly there is some risk) of popularity'.[3] It would not be readily accepted by those convinced anti-Germans who were Pitt's particular supporters.

Pitt had in fact carefully prepared the ground for the sending of troops, despite his frequent and artfully phrased denials that any such move was contemplated. Right at the beginning of the Coalition the *Con-Test* had begun the process. In March 1758, when pressure from Frederick was intense, the Spanish Ambassador had it on good authority that Pitt would eventually send troops, but would protect himself by having a motion moved in the Commons to test opinion without forcing the issue. Potter had made it clear to the group of Tories organizing support for Pitt over the Prussian treaty in April that it would be impossible to make a declaration in principle against sending troops to Germany. In the debate of 19 April Pitt emphasized that, while he did not know of any intention to do so, he did not preclude such a development if the troops could be useful to Ferdinand and served the common interest, not just that of petty states (i.e. Hanover). Pitt's frequent and flattering letters to Bute may also have been a smoothing of the way for the announcement of a decision made some time before, by May at the latest.[4]

Significantly he took no open step until after the prorogation of Parliament. Then, he took care to explain such an uncongenial move to those to whom he looked for support. He turned first to Leicester House and his personal friends. Bute, approached after Pitt had made his initial proposals, agreed on the understanding that a 'small body should not lead to a great one'. Pitt replied, 'A thousand real thanks for my noble friend's salutary caution. Be assured, I will not be drawn further than my own conviction, authorised and confirmed by your concurrence, shall suggest.' After the news of Crefeld Bute was perhaps a little warmer, agreeing that the number of men 'is in truth neither more nor less than what I had

---

[3] Pitt to Bute, [23 June 1758], 'Letters from Pitt to Bute', p. 154; Barrington to Newcastle, 24 June 1758, Add. MSS 32881, f. 35, quoted Fraser, 'The Pitt–Newcastle Coalition', p. 217.

[4] See above p. 90; D'Abreu to Wall, 3 Mar. 1758, *Corr. Chatham*, i, p. 297; Potter to Pitt, [Feb.–Apr. 1758], PRO 30/8/53, f. 98; Calcraft to Rigby, 20 Apr. 1758, Add. MSS 17493, f. 154, Neville parliamentary diary, 19 Apr. 1758, Berks. Record Office, D/EN 034/16; Newdigate Diary (transcript), 19 Apr. 175[8]; 'Letters from Pitt to Bute', pp. 148–53.

n secret wished to go'. Although he hoped that relations with 'russia would be improved as a result, he was still very suspicious of 'rederick. The Prince of Wales, probably more nearly reflecting 3ute's real views as well as his own, was much less happy about the lecision of 'your wavering friend'. He feared deeper involvement in a Continent war' which, when he came to the throne, would 1amper his forming a ministry which could 'have the opinion of the 0eople'. Yet, as Temple suggested, as long as there was no likelihood 0f Cumberland's being appointed to command the troops, Leicester 4ouse would not raise insuperable difficulties, especially if Pitt 0ontinued to press the coastal raids which they supported.[5]

Some of Pitt's personal supporters were also hesitant, if less so. In he euphoria of the success of the coastal expedition at Cherbourg, remple at first said the decision must depend upon circumstances .nd be justified by success. There had never been, he maintained, .ny undertaking in principle not to send troops. A few days later he vas more doubtful. Expressing sympathy with Pitt's difficulties and ome approval of the measure, he went on, 'though as one step 1ecessarily draws on many more, in any hands but yours, with such . master, such colleagues, and the whole of the plan of the war taken ogether, my reluctance would be extreme.' Beckford, also informed 0y Pitt of his decision, revealed some of the qualms Tories would eel. He set out the rival arguments he was hearing about the 0elative merits of coastal expeditions and armies sent to Europe, iving his support to the former. He recounted gibes that 'notwith-tanding his promise to parliament, Mr Pitt will be obliged to send n army into Germany'. Nevertheless he gave quite warm approval o the sending of cavalry; if infantry were sent, he warned, it would ause uneasiness.[6] Beckford was closer to Pitt than most of the 'ories. It was not at all certain that others would silence their 1ualms so readily.

For the moment, Pitt had no need to worry about the reaction of he Tories in Parliament. By the time they reassembled, in five nonths or so, he could well hope that events would have justified

---

[5] Bute to Pitt [reply to letter of 23 June], Prince of Wales to Bute, [*c.*2 July 1758], *etters from George III to Lord Bute*, p. 11 and fn. 1; Pitt to Bute, [23], 26 June 1758, _etters of Pitt to Bute', pp. 153, 155; Bute to Pitt, 28 June, Temple to Pitt, 3 July 758, *Corr. Chatham*, i, pp. 320–1, 324–5.
[6] Temple to Pitt, 29 June 1758, PRO 30/8/61, f. 27; Temple to Pitt, 3 July, eckford to Pitt, 10 July 1758, *Corr. Chatham*, i, pp. 324–5, 328–30.

him. Something of their likely immediate reactions, however, can b
gauged from controversy in the press. In particular, the *Monito*
provides a dramatic seismographic record of Tory shock. Further
the waves of controversy the shock set off over the next nine month
show how Pitt's popular support was reshaped by it. Again th
Monitor is central in this process.

Even as the *Monitor*'s confidence in Pitt's Administration ha
grown again from April onwards, it had continued to draw ver
carefully the proper limits to Continental involvement. Fear that
British army might be sent was never far from the surface.[7] Now, a
the decision to send troops became known and papers carrie
reports of their movements, this undertone of concern rose to
jarring note. Should the Minister who had delivered and inspire
the nation be over-ruled,

should we be threatened into the expensive and disabling measure c
transporting . . . troops into Germany . . .: should this Measure appear t
have been put off to this advanced time of the year, only because th
advisers thereof were afraid to bring it up on the tapis, during the sitting c
parliament: or should they . . . attempt to baffle the friends of their king an
country, by an argument drawn from the prerogative of the crown, t
command the national forces to any place or service: what might we nc
expect?

The answer: it would 'disgust the Nation' and bring disaster.[8]

From July until November the *Monitor* remained preoccupied witl
this development. In shocked reaction it drew back from positions i
had come to defend. It very soon rejected all arguments in favour o
British support for Prince Ferdinand's offensive, whether for th
sake of the liberties and religion of Europe, because of treat
obligations, out of special consideration for Hanover, or because th
troops were better employed than kept idly at home. These troop
had been voted for the British war against France. If they wer
inactive it must be due to factious opposition to their proper use. N
case was allowed for their use in Germany. It was suggested tha
Prince Ferdinand used his troops only in Hanoverian interests, nc
to assist Prussia and the Protestant cause as had been intended
Although the *Monitor* had so recently defended a proper Britisl
concern for the balance of power and religion and liberties c

---

[7] e.g. *Mon.* 138–9, 11–18 Mar. 1758.   [8] Ibid. 156, 15 July 1758.

Europe, it now tended to deny any British interest in events in
Germany, and even implied hesitation about the Prussian alliance
and Frederick's cause.[9] Such a rapid change of attitudes show just
how unacceptable the new moves were to those concerned primarily
with Britain's maritime and commercial policy. In strange contrast,
the *London Evening Post* took refuge in silence. In April, when the
Prussian Convention was before Parliament, the paper had reiterated its opposition to the sending of troops. Now, it merely reported
the troop movements, with no comment except a copy of the
Monitor's stern warning of 15 July. For most of the rest of the year,
indeed, it made little original comment on major political questions.
However, there can be little doubt that its silence was one of
embarrassment. The *Monitor's* response suggests that reports of the
City's quick recovery after some initial shock and of general
satisfaction with the sending of troops were misleading, at least
about those who had been foremost in support of Pitt.[10]

Interest in the sending of troops to Germany was naturally not
confined to those who had been most rigid in their opposition. A
widely copied article which seems to have originated with Probus in
the *Gazetteer* admitted that, while the nation was virtually unanimous in support of the King of Prussia and did not begrudge his
money, many seemed 'to repine at the sending of forces to Germany,
because they imagine it is done for the sake of Hanover, and fancy
they perceive something unconstitutional in it'. The *London Chronicle*
and *Lloyd's Evening Post* both gave extracts from the *Monitor's* first
explosive reaction, although the *London Chronicle* moderated the
warning considerably. Both also presented other points of view.
Indeed, the unusual range of material given to their readers
confirms the considerable interest aroused by the issue. But debate
did not persist long and Pitt's confidence that he had no reason to
doubt the 'publick approbation' was probably largely justified. Both
Probus in the *Gazetteer* and the author of the *Westminster Journal*, the
two most politically alert commentators in newspapers, gave the
sending of troops judicious approval in present circumstances and

[9] Ibid. 158–61, 29 July–19 Aug., 163, 2 Sept., 166, 23 Sept., 174, 18 Nov. 1758.
[10] *LEP*, 15–18 Apr., 18–20 July 1758; Symmer to Mitchell, 20 July 1758, Add.
MSS 6839, f. 100; Gordon to Newcastle, 21 July 1758, Add. MSS 32882, f. 33.

Probus apparently went on answering the *Monitor*'s arguments for some weeks.[11]

Yet the pockets of resistance to Pitt's Continental policy were not easily overcome. The *Monitor*'s reaction was undoubtedly influenced by a pamphlet which appeared late in July, probably in time to shape the *Monitor*'s first substantial comment on the issue on 29 July. This was *Things As They Are*, attributed, credibly, to Lord Egmont. It attacked the Prussian alliance as an unjustified reversal of Britain's natural alliances. This had brought on her the hostility of Russia and Austria, and embroiled her with an aggressive and insatiable ally against the rest of the German princes, which could only mean endless war. It had diverted Britain from her own just cause against France, and had brought no advantages, not even the protection of Hanover. Britain was merely doing France's work by saving Prussia and the balance of power in Germany. Almost as strongly, the pamphlet dwelt on the unfortunate effects of the Hanoverian connection, without which there would never have been a Prussian alliance and Britain would still have had true friends and well-considered Continental connections. Instead, she was making an insignificant contribution to an army not even commanded by one of her own generals.

Worst of all, the pamphlet linked Pitt with these mistakes. It mocked the 'speech-trade' and 'popular harangues, especially against Continental connections' by which he rose to power when the country was desperate. It reminded its readers that he had once before (in 1746) bargained popularity for office as he had done again in entering a discordant coalition (in 1757). He had missed the chance offered by his rise to power on popular acclaim to disentangle the nation once and for all from the Continent. Instead he had become the advocate of the most dangerous connection of all and now was sending troops as well as money. The victory of Crefeld had been exaggerated, the pamphlet claimed, 'by the mouths of the Tower-guns, and by a solemn thanksgiving', in order to make this

[11] *LC*, 18–20, 20–2 July 1758; *Lloyd's EP*, 17–19, 21–4, 24–6 July 1758; *UC*, 22–9 July 1758 (quotation); Probus quoted in e.g. *LC*, 18–20, 20–2 July, *Lloyd's EP*, 14–16 Aug. (in answer to *Mon.* 160, 12 Aug.), 25–8 Aug., *Westminster Journal* in *Lloyd's EP*, 24–6 July (no copies of the original article survive); on Pitt, see above p. 115. A flurry of renewed comment on the Habeas Corpus issue just when the troop movements were first reported may have been officially inspired to protect Pitt's patriot reputation. *LEP*, 11–13 July 758, *LC*, 13–15 July 1758, *Lloyd's EP*, 12–14, 14–17 July 1758.

move 'go down the more glib, with soldiers and people, under all the smoke and flash of that recent success'. It questioned all his supposed achievements in office, ridiculing especially the 'absurd and insignificant activity' of the coastal expeditions, given so much attention. And it ended by suggesting that the 'sense of the enlightened and impartial multitude begins to look with an equal eye on the veterans of corruption, and the pretenders to patriotism, on the worn out tool of a court, and the mushroom of a much abused popularity, ridiculously shot up to a cedar-height'. Both had achieved '*Nothing*, or *worse than nothing*'. Such were 'Things as they are'.[12]

This attack attracted attention for some weeks, showing again how sensitive the issue of Continental connections was. The *Critical Review*, with its Tory leanings, was obviously made uneasy by the pamphlet's arguments. It could only 'hope' that the sarcasms against the Ministry were unjust and undeserved, and concluded 'the public has a right to know, and no doubt, will know in due time, why those continental measures, which were so lately dammed to reprobation, are now resumed in the face of day, and carried on at such an enormous expence'. The *Monthly Review* was more clearly hostile to the pamphlet which it saw as a party effort designed to raise discontent. It deplored the ridicule of the 'active operations of the Ministry'. But it felt obliged to take some of the pamphlet's arguments seriously. The *Monitor* was influenced first by the pamphlet's anti-Hanoverianism and only later, on 2 September, by the criticisms of the Prussian alliance. Perhaps it realized only slowly that its readers still had difficulty in accepting the alliance as a British rather than a Hanoverian measure.[13]

The pamphlet was answered in mid-August by *Things Set In A Proper Light*. This work attempted a 'vindication of the character of the *heroic Frederic and our noble Patriot*'. However it consisted merely of

[12] *Things As They Are*, London, 1758, esp. pp. 25, 27, 29–31 (accusations against Pitt), 82 (Crefeld), 107, 112 (last three quotations). Egmont, prominent in opposition in the 1740s and author of the masterly *Faction Detected by Evidence of the Facts*, London, 1743 (a defence of Pulteney), and a wayward politician of Leicester House connections, had shown signs of dissatisfaction with Pitt. See above pp. 113–14.

[13] Birch to Royston, 29 July 1758, Add. MSS 35399, ff. 7–8; *MR*, xix, Aug. 1758, pp. 166–9; *CR*, vi, Aug. 1758, pp. 170–1; *LM*, xxvii, Aug. 1758, pp. 407–13; *GM*, xxvii, Aug. 1758, p. 379; *UC*, 2–9 Sept. (Probus), 9–16 Sept. 1758; *Mon.* 163, 2 Sept. 1758.

disjointed and weak denials of the main points of its antagonist, to which it gave greater publicity by quoting them at length, so much so that the *Monthly Review* thought it a collusive answer.[14] Yet, although replies to *Things As They Are* were unsatisfactory and although the criticism of the Prussian alliance and the sending of troops struck some responsive chord, virtually no one accepted the criticism of Pitt. People just did not believe that 'notwithstanding the protection of our own trade, the destruction of that of *France*, the ruin of her navy, and the destruction of her harbours, the expedition against *Cape Breton*, and our success in Africa, . . . [the Ministry] have done nothing, or worse'. In addition to these successes, news of the victory at Plassey in India had been received early in the year and evidence of vigorous preparations for more action further encouraged confidence.[15]

From the beginning the *Monitor* dissociated Pitt from the decision to send troops to Germany and exonerated him from blame. This was most obvious in the early paper of 29 July.[16] In setting out in dialogue form the arguments for and against the sending of troops, it put the arguments for into the mouth of Harry, representing Fox, his patron Cumberland, and all the 'faction' which supported a Pelhamite Continental policy. The arguments against were given to Will. *Things Set In A Proper Light* went further still and declared to the public that their 'darling minister' was 'not one of the number' who now advocated Continental connections, and that he persisted firm as ever 'against pursuing any such continental measures, as may be detrimental to England's interest'.[17] So by misrepresentation, deliberate or otherwise,[18] Pitt's reputation survived his most damaging move yet. Only his earlier skilful defence made the misrepresentation credible.

---

[14] *Things Set In A Proper Light*, London, 1758; Birch to Royston, 19 Aug. 1758, Add. MSS 35399, f. 17 (quotation); *CR*, vi, Aug. 1758, p. 171; *MR*, xix, Sept., 1758, p. 302.

[15] *GM*, xxvii, Aug. 1758, pp. 378–9 (quotation); cf. *MR*, as fn. 13. Other comment just ignored the criticisms. For the naval victories see above p. 106, and the destruction of harbours below p. 124. Operations against Louisbourg (Cape Breton) were begun again late in May under Amherst. In April/May Fort Louis at the mouth of the Senegal River was captured. For the effects of all this see *A Vindication of Mr Pitt*, London, [Mar.] 1758, pp. 55–6; *Mon.* 156, 15 July 1758.

[16] *Mon.* 158, 29 July 1758.   [17] *Things Set In A Proper Light*, p. 17.

[18] As Beckford knew of Pitt's part in the moves, it is hard to see the *Monitor*'s misrepresentation as innocent. However, those even closer to Pitt could, in other contexts, talk sincerely of 'numberless Cabals' and 'restless Faction' interfering with Pitt's 'salutary Councils'. e.g. Potter to Pitt, 20 Aug. 1758, PRO 30/8/53, f. 69.

Yet Pitt's rescue was not entirely due to misrepresentation. The timing of the decision to send troops to Germany was closely linked with the fortunes of the second expedition to the French coast, which set out on 1 June 1758. It had some preliminary success around St. Malo before reimbarking because of threatened opposition. After delays caused by stormy weather, the fleet made various threatening appearances of Le Havre, Caen, and Cherbourg before returning to Spithead to provision at the end of June.[19] Pitt made his surprise suggestion about troops to Germany during discussions about the orders to be given to the expedition's Commander, the Duke of Marlborough, after the reimbarkation at St. Malo. He had to insist that the expedition should stay on the French coast, and probably suggested the troops for Germany to avoid its diversion either there or to Flanders. He continued to insist that it should go out again after its return to port at the end of June. Later he even thought of strengthening it and still went on insisting that it should continue. Even after its failure at St. Cas early in September, on its third stage, he did not immediately abandon further plans for it and threatened to withdraw all troops on the Continent if he was not supported.[20]

Obviously Pitt saw this expedition, like that of the previous year, not only as a military exercise but also as a necessary diversion of attention at home from his developing Continental policy. His letters to Bute amply reflect his anxiety for its success.[21] His political allies saw it in the same light. Leicester House wholeheartedly supported the expedition as an alternative to German measures, while Temple and, later, George Townshend advised further efforts for political reasons. From the beginning Beckford attached great importance to the expedition and urged firmness. He reported at length the opinions of 'disinterested' men who saw it as an effective alternative to 'sending large bodies of men to Germany or the Low Countries' and as an answer to those who sought to 'lessen the popularity you have so justly acquired'.[22] Some public comment also saw the sending of troops to Germany and the expedition as

[19] Walpole, *Geo. II*, ii, pp. 304–7, 313–14, and Corbett, i, pp. 275–301, give accounts of the whole course of the expedition.

[20] Corbett, i, pp. 285, 288–9, 295, 296, 373–5; *Dodington*, p. 372, 7 [July 1758].

[21] Pitt to Bute, 8, 15, 16, 22 June 1758, 'Letters from Pitt to Bute', pp. 150–3.

[22] Bute to Pitt, [16 June], [2 July], Temple to Pitt, 3 July, G. Townshend to Pitt, 27 Aug., Beckford to Pitt, 10 July 1758, *Corr. Chatham*, i, pp. 318–19, 323–4, 346–7, 328–30.

alternative forms of action which were causing debate in the Ministry. As Pitt was clearly associated with the expedition, such comment helped to disguise his part in the decision to send troops to the Continent, although there were still notes of scepticism about the value of the expedition.[23]

Certainly the expedition attracted more attention than did the sending of troops.[24] Its early activity at St. Malo was enough to be treated ostentatiously as success, and accepted as such, at least in the City.[25] Its next stage, at Cherbourg early in August, was even more successful. The port was temporarily seized. Fortifications and harbour works were destroyed and armaments taken. When the expedition returned home, Pitt had the captured guns put on display in Hyde Park before they were taken with ceremony to be stored in the Tower. Townshend and Potter were exultant.[26] The sending of troops was forgotten, it seemed, by all but the *Monitor*. In marked contrast to its enthusiasm for the Rochefort expedition in the previous year, the *Monitor* and its readers were not now to be diverted from the shock of the new German policy by mere baubles of temporary successes on the coast of France, however stridently proclaimed.

Fortunately, the expedition was not the sole glimmer of success during the summer to encourage more confidence in the conduct of the war. There had been earlier naval and colonial victories. Ferdinand's triumph at Crefeld was ostentatiously celebrated by 'the Tower guns' and services of thanksgiving, as *Things As They Are* sceptically pointed out.[27] Most important of all, on 18 August,

[23] *AR,* i, 1758, pp. 65–6; *Lloyd's EP,* 7–10 July, cf. *OWC,* 8–15 July 1758. For scepticism see *LC,* 3–5 Aug., *Lloyd's EP,* 16–18 Aug. 1758.

[24] It was fully reported and commented on in *GM,* xxviii, May to Nov., which in June noted that it was 'much the subject of Conversation' (p. 253). See also e.g. *AR,* i, 1758, pp. 66–9; *UC,* 10–17 June, 12–19 Aug. 1758; *OWC,* 17–24 June, 12–19 Aug. 1758; *CR,* vi, July 1758, p. 79, Aug., p. 175; *LM,* xxvii, July 1758, pp. 348–51. All newspapers carried reports.

[25] Walpole to Mann, 18 June 1758, *Walpole's Corr.* xxi, p. 213; Watkins to Newcastle, 19 June, Gordon to Newcastle, 7 July 1758, Add. MSS 32880, f. 499, 32881, f. 197.

[26] Corbett, i, pp. 295–6; Walpole to Mann, 12 Aug., 9 Sept. 1758, *Walpole's Corr.* xxi, pp. 226, 238; Symmer to Mitchell, 12 Sept. 1758, Add. MSS 6839, f. 103; Potter to Pitt, 20 Aug. 1758, PRO 30/8/53, f. 69; Townshend to Pitt, 27 Aug. 1758, *Corr. Chatam,* i, pp. 346–7.

[27] See above fn. 15. *Things As They Are,* p. 82; Walpole to John Chute, 29 June, to Montagu, 6 July 1758, *The Letters of Horace Walpole,* iv, pp. 152, 153; *GM,* xxviii, July 1758, p. 336.

simultaneously with the reports of success at Cherbourg, came news from America of the capture of Louisbourg. A little later the standards captured there were ceremonially paraded to St. Paul's. All agreed on the central importance of America. *Things As They Are* had conceded that the fall of Louisbourg would provide real occasion for celebration.[28]

The news was rapturously received. In the press, in verse, and in pamphlets the victory was chronicled and celebrated and the value of the conquest extolled.[29] Its effect was the more potent because of the memory that Louisbourg had been won in the last war, only to be given back in the Peace of Aix-la-Chapelle in 1748. More formal expressions of triumph came in at least fifty addresses of congratulation, including one from London.[30] Almost universally the victory was attributed to Pitt's measures. The tide of popularity was indeed rising fast.

The victory brought to Pitt more than just general popularity. Above all else it drew attention away from distasteful Continental developments and made more effective the attempt to dissociate Pitt from them. It was evidence, seized with enormous relief, that British measures still prevailed. The *Monitor* did not ignore this victory and assessed its value in very high terms. The *London Evening Post* triumphantly if belatedly produced it as an answer to those who criticized all ministers. 'Now should we . . . compare *Things as they are*, with Things as they were about a Twelve-month ago, should we not, contrary to the deceitful Representations of an invidious Writer, find them mended, even to a Miracle.'[31] Pitt's City supporters returned warmly to him. They initiated the City Address which was intended as an expression of faith in him at the expense of the other Ministers. For this reason it did not pass without considerable debate, although Beckford had reported 'infinite joy more than I ever remember' over the victory in the City.[32] There and elsewhere

[28] Walpole, *Geo. II*, ii, pp. 311–12; Jenkinson to Grenville, *Grenville Papers*, i, p. 265; *Things As They Are*, p. 89.

[29] e.g. *LM*, xxvii, Sept. 1758, pp. 447–8; *GM*, xxviii, Aug. 1758, pp. 372, 384–9; *OWC*, 2–9 Sept. 1758; *LC*, 17–19 Aug., 12–14 Sept. 1758; *Lloyd's EP*, 13–15 Sept. 1758; *CR*, vi, Oct. 1758, p. 347, Nov., p. 437; *MR*, xix, Nov. 1758, p. 499.

[30] *London Gazette*, 26 Aug.–30 Dec. 1758.

[31] *Mon.* 162, 26 Aug., 165, 16 Sept., 168, 7 Oct. 1758; *LEP*, 29–31 Aug. 1758.

[32] Hodges to Pitt, 23, 30 Aug. 1758, PRO 30/8/40, ff. 143, 145; Birch to Royston, 26 Aug. 1758, Add. MSS 35399, f. 22; Beckford to Pitt, 26 Aug. 1758, PRO 30/8/19, f. 46. Beckford was not present when the Address was voted (Jour. Common Council, 61, f. 281) but this letter (f. 46) makes it clear that he approved its contents.

(for example Exeter and Chester) where the Addresses originated with or were influenced by Tories, they were used to emphasize again the importance of the colonial and maritime war. In such a strategy Louisbourg had held particular significance ever since its dramatic capture in 1745.[33] These Addresses ostentatiously praised 'British' victories in Africa and on the French coast as well as at Louisbourg. By contrast Continental victories were studiously ignored. With obvious reference to the fate of Louisbourg in 1748, and in line with demands in the 1740s, its permanent retention in the peace settlement to come was asked for in some Addresses. The amendment to this effect in Bath, proposed by 'an old Tory', embarrassed Pitt's lieutenant, Potter. Although it was defeated, the Address still provocatively expressed the joy of 'Englishmen who love their country' at seeing the 'Honour of the British Name so gloriously retrieved'. The terms of the proposed City Address were so extreme that Pitt thought it judicious to take steps to have them softened. Other places used different means to show their loyalties. Chester praised the King's choice of ministers, Salisbury the proper attention shown to true British interests which had led to unanimity among his people. Partisan notes were loudest in the Addresses of the first month after the news of Louisbourg.[34]

The *London Evening Post* urged all corporations to follow London's example in asking for the retention of Louisbourg. The *Monitor* joined wholeheartedly in these expressions of Tory orthodoxy. It made a point of denying that success at Louisbourg owed anything to the assistance Britain had given to Prussia. Its 'faction' argument, which it had already used to good effect to exonerate Pitt from responsibility for the sending of troops, was now strengthened, and widened. All measures which the paper disliked in both foreign and domestic affairs it now regarded as the result of the continuing influence of 'such as are left of the old pack', those who had held office in earlier administrations. The 'old pack' impeded and depreciated the wise policies of the present Ministry, which were

[33] Langford, *The Eighteenth Century*, pp. 124–6.

[34] See e.g. *London Gazette*, 22–6 Aug. (London), 29 Aug.–2 Sept. (Exeter), 2–5 Sept. (Norwich, Newcastle Merchant Adventurers), 16–19 Sept. (Chester), 19–23 Sept. (Salisbury, Dorchester), 23–6 Sept. 1758 (Bath). Only sixteen Addresses asked for retention but nine of these were among the first fourteen Addresses, to 19 Sept. Potter to Pitt, [n.d.] 1758, PRO 30/8/53, f. 75; Gordon to Newcastle, 30 Aug. 1758, Add. MSS 32883, f. 182.

constantly contrasted to those of the past.[35]

Such partisan exploitation of the victory was not allowed to pass without challenge. The parading of the colours was dismissed as out of proportion to the value of the victory. Some said it was more a loss to the French than a gain to the British. The Addresses urging the retention of Louisbourg were criticized as presumptuous intrusions into the royal prerogative. Emphasis on the importance of Louisbourg was interpreted as derogatory of Ferdinand's victory at Crefeld and for this reason the City's Address was said to have caused offence at Court. Other Addresses, notably the early one from Cambridge (where Newcastle was Chancellor), dwelt at some length on the benefits of Crefeld and Prussian successes as well as those of the British victories. In answer, the *Monitor* defended the right to address, and compared Crefeld and Louisbourg very much to the advantage of the latter, indignantly denying that its capture benefited only 'the mercantile part of the nation'.[36]

Despite these differences of opinion about the victory, Pitt's supporters had been immensely reassured. It did not matter that again they assumed too easily that he entirely shared their views. He was, for example, wary of the demand for the unconditional retention of Louisbourg. The triumphal parade of colours was enough to suggest to them his sympathy. Moreover Pitt's general popularity was strengthening. The *Monitor* was not alone in distinguishing him among the Ministers by its 'faction' argument and the gibes of *Things As They Are* seemed increasingly irrelevant. Potter was right to rejoice that the victory at Louisbourg could be a 'means of continuing to this undone Country your salutary Councils' despite the 'numberless Cabals' of 'restless Faction' in recent months.[37]

However, even in the first flush of colonial victory, the controversial issue of Continental connections was not forgotten. Events would show that Pitt was still vulnerable on this question. It was

[35] *LEP*, 12–14 Sept. 1758; *Mon.* 159, 5 Aug., 162, 26 Aug., 163, 2 Sept., 166, 23 Sept. (quotation), 174, 18 Nov. 1758. *LC*, 26–9 Aug. 1758 also strongly supported the London Address.

[36] e.g. *UC*, 2–9 Sept., 23–30 Sept. 1758; *GM*, xxviii, Sept. 1758, p. 432 (the By-stander); *Lloyd's EP*, 25–8 Aug. and *LC*, 26–9 Aug. both quoting *UC* (Payne's); Walpole, *Geo. II*, ii, p. 326; *London Gazette*, 9–12 Sept. 1758 (Cambridge Address); *Mon.* 162, 26 Aug. (quotation), 165, 16 Sept., 168, 7 Oct. 1758. Only eleven Addresses mentioned European victories, five of these Prussian ones only.

[37] e.g. *UC*, 19–26 Aug., 2–9 Dec. 1758; *OWC*, 2–9 Dec. 1758; Potter to Pitt, 20 Aug. 1758, PRO 30/8/53, f. 69.

fortunate that the crucial victory at Louisbourg came when it did. Otherwise the atmosphere would have been much more seriously soured by the chequered last stages of the expedition to the French coast. After its return from Cherbourg on 19 August Pitt ordered it to sea again as soon as possible. On 31 August it sailed for another attempt on St. Malo. Once again a successful landing was made at Lunaire Bay nearby, but, faced again with French opposition, this turned into a humiliating and incompetent retreat. Lives were sacrificed with nothing to show for them. From this the expedition returned home on 18 September for the last time.

Despite attempts at censorship of news from the expedition,[38] this débâcle triggered another lively pamphlet controversy like that of the previous year over the failure at Rochefort. Again the controversy concentrated on the conduct of the officers, chiefly that of the military Commander, Lieutenant-General Bligh.[39] But again as on the previous occasion, the debate widened to include matters that could be embarrassing to Pitt. Although criticisms of him were made quite early, especially for his choice of that 'superannuated gentleman', Bligh, as Commander, the political explosiveness of the controversy was first fully shown in *An Examination of a Letter* in November. Under the guise of a commentary on a previously-published letter which purported to be from Bligh to Pitt (but was speedily disavowed), the pamphlet mounted a powerful attack on Pitt. It questioned the feasibility and objectives of this expedition and the general capacity of such enterprises to meet their purpose, although in theory they might be true British measures. More important, on lines very similar to *Things As They Are*, it criticized Pitt bitterly and at length for his changes of front on Continental connections and for the disastrous effects of the alliance with Prussia. Again it questioned the soundness of Pitt's popularity and the sincerity of his appeal to the people. It suggested that when his fatal Continental connections had led inevitably to the sacrifice of Louisbourg for the sake of Prussia or Hanover, Pitt would revive his

---

[38] Corbett, i, p. 301.

[39] Calcraft to Fox, 21 Sept. 1758, Add. MSS 51398, f. 29; Jenkinson to Grenville, 30 Sept. 1758, *Grenville Papers*, i, p. 272; Birch to Royston, 23, 30 Sept., 21 Oct. 1758, Add. MSS 35399, ff. 34–6, 39–40, 53. For the works see *MR,* xix, Sept. 1758, pp. 311–12, Oct., pp. 405–6, Nov., pp. 499, 500, Dec., p. 579, 580; xx, Jan. 1759, p. 79; *CR,* vi, Sept. 1758, pp. 260–1, Oct., p. 344, Nov., pp. 435–6, 437, Dec., p. 523; vii, Jan. 1759, pp. 83–6.

arts of popular appeal to deceive the people yet again into believing that the loss was not his responsibility.[40]

In various ways other pamphlets questioned the usefulness of coastal expeditions.[41] The controversy, particularly *An Examination of a Letter*, attracted some attention in newspapers and magazines.[42] The *London Magazine* chose for quotation the part of this pamphlet most critical of 'our publick conduct' in regard to Continental connections. Although the *Monthly Review* briefly and contemptuously dismissed it, the *Critical Review* could again only 'hope' that future events would falsify the accusations against Pitt, which 'perhaps' had been carried to undue lengths.[43]

Such uneasiness shows that these attacks could still shake Tory faith in Pitt. True, the *Monitor* was stung at last into some interest in the expedition by the criticisms of Pitt's choice of Bligh as Commander and demands for a parliamentary inquiry into the circumstances of his appointment. In response, the *Monitor* took a line strikingly different from its attitude to Byng and over Rochefort, calling for humanity and restraint in attacks on the General. A month later it leapt to Pitt's defence again in reply to *An Examination of a Letter*, but only on the expedition. As significant as its defence were the gaps in that defence. It simply ignored the *Examination*'s major point, its criticism of Continental connections, except perhaps to attempt to divert it by taking up at some length the subsidiary charge that Bligh was appointed because better qualified officers preferred service in Germany. It turned the tables on Bligh's critics by

[40] *A Letter to His E[xcellenc]y L[ieutenan]t G[enera]l B[lig]h*, London, 1758, *MR*, xix, Oct. 1758, p. 406; *A Letter from the Hon. L[ieutenan]t G[enera]l B[li]gh, to the Right Hon. W[illia]m P[it]t, Esq; MR*, xix, Nov. 1758, p. 500; *CR*, vi, Nov. 1758, p. 435; *An Examination of a Letter Published under the Name of L[ieutenan]t G[enera]l B[li]lgh and addressed to the Hon. W[illia]m P[it]t, Esq.*, London, 1758, esp. pp. 23–6, 37–51, 61 (attributed by Walpole to Dodington, *Geo. II*, ii, pp. 325–6).

[41] *An Appeal to common Sense, CR*, vi, Nov. 1758, pp. 435–6, *MR*, xix, Nov. 1758, p. 500; *A Letter From A Member of Parliament in Town, To A Noble Lord In the Country, In regard to the Last Expedition to the Coast of France, CR*, vii, Jan. 1759, pp. 85–6; *MR*, xix, Dec. 1758, p. 579; *An Apology for W[illiam] P[itt] Esq; In Which The Conduct of L[ieutenant] G[eneral] B[lig]h is vindicated from all the Cavils thrown out against him*, London, 1759, esp. pp. 1–5, 8, 11–13 (an ironic defence, it would seem).

[42] e.g. *OWC*, 23–30 Sept., 4–11 Nov., 2–9 Dec. 1758; *LM*, xxvii, Oct. 1758, pp. 495–6, Dec., p. 654; *LEP*, 11–14 Nov. 1758; *LC*, 14–16 Nov. 1758; *GM*, xxviii, Nov. 1758, pp. 530–4, Dec., p. 598; xxix, Jan. 1759, pp. 36–7.

[43] *LM*, xxvii, Nov. 1758, pp. 547–9; *MR*, xix, Dec. 1758, p. 580; *CR*, vi, Nov. 1758, p. 435.

demanding a full inquiry by Ministry and Parliament into the behaviour of these officers. So again it took up a version of the 'faction' argument in response to the mediocre later performance of the expedition, while ignoring major charges against Pitt.[44]

Yet the controversy also shows how the potential disillusionment with Pitt was moderated by success, especially that at Louisbourg. The *Critical Review* cited this in answer to criticisms that Pitt's efforts were wrongly directed. Other comment mocked all the argument and volatility of opinion; Cherbourg and Louisbourg outweighed all failures. The general mood was captured early in the new year by the *Monitor* in a great paean of praise of victories which were the result of wise policies and new ways of attacking France, avoiding diversion into Continental war. Somewhat later, the *Monitor* was even able, albeit under the disguise of allegory, to take advantage of Pitt's growing reputation to deny rumours of further involvement in Germany. Despite some reports of 'peevishness' in the City, there was no threat of a major crisis, as there had been over Rochefort the previous year. In this sense Birch was right in his initial comment that criticism was moderated by Pitt's popularity, and so was Symmer in his early conclusion that affairs at home would not be disturbed by the controversy and there was 'not the least Appearance of the Ministers meeting with Opposition in the ensuing Session of Parliament'.[45]

The outcome of the controversy is well summed up in a late but very skilful contribution, *Plain Reasons For Removing A certain Great Man From His M[ajest]y's Presence and Councils for ever*. The pamphlet, apparently an attack on Pitt, in fact most effectively recapitulated, under ironic guise, his popular image which so much helped to rebut criticism. His support of 'popular' measures, together with his personal qualities and integrity, his vigorous war measures and his likely attitudes in peace negotiations were all dwelt on. The villains of the 'faction' argument were ironically turned into 'noble patriots', always ready to oppose him and remedy his errors. Especially interesting is the pamphlet's rendering of the charge that Pitt had

[44] *Mon.* 173, 11 Nov., 177, 9 Dec., 179, 23 Dec. 1758; 183, 20 Jan. 1759.
[45] *CR*, vi, Nov. 1758, p. 436; *LC*, 19–21 Oct. and *Lloyd's EP*, 18–20 Oct. 1758, citing the *By-Stander* 12; *Mon.* 182, 13 Jan., 192, 24 Mar. 1759; cf. *LEP*, 12–14 Dec. 1758; Gordon to Newcastle, 14 Feb. 1759, Add. MSS 32888, f. 116; Birch to Royston, 23 Sept. 1758, Add. MSS 35399, f. 34; Symmer to Mitchell, 6 Oct. 1758, Add. MSS 6839, f. 107.

followed the maxims of the Tories. It raised no doubts that he wholeheartedly accepted their reliance on naval warfare and suggested that he would not have sent any aid to the Continent, had not his predecessors made it inevitable by their policies. In other words, it used Pitt's popularity neatly to sidestep the central issue of his responsibility for Continental connections.[46] Its author's words in another work sum up the view of Pitt now becoming generally accepted: he was 'that great man, who had raised us from a very low state of political depression, not only in the eyes of all Europe, but in our own opinion, to make rapid progress to the highest state of national glory in which ever we had been.'[47]

Expeditions to the French coast were soon to be abandoned for the time being. Controversial though they had been and perhaps of dubious military value,[48] they had succeeded in their political purpose. They helped to maintain Pitt's reputation as a proponent of true British measures in the difficult period before victories provided more solid support.

Meanwhile the new session of Parliament had opened and it could be seen whether the controversies and varying fortunes of the past five months would affect it. Pitt, well aware of the strain of recent developments on his Tory support, had refused any further Continental commitments over the later summer and autumn. On the eve of the session, Dodington was reported to be acting as a 'Missionary to the Tories, to blow them up against the English Troops sent to Germany'.[49] Yet there were only occasional hints of uneasiness in Parliament over Continental issues and the failure of the expedition was not even raised.

[46] *Plain Reasons For Removing A certain Great Man From His M[ajest]y's Presence and Councils for ever*, London, 1759, esp. pp. 35–7. Attributed by Halkett and Laing to Alexander Carlyle, a Scottish divine of Inveresk, the pamphlet was much noted and approved. e.g. *CR*, vii, Mar. 1759, pp. 279–80; *MR*, xx, Mar. 1759, p. 275; *LM*, xxviii, Mar. 1759, pp. 118–20, *OWC*, 3–10 Mar. 1759; *UC*, 17–24 Mar. 1759; *LC*, 1–3 Mar. 1759; *Lloyd's EP*, 19–21 Mar. 1759.

[47] *Autobiography Of The Rev. Dr. Alexander Carlyle, Minister Of Inveresk Containing Memorials Of The Men And Events Of His Time*, ed. J. H. Burton, Edinburgh, 1860, p. 383.

[48] Corbett, i, pp. 303–4, argues that they were a considerable strategic success.

[49] Newcastle to Hardwicke, 2 Aug., additional memorandum, 10 Aug., Newcastle to Hardwicke, 19 Oct., Newcastle memorandum (Viry) (quotation), memorandum for the King, 10 Oct. 1758, Add. MSS 32882, f. 202, 32998, ff. 139, 140, 32884, f. 437, ff. 312–13, 308; Chesterfield to his son, 21 Nov. 1758, *Letters to His Son* [*by the Earl of Chesterfield*], ed. Oliver H. Leigh, 2 vols. in one, New York, [n.d.], ii, p. 251.

Pitt took the bull by the horns in a forthright speech in the debate on the Address in Reply. He stressed the great cost of what had to be done and challenged those who took advantage of setbacks by expressing disapproval in pamphlets to speak out then and there and propose other policies. His frankness seemed to bear results. The Address was moved by Lord Middleton and seconded by Sir Richard Grosvenor, 'a young converted Tory' who 'called Mr Pitt a blazing star'. Symmer saw this as an indication of some accommodation between the Tories as a party and Pitt. German measures were included in the general approbation: 'King of Prussia's victories worth all we have given: those he will gain worth all we shall give.'[50] No Tory supported the independent, Vyner, when he spoke against the Prussian Alliance in December. In answer Pitt stressed its importance. Nor did any Tory support Vyner's single dissenting voice when the Prussian subsidy was voted in January.[51] True, on one occasion Sir John Philipps 'reproached Pitt with Hanoverizing'.[52] In the debate on the Address, Beckford's approval of support for Continental allies was somewhat strained, and this did not pass unremarked by observers. He insisted that America should remain the primary object of the war and sought to limit the amount to be spent on the Continent to what had been sufficient the previous year. He received a most complimentary assurance on the first point from Pitt, although Pitt would not accept any limitation of the amount to be spent. Pitt's reassurance bore fruit in January when, in a short but troubled debate on the Hessian subsidy, Beckford showed a marked change of attitude. In answer to objections from a Tory, Northey, and an independent, Strange, and in support of Pitt's heated reaction, Beckford declared the subsidy 'was giving money to America by this diversion on the Continent of Europe and that if Hanover were lost, he would vote one hundred millions sooner than not recover it'.[53] Meanwhile Tory

---

[50] Walpole, *Geo. II*, ii, pp. 325–6 (first quotation); Walpole to Mann, 27 Nov. 1758, *Walpole's Corr.* xxi, pp. 256–7; Symmer to Mitchell, 24 Nov. 1758, Add. MSS 6839, f. 115; *Dodington,* p. 380, 23 [Nov. 1758] (second quotation). Walpole takes Pitt's reference to pamphlet writers to be to Dodington's *An Examination of a Letter.* See above fn. 40.

[51] Neville parliamentary diary, 14 Dec. 1758, Berks. Record Office, D/EN 034/17; West's account, 26 Jan. 1759, Add. MSS 32877, f. 351.

[52] Walpole, *Geo. II*, ii, p. 352.

[53] West's accounts, 23 Nov. 1758, 26 Jan. 1759 (quotation), Add. MSS 32885, ff. 524–5, 32887, ff. 351–3, 355; Symmer to Mitchell, 24 Nov. 1758, Add. MSS 6839, ff. 115–16; Walpole to Conway, 28 Jan. 1759, *The Letters of Horace Walpole,* iv, p. 233.

consciences had perhaps been eased by being able to display their principles in a vote of thanks to General Amherst and Admiral Boscawen for their part in the capture of Louisbourg. This was moved by Philipps and supported by Beckford.[54]

So Pitt seemed to have no trouble in holding the Tories. He could even make provocative use of parliamentary speeches to reassure actual and potential Continental allies, chiefly Hesse-Cassel and Bavaria. In December, for example, on the motion of thanks to Amherst and Boscawen, he firmly checked Philipps's and Beckford's enthusiasm for the retention of Louisbourg. It was too early to say, he maintained, what would or would not be restored at a peace. He avowed that 'he would not give up an iota of our allies for any British consideration'. This raised the possibility that once again Louisbourg would be sacrificed to European considerations and was certainly noticed outside the House. He had already stressed the importance of the Prussian alliance and of securing Bavaria.[55] On the other hand, when questions of policy and the susceptibilities of allies were not at stake, he was equally provocative in his courting of the Tories. He made a particular fuss, for example, over a demand from Hanover for extraordinary expenses. Contrary to normal practice, circular letters were sent to the Tories to attend when the demand was debated in the House. From this time Pitt began to emphasize that the cost of the war and the management of war finances were not his responsibility.[56] Already such disclaimers were achieving results with the Tories. Not without reason, therefore, did experienced observers comment throughout the session on its almost uninterrupted harmony.[57]

Out of doors, however, the Tories were much less happy. The

[54] Rigby to Bedford, 7 Dec. 1758, *Corr. Bedford*, ii, p. 371.

[55] Albert von Ruville, *William Pitt Earl of Chatham*, 2 vols., London, 1907, ii, pp. 18–20 (*re* Bavaria); note to the King, 15 Dec. 1758, Add. MSS 32886, f. 323 (*re* Hesse); Rigby to Bedford, 7 Dec. 1758, *Corr. Bedford*, ii, pp. 371–2; Symmer to Mitchell, 8 Dec. 1758, Add. MSS 6839, f. 118; Walpole, *Geo. II*, ii, p. 326 (quotation); Neville parliamentary diary, 14 Dec. 1758, Berks. Record Office, D/EN 034/17.

[56] Walpole, *Geo. II*, ii, pp. 331–2; Yorke, *Hardwicke*, iii, pp. 27–8; West's account, 3 Nov. 1758, Add. MSS 32885, f. 525; Mrs Montagu to Montagu, 28 Nov. 1758, *Elizabeth Montagu*, ii, p. 153.

[57] e.g. Walpole to Mann, 27 Nov. 1758, *Walpole's Corr.* xxi, p. 256; Walpole to Conway, 19 Jan. 1759, *The Letters of Horace Walpole*, iv, p. 229; Symmer to Mitchell, 9 Feb. 1759, Add. MSS 6839, f. 124; Richard Cox to Edward Weston, 7 June, 10 July 1759, HMC, *Tenth Report*, pt. i, pp. 315, 317.

Monitor continued to be concerned over Continental commitments
Commenting on the King's Speech it extolled British victories
attributing them to a total change in policy towards British
measures supposedly introduced by the new Ministry. Like Beckford in the House, it insisted on the primary importance of America
and the crucial significance of Louisbourg, which should never be
given up, whatever the cost. Such parallels suggest there was more
behind Beckford's uneasiness than appeared in debates. The *Monitor*
showed its concern more directly, in the midst of praise of Pitt's
measures, by confessing that it would rather have seen money spent
on hiring 30,000 Swiss troops than on sending British troops to the
Continent. Its praise emphasized the ways Pitt had found of
attacking France other than by the 'chimera' of a Continental war.[58]
Even when Beckford declared so warmly for the subsidies in
January the *Monitor* did not come out in support even of the Prussian
alliance.

Soon, however, the *Monitor* was pushed by hostile comment into
acceptance and defence of Pitt's Continental policy, back to and
then beyond the arguments it had developed in 1757–8. The process
was begun by a 'simile' written by Soame Jenyns, member of
Parliament and 'humorous poet'. The simile was a little verse skit on
the submission of the Tories to Pitt and their changed attitudes to
Continental policy. It was first circulated in manuscript, then
published in mid-February 1758 and taken far more seriously than
intended. It attracted considerable attention and at least three
replies.[59] Because it touched raw Tory nerves, it made Pitt so angry
that Hardwicke had to intervene to protect Jenyns's place at the
Board of Trade.[60] The *Monitor*'s reactions show that Pitt's fears were
not unjustified. After an angry spluttering introduction on the use

[58] *Mon.* 175–8, 25 Nov.–16 Dec. 1758, 182, 13 Jan., 196, 21 Apr. 1759. The paper
of 16 Dec. pointed out the value of Louisbourg to the trade and navigation of the
sugar islands, another reason for Beckford's interest.

[59] Symmer to Mitchell, 13, 27 Feb. 1759, Add. MSS 6839, ff. 126, 127; *MR*, xx
Mar. 1759, p. 279, calls it 'an ingenious little poem . . . which every body has seen, as
it has been copied into all the chronicles, Monitors, Magazines, &c'. The evidence
bears out this claim except for the daily papers and *LEP*. See also *AR*, ii, 1759, pp
439–40. For the answers see e.g. *MR* as above, *AR*, ii, 1759, pp. 442–3, *OWC*, 10–1
Mar. 1759.

[60] Newcastle to Hardwicke, 15 Feb. 1759, Add. MSS 35418, f. 82; John Gordon to
Newcastle, 28 Feb. 1759, Add. MSS 32888, f. 278; Walpole, *Geo. II*, ii, p. 35
(quotation).

and misuse of ridicule in political controversy, it printed the simile
in full. It did not deny the implicit charges against the Tories.
Rather it sought to justify their conversion by presenting its own
allegory contrasting the corrupt member of Parliament and the
honest independent. Out of the honourable union of the latter with
Pitt had come the offspring, Senegal, Louisbourg, Duquesne, and, in
expectation, America. In other words, in line with its own and other
earlier defences of Pitt, it emphasized British victories and skirted
the charges about the Continent.[61]

But it was not allowed to let the matter rest there. Its skirting of
Jenyns's attack on the consistency of the Tories provoked a reply, a
pamphlet addressed to the *Monitor* and entitled *The Honest Grief of a
Tory*. The pamphlet claimed to originate in Wiltshire and expressed
particular dissatisfaction (clearer in its sequel) with the behaviour of
William Northey, member for Calne. He was one of the Tory group
which had declared for Pitt in the previous session, although he had
recently expressed some reluctance over the Hessian subsidy.
Whether genuinely Tory or not, the pamphlet was bound to
exacerbate Tory uneasiness, for it brought the question of their
consistency firmly into the open. It praised the *Monitor* as 'the Voice
of those true Englishmen, who zealously called for, and of late
triumphed in a Change, as they supposed, of Men and Measures'.
'Our whole party, therefore,' it said, 'is interested in your continuing
firm on the same honest Principles and Pursuits.' Why then had the
Monitor not vindicated the Minister and the Tories more effectively
against the charge of Hanoverian measures? Perhaps it, too, had
forsaken its principles, and had 'basely become the Defender of
Germanized Measures and Ministers. Nay more, a nauseous Flat-
terer.' Like all ministers, Pitt had in fact succumbed to the
temptations of power and anyway could not be given all the credit
for successes. He did not deserve the *Monitor*'s excessive adulation.
Worst of all, earlier *Monitors* were quoted to highlight the inconsistency of Tory support for Pitt in view of his German measures—not
just money but men, and the men sent to be commanded by a
foreigner. The country's situation was now worse, the pamphlet
maintained, than it would have been had Fox been in control,

---

[61] *Mon.* 187, 17 Feb. 1759 (quoted in *LC*, 27 Feb.–1 Mar. 1759, *Lloyd's EP*, 16–19
Feb. 1759). In contrast *LEP* ignored the simile until it could dismiss the criticisms
caustically in the context of the conquest of Guadeloupe (13–15 Mar. 1759).

because the so-called '*blessed Union*' of Pitt and the Tories removed the opposition which would at least have limited such measures. All the defences and disguises of Pitt's behaviour, so effective until now, were ruthlessly stripped away and his coalition with Newcastle was set in its 'true' light. The Minister could not even be called virtuous because he had ended corruption; it continued apace, 'dispensed by the same Hand as heretofore, by the well tutored Scholar of Walpole and his own Brother Pelham'. Even the Tories now enjoyed it. This was the '*blessed Union*'; corruption of Whig and Tory alike. '[I]n simple, honest Truth, his G[race], and his Corruption, are the main Supports of P[itt] and his Virtue'. The only hope was that perhaps 'our Clamours will secure a Remnant . . . who will so far succeed, as to lessen these continental Expences, and delay our Ruin'.[62]

The *Monitor* could hardly avoid such a challenge both to itself and Pitt. It took it up in 'The MONITOR'S Vindication of his *constitutional* Principles', a cogent paper and a milestone in the *Monitor*'s political development. It began by disavowing a party label, not because it had changed its principles but because party distinctions were irrelevant under an Administration 'that disdains the aid of party'. Only bad ministers sought to 'keep up a party'; party divisions appeared only when the national interest was not pursued. Naïve anti-Court reactions, founded on the belief that 'such as join with a minister, must be sunk forever in a mass of corruption', were also inappropriate. Who could deny that honour was due to Pitt for the benefits he had brought to his country? Of course others contributed to the successes. Yet it was not idolatry, the author contended, to acknowledge that such advantages '*reflect a dazzling splendor on his character*'.

Then the paper came directly to the heart of the matter. The present operations in Germany, it admitted, had been particularly criticized. Yet they were no mere sacrifice to Hanover and Prussia motivated by a wish on Pitt's part to flatter his master, but a defence of British interests in the 'preservation of a bulwark to arbitrary power and universal monarchy on the continent'. To its former arguments, now revived, about Britain's proper concern for the liberties and religion of Germany and the balance of power, a

---

[62] *The Honest Grief of a Tory, Expressed in A Genuine Letter From A Burgess of* [*Calne*], *in Wiltshire, To The Author of the Monitor, Feb. 17, 1759*, London, 1759 (dated 23 Feb.—quotations from pp. 4–5, 14, 23, 24, 35).

powerful new one was added. 'Look at our exports: examine the extent of our trade to Germany. Should the Rhine, the Elb, the Weser, the Oder and the whole navigation of Germany be reduced under the power of France, our manufactures and merchandize; our colonies and settlements would feel their loss severely.' The paper's other main answer to the criticism was, as before, that the 'aid sent on this important occasion, differs widely, both in its kind, and its object, from our former connections with the continent'. Britain was not now entering as a principal, nor sacrificing her interests and the exertion of her natural powers. Further, there was no reason to doubt the rectitude of the measures which the Almighty daily blessed with success.[63]

Still the debate did not rest. The *Honest Grief* was followed by *A Second Letter From Wiltshire To The Monitor*. This affirmed links with a disillusioned Tory club in Calne and with the *Honest Grief*, for which it claimed 'the Sale of two large Impressions in a few Days'. Again it criticized the *Monitor* for panegyrics on Pitt and again it concentrated on the German war. It rejected all the *Monitor*'s arguments in favour of the aid now being given to Germany, including the new one concerning trade. On all of them it condemned the *Monitor* even more effectively than its predecessor by quoting the former's own earlier words, the 'true' doctrine of Toryism. It also elaborated accusations against Pitt that were to grow in importance, that he was blithely careless of the expenses of war regardless of the remonstrances of his colleagues (Legge was referred to), and that he precipitately initiated grandiose ill-conceived designs. The letter ended by hoping that the favourable reception given to the *Honest Grief* was a sign that 'the Nation is returning from the wanderings of an unaccountable Passion for his Minister, to the sober dictates of good Sense and Reason.'[64]

In answer the *Monitor* reiterated its revived arguments for British intervention in Germany, noting defensively that public faith required the fulfilment of treaties and that any evil in the present measures was due to the difficulties created by past ministers. It celebrated again the successes Pitt had achieved. It attempted to

---

[63] *Mon.* 190, 10 Mar. 1759. According to Pares, 'American versus Continental Warfare', pp. 438–9, the argument from trade was justified and well-established among apologists for Continental war.

[64] *A Second Letter From Wiltshire To The Monitor, On the Vindication Of His Constitutional Principles*, London, 1759 (dated 18 Mar.—quotations from p. 32).

answer what seems to have been a growing swell of criticism of the mounting cost of the war as well as of the extension of German measures.[65] So, in response to these two pamphlets, it confirmed its conversion from its early stand against Continental connections and its rejection of the waverings of 1758. However much it might claim that the present Continental measures were fundamentally different from those of the past, the change was remarkable. The *Monitor* was now wholeheartedly committed not only to Pitt, but also to the full extent of his Continental policy.

In contrast to the attention given to the *Simile* which sparked it off, this whole exchange did not attract any extraordinary interest. For most people, it would seem, the issue of Continental connections was a peripheral one, irrelevant beside the growing successes in war. Most of the answers to the *Simile* skirted the question. The *Monthly*'s reviewer treated both pamphlets less than seriously and virtually ignored or dismissed this central point of their attack.[66] The exchange was a domestic one amongst Tories (if the claim of the pamphlet-writers to be genuine Tories can be accepted at face value).

It is none the less important. Although, as the *Honest Grief* admitted, the *Monitor* had been respected as a Tory spokesman, it could not carry all with it. The *Critical Review* comments on the two pamphlets bore witness to the uneasiness they caused, although it affirmed its faith in Pitt. A split was clearly developing in that Tory support which Pitt had wooed so carefully, between the old school, strict in their independence and adherence to ideological stands, and those who were tired of continual opposition and were prepared to follow Pitt.

It is not difficult to explain why the division occurred as it did. In the City the benefits of war were beginning to be widely appreciated. War financing and remittance of money to allies meant unparalleled opportunities for investment and profit for the moneyed élite. Campaigns abroad gave similar openings for Government contractors. Many more of the City's mercantile classes profited from privateering. In the longer term they were to benefit from the boost

[65] *Mon.* 199, 12 May 1759, 192, 24 Mar., and 196, 21 Apr. 1759, refer to criticisms of Pitt.

[66] The pamphlets were noticed in *LM*, xxviii, Mar. 1759, pp. 131–2; *MR*, xx, Mar. 1759, p. 268, Apr., p. 379; *CR*, vii, Mar. 1759, pp. 280–1, Apr., p. 382. The *Honest Grief* only was noted by *LC*, 26 Feb.–1 Mar. 1758, alone among the newspapers.

to almost all areas of overseas trade, and domestic prosperity was rising.[67] Not only the merchants but the many others of London's population which depended on trade for their livelihood stood to gain. Even by 1758–9 some of this was already apparent. The Speech from the Throne at the opening of the new session of Parliament drew attention to the flourishing state of commerce 'not to be paralleled during such troubles'. In February 1759 twenty merchants presented an address of thanks to Pitt for his measures to protect American trade. He not only won victories but was actively concerned about trade.[68] Not surprisingly, then, enthusiasm in the City for the war and for Pitt and opposition to any early unsatisfactory peace were growing.[69]

The *Monitor*, too, noticed the prosperity of trade and developed its new commercial argument for interest in Europe.[70] More decisively than anything else, the changing attitude in the City opened the way for the Tories to take the lead again in popular circles there, as Sir John Barnard's leadership came to its final close.[71] They were already known as Pitt's supporters. Now that he was winning wider popularity they too could profit. The much more frequent if largely incoherent outpourings of John Gordon to Newcastle in this year often dwelt on the growing strength and changing views of the 'faction', particularly its keenness for war and its praise of Pitt at the expense of other Ministers. Newcastle was impressed enough to note to report to the King

Accounts from the City
The hot ones, Mr Pitt's friends . . .
That the whole dispute is between the old and the new, Administration:—
And the old Administration cramp Mr Pitt in his measures, and prevent him from doing or succeeding, as he otherwise would do.[72]

[67] Rogers, 'London Politics', pp. 235–9; T. S. Ashton, *Economic Fluctuations in England 1700—1800*, Oxford, 1959, pp. 60–1, 96–7, 149–50.

[68] *Parl. Hist.* xv, c. 930; address from the merchants of London, 6 Feb. 1759, PRO 30/8/48, f. 186; Rogers, 'London Politics', pp. 239–40.

[69] Walpole to John Chute, 29 June, to Montague, 6 July, to Conway, 2 Sept. 1758, *The Letters of Horace Walpole*, iv, pp. 152, 153, 183; Symmer to Mitchell, 12 Sept. 1758, Add. MSS 6839, f. 103; Birch to Royston, 30 Sept. 1758, Add. MS 35399, f. 39; Watkins to Newcastle, 8 Dec. 1758, Add. MSS 32886, f. 223.

[70] *Mon.* 177, 9 Dec. 1758, 182, 13 Jan., 190, 10 Mar. 1759.

[71] In July 1758 he was granted leave to resign as Alderman. *LC*, 18–20 July 1758. Cf. above, pp. 11, 55.

[72] Gordon to Newcastle, 31 Jan., 20, 26 Mar., 6, 24 Apr., 20 May 1759, Add. MSS 32887, ff. 438–9, 32889, ff. 157–60, 243, 388–9, 32890, ff. 322, 32891, ff. 210–11; Newcastle's memorandum for the King, 20 Mar. 1759, Add. MSS 32889, ff. 155–6.

The City Tories, then, had sound reason to continue to support the war and Pitt, regardless of principle.

The country Tories, on the other hand, along with other land-owners, bore much of the cost through the increased land tax, without reaping many of the benefits. They might rejoice in victories, but they had good cause still to be suspicious of expensive extension of the war on the Continent. The traditional ideology still had some point for them. So it was in the City rather than among the Tories generally that Beckford and the *Monitor* eventually found the political opening which they could exploit for Pitt.[73]

For his part, Pitt seemed deliberately to aggravate this important division among his supporters by his reckless courting of Beckford over an issue that touched the latter closely, one that had been controversial in the last war too. This was the tax on sugar projected by Legge in 1759. Such a tax was being discussed in the City from late 1758 and was generally welcomed. Sugar prices were high and a further tax seemed an obvious way to take some of the burden of the war off the landed classes.[74] As soon as the tax seemed likely, Beckford took up the cudgels 'to parry the Blow aimed at the Colonies'. By the time the proposal came before the House in definite form at the end of February Beckford was 'at the head of the powerful Body of Sugar Planters, Merchants, &c', in opposition to it. When an appeal to Legge failed, Beckford turned to Pitt. Although Pitt insisted that Beckford should drop a controversial suggestion of an excise on tobacco, he gave his support on the major issue and even to Beckford's reluctance to accept a compromise tax on all dry goods including sugar. In the House on 9 March, when Beckford's opposition to this tax was greeted by 'horselaughs', Pitt

made an extravagant panegyric on Beckford, who, he said, had done more to support government than any minister in England; launched out on his principles, disinterestedness, knowledge of trade, and solidity; and professed he thought him another Sir Josiah Child [whom Beckford had quoted].

[73] The *Monitor*, rather than activity in the corporate bodies, was still Beckford's chief influence there, and Gordon refers to its contribution to the growing strength of the 'faction' (to Newcastle, 20 May, cf. 20 Mar. 1759, Add. MSS 32891, f. 211, 32889, ff. 157–8.

[74] Watkins to Newcastle, 28 Nov., 8, 19 Dec. 1758, Add. MSS 32886, ff. 80, 223, 401.

'He looked upon the honour of his acquaintance as one of the glories (though he had but few glories) of his life.' In face of the scepticism of the House the praise was repeated.[75]

Not only did such opposition to a sensible Government measure give serious offence to Pitt's colleagues. The *Honest Grief* and the *Second Letter From Wiltshire* show, and Newcastle confirms, that this was another cause of the split in Tory support for Pitt. His 'subservience' to Beckford and to a lesser extent to Sir John Philipps, and his courting of the West Indian interest at the expense of what seemed like a fair relief to the landed classes were bitterly disliked—and not only by the Tories. His general reputation was considerably if only temporarily harmed, even in some sections in the City. The controversy in the last war should have taught Pitt the risks. Beckford hardly seems worth such costs.[76] Further, it was not only for pamphlet writers that the excuses for Pitt's coalition with Newcastle and his use of it to evade responsibility for unpopular decisions were wearing thin. Some Tories were beginning to see that 'if there is no Blood drawn, it is a sham Battle;' and that whenever 'there is an odd thing done . . . it is presently covered with a pretended quarrel'. The latter part of the session brought other evidence of Tory divisions. For example, most of the Tories supported the Bill to increase the salaries of the judges, but Beckford, in accord with Pitt, spoke against it. By June, Sir John Glynne, who had brought in the motion for shorter parliaments in February 1758, was outspokenly against Pitt.[77]

Although it is impossible to define the precise extent of the split between the City and country Tories, there is no doubt that the debate over Continental connections, brought to the fore by Pitt's

[75] Symmer to Mitchell, 2 Feb. 1759 (first quotation), 27 Feb. 1759 (second quotation), Add. MSS 6839, ff. 122–3, 127; West's account, 9 Mar. 1759 (last quotation), Add. MSS 32888, f. 428; Beckford to Pitt, [Feb. 1759], PRO 30/8/19, f. 107; Walpole, *Geo. II*, ii, pp. 350–2 (third quotation).

[76] *The Honest Grief of a Tory*, p. 38; *A Second Letter from Wiltshire*, pp. 8, 31; Newcastle's memorandum for the King, 12 Mar. 1759, Add. MSS 32889, f. 16; Lady Anne Egerton to Bentinck, 13, 23 Mar. 1759, Eg. 1719, ff. 32, 34; Watkins to Newcastle, 22 Mar. 1759, Add. MSS 32889, f. 192.

[77] Campbell to Fox, 6 Apr. 1759, Add. MSS 51407, f. 58 (quotation); West's account and list of speakers, 14 May 1759, Add. MSS 32891, ff. 129, 130; Hardwicke to Newcastle, 29 Apr. 1759, Yorke, *Hardwicke*, iii, p. 55 and fn; Walpole, *Geo. II*, ii, pp. 354–5; R. Kenyon to Lloyd Kenyon, 25 June 1795, HMC, *Fourteenth Report*, app. iv, p. 496. See above p. 107.

decision to send British troops to Germany, showed up some important changes in the nature of Pitt's popular support. The events of 1758 also brought another change in his political situation. The controversy over the last stages of the expedition to the French coast created a breach between him and Leicester House. Leicester House had been closely identified with all stages of the expedition. The young Prince Edward had gone with it to Cherbourg and there had been close consultation with the Commanders even to the extent of influencing their plans without the knowledge of the Ministers. The Prince of Wales and Bute were indignant at the cold attitude taken to Bligh on his return, especially by the King. They were even more angered when Pitt refused to dissociate himself from the general attitude. This merely capped a succession of supposed slights by Pitt over the communication of information, together with differences over German policy, and resulted in a decisive break in relations.[78]

Pitt seemed to care little about either development. As military success, together with flexibility of policy, warmed his relations with his colleagues and the King as well as with the City and the general public, the loss of his old supports appeared to matter little. Perhaps they were not now worth the skill and effort he had expended on them earlier, especially as major questions of war strategy were involved. But the Prince of Wales bitterly reflected that Pitt was forgetting the future, 'when he must expect to be treated according to his deserts'.[79] Time and the fortunes of war would reveal whether his calculations were correct.

[78] Bute to Pitt, 25 Sept. 1758 and note on Pitt's reply [lost], 'Letters from Pitt to Bute', pp. 163–6; Prince of Wales to Bute, 30 Sept. 1758, and note, *Letters from George III to Lord Bute*, pp. 15–16.

[79] Prince of Wales to Bute, 8 Dec. 1758, quoted 'Letters from Pitt to Bute', p. 166.

V

The Years of Victories 1759–1760

In the short term the fortunes of war were indeed to bring Pitt's popularity to its peak. In 1759—the great year of victory—the tide of the war turned decisively. The year 1760 saw yet more success. In North America, the centre of British interest, Pitt's offensive strategy won the major victories. Niagara, Ticonderoga and Crown Point, key fortresses in the attack on the French, fell to the British. This was known in London in August 1759. Two months later, in October, came news that provided the triumph of the year. Quebec had been taken, after a long and often disheartening siege. This victory was capped in 1760 by the capture of Montreal, bringing almost complete control of Canada. In the West Indies, a subsidiary operation in the American war failed its main target among the French sugar islands, Martinique, but did take Guadeloupe in May 1759. India was a secondary theatre for both sides. But here again the British prevailed against both the French and the Dutch on land and sea, although Pondicherry, the last French stronghold, was not captured until January 1761. In all, Pitt's war leadership reaped decisive colonial success. Britain was emerging as the strongest colonial power.

On the home front, the main preoccupation of 1759 was the prolonged fear of invasion by the French. This threat, made in desperation, became serious in the middle of the year. It was deflected at length by the great victory of Prince Ferdinand at Minden on the Weser in August, and by two naval successes. Minden saved Hanover for another year and prevented the French from concentrating on the invasion of Britain. In August, Boscawen's defeat of the Toulon fleet off Lagos in south-west Portugal prevented the concentration of French naval resources; in

November, when at last the main French fleet slipped out of Brest, Hawke put a final stop to serious invasion plans by defeating it at Quiberon Bay. The last effort, an attempted landing in Ireland in February 1760, proved a very damp squib.

Pitt's deft handling of the invasion threat added considerably to his reputation. Early in the year, to Newcastle's despair, he apparently refused to take the threat seriously or to be drawn from his own plans for the war. He was resolved to meet the invasion, if it did materialize, with naval rather than military measures. For these he made vigorous preparations, and he had no wish to undermine morale by alarmist moves.[1] By May, however, he had growing intelligence of French plans and the situation in Germany was deteriorating. Ferdinand was steadily retreating before the French and Frederick showed little inclination to help. In response, Pitt's attitude to the threat of invasion changed. On 30 May he presented a Royal Message to the House of Commons concerning the invasion threat and the possibility that the Militia might have to be embodied. In the latter part of June, when the crisis grew still more severe, the counties which were ready were ordered one by one to call out their men.[2] By this time, however, Pitt's contempt for the French threat together with these preparations had encouraged public confidence. The mood was in marked contrast to that of 1757. Confidence grew as the summer advanced. The bombardment of French preparations at Le Havre by Admiral Rodney in July added to the effect. There were some scares, but morale was generally high, money easily raised, and Pitt's reputation rose.[3] Eventual success in turning the threat proved him right again in public eyes.

The use of the Militia redounded further to Pitt's credit. Part of his reluctance to admit the invasion threat perhaps sprang from doubts about the Militia, which would have to be embodied if the threat was real. In popular eyes he was the champion of the Militia. Yet there was good reason to fear further riots like those of 1757 if it were embodied on a large scale and for any length of time. There were equally good reasons to doubt its military effectiveness. When the Royal Message of 30 May gave enthusiasts for the Militia a chance to suggest an additional Address in Reply, asking the King

---

[1] Corbett, ii, pp. 4–5, 10–16; Western, pp. 154–6.

[2] Corbett, ii, pp. 17–18; *Parl. Hist.* xv, cc. 939–41; Western, pp. 156, 447.

[3] e.g. *GM*, xxix, July 1759, pp. 341–2, is full of confidence. See also below fn. 6.

to urge lords lieutenant to do their utmost to implement the Militia Act fully, Pitt seized the chance to make a patriotic stand. He strongly supported the move, although he defended the lords lieutenant.[4] When embodiment at length began, late in June, his last doubts were removed by the enthusiastic response of the country, shown most strikingly at the review of the Norfolk Militia by the King on 17 July. From this time onwards, whether for reasons of politics or military defence, Pitt warmly supported the active use of the Militia. At the opening of the next session of Parliament he praised its contribution to meeting the invasion scare: without it troops would have had to be withdrawn from Germany. Once again, Pitt had made adroit use of an unpromising situation. Newcastle, in contrast, was embarrassed, even though he had in fact pressed Pitt for embodiment. He was torn between his fear of invasion and his distaste for the Militia. City demands for its embodiment bothered him, as did gibes at the dilatoriness of the counties in which he had influence and manœuvres there to outwit him.[5]

Pitt's attitude was reflected in public discussion of the possibility of invasion, which dominated the papers. Some took the threat more seriously than others but all agreed on the importance of the Militia.[6] The *Monitor* first ignored and then belittled the threat. When the danger had to be acknowledged, it urged the Militia as the appropriate answer, pushed for inquiries into opposition to the Militia, and extolled its virtues in tune with the national mood. The *London Evening Post* also belittled French intentions and harped incessantly on the Militia in both news and comment.[7] Although Gordon associated such views particularly with 'the faction', the City in general shared them, mocking the threat as a joke and a trick to divert Britain from her plans. It also called for the embodiment of the Militia. The City's failure to address the King over Boscawen's victory off Cape Lagos was 'ascribed to an unwillingness to touch

[4] Rigby to Bedford, 30 Mar. 1759, *Corr. Bedford*, ii, pp. 382–4.

[5] Pitt to Lady Hester Pitt, 17 July 1759, *Corr. Chatham*, ii, pp. 4–5; Western, pp. 157–60.

[6] e.g. *Gaz.*, 31 May, 1, 7 June 1759, *LC*, 7–10, 10–12, 21–4 July, 14–16 Aug. (all from *Westminster Journal*), 26–8 July 1759; *OWC*, 26 May–2 June, 2–9 June, 7–14 July, 11–18 Aug., 18–25 Aug. 1759; *UC*, 7–14 July, 1–8 Sept. 1759; *RWJ*, 21 July 1759; *LM*, xxviii, June 1759, pp. 293–4, 304–5 (but cf. July, pp. 347–8, 381–2, from *Westminster Journal*).

[7] *Mon.* 182, 13 Jan., 202, 2 June, 207, 7 July, 209, 21 July, 214, 25 Aug., 222, 20 Oct. 1759; e.g. *LEP*, 9–12, 28–30 June, 12–14, 26–8 July, 9–11 Oct. 1759.

upon the topic of an invasion, which can scarce be avoided on such an occasion, the rulers of the Corporation still affecting to talk with contempt of all apprehensions of danger from attempts of that kind'. At the opening of the next parliamentary session, Beckford complimented the Militia for having made it possible to 'laugh at invasion' without calling on foreign troops, in contrast to 1756.[8]

Pitt's primary reliance on naval measures to meet the threat of invasion posed an awkward question bearing on his reputation. If naval measures were to be effective, the benevolent neutrality of other naval powers, the Dutch, Danes, Swedes, Russians, and Spaniards, was essential. They were also important to Great Britain as trading partners or investors in the public funds. Yet their benevolence, especially that of the Dutch, was seriously threatened by British attitudes to their carrying of French trade. The French West Indian trade in particular had been thrown open to neutrals in order to save it from extinction. In reply, the British courts asserted more forcefully than ever the right of search and seizure of enemy goods. With this support, British naval cruisers and privateers began to seize Dutch ships with little regard for what remained of neutral rights, to have the courts declare them lawful prize. The consequence was a torrent of Dutch protests during 1758. If no concessions were made in response to these, an open break seemed only a matter of time, especially with the removal by death of the moderating influence of the Princess Royal, eldest daughter of George II and Dowager Princess of Orange.[9]

This question had greatly interested public opinion for some time. From March 1758 the stream of news and comment on it had grown steadily in pamphlets and newspapers, until it became the most persistently and widely discussed political issue of the time. All the comment was hostile to the Dutch.[10] The *Monitor* was prominent in the cause from the autumn of 1758 well into 1759. Of course it spoke

[8] Watkins to Newcastle, 27 June, 19 July, Gordon to Newcastle, 6, 8 July, 24 Sept., 10, 14 Oct. 1759, Add. MSS 32892, f. 270, 32893, f. 146, 32892, ff. 446, 478, 32896, ff. 68, 432, 32897, f. 81; Symmer to Mitchell, 13 July 1759, Add. MSS 6839, f. 147; Birch to Royston, 29 Sept. 1759, Add. MSS 35399, f. 109 (quotation); West's account, 13 Nov. 1759, Add. MSS 32898, f. 223.

[9] Walpole, *Geo. II*, ii, pp. 316–18, 343; Corbett, ii, pp. 5–7.

[10] *MR*, xviii, Mar. 1758, p. 264, xix, Dec. 1758, pp. 542–9, xx, Jan. 1759, pp. 56–8; *CR*, vi, Dec. 1758, pp. 519–20. References in magazines and newspapers are too numerous to cite.

to a mercantile audience in the City most keenly interested in the
issue. Its views were spiced by a sharp commercial jealousy.
Nevertheless it arguments are a fair indication of the general range.
They were based variously on the obligations of the Dutch to Great
Britain by treaty and by ties of friendship and gratitude, ties which
they were said to have often perfidiously betrayed or used only to
their own advantage, on their common interest with Great Britain in
resisting the French, and on the demands of the law of nations.[11]
The *Monitor*'s unwavering hostility to the Dutch and calls for strong
action against them were widely shared, noticeably by the two
Reviews, united for once on a public question. In the latter part of
1759 the issue was kept to the fore by a number of appeals heard by
the Privy Council in cases of prizes seized by privateers.[12] Such
warmth of opinion was scarcely to be ignored, especially when the
Monthly Review thought that on 'a point, so national and important,'
it was 'a happy presage of success, that our ministers *dare* to do
justice to their country'.[13]

At first Pitt supported the commercial interest and general
opinion by opposing any concessions to the Dutch. Yet by November 1758, when Beckford raised the issue in the Debate on the
Address, Pitt had recognized its delicacy. In his reply, he spoke
about the need to check abuses by British privateers as well as
Dutch breaches of neutrality.[14] By the early months of 1759 the
situation was acute. Public interest was still intense but the invasion
threat demanded some concessions to the neutral powers. Otherwise
they might well combine to protect their rights and challenge British
control of the Channel. To Newcastle's intense relief, Pitt accepted
the need for concessions, at least to the extent of supporting the
passage in May of an Act restraining the actions of British privateers. This he did against his own supporters, notably Beckford.
Acting as spokesman for the mercantile community, Beckford
opposed the measure, despite an earlier promise to Pitt to take his
line and despite Pitt's very recent support over the sugar tax. His
objections all tended to keeping privateering as free as possible and

[11] *Mon.* 167, 30 Sept., 169, 14 Oct., 171, 28 Oct., 172, 4 Nov., 180, 30 Dec. 1758,
181, 6 Jan., 184, 27 Jan., 186, 10 Feb., 188, 24 Feb., 191, 17 Mar., 194, 7 Apr. 1759.

[12] e.g. *GM*, xxvii, Aug. 1758, p. 392, Nov., p. 551.

[13] *MR*, xx, Jan. 1759, p. 58.

[14] Walpole, *Geo. II*, ii, pp. 317–18; West's report, 23 Nov. 1758, Add. MSS 32885,
f. 525.

open to smaller ships. Pitt answered him fully, making his first appearance after another attack of gout to do so. Pitt's intervention did much to secure the passage of the Act with only minor concessions to the opposition. It certainly won away from Beckford the support of many Tories.[15]

Thus Pitt did not sacrifice policy to popularity. Nevertheless, within the limits of necessary policy, he protected his popularity carefully. Not only were there some concessions to the opposition. Pitt also exercised considerable tact in answering Beckford, both in the Address in Reply debate in November and in debates on the Bill. Furthermore, he made it clear that he stood firm over the larger issue of the right to seize enemy trade carried by neutrals. In particular, he and his supporters strongly opposed, in public and private, the judgement on appeal in the case of the *Maria Teresa*, which attracted much attention. In March 1759, just before the Privateer Bill came before Parliament, her owners were acquitted on charges of illegal trading.[16] Once again, Pitt was using the tactic of distinguishing the elements in the Ministry to the advantage of the patriots, and blame was focused on Hardwicke and Mansfield.[17] Such stands may not have been merely political, but their tactical success was shown both in the attitudes of many Tories in Parliament and by the *Monitor*. It did not take up the Privateering Act at all. And Beckford, of course, was not seriously alienated from Pitt over the incident. The Privateering Act certainly brought no end to uneasy relations between the British and the Dutch or to public interest in them. But for the moment an open breach was averted without damage to Pitt's reputation.

The most controversial event of 1759–60, at least as measured by the number of pamphlets it provoked, did not directly affect Pitt's reputation. Lord George Sackville, Commander of the British cavalry at the battle of Minden, was accused of deliberate delay in

[15] Beckford to Pitt, [after 24 Mar. 1759], PRO 30/8/19, f. 115; West's accounts, 30 Apr., 4 May 1759, Hugh Valence–Jones to Newcastle, 4 May 1759, Add. MSS 32890, ff. 401–2, 486–7, 488–90; Charles Frederick to Lord George Sackville, 5 May 1759, HMC, *Stopford-Sackville*, i, p. 55; Richard Pares, *Colonial Blockade and Neutral Rights, 1739—1763*, Oxford, 1938, pp. 26 fn. 2, 46–8, 258–9.

[16] *Dodington*, p. 385, 22, 29 [Mar. 1759]; *GM*, xxviii, Mar. 1759, pp. 144, 145.

[17] Memorandum for the King, 12 Apr., consideration of the present state of affairs, 19 Apr. 1759, Add. MSS 32890, ff. 35, 143; Pares, *Colonial Blockade and Neutral Rights, 1739–1763*, pp. 105–7.

obeying Prince Ferdinand's orders to advance. The long-drawn-out controversy over this accusation, Sackville's subsequent behaviour and treatment, and his eventual court martial, aroused very great public interest.[18] The *Monitor*'s initial hostility to Sackville, apparently in accord with Tory attitudes in the City,[19] might have presaged another Byng-like clamour, had circumstances abroad not been so felicitous. As it was, this initial hostility was quickly moderated, probably out of deference to Pitt. The *Monitor* showed little further interest.[20] Pitt suffered no embarrassment from the controversy, although it confirmed his breach with Leicester House, which took up Sackville's case.[21]

In short, the events of 1759–60 did much to confirm and very little to challenge Pitt's popularity. Now indeed he could be said to be popular in both the general and the particular sense of the word. In the eighty addresses of congratulation to the King on the victories of the year that poured in between October 1759 and the end of January 1760 there were few attempts to make political points or to distinguish among the victories as there had been in 1758. Early in 1759 Walpole noted that it was 'as much the fashion to couple' the two words 'ministerial' and 'patriot' 'as it was formerly to part them'. In September, before the greatest victories were achieved, Symmer reported that the successes already won 'have consolidated the Power of the Minister, who has been active in those measures, and raised him above all Opposition'. Newcastle described him as 'more popular every day than ever'. In November, when justifying to the King his alliance with Pitt in the midst of one of Pitt's displays of unreasonableness, Newcastle attributed entirely to him 'the unanimity of the people, the popularity, the Common Council [of London], etc.', without which the war could not have been carried on with such expense. Hardwicke was also convinced that without Pitt the Administration could neither carry on the war nor make peace. Thomas Percival reflected general opinion when he wrote the 'glorious success of this year I ascribe solely, and under God, to Mr

[18] For these events see Walpole, *Geo. II,* ii, pp. 361–7, 379–81, 413–17. They provoked far more pamphlets than any others of this period.

[19] Gordon to Newcastle, 16 Sept. 1759, Add. MSS 32885, f. 434; cf. *LEP*, 11–13 Sept. 1759 and Newcastle's memorandum of a conversation with Viry, 2 Oct. 1759, Add. MSS 32896, f. 223.

[20] *Mon.* 216, 8 Sept., 219, 29 Sept. 1759, 250, 3 May 1760.

[21] McKelvey, pp. 103–7.

Pitt'.[22] Public comment in its various forms expressed the same opinion with exuberant patriotism. In local as well as metropolitan papers Pitt was the great national hero.[23]

In the City general opinion was now warmer than ever for Pitt, with good reason. All over the world victories were creating opportunities for British trade. After a period of depression in the early 1750s, exports reached unprecedented levels from 1759 to 1761.[24] The Atlantic economy was booming. The sugar trade from the West Indies prospered, protected by convoys, and benefited from the dislocation of French production and trade. Despite the competition of prize sugars and of the produce of Guadeloupe after May 1760, the sugar market in England remained remarkably buoyant. The Navy in West Indian waters stimulated rum production. Captured territories there and in Africa gave slave traders rich openings. The tobacco trade from the southern American colonies expanded rapidly too.[25] More important was the dramatic growth of North American trade. This was fast becoming the new dynamic in English economic growth as the expanding colonial population demanded a wide variety of manufactured goods. The period of the Seven Years' War saw the most rapid rise in exports to America. It may well be that the rise was artificially induced by the demands and the spending power of large fleets and armies sent to the colonies. British merchants and industrialists benefited none the less. The conquest of Canada opened the frontier fur trade to the British in place of the French.[26] It was little wonder that America

[22] *London Gazette*, 16–20 Oct. 1759—22–6 Jan. 1760; Walpole to Mann, 4 Mar. 1759, *Walpole's Corr.* xxi, p. 277; Symmer to Mitchell, 14 Sept. 1759, Add. MSS 6839, f. 146; Newcastle's 'business with Lord Mansfield', 4 Sept. 1759, Add. MSS 32895, f. 156; Newcastle to Hardwicke, 25 Oct. 1759, quoted Torrens, ii, p. 529; Hardwicke to Newcastle, 23 Sept. 1759, Yorke, *Hardwicke*, iii, p. 60; Percival to [unknown], 16 Nov. 1759, HMC, *Fourteenth Report*, pt. iv, p. 496.

[23] On Yorkshire, see C. Collyer, 'The Rockingham Connection and Country Opinion in the Early Years of George III', *Proceedings of The Leeds Philosophical and Literary Society*, vii, iii (Mar. 1955), 252 and n.5.

[24] Ashton, pp. 60, 149; B. R. Mitchell and Phyllis Deane, *Abstract of British Historical Statistics*, Cambridge, 1962, p. 280.

[25] Ralph Davis, 'English Foreign Trade, 1700–1774, *Economic History Review*, xv, 2 (Dec. 1962), 291, 297; Rogers, 'London Politics', pp. 237–8.

[26] Davis, pp. 290, 296; Rogers, 'London Politics', p. 238; Robert Paul Thomas, 'A Quantitative Approach to the Study of the Effects of British Imperial Policy upon Colonial Welfare: Some Preliminary Findings', *Journal of Economic History*, xxv, 4 (Dec. 1965), 618–19.

was so generally regarded as the centre of the war effort.

Other parts of the world offered opportunities too. Good fortune in India allowed the British to capture the China tea trade and City Tories like Blakiston and Beckford, supported by Sir John Philipps (and the *Monitor*), helped to open it to individuals outside the East India Company.[27] The gum trade of Senegal was taken over from the French. In Europe, Portugal prospered on the profits of Brazilian sugar while French production was disrupted and Portuguese imports of British textiles grew. British trade with Europe in general was still substantial, although not growing in importance like colonial trade. When there was war in Germany exports there always increased. Woollen manufacturers benefited particularly.[28]

In such circumstances differences in the City were forgotten. The *Monitor* and Beckford now spoke confidently for wider City interests than just the Tories, over the Dutch issue for example, and the invasion threat. The *Monitor* also spoke for all commercial interests as its praises of Pitt grew through 1759. They reached a climax on 1 December, inspired both by the enumeration of triumphs in the King's Speech at the opening of Parliament on 13 November and by the day of thanksgiving observed on 29 November. The people, it claimed, were 'so thoroughly convinced of [his merit], that all the power of darkness will never be able to deprive him of their confidence and applause'. Regular paeans of praise of the great victories and of Pitt's major responsibility for them continued through 1760.[29] So Beckford could now openly bring his influence in the City through the *Monitor* into line with his own well-established commitment to Pitt. There was no longer any need for the equivocations made necessary by earlier doubts among some opinion in the City. In 1759–60 the *Monitor* was clearly recognized as the mouthpiece of Beckford's support for Pitt. More than ever it became a means of harnessing City opinion to Pitt's political chariot. The mood of the City also resounded jubilantly in its Address on the fall of Montreal in October 1760 which Pitt received exultantly as

[27] Rogers, 'London Politics', p. 239; Lucy S. Sutherland, *The East India Company in Eighteenth-Century Politics*, Oxford, 1952, pp. 30–1; *Mon.* 193, 13 Mar., 195, 14 Apr., 198, 5 May 1759.

[28] Rogers, 'London Politics', pp. 238–9; Davis, pp. 287–9; Pares, 'American versus Continental Warfare, 1739–63', p. 439.

[29] e.g. *Mon.* 208, 14 July (quotation) 225, 10 Nov., 226, 17 Nov., 228, 1 Dec. 1759, 272, 4 Oct., 274, 18 Oct. 1760.

promising 'a million in every line' for the vigorous prosecution of the war.[30] The same spirit rang out in the glowing inscription on the foundation stone, laid on 31 October 1760, of the new bridge at Blackfriars, known for some time as Pitt's bridge.[31]

As a result of his wide popularity, Pitt appeared to dominate politics and, whatever the tensions behind the scenes, to impose a unanimity apparent to all.[32] Of the year 1759, Walpole wrote

Intrigues of the cabinet, or of parliament, scarce existed at that period. All men were, or seemed to be, transported with the success of their country, and content with an administration which outwent their warmest wishes, or made their jealousy ashamed to show itself.

Of the session of 1759–60 he said, 'the winter was not memorable for any parliamentary debates'.[33] At the opening of the session a grand encomium by Beckford, emphasizing the victories of the year, gave Pitt the opportunity to dwell on the unity of the Ministers and the unanimity of the people. With specious modesty he disclaimed any special credit for the victories.[34]

The political strength popularity gave is perhaps best illustrated in the protracted and intensely strained squabble over Lord Temple's Garter, from August to November 1759. Temple was determined to have the vacant Garter. Pitt wanted Temple to have it as a mark of recognition of his own services and his standing in the Administration. The King, still smarting under Temple's insult of 1757 over Byng, was equally determined to refuse. Throughout, Newcastle and Hardwicke supported Pitt's claim as strongly as they dared and dreaded any thought of his resignation, which they considered a real possibility. As Walpole put it, 'apprehending the power of his popularity' they were determined not to break with

[30] Jour. Common Council, 62, ff. 139–40 (Beardmore, one of the *Monitor*'s authors, was on the committee to draw up the Address); *GM*, xxx, 1760, p. 479; Pitt to Grenville, 18 Oct. 1760, *Grenville Papers*, i, p. 355. Newcastle sceptically pointed out that those who addressed were not those who provided money (to Hardwicke, 18 Oct. 1760, Add. MSS 32913, f. 187).

[31] *GM*, xxx, Nov. 1760, p. 538.

[32] Richard Cox to Weston, 7 June, 10 July 1759, HMC, *Tenth Report*, pt. i, pp. 315, 317; Lyttelton to W. H. Lyttelton, 4 Dec. 1759, *Mems. Lyttelton*, ii, p. 621; Symmer to Mitchell, 8 Jan. 1760, Add. MSS 6839, f. 155.

[33] Walpole, *Geo. II*, ii, pp. 340, 410.

[34] Ibid., p. 389; West's account, 13 Nov. 1759, Add. MSS 32898, f. 223.

him. Reactions in the City to rumours of resignations did something
to prove them right. The King was not so sure of Pitt's indispensa-
bility, although their antipathy had long since been mitigated by
Pitt's ready adoption of German measures.[35] Yet over this major
issue of patronage, still very much a prerogative matter, the King
had eventually to give in, when Temple briefly resigned and Pitt
seemed likely to go with him.[36]

* * * * * *

Yet Pitt's popularity, immeasurably strengthened though it was,
was still open to challenges which might well make it transient and
unreliable. Nothing better illustrates this than the *Monitor*'s commentary. It was not interested in the progress and events of the war
as such. It paid little attention to the details of the invasion threat or
to the course of the war in Germany. More remarkably it showed no
great interest in the West Indian expedition which Beckford had
advocated. Even the greatest triumph of 1759, the capture of
Quebec, received relatively little notice. Almost immediately the
paper turned to rebuttal of 'factious' derogation of the victory and
Wolfe's achievement. Similarly in 1760 it was little interested in the
further great victories in India and America. Its only comment on
the taking of Montreal came in praise of the City Address of
congratulation.[37] Rather than the details of events and triumphs the
paper was interested in points of controversy which concerned the
City interests and Pitt. In seeking to turn what it could to his
advantage, it had not only to praise but even more to defend him
against what seemed to be substantial criticisms. Still the dominant
issue was policy on the Continent. This was aggravated as Frederick's difficulties multiplied rather than decreased and he adopted
a defensive attitude for the first time. The Army under Ferdinand in
the West seemed subordinated to Prussian interests.[38] Ferdinand's
victory at Minden only temporarily allayed criticism of German
affairs, which was coupled with a growing groundswell of criticism

[35] Walpole, *Geo. II*, ii, p. 354; Watkins to Newcastle, 19 Nov. 1759, Add. MSS
32898, f. 370; Newcastle to Hardwicke, 25 Oct. 1759, quoted Torrens, ii, p. 529.

[36] For accounts of the incident see Walpole, *Geo. II*, ii, pp. 391–2; Yorke, *Hardwicke*,
iii, pp. 23–6 and letters Aug. to Nov., esp. Hardwicke to Newcastle, 23 Sept. 1759, pp.
57–91; Torrens, ii, pp. 515–17, 519–22, 529, 532–4.

[37] *Mon.* 223, 27 Oct. 1759, 275, 25 Oct. 1760.

[38] Walpole, *Geo. II*, ii, pp. 359, 410; Corbett, ii, pp. 26, 77–8.

of the cost of the war. In May 1759 the *London Chronicle* calculated
the cost of Britain's part in the German war as £3,289,954,
compared with £823,759 in 1757. In 1760 a similar calculation
would have reached more than £4,000,000. Some of the consequent
criticism was now coming from opponents in national politics,
supporters of former governments or adherents of Leicester House,
as well as from Tories. Gordon provides voluminous if confused
evidence that it was to be heard also in the City and even among
those who had been advocates of the war. Successes in other
spheres, notably Quebec, merely stimulated it.[39] In reply, the
Monitor was at the heart of Pitt's defence as spokesman for his
Continental policy, particularly the Prussian alliance.

A bout of abusive and detailed controversy was occasioned in
June and July by two pamphlets, directed straight at Pitt, *A Letter
From The Duchess of M[a]r[lborou]gh, In The Shades, To The Great Man*[40]
and *A Defence Of The Letter*.[41] With arguments strongly reminiscent
of *Things As They Are* in the previous year, although not so
anti-Hanoverian, both pamphlets attacked Britain's involvement on
the Continent, particularly in alliance with Prussia, and blamed Pitt
for his support of this involvement. Neither avowed any party label.
Indeed, any party bias was denied by the *Letter*. However, Tory
connections are suggested by the high praise in the *Defence* of the
Monitor's former stands and equally bitter criticism of its change of
views and 'excessive' praise of Pitt,[42] together with the traditional
arguments against Continental involvement. Here, it seems, is more
evidence of bitter division in Tory ranks.

The first pamphlet criticized Pitt more vehemently than ever for

[39] *LC*, 29–31 May 1759; for the criticism see e.g. Dodington to Sewallis Shirley, 15
Sept. 1759, *Dodington*, pp. 387–8; Walpole, *Geo. II*, ii, pp. 359–60; Gordon to
Newcastle, 27 Apr., 7 May, 25 July, 28 Aug., 21 Oct., 13, 28 Nov. 1759, 16 Jan. 1760,
Add. MSS 32890, f. 370, 32891, f. 25, 32893, f. 264, 32894, f. 509, 32897, f. 273, 32898,
ff. 227–8, 32899, f. 167, 32901, f. 323.

[40] London, 1759. The title is explained in the opening pages (1–5). The Duchess of
Marlborough had left a legacy of £10,000 to Pitt because of her admiration of his
opposition to Walpole (Rosebery, pp. 233–4). She is now represented as having had
her good opinion of him challenged by the reports of his later behaviour given by
recent arrivals 'in the shades'.

[41] *A Defence Of The Letter from the Dutchess of M[arlboroug]h in the Shades to the Great
Man . . . In Answer to The Monitor's Two Papers, Of the 23rd and 30th June, 1759*, London,
1759.

[42] Ibid., p. 57.

his changes of front over Continental policy, stripping away the strategems he used to disgsise them. After his last return to office he could, it said, have rejected old measures on the strength of his popularity. Instead, having climbed to power by means of popularity, he then spurned it. He was not, as he complained, sacrificed to his new friends. Rather, he had unnecessarily sacrificed the people to them, while the people had been deceived by 'designingly blustering airs', for example over ill-conceived expeditions, in place of true spirit and business. Further, he had mishandled Continental involvement so badly as to align Britain with a country condemned by all Europe and now so weak as to endanger all Britain's gains. Thus British efforts against France had been diverted from their true course. The victories won despite all were no special credit to Pitt. Of what use, the pamphlet asked, was unanimity in councils if the unanimity was so wrongly directed? 'What has this great man done for the nation which had put it into his power to do so much?[43]

In reply, the *Monitor* sprang to the defence of the Prussian alliance, this time with no hesitation except a momentary if tell-tale confession that it would have been better if there was 'no necessity for our interfering between the Belligerents on the continent'. At present, however, it said, the Prussian alliance was necessary as an alternative to Austria, which had deserted Britain. The alliance was also good in itself, on grounds of religion, of Britain's trade in Germany, and because Prussia was fighting for the rights of small states against the common enemy, not for conquests (*sic!*). It had allowed Britain to continue her own efforts in her own sphere all the more gloriously. It was not true, the *Monitor* argued in detail, that the alliance had brought more difficulties to both Prussia and Britain [44] To this substantial extent the *Monitor* defended Pitt. But it did little to answer the charges that Pitt had 'veered right round' and misused his popularity.

In answer, the second pamphlet elaborated the arguments against involvement in Europe. It rejected those based on the balance of power, religion or obligation to Hanover, but ignored Britain's trading interests. Especially it argued against involvement in the form of the Prussian alliance. It held clumsy British diplomacy rather than the disloyalty of Austria responsible for the reversal of

---

[43] *A Letter*, esp. pp. 23 (first quotation), 32, 33, 38, 40, 72, 74, (second quotation).
[44] *Mon.* 205, 23 June, 206, 30 June 1759 (quotation).

alliances which had upset the whole European and German situation and put Britain on the wrong side morally. Prussia had shown no real enmity towards France, the pamphlet said, but had concentrated on her other enemies. Britain, not France, had been weakened as a consequence. The victories which she had nevertheless achieved merely served to emphasize that her true medium was the sea. Popular support for the Prussian alliance was the result of misrepresentation of its benefits and misguided faith in Pitt. In supporting the alliance Pitt had either succumbed to the 'court-passion' or been blinded by a few insubstantial successes. Either way his reputation as a patriot and statesman was thrown in doubt.

The *Monitor* kept up the controversy in even more detail in August and September. It concentrated on two further main points of the opposition: that Prussia was by true inclination a friend of France and that the Queen of Hungary was to be pitied because she had been deserted by Britain rather than blamed for reaching an accommodation with France.[45] Its continuing and detailed concern shows how important it thought this controversy. These were no mere murmurs of discontent but deep-seated dissatisfactions, felt especially but not only by Tories[46] and closely affecting Pitt's reputation. Varying reactions to the controversy are well illustrated in the Reviews. The *Monthly* condemned the attack on Pitt as 'malice, falshood, contradiction, and absurdity'. This was the main thing it noted about the first pamphlet. It abruptly dismissed the charges of hypocrisy and praised Pitt for following the voice of the people, not only in colonial but also in Continental operations and the alliance with Prussia. It had no doubts about his 'virtue and ability'. The second pamphlet it dismissed even more cursorily as 'the spawn of personal malice, or private interest'. The *Critical Review*, however, was torn between commitment to Pitt and opposition to Continental connections. The 'severe invective against a certain great man' in the first pamphlet was 'unjust', it claimed, but nevertheless 'replete with many melancholy truths, relating to our continental measures and German allies'. It could not imagine that such measures had ever been adopted by a British statesman who with

---

[45] *Mon.*, 211, 4 Aug., 217, 15 Sept. 1759.
[46] e.g. Gordon to Newcastle, 26 June 1759, Add. MSS 32892, f. 237.

a real spirit of patriotism, and irresistible power of eloquence, hath so often combated these pernicious connections, and whose chief praise it is, to be deemed the minister of the people.

In its notice of the second pamphlet the Review's dilemma was even more apparent. Here it strongly denied that '*the war which we maintain in Germany, is a necessary diversion in favour of Great-Britain*'. Yet it defended Pitt's 'talents and incorruptibility' and refused to believe him 'guilty of engaging in any measures destructive of the true interest of Britain'.[47]

The first pamphlet was noticed by some newspapers, all comment being hostile. Probus in the *Gazetteer* answered at some length the 'ill-designed' tract's criticisms of Pitt and especially of Prussia. It was a strange experience for the *Monitor* to be on the same side as the *Gazetteer*, and hardly reassuring to Tory waverers. *Lloyd's Evening Post* quoted the *Monitor*'s first answer to the Duchess. The *London Evening Post* contented itself with a few gibes, the most direct copied from the *Gazetteer*, but its diffidence did not spring from embarrassment any longer. Like the *Monitor* it was now firmly committed to Continental connections. Although the *London Magazine* extracted some of the most embarrassing of the first pamphlet's criticisms of Pitt, it seems that the *Monthly Review's* contempt was the general reaction.[48]

But for some at least, the issue of Continental policy was still closely connected with Pitt's popular reputation. Even the French, apparently, tried to use it to undermine his standing.[49] The uneasiness of Pitt's Tory supporters was not, however, the main reason for the importance the *Monitor* attached to this controversy. Continental connections in the form of the Prussian alliance were indeed the crucial strategic issue of the war, the more so as the difficulties of the King of Prussia became extreme. Everyone agreed that for Britain this war was being fought for colonial and mercantile objectives. Yet British achievements outside Europe were threatened by the tenuous situation of their ally, pressed on all sides by his enemies.[50]

---

[47] *MR*, xx, June 1759, pp. 561–2, xxi, Aug., pp. 179–80; *CR*, vii, June 1759, p. 557, viii, Aug., pp. 164–5.

[48] *Gaz.*, 9 (quotation), 12, 14 June 1759; *Lloyd's EP*, 25–7 June 1759 (no copies of either paper survive for July); *LEP*, 26–8, 28–30 June, 14–16 Aug., 8–11 Sept. 1759; *LM*, xxviii, June 1759, pp. 312–15.

[49] *CR*, ix, Jan. 1760, pp. 67–9.   [50] Walpole, *Geo. II*, ii, pp. 369–72.

Sacrifices might well have to be made in any peace settlement to rescue him.[51] To some people this seemed a good reason to abandon him and to reject again all costly European entanglements. But for Pitt, Continental involvement had become one of the pillars of his war plans. He looked for more than mere preservation of what had already been won and wanted to keep French energy diverted in Europe so that victory elsewhere could be complete. The City, dazzled by victories and led on by hopes of commercial gain, followed him in this reasoning. It was the desperate fear that prosecution of the war to its proper conclusion might be interrupted which lay behind the ever more bitter accusations of 'faction' running monotonously through all the *Monitor's* commentary now. Sometimes these complaints of faction were the same old Tory complaints against Newcastle and his associates. Sometimes, however, they were overlaid with bitterness against former allies in the Tory ranks who were now opponents.[52] In either case the fear was the same, that war policy would be diverted and an early unsatisfactory peace made based on present gains. The accusations were no longer just a rhetorical device to divert blame from Pitt.

Despite the difficulties and criticisms, Pitt committed himself even more fully and openly to the German war in later 1759 and 1760. He assured Ferdinand 'he shall have what reinforcements, what ammunition he pleases—tell him I will stand or fall with him'. He announced to the new session of Parliament that 'he had unlearned his juvenile errors, and thought no longer that England could do all by itself'. The war had to be carried on in its totality, he said, if a proper peace could not be obtained. He spoke too of the need to reinforce Ferdinand's army. In January, April–May and July further troops were sent.[53] Yet this was an uncomfortable issue in Parliament. The undercurrent of criticism of the German war reached a peak in the early weeks of the session, as Frederick's dire situation was pondered on.[54] The Tory country gentlemen were divided but on the whole opposed to the sending of more troops. Behind the apparent euphoria and unanimity of the session there were notes of concern about the growing cost. An exchange between Sir John Philipps and Pitt, for example, in the debates on the Army

---

[51] Cf. *AR*, ii, 1759, pp. 45, 56.   [52] e.g. *Mon.* 221, 13 Oct., 228, 1 Dec. 1759.

[53] Walpole, *Geo. II*, ii, pp. 381 (first quotation), 390 (second quotation); West's account, 13 Nov. 1759, Add. MSS 32898, ff. 223–4; Corbett, ii, pp. 80, 83, 85.

[54] Lady Anne Egerton to Bentinck, 10 Dec. 1759, Eg. 1719, f. 81. See below p. 169.

estimates, turned to the question of economy and brought Pitt to declare that 'to push expence was the best oeconomy'. In contrast to Philipps, Beckford was ostentatiously helpful over a Government loan and publicly avowed his approval of arrangements for supply before Philipps and others. Later in the session there were further hints of difficulties with some Tories.[55]

Pitt clearly realized the challenge to his popularity.[56] He took his usual care to disguise his moves over the sending of troops. He wanted to appear 'to be ravished to it' and to impose conditions, although in fact he was co-operative. In July he wrote somewhat apologetically to Temple about the latest reinforcements.[57] As before, his tactics of disguise included taking up 'popular' issues which conveniently arose. The consequent confusion annoyed Newcastle and the King, who for once saw that his motives were 'to enable *Himself, with the Tories*,' with scant regard for 'our Friends, who compose the Majority of the House of Commons' of which he was supposed to be the Leader.[58]

One such measure was a bill concerning the enforcement of the property qualifications of members of Parliament, a measure of the Tory country gentlemen in the tradition of place and pension bills. The Bill was introduced in February by Sir John Philipps and Beckford. They had first asked Pitt for assurances that the Administration would not oppose the measure 'in consideration of the assistance, which *they* had given to the King's measures'. Pitt declared his support and created some uncomfortable moments over the measure. However, he left the Government line to Newcastle.[59] Newcastle disliked the Bill, especially because of the difficulties it would cause in the approaching general election. But neither he nor

[55] Western, p. 168; Lord Talbot to Dodington, 25 Aug., 1 Sept. 1760, HMC, *Various Collections*, vi, pp. 46, 47; Walpole, *Geo. II*, ii, p. 397 (quotation); Lyttelton to W. H. Lyttelton, 4 Dec. 1759, *Mems. Lyttelton*, ii, p. 621; West, memorandum to Newcastle, 15 Jan. 1760, Add. MSS 32901, f. 305; Lady Anne Egerton to Bentinck, 25, 27 Mar. 1760, Eg. 1719, ff. 102, 104.

[56] Newcastle to Hardwicke, 31 Oct. 1759, Add. MSS 35419, f. 43.

[57] Newcastle to Devonshire, 8 Apr. 1760, memorandum for the King, 2 May 1760, Add. MSS 32904, f. 260, 32905, f. 242; Hardwicke to Newcastle, 10 Apr. 1760 (quotation), Yorke, *Hardwicke*, iii, p. 245; Pitt to Temple, 22 July 1760, *Grenville Papers*, i, p. 347.

[58] Newcastle to Hardwicke, 15 Mar. 1760, Add. MSS 32903, f. 297.

[59] Newcastle to Hardwicke, 26 Jan. (quotation), 20 Feb. (2 letters), 4 Mar. 1760, Add. MSS 32901, f. 479, 32902, ff. 280, 282, 32903, f. 82.

Pitt really wished to disrupt the Administration over it. Newcastle saw to it that a modified version was eventually passed, despite opposition from his more hot-headed younger supporters.[60] Pitt made as much capital as he could out of the Bill and its difficulties. He objected to the modifications and took the usual line that he could do nothing in face of Newcastle's control of the House. In the final debate on 21 April he represented the measure as a small return to the landed interest who had given fifteen millions a year for the war. In fact, not all Tories, let alone all country gentlemen, approved the Bill. In the House of Lords Temple gave ostentatious support which irritated Hardwicke. Such hints of acrimony were designed mainly for public consumption. When the Bill eventually became law on 22 May Newcastle was probably right in regarding it as a sign of the basic unity of the Administration.[61]

The other popular measure which Pitt took up was the Militia. Two matters concerning it caused contention in the 1759–60 session: the extension of the scheme to Scotland and the question of some relief from the central Government for the family allowances each county paid its militiamen while its Militia was embodied. The proposal for a Scottish Militia was defeated in April. It was opposed by Newcastle and his 'young friends' and supported only halfheartedly by Pitt. Beckford was among the supporters and Newcastle expected 'all the City' to be for it.[62] The more seriously contentious issue of the financial burden on the counties brought Pitt and Newcastle into such violent dispute as to threaten a breach. Pitt demanded a measure as a *quid pro quo* for agreeing to the German reinforcements of April–May, which would increase the need to keep the Militia embodied. In the House, however, he was not as clear in support as Beckford and showed some concern for the unity of the Administration. The compromise Bill introduced by Pitt's cousin, Jack Pitt, was at first rejected by the Commons and eventually passed in severely emasculated form. Pitt, however, had

---

[60] Newcastle to Kinnoull, 15 Feb., 1 June 1760, Newcastle to Hardwicke, 4, 5, 15 Mar. 1760, Add. MSS 32902, f. 194, 32907, f. 16, 32903, ff. 82–3, 98, 298; Walpole, *Geo. II*, ii, pp. 435–6.

[61] Newcastle to Hardwicke, 4, 5 Mar. 1760, West's account, 21 Apr. 1760, Add. MSS 32903, ff. 82, 98, 32905, ff. 14–15; Walpole, *Geo. II*, ii, pp. 436–7; Newcastle to Kinnoull, 1 June 1760, Add. MSS 32907, f. 16.

[62] Western, pp. 162–7; Newcastle's memorandum for the King, 15 Apr. 1760, Add. MSS 32904, f. 388.

been encouraged, indeed compelled, to commit himself further to the Militia and to the larger question of prolonging its life when the current legislation expired.[63] This became the major militia question through 1760. Militia zealots became very warm. Newcastle and the old King were very agitated. The King was even prepared to risk Pitt's resignation over it. Again, however, neither Pitt nor Newcastle wished to press the issue too far. A compromise was reached whereby the militia legislation was to be extended for the duration of the war only. In the new reign even this was put off. On the strength of a flattering reference to the Militia in the King's Speech at the end of 1760, Pitt was able to persuade his friends to accept the situation.[64]

Undoubtedly Pitt acted on both the Qualification Bill and the militia questions partly to offset the unpopularity of his Continental measures among the Tory country gentlemen. (There was also the practical need to check the declining popularity of the Militia arising from its long embodiment.) Militia and constitutional questions still mattered to some of his supporters. Indeed Pitt admitted to Hardwicke that he had been driven to support the continuation of the Militia against his better judgement, 'by the jealousy raised that he had abated of his zeal for the measure itself'.[65] Yet the *Monitor* paid the measures, particularly those concerning the Militia, scant attention despite Beckford's support for them.[66] Pitt had the loyalty of the City now because of his conduct of the war and not mainly as defender of the constitution, as had been the case in 1756–7. For the rate-paying country gentlemen the issues might have been more relevant. Even for them, however, there is reason to believe that the long embodiment was causing the Militia to lose its popularity as a 'country' nostrum. What agitation there was lacked depth and intensity.[67] Nevertheless Pitt had used the issues for what they were worth. In general, and on these issues particularly, the session had

[63] Western, pp. 169–73; West's account, 8 May 1760, Add. MSS 32905, f. 339.

[64] Western, pp. 175–80.

[65] Ibid., pp. 168–70; Hardwicke to Newcastle, 29 Oct. 1760, Yorke, *Hardwicke*, iii, p. 309.

[66] It warmly supported the Qualification Bill but took it up late and did not persist (*Mon.* 243, 15 Mar., 252, 17 May 1760). It noticed militia questions only once, the Scottish Militia on 22 Mar. 1760. *LEP* was similarly reticent but there was discussion in other papers.

[67] Western, pp. 174–5. The issues provoked only two pamphlets, see *CR*, ix, Mar. 1760, pp. 240–1; *MR*, xx, May 1760, pp. 433–4.

proved the parliamentary strength of Newcastle's friends rather than Pitt's. Newcastle had allowed some gestures to be made but the concessions which kept the Administration's supporters united had come mainly from Pitt.[68] Perhaps the gestures alone were sufficient for his purpose.

From the end of 1759, a new issue arose just as vital to Pitt's reputation as that of Continental connections. At this time the first serious discussion of the possibility of peace began. Frederick had for some time been advocating an early peace. Hardwicke and Newcastle also favoured peace at least from the time of the capture of Louisbourg in 1758. They were alarmed at the prospects of financial difficulties and political opposition to a campaign to save Hanover. France's colonial losses, the increasing hopelessness of the invasion attempt and especially the desperate state of her finances inclined her Chief Minister, Choiseul, towards a separate peace with Britain, to be brought about by Spanish mediation. Spain's interest was quickened by the ambitions of her new King, Charles III, to play a role in Europe and by fear of the major change in the balance of power in America resulting from the fall of Quebec. Approaches to Britain were at first rebuffed by Pitt who wanted to make the most of French difficulties. He acted with some caution, though, when he realised the potential threat of Spanish fears. Offers of Danish mediation were likewise refused. After the battle of Minden in August 1759, however, Pitt first began to think seriously that an early peace might be desirable, especially as Frederick's situation continued critical. Means were therefore found to counter these French and Spanish pressures towards a separate peace. Taking up an idea originally suggested by Frederick, the British proposed that, at the end of the campaign when Quebec was likely to have been taken, a joint declaration with Prussia in favour of a general peace congress should be made. This declaration was formally made on 25 November to the representatives of the belligerent powers at The Hague. It initiated long months of fluctuating and eventually fruitless negotiation.[69]

Pitt's attitude to these negotiations was crucial to their progress. As both Hardwicke and Kinnoull observed, any peace would have

---

    [68] Newcastle to Kinnoull, 1 June 1760, Add. MSS 32907, ff. 16–17.
    [69] Mitchell to Newcastle, 20 May, to Holdernesse, 24 May 1759, *Mems. Mitchell*, ii, pp. 63, 66; Corbett, ii, pp. 72–7; Yorke, *Hardwicke*, iii, pp. 142–6.

to be endorsed by him to be acceptable to public opinion.[70] There is every reason to believe that after the conquest of Quebec he was seriously interested in peace and moderate and flexible about the means of obtaining it and the terms to be demanded. His despairing conversation with Lady Yarmouth in September 1759, prompted by the deteriorating German situation, would suggest that he had hoped soon to be able to negotiate a peace from strength, based on conquests in America, the West Indies, and Africa. Certainly Newcastle was convinced in October that he 'seemed really desirous of peace this winter and upon reasonable terms'. Pitt had carefully avoided any commitment to retain Louisbourg and was not talking of insisting on Quebec. Rather he appeared to be thinking of holding only those captured points in North America essential to the security of the British colonies—such as Crown Point and Niagara. Outside North America he wanted to keep Senegal and Gorée. Sometimes he seemed indifferent about Guadeloupe but certainly wanted to retain some of the French islands, probably including it.[71] Hardwicke, too, a more sober judge, thought his ideas quite reasonable, far from the extremes of popular opinion which was insisting on holding everything and reducing France to nothing. Pitt's terms were more moderate, too, than the King's. He was against peace at this time because there was no hope of territorial gains for Hanover and therefore stood out for high terms in America.[72] A lengthy reference was made to the hope for peace in the King's Speech in November, apparently on Pitt's initiative and certainly with his approval. In the debate on the Address he spoke cautiously about the prospects, emphasizing the delicate state of the overall struggle against France, but Walpole at least was convinced of the sincerity of his interest. Certainly at first he worked actively for peace and as late as February 1760 Newcastle thought that he seemed earnest for it.[73]

[70] Hardwicke to Newcastle, 24 Oct., Kinnoull to Newcastle, 30 Oct. 1759, Add. MSS 32897, f. 350–1, 501.

[71] Newcastle to Hardwicke, 19 Sept., 31 Oct. (quotation) 1759, Yorke, *Hardwicke*, iii, pp. 58, 242; memorandum, 12 Oct. 1759, Add. MSS 32897, ff. 32–3; Rogers, 'London Politics', p. 246.

[72] Hardwicke to Newcastle, 16 Oct. 1759, Yorke, *Hardwicke*, iii, p. 239; heads of Mr Pitt's conversation, 17 Oct. 1759, Add. MSS 32897, f. 174.

[73] Newcastle to Pitt, 3 Nov. 1759, *Corr. Chatham*, i, p. 448; *Parl. Hist.* xv, c. 949; West's account, 13 Nov. 1759, Newcastle to Kinnoull, 15 Feb. 1760, Add. MSS 32898, f. 223, 32902, f. 194; Symmer to Mitchell, 13 Nov. 1759, Add. MSS 6839, ff. 150–1; Walpole, *Geo. II,* ii, pp. 390–1; Hardwicke to Newcastle, 5 Jan. 1760, Yorke, *Hardwicke,* iii, pp. 242–3.

By this time, however, a major public debate had developed over the peace negotiations. Talk of the possibility of peace had gradually grown in the newspapers through 1759. Up to the time of the joint Anglo-Prussian declaration this discussion had not been very precise either on the desirability of peace or the terms which should be negotiated, although there was almost universal urging of a strong peace. This was the basis for Hardwicke's comment that popular opinion was insisting on holding everything and reducing France to nothing.[74] What few clues there were before November on the terms to be demanded suggest that ambitions were growing with victories. There was still some talk, like that at the beginning of the war, about settling the limits of territories in North America so clearly and defensibly that all disputes would be at an end.[75] But ideas of what were acceptable limits were changing and talk of excluding the French altogether was growing. At the very least the mood was that expressed in the *Annual Register* for 1759: 'it will depend more upon our own sentiments of convenience what part of North America we shall leave to France, than to any efforts they may make in that part of the world.'[76]

In the City, in contrast to the report of Birch in September 1758, Gordon commented frequently in 1759 on the desire for peace. He did, however, admit that City opinion was divided and that there was still an ardent pro-war party. He usually identified this with 'the faction' or 'the merchants' who were making profits from the war. It was the moneyed interest that was keen for peace.[77] The *Monitor* can be taken as typical of the views of the pro-war party. From the beginning it had regarded the war as a fight to the finish to

[74] e.g. *UC*, 5–12 May, 18–25 Aug. 1759; *OWC*, 12–19 May, 26 May–2 June, 2–9 June, 18–25 Aug., 17–24 Nov. 1759; *LC*, 26–8 June, 6–9, 9–11 Oct. 1759; *LEP*, 11–13 Oct. 1759.

[75] *GM*, xxviii, Sept. 1758, p. 430, cf. *UC*, 16–23 Sept. 1758; *GM*, xxix, Oct. 1759, p. 466; *LEP*, 6–8 Dec. 1759. Pares, 'American versus Continental Warfare', p. 450, seems wrong when he suggests that public opinion intended the total expulsion of the French from North America from the beginning of the war.

[76] *GM*, xxix, Aug. 1759, p. 376; *Considerations On The Importance of Canada . . . Addressed to the Right Hon. William Pitt,* London, [Oct] 1759; *AR*, ii, 1759, p. 45.

[77] Birch to Royston, 30 Sept. 1758, Add. MSS 35399, f. 39; Gordon to Newcastle, 7 May, 18 June, 6 July, 28 Aug., 29 Oct., 13, 20, 28 Nov. 1759, Add. MSS 32891, ff. 25, 131, 32892, f. 446, 32894, f. 510, 32897, ff. 468–9, 32898, ff. 227–8, 405, 32899, f. 167; Symmer to Mitchell, 13 Nov. 1759, Add. MSS 6839, f. 150. For an explanation of the attitudes of the moneyed interest see below p. 188.

reduce the power of France. It was a just war fought in self-defence which no ambiguous patched-up peace should interrupt. As early as April 1758 the *Monitor* argued that any peace must be made on the principle of *uti possidetis*. As the issue came more to the fore the *Monitor*'s hostility to an early peace became increasingly clear. A peace made before the objects of the war were fully achieved and when Britain was still able to press on vigorously with conquests would be 'untimely'. No conquests should be given up. Over and over again the dangerous ambitions and perfidy of France were emphasized and the need to reduce her power completely was increasingly stressed. When, in 1759, the *Monitor* became the spokesman for the Prussian alliance, it also insisted there be no abandonment of Prussia.[78] The paper had few precise ideas on European terms. But over colonial conquests, as the months passed the *Monitor*'s ambitions grew. By October, still before the news of the conquest of Quebec and almost certainly under the influence of a pamphlet, *Considerations On The Importance of Canada*, France was to be excluded entirely from the American fisheries and, if possible, from the trade in fish and fur.[79]

The major debate stimulated by the joint Anglo-Prussian declaration in November 1759 brought the question of the kind of peace to be demanded right to the fore and showed that the views of the *Monitor* were pretty widely held. It was begun by *A Letter Addressed To Two Great Men*. Attributed by many contemporaries to Lord Bath, this pamphlet was almost certainly written by his protégé and chaplain, John Douglas, probably with Bath's advice. Perhaps because of its supposed authorship, it attracted considerable attention, especially, according to Walpole, in the City, where its views were 'much adopted'.[80] For the first time in public debate the pamphlet raised the possibility of the total exclusion of the French from Canada. In this it was soon followed by the *Monitor*, responsive

---

[78] *Mon.* 145, 29 Apr., 175, 25 Nov. 1758, 182, 13 Jan., 196, 21 Apr., 202, 2 June, 206, 30 June, 214, 25 Aug., 217, 15 Sept., 218, 22 Sept., 220, 6 Oct., 222, 20 Oct., 224–5, 3–10 Nov., 227, 24 Nov. 1759.

[79] *Mon.* 214, 25 Aug., 220, 6 Oct. 1759; see above fn. 76.

[80] *A Letter Addressed To Two Great Men, On The Prospect of Peace; And on the Terms necessary to be insisted upon in the Negociation,* London, 1759. Newcastle to Hardwicke, 29 Dec. 1759, Add. MSS 32900, f. 401; Jenkinson to Grenville, 25 Dec. 1759, *Grenville Papers*, i, p. 334; Mrs Montagu to Lyttelton, 15 Jan. 1760, *Elizabeth Montagu*, ii, p. 179; Walpole to Montagu, 14 Jan. 1760, *Walpole's Corr.* ix, p. 270; Walpole, *Geo. II*, ii, pp. 411–12. The pamphlet was noticed in all newspapers and magazines.

as ever to the arguments of pamphlets, although at the moment it was initiating little because it was preoccupied with matters of special concern to itself. The effect of the pamphlet was most remarkable on the *London Evening Post*. Hitherto the paper had been vague about peace terms. Now, through a new correspondent, Albion, it came out quickly and strongly for holding all Canada.[81]

The *Letter*'s most obvious effect was to initiate the prolonged public debate, continuing until peace was finally concluded in 1762, over which colonial conquests Britain should retain. 'Canada versus Guadeloupe' was the major issue. It was to be argued with much zest and sometimes considerable sophistication, the balance of opinion tending towards Canada.[82] The *Letter* considered that other conquests were not as important as Canada and might possibly be relinquished, although the preference was for keeping all. Again, at first the *Monitor* followed suit. By February, however, probably influenced by another pamphlet, the *Monitor* rejected any distinction between 'necessary' and 'unnecessary' conquests. France should be weakened as much as possible and therefore the already-captured French sugar islands should be retained and Martinique conquered. 'Our dispute is about the extent of trade: whether the trading genius of Britain or of France shall prevail', the *Monitor* had already declared. Now it let its greed for commercial gain carry it out of line with the views of many West Indian interests, which favoured the return of the sugar islands out of fear that British markets would otherwise be over-supplied. Many others in the City, however, must have shared the *Monitor*'s ambitions. Patriotic fervour appealed more than sophisticated argument to the middling sort who were its readers, and readers of the *London Evening Post*, which was even quicker to argue for the retention of all conquests.[83] Other papers less insistent on keeping all seem also to have favoured Canada, just

81 *Mon.* 232, 29 Dec. 1759; see below p. 175. *LEP*, 5–8, 8–10 Jan. 1760, cf. 6–8, 25–7 Dec. 1759.

82 See W. L. Grant, 'Canada versus Guadeloupe, an Episode of the Seven Years' War', *American Historical Review*, xvii, 4 (July 1912), esp. 135–9; Namier, *England*, pp. 273–82.

83 *Mon.* 217, 15 Sept. 1759 (quotation), 233, 5 Jan., 237, 2 Feb. 1760. *An Answer to the Letter to Two Great Men*, *CR*, ix, Feb. 1760, p. 155, *MR*, xxii, Jan. 1760, pp. 71–2; Grant, pp. 735–6; Namier, *England*, p. 278. e.g. *LEP*, 5–8, 8–10, 10–12 Jan., 7–9 Feb. 1760. Rogers, 'London Politics', p. 270.

as many of the addresses of congratulation attached special importance to the victory at Quebec.[84]

Such public debate over possible peace terms was very relevant, as the *Monthly Review* pointed out,[85] to the acceptability of any peace which might be made. It increased the likelihood that not everyone could be satisfied. But more important than detailed argument over terms were the general questions whether Britain should try to secure a moderate or a demanding peace, and whether she should return any conquests at all. The public might be divided over the relative merits of Canada and Guadeloupe. On these general issues, despite some judicious contributions to the contrary,[86] comment was virtually unanimous in favour of a strong peace making few concessions. Arguments about the cost and increasing burden of the war were discounted. It was only in Change Alley, said the *London Evening Post*, that anyone wanted peace; the stocks might tremble but trade still flourished. Responsive chords were struck by discourses on the exhausted state of France and her perfidy and ambition, and a retributive peace to end the just war which Britain was fighting with the obvious blessings of Providence was considered both possible and desirable.[87]

The prevailing tone of the debate on peace terms certainly created problems for the Ministers and especially for Pitt. The year before, *Plain Reasons* had pointed out how a patriot minister was expected to behave in peace negotiations: he would be firm on the honour of England and allow no concessions to the enemy's trade or naval power.[88] Now public opinion was ahead of Pitt, especially on the exclusion of the French from North America. Chesterfield, sympathetic to that opinion, forecast a 'harvest of disaffection' if Quebec were sacrificed. The 'germ of discontent' was already great at the mere supposition. No wonder that Pitt was said to be angry over the *Letter*.[89]

[84] e.g. *LC*, 5–7, 21–3, 26–8 Feb. and 7–9, 9–12 Feb. quoting Simplicius from *Gaz.*

[85] *MR*, xxii, Jan. 1760, p. 50.

[86] Most notably, *Remarks On The Letter Addressed To Two Great Men*, London, 1760; and *A Letter To The People of England, On The Necessity of putting an Immediate End to the War*, London, 1760, cf. *GM*, xxx, Feb. 1760, pp. 95–6.

[87] e.g. *MR*, xxii, Jan. 1760, pp. 50–3; *CR*, ix, Jan. 1760, pp. 71–3, Feb., p. 157; *LM*, xix, Feb. 1760, pp. 72–6; *LEP*, 1–4 Mar. 1760. Almost the only contrary voice in the newspapers was the *Westminster Journal*, e.g. 1 Dec. 1759, and in *UC*, 12–19 Jan., 8–15 Mar., *LC*, 22–4 Jan. 1760. It is not possible to assess the attitude of *Gaz.*

[88] *Plain Reasons*, p. 9.

[89] Chesterfield to his son, 25 June 1759, *Letters to His Son*, ii, p. 267; Mrs Montagu to Lyttelton, 15 Jan. 1760, *Elizabeth Montagu*, ii, p. 179.

In these circumstances it seems that Pitt was influenced in his attitude to the negotiations by public opinion and especially his friends in the City. Certainly it was his insistence on the formal inclusion of Prussia in the negotiations that ended any hope that they would become substantial. The refusal of Austria to contemplate negotiations before Prussia was finally crushed made a general congress impossible. Choiseul continued his efforts to initiate separate negotiations with Britain. Discussions were begun at the Hague in January 1760 between the British and French, but Britain's insistence on the inclusion of Prussia did not give Choiseul a sufficient loophole to desert his ally and the discussions came to nothing. When at last the answers to the joint declaration were given in early April they were, as expected, tantamount to a refusal of a general congress. By May negotiations were over.

There was no *prima facie* need for Pitt to insist on Prussia's inclusion. True, in June 1759 he had promised Frederick that '*no peace of Utrecht* will again stain the annals of England', but this did not bind him to demand the participation of Prussia at all stages. Frederick was certainly not against separate negotiations, even a separate peace.[90] Pitt's insistence was clearly a disguise for other reasons for changing his mind over the desirability of peace. It seems that now, for the first time, he considered an eventual settlement based on fundamental changes in North America, perhaps the retention of all Canada, might be possible. This would, of course, require another campaign to complete the conquest. The increasing difficulties in the way of peace, together with various pieces of intelligence suggesting that France regarded Canada of little value, may have contributed to his changed attitude.[91] More certain, however, was the influence of public opinion, as it became clear that any suggestion of restoring American conquests would compromise his popularity. Certainly in April, by which time there was a clear divergence between Newcastle and Pitt on further negotiations and Pitt was vehemently insisting on the continuation of the war, Hardwicke explained his change of attitude in this way.

---

[90] Pitt to Mitchell, 12 June 1759, *Corr. Chatham*, i, p. 411; Mitchell to Holdernesse, 16 Jan., 12 Feb. 1760, *Mems. Michell,* ii, pp. 124–5, 134.

[91] e.g. Mitchell to Holdernesse, 16 Jan. 1760, *Mems. Mitchell,* ii, p. 123. *A Letter Addressed To Two Great Men,* pp. 30–1, argued that France thought Canada of little value.

Your Grace says that you begin to be of my opinion about Mr Pitt's disposition as to peace. I never said that he might not wish it, but I have said, and do think, that he hardly knows how to set about it. He sees that in order to obtain peace, so much of our acquisitions must be given up; and the populace, who have been blown up to such an extravagant degree, and of whom he is willing to quit his hold, will be so much disappointed, that he is ready to start at the approaches to it.[92]

The nagging debate over the Continental war persisted as a substantial undertone to the peace discussion. Sometimes it became the major preoccupation. One of the most striking features of the *Letter Addressed To Two Great Men* was its apparently wholehearted defence of current Continental policies as substantially different from the reprehensible measures of the past. They had 'contributed more than perhaps we could expect, to our success in *America*, and other Parts of the World'. 'It is entirely owing to the *German* Part of the War that *France* appears thus low in the political Scale of Strength and Riches.' So Britain should continue all possible support, even to the extent of rescuing Prussia by relinquishing British colonial conquests (other than Canada). Such an outspoken and perhaps deliberately provocative defence could not but stimulate replies along the usual anti-Continental lines.[93] Indeed no other pamphleteer in the peace debate attempted any substantial defence of Continental measures, although some newspapers did.[94] The *Monitor* was too preoccupied to take up the challenge at this time. Not surprisingly, there was universal opposition, even among those sympathetic to the Continental war, to any sacrifice of British conquests for her European allies.

The situation on the Continent grew even worse during 1760. There were grave and well-founded doubts whether Frederick could mount and survive the further campaign which had become inevitable by May. He managed to struggle on, his gloomy situation only temporarily relieved by some brilliant moves. On 8 October the

---

[92] Newcastle to Hardwicke, 9 Apr., Hardwicke to Newcastle, 10 Apr. 1760, Yorke, *Hardwicke*, iii, pp. 244–5.

[93] *A Letter Addressed To Two Great Men*, pp. 37, 38 (quotation), 39–41 and e.g. *A Letter From A Gentleman In the Country To His Friend in Town, On his Perusal of a Pamphlet Addressed to Two Great Men*, London, 1760, the most notable answer not already cited.

[94] e.g. *LEP*, 16–19 Feb., 1–4, 4–6 Mar. 1760; *OWC*, 22–9 Dec. 1759 (Probus from *Gaz.*), *LC*, 27–9 Dec. 1759, 1–3 Jan. 1760 (from *Westminster Journal*, q.v. 22 Dec. 1759) but cf. 12–15 Jan. 1760.

Russians took Berlin. The year's campaigns ended with a victory at Torgau which enabled Frederick to recover all of Saxony except Dresden. His resources, however, were still desperately over-extended. In the west, Ferdinand's campaign brought little comfort. He faced superior French forces and only their dissension saved him from decisive defeat. As it was, 'the French soon over-ran Hesse, seized Gottingen and Munden, and were at the eve of possessing Hanover'. In October Ferdinand was defeated in an attempt to overcome the very weak French garrison of Wesel. Any offensive seemed beyond his powers.[95]

Yet an offensive of some kind was essential. It was no longer simply a question of diverting France to allow victories elsewhere. France had to be defeated to secure the victories already won. If she could retain some offensive strength on the Continent a compromise peace would be unavoidable, not just out of compliance with the King's Hanoverian susceptibilities but out of a realization of British interests in Europe. In face of disappointments even Pitt began to doubt that the European sphere could meet the demands his strategy put on it. Another request for reinforcements was refused with some asperity and in September Pitt declared to Newcastle that 'without a battle [i.e. a decisive encounter not just a holding action] I will not be for the continuance of the measures in Germany another year'.[96]

In an attempt to give relief in Germany, in September the idea of a diversionary raid on the French coast was revived. Against Newcastle's inclination, Belle-Île in the northern Bay of Biscay was decided on as the objective and the aim was to conquer it as a bargaining counter in peace negotiations and as a deterrent to Spain. Planning proceeded, albeit uncertainly in view of the lateness of the season and the lukewarmness of officers and other ministers. Not until late November, after the death of the King had caused another disruption, was the expedition finally postponed. The threat of action had some diversionary effect, but too late to help Ferdinand much. To some extent, like earlier raids, it also served a propaganda function at home, especially in the City, but that was where propaganda was least needed.[97]

[95] Walpole, *Geo. II*, ii, pp. 443–51 (quotation p. 451); Corbett, ii, p. 104.

[96] Newcastle to Hardwicke, 13 Sept. 1760, quoted Corbett, ii, p. 95.

[97] Corbett, ii, pp. 95–103; Walpole to Mann, 5 Oct. 1760, *Walpole's Corr.* xxi, p. 438; Birch to Royston, 18 Oct. 1760, Add. MSS 35399, f. 184.

The setbacks on the Continent, in marked contrast to successes elsewhere, sharpened criticism of the cost and burden of the German war. The note of concern behind the euphoria in the parliamentary session found its way even into the *London Evening Post* by mid-1760. The *Westminister Journal* was 'forming itself into a direct opposition to Mr Secretary Pitt', attacking him for inconsistency over Continental policy.[98] As criticism grew, in the summer and autumn of 1760 the *Monitor* returned to defence of the Continental war. In doing so it acknowledged the force of the criticism. This war was indeed 'the most chargable and extensive, that we have ever been engaged in'. There was much room for contrast between the measures of 1760 and those of previous years, rightly praised for their frugality and proper understanding of British interests on the Continent. The present state of Britain rightly attracted the attention of 'every friend to his country'. Nevertheless this situation was the necessary and logical consequence of pursuing the aim of the war, the reduction of French power. First, French trade and navigation had been destroyed. Now her influence on the Continent had to be restricted. If it were not, she would be able to obstruct British trade and eventually turn all her strength against Britain, so that not even America would be secure. Thus, the *Monitor* concluded, 'a measure, which at the beginning of the war was bad, is now, by becoming necessary, just and good'. Throughout, the Ministry's measures had been consistent and harmonious, complementary to each other in destroying French power. The war had been conducted 'on a better plan and with greater vigour, than any this nation has entered into of late years'. Pitt did not deserve the fickle treatment of public opinion which had swung from showering gold boxes and toasts to ungrateful attacks.[99]

So Pitt's propagandists showed themselves fully aware of the crucial importance of the European war to British interests as Pitt saw them. The *Monitor*'s defence was reiterated in answer to *A Letter to the MONITOR, by an Assembly of Brethren called QUAKERS*. This strange document recapitulated traditional suspicions of Continent-

---

[98] e.g. *LEP*, 5–7 Aug. 1760 (a long article copied from the *Grand Magazine* for July); Birch to Royston, 23 Aug. 1760, Add. MSS 35399, f. 146 (quotation). The *Westminster Journal* had been showing doubts about Pitt since Jan. See *UC*, 29 Dec. 1759–5 Jan. 1760, 26 Jan.–2 Feb., 5–7, 16–23 Feb. 1760.

[99] *Mon.* 257, 21 June (second and third quotations), 274, 18 Oct. 1760 (other quotations).

al involvement and waxed sarcastic at the *Monitor's* betrayal of patriot principles. The *Letter* also argued with considerable detail, which could have been embarrassing to Pitt, that in the campaigns of 1759 and 1760 British efforts had been diverted from the naval and colonial war and the conquest of Canada by German measures.[100] The *Monitor's* developing defence did little to abate the growing debate over the cost and burden of Continental connections, but at least it brought a warm response in the City.[101]

There was little to suggest yet that Pitt's political strength was affected by this debate. Despite the rubs and annoyances that Pitt's uncertain temper and devious political tactics caused, Newcastle and Hardwicke were still anxious to appease him, as the parliamentary session had shown. Such strength depended, however, on Pitt's popularity. His position had still not been buttressed by any more traditional supports. The breach with Legge, first opened during the Coalition negotiations in 1757 and widened since, most obviously by differences over taxes, was now complete and irrevocable. Relations with Leicester House had steadily worsened. Over the Prince's desire to do something in the invasion crisis of 1759 Pitt's attitude was found unacceptable.[102] The Sackville affair strained relations further and the Prince and Bute were again affronted that Temple resigned without consulting Leicester House. An attempted reconciliation in April 1760 came to nothing. The Prince was now utterly convinced that Pitt was 'the most ungrateful . . . most dishonorable of men' and hoped that England would soon see that 'her popular man is a true snake in the grass'.[103] While the old King lived, the breach weakened Leicester House rather than Pitt. But the King could not live much longer.[104]

Pitt's popularity had certainly been immeasurably widened by victory in war. Yet, in the general sense of the good opinion of the political nation, popularity was intangible and could be ephemeral.

---

[100] *Mon.* 268–9, 6–13 Sept. 1760; *GM*, xxx, Aug. 1760, pp. 274–7, prints the letter. According to *Mon.* it was first published in the *Edinburgh Evening Courant* of 18 Aug., but it also appeared in *LC*, 7–9 Aug. 1760, with *Mon.* 275, 21 June, which prompted it.

[101] See above pp. 151–2.   [102] McKelvey, pp. 95–102.

[103] See above pp. 148–9; Prince of Wales to Bute, *c.* 16 Nov. 1759, 4 May, ?5 Oct. 1760, *Letters from George III to Lord Bute*, pp. 34, 45 (first quotation), 47 (second quotation); Namier, *England*, pp. 104–9.

[104] McKelvey, p. 121.

The undercurrents of opinion in 1759–60 had shown some of the potential dangers. The war was increasingly expensive, but it would be difficult to end by a peace which would satisfy public opinion. When peace came, much would still be expected of a patriot minister. The *Letter Addressed To Two Great Men* had emphasized the constitutional reforms peace would make possible. Drawing deftly, if ironically, the patriot picture of Pitt's career, and reminding him of his 'repeated Promises, and Declarations', the *Letter* adjured him 'not to Disappoint the Confidence the Public places in your future Endeavours to prop the sinking Constitution'. Many hoped for a new order from the national hero.[105] If these undercurrents of potential dissatisfaction visible in 1759–60 should rise in a tide that could wear away the wider superstructures of general popularity, would the piles, the tangible supports of popularity in the eighteenth-century sense, remain firm?

One, the Tories, had already been weakened by these very currents. In the other, the City, there were some signs of them. Complaints against the cost of the German war continued to be heard there, even among City Tories. Sir John Philipps's influence had always been strong with them and now it was increasingly moving in a different direction from Beckford's.[106] Further tensions in Tory circles were manifested in an obscure but strenuous and lengthy attempt to prevent the election of Alderman Blakiston, now a firm ally of Beckford, as Lord Mayor in 1760. This attempt appears to have emanated from some Tories warmly inclined to Sir John Philipps and to have been connived at by Newcastle. It was especially important because of the imminence of a general election in which Sir John Barnard would no longer be a candidate and was linked with election plans. Philipps's Tory friends wanted him as a candidate.[107]

Despite such undercurrents, the City was stouter than ever for

[105] *A Letter Addressed To Two Great Men*, pp. 47–9, 50 (quotations); cf. Collyer, p. 252. Even *Mon.* had not forgotten its constitutional programme; see e.g. 252, 17 Mar. 1760, cf. *LEP*, 16–19 Feb. 1760.

[106] Gordon to Newcastle, 26 June, 12 Sept. 1760, Add. MSS 32907, ff. 384–5, 32911, ff. 257–8; Calcraft to Harvey, 29 July 1760, Add. MSS 17495, f. 85. On Sir John Philipps's influence see Gordon to Newcastle, 7 July 1758, f. 197, 12, 15 July 1759, Add. MSS 32881, f. 197, 32893, ff. 13–14, 64.

[107] Anon. to William Guthrie, 5 June, anon. to Newcastle, [8 June], 25 Sept., West to Newcastle, 29 Sept. 1760, Add. MSS 32906, f. 488, 32907, f. 110, 32912, ff. 96, 231; Birch to Royston, 9 Aug., 27 Sept. 1760, Add. MSS 35399, ff. 140, 166.

Pitt and his connections there remained strong. His relations with James Hodges, the Town Clerk, were developing. The City Addresses on the Prince of Wale's majority in 1759 were concerted by Hodges with Pitt to be acceptable to him, and Hodges was knighted for his efforts. Pitt took Hodges's advice that some attention should be paid to the popular Lord Mayor, Sir Richard Glyn, who duly received a baronetcy during 1759.[108] But Beckford and the *Monitor* were still Pitt's main allies in the City. The *Monitor*'s unwavering support for him was important in moderating Tory doubts. At the same time as John Gordon told Newcastle of tensions among the City Tories he also referred to 'the faction's' desire to have Beckford 'a continual member' of Parliament. Beckford's activity was now extending beyond the *Monitor*. In 1759 he took a leading part in the opening of a subscription list in the City to encourage enlistment in the Army, a move which originated with the Half Moon Club as a gesture of support for Pitt. Beckford's subscription of £105, one of the largest, attracted some notice.[109] In 1760 Beckford helped to defeat the opposition to the election of Blakiston. In the earlier annual election of sheriffs which was part of the struggle, Beardmore, one of the authors of the *Monitor*, was a leading agitator for the successful candidate.

One issue in early 1760 showed very clearly Beckford's growing influence in the City and, like the sugar tax of the year before, demonstrated the value Pitt placed on Beckford's support. Late in 1759 the question of whether the prohibition on the distilling of gin from grain should be continued came under consideration by Treasury officials and the House of Commons and was much discussed in the press. The prohibition had been introduced in 1757, largely to alleviate the shortage of grain. It had, of course, been to the advantage of other distillers, particularly the distillers of rum from colonial molasses. When proposals to replace the prohibition by a large additional duty on all spirituous liquors, with incentives

[108] Hodges to Pitt, 14 Mar., 2, 14 June, 12, 30 Oct. 1759, PRO 30/8/40, ff. 141, 139, 137, 135, 134; Gordon to Newcastle, 17 Aug. 1759, Newcastle's memoranda for the King, 19 Aug., 5 Sept. 1759, Add. MSS 32894, ff. 268, 296, 32895, f. 179; Jour. Common Council, 62, f. 56 (resolution of thanks to Glyn, 4 Dec. 1759). On Glyn, see above pp. 55–6 fn. 91.

[109] Jour. Common Council, 62, ff. 32–4, 35, 113–16; Birch to Royston, 18 Aug. 1759, Add. MSS 35399, ff. 80–1; Beckford to Pitt, 23 Aug. 1759, PRO 30/8/19, f. 50; Gordon to Newcastle, 12 Sept. 1760 (quotation), Add. MSS 32911, f. 258.

for the export of corn spirits, were introduced into the Commons early in 1760, these other distillers found themselves threatened with a serious disadvantage.[110]

Beckford naturally sprang to the defence of the West Indian interest. He took a leading part in opposition to the changes at all stages in the House.[111] In the City a petition to the House of Commons against the opening of the distillery was eventually agreed to on 13 March, after a first attempt had failed. The eventual success is probably a measure less of the strength of the colonial and slave trade interests affected than of Beckford's growing influence on Common Council, where the overseas trading oligarchy was not predominant. A separate petition from City merchants was circulating. Beckford's influence was not strong enough, however, to carry a spur-of-the-moment motion, much later in the Common Council meeting, for a similar petition to the Lords.[112] The *Monitor* took up the issue earlier and much more fully than it did the sugar tax the year before, and was preoccupied by it at the expense of other issues of much wider appeal from December 1759 to April 1760. That Beckford felt able to use the *Monitor* on a matter of narrow self-interest not vital to the City as a whole, or even to the popular opinion to which it had been so sensitive earlier, seems also to reflect a confidence about the strength of his influence.[113]

Beckford also sought and won Pitt's support. From February onwards Pitt backed Beckford's objections fully, both publicly and in ministerial discussion, in opposition not only to Newcastle but to his closest colleagues, particularly George Grenville. Pitt pressed his opposition with little regard for the difficulties of war finance. On a matter which, like the sugar tax, saw a conflict between landed and

[110] e.g. J. Page to Newcastle, 30 Nov. 1759, John Ramsay to Kinnoull, 30 Nov. 1759, Newcastle to Page, 27 Dec. 1759, Add. MSS 32899, ff. 211–12, 213–14, 32900, f. 358; *Commons' Journal*, xxviii, pp, 632, 666, 673, 676, 689, 704, 708, 718, 723–4, 740, 746; *GM*, xxix, supplement 1759, pp. 630–1.

[111] *Common's Journal*, xxviii, pp. 761, 770, 773, 777, 786, 817, 821–2, 829; West's accounts, 24, 25 Mar. 1760, Add. MSS 32903, f. 497, 32904, f. 26; Beckford to Pitt, 22 Mar. 1760, PRO 30/8/19, f. 61.

[112] Jour. Common Council, 62, ff. 95–6, 97; *PA*, 10, 31 Mar. 1760; Watkins to Newcastle, 17 Mar., Gordon to Newcastle, 18 Mar. 1760, Add. MSS 32903, ff. 338, 365. On the composition of Common Council see above, pp. 8–9.

[113] The issue did attract much discussion in the press, rivalling the question of peace in space devoted to it. *LEP* followed *Mon.* in opposing the reopening of corn distilling.

commercial interests, he showed no concern about possible offence to other Tory allies. Yet he was courting them in this very session on other issues. Pitt's support for Beckford was hampered only by illness, not by any discretion.[114]

Beckford lost the fight and the measure was passed without major modification. But in the course of the struggle he had demonstrated his influence in the City and his connection with Pitt. Whether either was in this case well directed for Pitt's larger political ends is questionable. Certainly Beckford and the *Monitor* could bring Pitt rich dividends in the City as its response later in 1760 showed. Pitt could hardly be sure, however, that they would be solid enough support for his essential popularity should circumstances change.

[114] Beckford to Pitt, [n.d.], 19, 26 Feb., 22 Mar. 1760, PRO 30/8/19, ff. 85, 57, 59, 61; Newcastle to Hardwicke, 4 Mar., Hardwicke to Newcastle, 5 Mar., Watkins to Newcastle, 17 Mar. 1760, Add. MSS 32903, ff. 82, 100, 338.

VI

The New Reign 1760–1761

Suddenly, on 25 October 1760 George II died, and the relative stability of the political world since 1757 was threatened. On the surface there were few changes. Urged by Hardwicke, Newcastle briefly considered resignation, but most of his friends, including his contacts in the City, easily persuaded him to stay.[1] Like the old King, the young George III and his adviser, the Earl of Bute, accepted, albeit reluctantly, that there was no immediate alternative to the Coalition. They realized that the war which had brought such spectacular success could not be ended precipitately. The tutoring of the City Address to this effect was hardly necessary.[2] Room was found for Bute, first as Groom of the Stole with a place in the Cabinet and then, in March 1761, as Secretary of State, without displacing the leading Ministers. Walpole could write of all being settled again in the 'old channel'.[3]

Soon, however, Walpole was expecting difficulties. Beneath the surface the new situation created all sorts of new strains for the old Ministers.[4] It meant a marked change for Pitt. Until now, he had exploited Newcastle's devotion to the burdens of office and unwillingness to precipitate a separation and had used Newcastle's influence with the King and large majority in the House of Commons to secure his own control of policy. At the same time he

---

[1] Hugh Valence Jones to the Duchess of Newcastle, 28 Oct. 1760, Yorke, *Hardwicke*, iii, p. 307; Watkins to Newcastle, 31 Oct. 1760, Add. MSS 32913, f. 497.

[2] Jour. Common Council, 62, f. 159, 28 Oct. 1760.

[3] Walpole to Mann, 1, 14 Nov. 1760, *Walpole's Corr.* xxi, pp. 448, 451; cf. Holdernesse to Mitchell, 28 Nov. 1760, *Mems. Mitchell,* ii, p. 210.

[4] Walpole to Mann, 2 Jan. 1761, *Walpole's Corr.* xxi, p. 465; see Browning, pp. 274–5, 278 for Newcastle's difficulties.

had often turned Newcastle's dominance with King and Commons into a skilful disguise of his own responsibility for policies that would damage his popularity. Success in the war and his own increasing standing with the King made him, towards the end of the old reign, more open about the real situation.[5] But controversy about the German war still made some subterfuge desirable. Now he was offered again, on the very day of the King's accession, a renewed alliance with Bute.[6] This union of favourite with popular war Minister could well have been the best recipe for stability in the new reign. Nevertheless, it was still quite unacceptable to Pitt.

For one thing, alliance with Bute would not guarantee Pitt that sole control of policy he had enjoyed through Newcastle. The events of the day dramatically illustrated that. The King's first speech to the Privy Council had referred to this 'bloody and expensive' war and the need for an 'honourable and lasting peace'. Only with great difficulty did Pitt secure a change in the printed version to 'an expensive but just and necessary war' and an 'honourable peace, in concert with our allies'.[7] Further, whatever the political advantages, Pitt was not prepared to modify his view of the proper conduct of the war to suit a political ally. He would 'act as an independent minister or not at all'.[8] As Symmer acutely observed, 'the C[ouncillo]r whose Power is founded in Popularity, and whose Passion is to act without Controll, will not easily descend from the Heighth to which his Achievements have raised him, and enter into Concert with others in relation to measures which he has hitherto had all the Glory of'.[9] Finally, alliance with Bute would not offer Pitt that disguise of unpopular moves which alliance with Newcastle had given. Bute might control the King, but by no stretch of the imagination could he be represented as directing the House of Commons, as having pushed Pitt into Continental war or as being in other ways responsible for the increasing war burden. Neither the old alliance nor the newly proffered one could now adequately serve Pitt's purpose.

[5] Conversation Viry and Newcastle, 8 Aug. 1760, quoted Namier, *England*, p. 108.

[6] Brooke, p. 76.

[7] Newcastle to Hardwicke, 26 Oct. 1760, Yorke, *Hardwicke*, iii, pp. 304–5; Walpole, *Geo. III*, i, p. 8.

[8] Quoted Brooke, p. 76; cf. Pitt's remark, Apr. 1760, quoted Namier, *England* p. 106, 'I would never have been Minister to act in collusion with any P[rince] and M[inister]', and later remarks quoted Williams, ii, pp. 65–6.

[9] Symmer to Mitchell, 16 Jan. 1761, Add. MSS 6839, ff. 205–6.

Pitt's awareness of the challenge to his command of the situation was shown in his continuing suspicion of Bute. Bute's appointment as Secretary of State in March was presented to Pitt as a virtual *fait accompli*. Beckford and Temple might ostentatiously express satisfaction with the appointment but there can be no doubt that it increased Pitt's uneasiness. Walpole certainly saw it as a direct challenge to his control of policy.[10] For a while, his awareness of the challenge from Bute made him more co-operative towards his ministerial colleagues. This was shown quite remarkably over the new duty of three shillings a barrel on strong beer and ale, made necessary by the ever-increasing demands of the war. The duty aroused hostility in the City and elsewhere, at first reflected in the *Monitor*. Pitt must have been aware of the likelihood of such hostility. Yet, although George Grenville intended to oppose the duty in the Commons, Pitt made a point of supporting it and even eulogized the Treasury. (The *Monitor* dutifully moderated its views).[11] Pitt's amiability did not last long, however, especially after Newcastle's part in the appointment of Bute as Secretary.

Even worse for Pitt than the challenge of Bute, his patriot beacon was in danger of being outshone by that of a patriot king. The accession of the young King, born and educated in England and 'glorying in the name of Britain', was enthusiastically greeted by the public papers and closer political observers alike.[12] Some outspoken criticism of Bute and the Princess Dowager in publicly displayed handbills, echoed by theatre crowds, proved as yet only flashes in the pan, although there were a few further ominous notes after Bute became Secretary of State in March.[13] To the King, the patriot

[10] Hardwicke to Newcastle, 29 Oct. 1760, Yorke, *Hardwicke*, iii, p. 308; cf. Newcastle to Hardwicke, 20 Jan., Hardwicke to Newcastle, 20 Jan., memorandum (Viry), 21 Mar. 1761, Add. MSS 32917, ff. 435, 429, 32920, f. 381; Devonshire's diary, 17, 24 Nov. 1760, quoted *Letters from George III to Lord Bute*, p. 49; Walpole to Mann, 17 Mar. 1761, *Walpole's Corr.* xxi, pp. 487–8; Namier, *England*, pp. 163–7; Williams, ii, pp. 65–6.

[11] Newcastle to Hardwicke, Hardwicke to Newcastle, 17 Dec., Newcastle to Devonshire, 19 Dec. 1760, Thomas Frances to Newcastle, 14 Feb. 1761, Add. MSS 32916, ff. 148, 150, 208, 32918, f. 517; *Dodington*, p. 417, 2 [Feb. 1761]; *Mon.* 285, 3 Jan., 290, [7] Feb. 1761.

[12] e.g. *Mon.* 276–8, 25 Oct.–8 Nov. 1760, 297, 28 Mar., 299, 11 Apr. 1761; *LM*, xxix, 1760, preface to collected edn.; Lyttelton to Mrs Montagu, 31 Oct. 1760, *Elizabeth Montagu*, ii, p. 212.

[13] Walpole to Montagu, 24 Nov. 1760, *The Letters of Horace Walpole*, v. p. 4; Lady Frances Williams to Mrs Montagu, 19 Nov. 1760, *Elizabeth Montagu*, ii, p. 216; *LM*, xxx, Mar. 1761, pp. [117–18], May, pp. 259–61 (also in *OWC*, 9–16 May 1761); *Mon.* 280–3, 25 Nov.–20 Dec. 1760; 295, 14 Mar., 298, 4 Apr. 1761.

precepts that had for so long echoed emptily around Leicester House were no empty platitudes; they had been an integral part of his education.[14] Within a few days of his accession he issued a Proclamation against vice. Economies were introduced in the Household and the use of Treasury money in the election campaign was forbidden. More substantially, the King was truly devoted to the patriot ideal of uniting all parties. Soon Tories from the Cocoa Tree coffee house, who had not been to Court for more than a generation, were flocking to kiss hands. Tories were made peers and appointed to the Household. Some were said to be 'partisans' of Pitt, their much-noticed appointments signs of a union between Pitt and Bute. However, the appointments were not made on Pitt's initiative or even in consultation with him.[15]

Moreover, Leicester House was known never to have abandoned its hostility to Continental connections as Pitt had done. It was also known that the King and Bute were not in favour of pushing on the war at all costs. They had long felt that it would hinder an auspicious beginning to the new reign.[16] They would have to feel their way carefully towards any change in policy but if the criticism of the war should continue to mount they could well step out to lead it. Egmont thought he could detect uneasiness about this possibility right from the beginning among Pitt and his associates.[17] In one way or another, Pitt's platform was being taken from under his feet and his erstwhile allies subverted. Not only the Tories but others, for example Richard Glover who had been an important link with popular City opinion in 1756–7, found the patriot King a more promising prospect than the patriot Minister.[18]

A further pamphlet from John Douglas in March 1761 soon encouraged such people to rejoice in 'the patriotism and virtue which now adds fresh lustre to majesty'. In his *Letter Addressed To*

[14] Brooke, pp. 56–8; McKelvey, pp. 85–7.

[15] Egmont's account [of events 25 Oct.–3 Dec. 1760], 'Leicester House Politics, 1750–1760, from the papers of John, Second Earl of Egmont', ed. A. N. Newman, *Camden Miscellany,* xxiii, fourth ser., vii, p. 226, 16 Nov. 1760; Mrs Montagu to Montagu, 20 Nov. 1760, *Elizabeth Montagu,* ii, p. 217; Lady Anne Egerton to Bentinck, 5 Dec. 1760, Eg. 1719, f. 169; Walpole to Montagu, 11 Dec. 1760, *The Letters of Horace Walpole,* v, p. 10; Walpole to Mann, 2 Jan. 1761, *Walpole's Corr.* xxi, p. 465 and fn.; Walpole, *Geo. III,* i, pp. 12, 13, 18, 19, 22–3.

[16] e.g. Prince of Wales to Bute, *c.*2 July 1758, *Letters from George III to Lord Bute,* p. 11.

[17] Egmont's account, 6 Nov. 1760, ed. Newman, p. 224.

[18] *Dodington,* p. 406, 21 [Dec], Dodington to Bute, 22 Dec. 1760

Two Great Men, Douglas had expatiated at some length on the need for domestic reforms after the conclusion of peace. Now, in *Seasonable Hints From An Honest Man*, he dwelt on the grounds for hope from the new King, despite his accession in the midst of a costly war and the claims of 'confederacies' and 'connections' of ministers and placemen. The new reign could bring an end to corruption and undue influence over Parliament. When peace came, there could be relief from the burden of the National Debt and proper concern for economy in government. Already, Douglas pointed out, the King had shown his determination to abolish party distinctions despite the indignation of those who had monopolized office, and had ordered public officers not to meddle in elections.[19] Scarcely-concealed gibes at both Pitt and Newcastle emphasized the ironic note behind the expressed pleasure that the old Ministers had been continued in office to use their great abilities in extricating the nation from its difficulties. The pamphlet illustrates particularly well how Pitt's defences were undermined. No one, said Douglas, could seek to divert blame for the great cost of the war on to the new King, nor could any minister in power in the last reign find a means to inflame the people against measures begun then, such as the Continental war.[20]

Although widely regarded as a Court manifesto, this pamphlet created nothing like the stir of the *Letter Addressed To Two Great Men*.[21] Nevertheless, reactions to it clearly demonstrate the appeal, especially to Tories, of its criticisms of ministerial despotism so obviously directed against the Old Corps of the Whigs, and its hopes of the new King. The *Critical Review* responded sympathetically, especially to the criticisms. The whiggishly inclined *Monthly Review* was suspicious of the motives for the attack on ministerial juntos and sensitive to the implied criticism of the present Ministers, although

[19] See above p. 173. [John Douglas], *Seasonable Hints From An Honest Man On the Present Important Crisis Of A New Reign And A New Parliament*, London, 1761, esp. pp. 18–28, 38, 43–4, 50–1 (quotation), 52–60. On the dangers of 'ministerial despotism' see also [Owen Ruffhead], *Reasons Why The Approaching Treaty of Peace Should Be Debated in Parliament*, London, 1760, *Ministerial Usurpation Displayed*, London, 1760, *Ministerial Influence Unconstitutional: or the Mischiefs of Public Venality*, *CR*, xi, Mar. 1761, p. 253, *MR*, xxii, Apr. 1761, pp. 272–3.

[20] *Seasonable Hints*, pp. 4, 6–7, 35–6, 16–17.

[21] Walpole, *Geo. III*, i, p. 42; Brewer, *Party Ideology*, p. 146. Brewer, p. 176, says it sold 2,000 in its first edn. but it aroused little response in the newspapers and no answering pamphlets. *LC*, 17–19, 24–6 Mar. 1761 gave two extracts with approving comment.

it concurred in the need for reforms. The *London Magazine* chose to extract those parts of the pamphlet urging reform. Most interesting of all was the reaction of the *Monitor*. It had already expressed high hopes of the new King and had begun to advise its readers over the choice of a new independent parliament. Now it took up with unabashed plagiarism the 'late writer's' urgings against ministerial despotism and insistence on the pleasing prospects of the new reign. However it departed from its model enough to reject any complaints against the measures of the present Administration.[22]

Pitt's support was much more urgently threatened by an earlier and quite independent pamphlet. The accession of the new King almost coincided with the publication, in November 1760, of Israel Mauduit's famous *Considerations On The Present German War*. This pamphlet by a hitherto virtually unknown author powerfully expounded the arguments against Britain's current involvement in Germany which, Mauduit maintained, served no British interest nor was necessary to fulfil any obligation. It was a diversion of British efforts, not of the French as was usually maintained. It had involved Britain in the unequal Prussian alliance under which she paid subsidies—dubbed tributes—and received nothing in return. Instead, in true traditional style Mauduit urged that the war should be prosecuted vigorously at sea and in the colonies (or if it must be fought by land, by direct attacks on the heart or flanks of France). Such a strategy would disable the French Navy for ever and so lay the basis for a secure peace which would enable Britain thereafter to be indifferent to all Continental questions.[23]

There was little new here. Rather Mauduit gave new cogency to well-established arguments, in a cool utilitarian tone remarkably free from the ideological prepossession usual in attacks on the Prussian alliance or the connection with Hanover. The pamphlet was not, however, without political point. It waxed bitter on the forgotten assurances that no British troops would be sent to Germany, and called on those who, it said, would disavow German

---

[22] *CR*, xi, Mar. 1761, pp. 233–7; *MR*, xxii, Mar. 1761, pp. 192–8; *LM*, xxx, Mar. 1761, pp. 115–16; *Mon.* 298–9, 4–11 Apr. 1761.

[23] [Israel Mauduit], *Considerations On The Present German War*, London, 1760, esp. pp. 38–42, 46–50, 57, 75–6, 115–27. Israel Mauduit (1708–87) was a dissenting minister turned woollen draper in the City of London, who had already written on the Minorca crisis and was later to interest himself in American affairs. In 1763 he was given a place in the Customs in Southampton.

measures when they had ruined the country, to disavow them now, fight the war in a practical way, save themselves and the public and so reach a greater popularity.[24]

There was unfounded speculation that the pamphlet had the support of men in high office. Much to his disgust the author was soon known.[25] By all accounts his work had an impact greater than that of any other piece of publicity of the war years. The *Critical Review*, in a survey of opposition papers in 1763, remarked that 'Mr Pitt, during his administration, can scarcely be said to have experienced an attack from the press, till the *Considerations of the German War* appeared'. It went through five editions in three months, with a total printing of 5,750, substantially greater than that of other influential pamphlets of the decade. With some reason the *Gentleman's Magazine* called it a 'very popular' pamphlet. Sir Horace Mann deplored its influence abroad.[26] It certainly sparked off an immediate and considerable literary controversy.[27] A spate of pamphlets appeared; the *Gentleman's Magazine* and particularly the *London Magazine* carried extracts from contributions to the debate every month from November to March. Most newspapers, especially the *London Chronicle*, also gave it extraordinary attention, both noticing pamphlets and making their own comment.

So far as a general reaction can be assessed from these pamphlets and reviews of them, it seems to have been one of some perplexity. Contrary to the impression usually given, even by contemporaries,[28] support for Mauduit was by no means as clear-cut as the wide circulation of his work might suggest. Its popularity came from very effective writing rather than the acceptability of its argument. The *Critical Review*, commenting on one of the answers, mentioned the

[24] Ibid., pp. 44–5, 51.

[25] Symmer to Mitchell, 3, 27 Feb. 1761, Add. MSS 6839, ff. 210, 212; Lady Anne Egerton to Bentinck, 25 Nov. 1760, Eg. 1719, f. 158; [Israel Mauduit], *Occasional Thoughts On The Present German War. By the Author of the Considerations on the same Subject*, London, 1761, p.v. Symmer's suggestion, followed by Walpole (*Geo. III*, i, p. 25) and the *DNB*, that Hardwicke wrote or countenanced the pamphlet, is not convincing. (Cf. Pares, 'American versus Continental Warfare, 1739–63', p. 462, fn. 2).

[26] *CR*, xvi, Oct. 1763, p. 280 (reviewing collected edn. of the *North Briton*); Brewer, *Party Ideology*, p. 146 (cf. total printing of 3,250 for Burke's *Thoughts on the Cause of the Present Discontents*); *GM*, xxx, Nov. 1760, table of contents; Mann to Walpole, 10 Jan. 1761, *Walpole's Corr.* xxi, p. 469.

[27] Summarized in *AR*, iii, 1760, pp. 51–5.

[28] Walpole, *Geo. III*, i, p. 25; Corbett, ii, p. 144.

storm raised *against* the *Considerations*, yet the answer itself spoke of the total change of opinion wrought *by* Mauduit. The *Monthly Review* noted the violent swings of opinion on the German war, commenting that the public was greatly divided over it.[29] Neither of the Reviews themselves showed the definite reaction their earlier views would suggest. The *Critical* did show rather more hostility to the German war, while the *Monthly* responded sharply to criticisms of Pitt. But both praised the *Considerations*, summarized its argument sympathetically, and then assessed pamphlets on both sides with detachment. Of the newspapers, the *Gazetteer* was studiously impartial. The contributions to the sustained debate in the *London Chronicle* were often strongly partisan, but on both sides. In numbers if not in weight of argument the balance was probably against Mauduit. The *London Evening Post* gave the debate little attention, as on earlier occasions when it had been embarrassed. Although shaken, it continued to defend the Continental war.[30]

The pamphlet answers provoked by Mauduit were quite unequal to their target. At worst, they either flatly contradicted him or argued absurdly;[31] at best, they were mere point-by-point refutations, larded with substantial quotation of the *Considerations* and lacking in overall coherence.[32] The better ones, however, did make something of the chief loophole in the argument of the *Considerations*, the importance to Britain of European trade, which unchecked French dominance on the Continent could endanger. Such dominance, they pointed out, could also enable France to threaten invasion of Britain. Thus the answers emphasized the unity of the different theatres of the war. Those pamphlets which joined Mauduit in hostility to the German theatre were on the whole equally

[29] *CR*, xi, Jan. 1761, p. 79; *Reasons In Support of the War in Germany*, London, 1761, pp. v–vi. *MR*, xxiii, Dec. 1760, pp. 493, 487.

[30] *MR*, xxiii, Nov. 1760, pp. 379–80, xxiv, Jan. 1761, pp. 165–6, Apr., p. 272; *CR*, x, Nov. 1760, pp. 403–4, Dec., p. 479, xi, Jan. 1761, p. 72, Mar., p. 254; *Gaz*. 29, 30, 31 Dec. 1760 (no copies survive for early 1761); *LC*, e.g. 27–9 Nov., 2–4, 16–18 Dec. 1760, 15–17, 20–2 Jan., 12–14, 14–17, 17–19 Feb., 3–5, 5–7, 7–10, 10–12 Mar. 1761; *LEP*, 13–15, 29–31 Jan., 14–17 Feb. 1761 and see below fn. 48.

[31] e.g. *CR*, xi, Mar. 1761, pp. 253–4, May, p. 411; *MR*, xxiv, June 1761, pp. 438–9.

[32] e.g. *A Full and Candid Answer to a Pamphlet, entitled, Considerations On The Present German War*, London, 1760; [Owen Ruffhead], *The Conduct Of The Ministry Impartially Examined*, London, 1760; *Reasons In Support of the War in Germany*, London, 1761. Birch (to Royston, 11 Sept. 1764, Add. MSS 35400, ff. 168–9), citing Douglas as his authority, associated Pitt with this answer.

unremarkable.[33] Two of them well illustrate the perplexed response. The *Remarks On Two Popular Pamphlets*[34] attacked involvement on the Continent in general and Pitt's changes of attitude over it. But it also violently attacked the *Considerations* for renouncing the ties of honour and obligation which, in the author's view, required Britain to take part in this German war. The second and much more noteworthy, *The Plain Reasoner,* thoroughly disliked the present operations in Germany because of their wasteful expense and inconclusiveness. Yet it thought the Prussian alliance was originally a well-conceived response to the French threat to Hanover. The alliance would have been effective but for the quite unexpected alliance of France with the Empire and Russia which forced Prussia to fight for its own interests rather than those of Britain. This author did recognize the unity of the war and the threat to Britain of French dominance on the Continent. He wanted to see Britain disengaged but was at a loss to suggest convincing ways to meet this threat without being drawn into Continental connections. In general he was puzzled by the inconclusiveness of the war and wanted vigorous action to end it.[35]

In contrast to most earlier exchanges on this topic, in the pamphlet debate provoked by Mauduit the merits of the argument were emphasized more than the political points to be made out of it. Mauduit did make his points against Pitt, and Egmont did so much more in his long-drawn-out *Things As They Are Part the Second.* On the other hand, *The Plain Reasoner,* on the same side of the question, was not unsympathetic to Pitt, while defence of Pitt was not a major concern of the replies to Mauduit. Nevertheless, the debate, in crystallizing the question when public uneasiness was already mounting, could not but be embarrassing to Pitt. The *Considerations* may not have wrought the total conversion which its undeniable impact suggested, but it certainly increased anxiety and made the

[33] *MR*, xxiv, Jan. 1761, pp. 86–7, Apr., pp. 272, 274–5; *CR*, xi, Jan. 1761, p. 77, Mar., p. 254. Even Egmont's *Things as They Are Part The Second,* London, 1761, was much less effective than the first part, a long-drawn-out survey of the causes of the war, bitterly hostile to Prussia and to Pitt.

[34] London, 1760.

[35] *The Plain Reasoner: Or, Further Considerations On The German War,* London, 1761. The author attempted to pass himself off as Mauduit (p. 1) but although the British Library Catalogue, the *DNB* and Halkett and Laing take him at his word, contemporaries were not gulled (*MR*, xxiv, Jan. 1761, p. 87, *CR*, xi, Jan. 1761, pp. 76–7). His arguments certainly do not support the attribution.

task of the Ministry in prosecuting the German war even more difficult.[36]

To enhance the impact of the debate, the prospect in Europe was very grey. In March 1761 the long-discussed British attack on Belle-Île was at last undertaken. Successfully completed by 8 June, it was accompanied by much controversy about its usefulness. But in Germany, although Ferdinand began the campaign with some vigour and success, he faced vastly superior forces. In the end he had to abandon all Hesse to the enemy. Frederick, after the great victory over the Austrians at Torgau on 3 November 1760, was able to do little else against his enemies from all sides. The Austrians and Russians wintered in his dominions. It was clearer than ever that his resources were severely strained and that he was unlikely to be able to hold out much longer.[37] In all, circumstances seemed to be ripening for an initiative by the new Court. Indeed, early in 1761 Bute was being urged by Dodington to put himself at the head of those supporting an immediate withdrawal from the German war and the making of a separate peace; but Bute's cautious assessment of the drift of public opinion prevented any open move.[38]

The debate stimulated by Mauduit had its echoes in Parliament. On 22 December, when Pitt moved the Prussian subsidy for the year, Sir Francis Dashwood, an independent of some standing, briefly but pointedly raised the arguments of the *Considerations*. The subsidy was voted but his arguments were felt to be 'unanswerable'. 'A certain little book, that was found somewhere or other, has made a great many orators in this House', retorted Pitt.[39] In February, £300,000 had to be voted to Hanover for forage expenses. Again it was passed, without a division, but again not without some bitter comment. Among others, Dashwood was now joined in complaint by Beckford and by George Cooke, member for Middlesex, another Tory who had committed himself to Pitt in 1757. There was unfavourable comment in both Lords and Commons, over the £400,000 demanded by Hesse for indemnification under

[36] Symmer to Mitchell, 19 Dec. 1760, 30 Jan. 1761, Add. MSS 6839, ff. 203, 208.

[37] Yorke, *Hardwicke*, iii, pp. 267–8.

[38] *Dodington*, pp. 411, 2 [Jan.,], 413, 9 [Jan.], 414–15, 16 [Jan.], 417, 2[Feb. 1761].

[39] Rigby to Bedford, 22 Dec. 1760, *Corr. Bedford*, ii, p. 426 (Russian is a mistake for Prussian). The context makes it clear that the pamphlet referred to was the *Considerations*, not the answer to it identified in the footnote). Pitt, quoted Williams, ii, p. 68.

the secret articles of its last subsidy treaty (for resisting which Legge at last provoked his own dismissal in March).[40]

Early in the session, when the budget was opened, Pitt declared strongly for the continued prosecution of the war. But he angrily checked Beckford in the debate on the Address in Reply when Beckford proposed even more vigour than before, especially in Germany. It was noted that Pitt spoke only very briefly in support of the Prussian subsidy.[41] In response to the criticism, he now sought to divert blame for the cost of the war, particularly in the sensitive German theatre, on to Newcastle and the Treasury. To Newcastle he made accusations of extravagance, mismanagement and deliberate obstruction of the war. Newcastle and others were trying, he said, to 'blow up the People' against the war. He threatened to declare his opinion and promote inquiries in the Commons. His gout prevented him from attending the Hanoverian forage debate, but he was very anxious to be present for the 'Hessian Affair'.[42] Pitt did not carry out his threat, but Beckford and his other Tory supporters followed his tactics in the House. Beckford's complaints against the expense of the war on these two occasions were directed at Newcastle's supposedly deliberate mismanagement designed to make continued fighting impossible. According to one report, however, Beckford was 'supported very coldly . . . Sir J. Philips not speaking'.[43]

Pitt continued to press both Newcastle and the King, blaming faults in the commissariat for Ferdinand's lack of success and again accusing the Treasury of deliberate obstruction. As a result, a long inquiry into the commissariat was instituted in the Treasury on both the King's and Newcastle's orders.[44] But the point of Pitt's com-

[40] Lady Anne Egerton to Bentinck, 17 Feb. 1761, Eg. 1719, f. 210; Walpole, *Geo. III*, i, pp. 29–31.

[41] Mrs Montagu to Montagu, 22 Nov. 1760, *Elizabeth Montagu*, ii, p. 220; Symmer to Mitchell, 19 Dec. 1760, Add. MSS 6839, ff. 203–4; Walpole, *Geo. III*, i, p. 18; Rigby to Bedford, 22 Dec. 1760, *Corr. Bedford*, ii, p. 426. Browning, p. 277, says Pitt refused to promote the renewal of the subsidy; perhaps he did threaten to refuse, but he certainly did move the subsidy, albeit without warmth.

[42] Memorandum, 12 Feb., Newcastle to Hardwicke, 21 Feb. 1761, Add MSS 32918, f. 467, 32919, f. 176.

[43] Walpole, *Geo. III*, i, pp. 29–31; Charles Yorke to Newcastle, 16 Feb. 1761, Add. MSS 32919, f. 38 (quotation).

[44] Newcastle to Hardwicke, 17 Apr. 1761, Add. MSS 32922, f. 21; Walpole, *Geo III*, i, p. 44; Browning, pp. 277–8.

plaint was political not administrative. He was trying to turn against Newcastle not only the public criticism of the German war but also the growing unpopularity of Ferdinand for supposed malversation of English funds.[45]

Despite this intransigent front, however, even Pitt was not unaffected by changing circumstances, military and political, and the growing outcry of public opinion. Over the last unsuccessful year he had made difficulties over continued reinforcements to Germany. In March 1761, in the negotiations with Bute over his becoming Secretary of State, Pitt declared his willingness to abandon the Continental war if the King wished, although he thought it the right policy.[46] His sincerity was never put to the test because other issues intervened.

Reactions in the City to the rising criticism of the German war gave Pitt yet more cause for concern. The euphoria induced by the economic boom from 1759 was beginning to wear thin. Colonial victories might widen trading opportunities but war also imposed strains such as increased freight and insurance charges, shipping losses and the need to travel in convoy. Trade to Europe was interrupted, especially in the Baltic. More important, the increasing demands of war finance led to a shortage of private credit evident as early as 1759 and affecting over-extended merchants. By 1760 rates of exchange were moving against Britain. They were very low by early 1761, to the detriment of Government remitters and contractors. Even some great merchant financiers were failing.[47]

In such circumstances, the Mauduit debate had major repercussions in the City. The unsuccessful German war, now costing, as Newcastle complained, £340,000 a month without the Prussian subsidy (£670,000 a year),[48] was easiest to blame for such strains. One of Gordon's letters to Newcastle in December spoke of arguments to support a rising wish for peace in a way that clearly reflected Mauduit. He reported that some were saying that 'a great minister had deviated, from the doctrine he commenced with, to become so popular'. Clearest evidence of the strength of the City's

---

[45] *Dodington*, pp. 414–15, 16 [Jan. 1761]; Lady Anne Egerton to Bentinck, 3 Feb. 1761, Eg. 1719, f. 202.

[46] Newcastle to Hardwicke, 9 Apr. 1760, Yorke, *Hardwicke*, iii, p. 244; Newcastle to Devonshire, 13 Mar. 1761, Add. MSS 32920, f. 169.

[47] Ashton, pp. 56, 124, 125; Rogers, 'London Politics', pp. 235, 251.

[48] Browning, p. 276, citing a document of Apr.–May 1761.

immediate reaction to Mauduit comes from the *Monitor*. It took up the King's emphasis on his British origins as an occasion to express the hope that Continental connections would become less influenced by German considerations and more in accord with the Act of Settlement. Even more remarkably, in three papers in January 1761 it opposed the German war with explicit reference to Pitt. A change from the ruinous measures of the past had brought much success, it said. Yet a reversion to them was threatened:

the last year's expence; the particular attention paid to the increase of our land-forces in Germany; the inconsiderable efforts made with our navy, and the more inconsiderable progress made by the vast army in British pay upon the continent, are bad symptoms of a relapse. . . . To proceed further might bring on such a paroxism, as to shake the constitution in such a manner, as never to recover its former strength and firmness.

Already the *Monitor* saw the relapse affecting fortunes of war: 'from the moment Britain altered her resolution not to send a man into Germany, and engrafted the cause of Prussia and of other German friends, upon the stock of the British contest with France in America, the event of the war became visibly uncertain.' France had succeeded in embroiling Britain on the Continent against a major coalition, disuniting the people and making them clamorous for peace. And in peace negotiations concessions would be asked from Britain in return for the restitution of the losses of her allies. Britain should revert to a middle line, the *Monitor* said, practising a 'seasonable desisting' from attachment to the Continent which alone could serve her interests and save her from the misery of her allies.[49]

This marked reversion from the *Monitor*'s defence of the Prussian alliance and German war in 1759–60 to its earlier views did not last beyond these three papers. The paper soon turned to other things, such as the beer tax and the election of 1761. The occasional doubts it continued to express were put more gently, without open criticism of Pitt, and it was brought back to support him by fears of ministerial changes.[50] But the very intensity of the brief reaction, together with the *Monitor*'s avoidance of foreign policy topics which

[49] Gordon to Newcastle, 11 Dec. 1760, Add. MSS 32915, ff. 401–2; *Mon.* 280, 29 Nov. 1760, 286, 10 Jan., 288, 24 Jan. (first quotation), 289, 31 Jan. 1761 (other quotations). Cf. *LEP*, 4–6 Nov. 1760, 24–7 Jan. 1761.

[50] *Mon.* 291, 14 Feb., 297, 28 Mar., 298, 4 Apr., 308, 13 June 1761.

had been its staple, suggests the strength of the anti-war swing in the City. Even the *Monitor* had to take account of it.

There is no doubt that such reactions posed some threat to Pitt's interests in the City but it is difficult to assess how much. Dodington had reports in January that 'Mr Pitt goes down fast in the city' but was not optimistic enough to accept them at face value.[51] Beckford, more strikingly recognized than ever now as Pitt's ally,[52] faced fluctuating fortunes. His growing leadership in City affairs was demonstrated in attempts to reorganize the Militia there at the turn of the year 1760–1. The City Militia, which had been excluded from the provisions of the Act of 1757, was felt to be inefficient and a disgrace to the City. In December 1760 a committee of Common Council was appointed to consider the matter. Beckford and Beardmore were both on it but the lead was taken at first by John Paterson, Hodges's rival for the position of Town Clerk in 1757 and a connection of Mansfield's. On 20 December the committee reported in favour of petitioning the King to grant the commission of lieutenancy for the City Militia to the Lord Mayor, Aldermen, and Common Councilmen. This was a delicate matter. Aldermen were already *ex officio* on the commission, but the Crown had hitherto used its power to appoint from outside the City corporate bodies to offset Tory influence. The committee's suggestion was accepted only after considerable debate, and it was ordered to draw up a petition. Now Newcastle became greatly alarmed, melodramatically seeing the intrusion on the prerogative as parallel to the events of 1642. With Bute's help, he organized a careful attempt to avoid the petition's being presented, or at least to moderate its terms, fearful all the time that Pitt would take the question up in concert with his 'Friends in the City'.[53] But in the end Newcastle's efforts were to no avail. He managed to moderate the aims of some most closely

[51] Paper read by Mr Dodington to Lord Bute, 16 Jan. 1761, quoted John Adolphus, *The History of England, From The Accession To The Decease of King George The Third*, 7 vols., London, 1840–5, i, p. 571.

[52] e.g. *Dodington*, p. 417, 2 [Feb. 1761]; memorandum (Viry), 21 Mar. 1761, Add. MSS 32920, f. 381.

[53] Jour. Common Council, 62, ff. 179–80, 181–2; memorandum, 24 Dec., Newcastle to Hardwicke, 24 Dec., Sir William Baker to Hardwicke, Hardwicke to Newcastle (quotation), Newcastle to Mansfield, 26 Dec. 1760, Dickinson to Mansfield, 19 Jan., Newcastle to Hardwicke, 20 Jan., Hardwicke to Bute, 20 Jan., Hardwicke to Newcastle, 20, 23 Jan. 1761, Add. MSS 32916, ff. 290, 298, 335, 333, 338, 32917, ff. 439, 435, 431, 429, 32918, f. 31; Rogers, 'London Politics', pp. 314–15.

involved. But, despite reports to the contrary, by the latter part of January at the latest Beckford was very much in control of the affair, with the warm support of Lord Mayor Blakiston and the knowledge of Pitt. Beckford was actually in communication with Bute over it. With Pitt's encouragement he took the lead in the Common Council meeting of 11 February when, after some debate, the petition was carried by a large majority of councilmen.[54] The City's petition was never granted, perhaps because of Pitt's resignation in October 1761. A new commission composed like former ones was eventually drawn up.[55] Nevertheless the affair does indicate Beckford's increasing strength in Common Council in 1760–1, in alliance with Hodges now and as Pitt's man. His intervention was regarded as crucial by Hardwicke, Bute, and Newcastle.

Yet Beckford had to face substantial opposition in the City in the general election of March–April 1761. He was challenged at the nomination meeting for neglecting his duty as an alderman. For an hour he faced the groans and hisses of the audience before being able to plead in excuse his duties in the House of Commons and as a Militia officer. Although these criticisms at the Livery meeting do not suggest so, it was as Pitt's friend that he was both opposed and supported. He himself claimed 'the honour to have those for Enemies, who are not well wishers to Mr Pitt'. In fact Richard Glover, at Dodington's instigation, had been stirring up opinion against 'The German War and *The German Minister* Mr Pitt'. With other merchants, he promoted the candidature of Thomas Harley, an American merchant, and opposed Beckford's nomination. Harley, like Beckford, was nominated on the official list and eventually came second in the poll. Beckford, although he solicited all possible support, including that of the Ordnance Office and the Board of Works, came only third, as in 1754. At one stage he was even lower. He had clearly not yet attained anything like the status of Sir John Barnard as a popular leader. Indeed the Livery's distaste for politicians was shown decisively when Sir Robert Ladbroke, who stood as an independent candidate above factions when not nominated on the official list, topped the poll. It was obvious that the liverymen, among whom wealthy financiers and merchants and

[54] Jour. Common Council, 62, ff. 196–7; Mansfield to Harwicke, 31 Jan., 11 Feb., Hardwicke to Newcastle, 1 Feb. 1761, Add. MSS 35596, ff. 238, 241, 32918, f. 177; Hodges to Pitt, 6 Feb. [1761], PRO 30/8/40, f. 132; *PA*, 12, 18 Feb. 1761.
[55] Rogers, 'London Politics', p. 316.

Court patronage had some influence, were not as firm for Pitt as
Common Council. The situation could have been worse had not the
Whigs been divided among themselves and Court influence split
between Bute and Newcastle. There was indeed reason for alarm
when the great war Minister's avowed ally could not rise higher
than third on the poll in the City which had become the bastion of
that Minister's popularity. At least there was some consolation that
Sir Richard Glyn, a supporter of Pitt, rose to win the fourth City seat
on the last day of the poll.[56]

Moves connected with Sir John Philipps provide further indirect
evidence of tension among the popular elements in the City which
must have had political overtones. Despite the rumours of the
previous year, Sir John was not a candidate in the election.
However, in February he and George Cooke, the Tory member of
Parliament who had spoken out against the vote to Hanover for
forage expenses, were granted the freedom of the City for their
services in promoting its business in Parliament. The vote was only
narrowly passed, by thirty-eight to thirty-three. The opposition was
ostensibly on the grounds that no notice of the motion had been
given, and when Sir John initially refused to accept the freedom
because of the opposition, the first vote was confirmed unanimously
in May. However, in view of Philipps's coolness for some time over
the war and Cooke's recent outspokenness, together with criticism of
Beckford for neglecting his City duties, it is hard not see these moves
as connected with opposition to Pitt and Beckford. Indeed Beckford
opposed the freedom at least to the extent of supporting the demand
that notice of such motions should be given.[57]

That Common Council could still be rallied by Beckford to Pitt's
cause was shown in June, in the City Address on the capture of
Belle-Île, which was deliberately intended as a compliment to Pitt
and his policies. Beardmore was on the committee which drew up
the Address. Its lavish praise of the conquest, its hopes of forcing
France to an acceptable peace, but its assurances of continued

[56] *PA*, 20 Feb., 5, 23, 25, 30 Mar., 3 Apr. 1761; *LEP*, 3–5 Mar. 1761; Beckford to Pitt, 5
Mar. 1761, PRO 30/8/19, f. 67; Beaven, i, p. 292 (cf. *LEP*, 28–31 mar. 1761); Newcastle to
Devonshire, 13 Mar., Fludyer to Kinnoull, Kinnoull to Newcastle, 30 Mar., Watkins to
Newcastle, 24 Apr. 1761, Add. MSS 32920, f. 169, 32921, ff. 190, 184, 32922, f. 187;
Rogers, 'London Politics', pp. 248–51, 311–13, 404–6; Beaven, i, p. 280.

[57] See above p. 173; Jour. Common Council, 62, ff. 203–4, 221, 228–9; *PA*, 19 Feb.
1761; Maitland, ii, pp. 34–5.

support for a just and necessary war were all rightly considered to reflect the views of Beckford and Beardmore.[58] Success at Belle-Île was especially welcome as the result of the use of British forces not in Germany but directly against France as both Mauduit and the *Monitor* had recommended.

Reassuring as this might be, divisions in the City were obviously reappearing as the strains of war dimmed the glow of victory. Pitt had good reason to be worried about opposition to Beckford and angry about Glover's efforts to stir up trouble.[59] Not just his general reputation or his Tory allies, but the very heart of his popular interest, its basis in the City, was being threatened. His colleagues, Bute and Newcastle, still assessed his strength and the danger of challenging him primarily in terms of his popularity. They differed in their assessments from one time to another but in retrospect there is much to confirm the conclusion that 'His Credit, and Popularity were much sunk'.[60] In every way then—in control of policy, in relations with his ministerial colleagues and in his popular support —Pitt's political position was made distinctly vulnerable in the new reign.

Although some of the trends making this so were of longer standing, the combination of circumstances which made them dangerous occurred quite suddenly in 1760–1. It is little wonder that the air was thick with rumours that Pitt might resign. At the very beginning of the reign Egmont spoke of the possibility that he might be pushed out, or that he might 'throw himself out' to make the most of the difficulties of concluding a satisfactory peace. Pitt himself contributed to the rumours by hints of resignation in frustration at his impotence.[61] Early in March Walpole reported that some thought his refusal to allow Temple to become Lord Lieutenant of Ireland was due less to his need for Temple's support in the Lords than to his own intention to resign soon. Later in the month, at the

---

[58] Hodges to Pitt, 15 June [1761], PRO 30/8/40, f. 130; Birch to Royston, 27 June 1761, Add. MSS 35399, f. 209; Jour. Common Council, 62, ff. 236–7; *London Gazette*, 16–20 June 1761.

[59] Newcastle to Devonshire, 13 Mar., Hardwicke to Newcastle, 18 Apr. 1761, Add. MSS 32920, f. 169, 32922, ff. 41–2.

[60] Newcastle's accounts of conversations with Bute, 10 Mar. (quotation), 21 Apr. 1761, Add. MSS 32920, ff. 67–8, 32922, f. 110.

[61] Egmont's account, 30 Oct., 6 Nov. 1760, ed. Newman, pp. 220, 224 (quotation); *Dodington*, p. 417, 2 [Feb. 1761]; memorandum 12 Feb. 1761, Add. MSS 32918, f. 468; Williams, ii, pp. 65–6.

time of Bute's appointment as Secretary of State, Walpole again commented that 'everybody expected disgust would soon oblige Mr Pitt to resign.' In discussion with Newcastle in March, Bute professed not to fear any threat of Pitt's reviving his popularity because he knew 'Mr Pitt would never go into Opposition; But, in all Events, would retire with some honourable Provision.' However, Hardwicke, with his customary realism, discounted any talk of a resignation of Pitt or Temple in the storms over the Treasury in April, because now there was no reversionary interest to turn to.[62]

The event so much talked of was precipitated not by difficulties over the German war, but by the major preoccupation of 1761, the negotiations for peace and the growing enmity of Spain which became obvious in the course of them. In 1760, Pitt's attitude, confirmed if not shaped by public opinion, had been a major cause of the breakdown of negotiations. Now, in changed circumstances, renewed negotiations set him a more difficult problem. On the one hand, it was not certain that successful negotiations would redound to his credit and advantage. They would make him much less necessary to the King and Bute and could well result in a marked turn of popularity towards them, leaving him high and dry. On the other hand, Pitt could not be sure now that a confident assertion of a strong line against peace would carry the day, as in 1760, and it was not at all clear whether such a line would still be popular. So the question of peace added to Pitt's difficulties.

Late in 1760, Frederick's desperate situation led him to suggest renewed contacts with France for a separate peace out of which he thought a general peace would grow.[63] The French Minister, Choiseul, also now seemed eager for peace, which France equally appeared to need. Approaches resulted in the exchange of the English and French agents, Stanley and Bussy, in May. A congress of all the belligerents was opened at Augsburg. The crucial exchanges were those between France and Britain. Over the next two

---

[62] Walpole to Mann, 3 Mar., cf. Walpole to Montagu, 13 Mar. 1761, *Walpole's Corr.* xxi, p. 485, ix, pp. 340–1; Walpole, *Geo. III*, i, p. 33; Newcastle's account of a conversation with Bute, 10 Mar. 1761, Add. MSS 32920, f. 67 (cf. his account of a conversation with Pitt, 10 Apr. 1761, Add. MSS 32921, f. 382); Hardwicke to Newcastle, 18 Apr. 1761, Yorke, *Hardwicke,* iii, p. 317.

[63] Newcastle to Harwicke, 3 Dec. 1760, Yorke, *Hardwicke,* iii, pp. 313–14. The best brief outlines of the negotiations are Corbett, ii, pp. 141–2, 148–96, and Williams, ii, pp. 80–102.

months, proposals and counter-proposals went backwards and forwards against a background of continuing British successes. Belle-Île fell in June, in July the news of the fall of Pondicherry and Dominica was received and a heartening victory was won by Ferdinand in Westphalia. By mid-July, broad agreement seemed possible on colonial terms. Britain proposed to retain all Canada, Senegal and Gorée, and some of the neutral West Indian islands but to return Guadeloupe and exchange Belle-Île for Minorca. The negotiations had come to turn partly on how Britain's and France's role in the German war should be ended (Britain refused to abandon Frederick). But the chief issue was the extent of the French exclusion from the North American fisheries. On this, negotiations became more and more deadlocked. Although both sides regarded the fisheries as crucial to naval power because they were a training ground for sailors, by this time they had become more a test of how far each side was prepared to go in pursuit of peace.

The course of the negotiations also revealed differences of opinion among the English Ministers on these basic questions. At one extreme the Duke of Bedford, recently returned from Ireland and invited by the King to attend Cabinet, emerged as the spokesman for the view that it was unwise to humiliate France too far and thus provoke the jealousy of other powers. Newcastle was as usual, and with good cause, concerned over the cost of the war and on some points he and Hardwicke supported Bedford. Bute on the whole took a firmer position; he (and the King) wanted peace, but on the best terms possible, for reasons of popularity if nothing else. Bute's caution about undue concessions, induced by nervousness about public reaction, was very apparent during the negotiations.[64] For much of the time it led him to support Pitt who, as might be expected, took the firmest line of all.

Pitt did not just obstruct, however. Initially, it is true, he seemed reluctant to negotiate.[65] Throughout, even while negotiating, he insisted on going ahead vigorously with plans for further operations, which led to the various British victories punctuating the negotia-

---

[64] e.g. *Dodington,* p. 417, 2[Feb. 1761]; Bute to Bedford, 12 July 1761, *Corr. Bedford,* iii, pp. 29–34; Lord Holland's Memoir [on the Events attending the death of George II And the Accession of George III], *The Life and Letters of Lady Charlotte Lennox 1745–1826,* ed. Countess of Ilchester and Lord Stavordale, 2 vols., London, 1901, i, pp. 51–2; Fox to Calcraft, Sept. 1761, quoted in Williams, ii, p. 85 fn. 1.

[65] Corbett, ii, pp. 142–3.

tions and promised even more success.[66] Certainly Pitt wanted a peace which would secure as many as possible of the advantages Britain had won in the war. But he did not insist on keeping everything. In December 1760 he

laid it down that we must give up considerably, but we must retain a great deal at the same time. He divided his propositions then, either to retain all Canada, Cape Breton and exclude the French from their fishery on Newfoundland, and give up Guadeloupe and Gorée; or retain Guadeloupe and Gorée with the exclusion of the French fishery on Newfoundland, and give up some part of Canada and confine ourselves to limits of the lakes etc.

By April 1761 he had decided on retaining the whole of Canada, Cape Breton, and especially the exclusive rights to the fisheries.[67] It is possible that his attitude hardened further. He may have come to see the chance of destroying French naval power for ever by further conquests, and of laying her 'on her back' rather than just bringing her 'to her knees'.[68] Certainly he was firmly against any concessions to France over the fisheries and characteristically imperious both with his colleagues and the French. Nevertheless, it seems that on balance he would have been glad of a peace if it were possible on what he considered reasonable terms. He had no reason to dissemble to Temple, to whom he declared at a late stage in the negotiations that the 'Duc de Choiseul does me no small injustice in supposing, as he does, that I wish nothing but to continue war, at any rate.'[69]

This tough if not totally unyielding attitude to peace was undoubtedly shaped in large part by Pitt's conception of the national interest and of the purpose of the war. Undoubtedly also, it was shaped partly by political considerations, his wish to assert and test his control of policy in changed circumstances, and concern for his popular reputation. It was no easier for Pitt than for Bute to determine how the peace negotiations would affect his popularity.

---

[66] e.g. Corbett, ii, pp. 143, 154–5.

[67] Newcastle to Hardwicke, 3 Dec. 1760, 17 Apr. 1761, Yorke, *Hardwicke*, iii, pp. 314, 315–16.

[68] Corbett, ii, p. 143; Williams, ii, p. 84 (quotation).

[69] Newcastle to Hardwicke, 1 Aug. 1761, Add. MSS 32926, f. 129; Jenkinson to Grenville, 28 July 1761, Pitt to Temple, 10 [Aug.] 1761, *Grenville Papers*, i, pp. 380, 385–6, Sir George Colebrooke, *Retrospection: [Or Reminiscences Addressed To My Son— Henry Thomas Colebrooke, Esq.]*, 2 pts., London, 1898, 1899, i, pp. 41–2 fn.

The reaction to Mauduit's work suggested that perhaps there was a growing wish for relief from the burdens of a war which seemed to have won quite sufficient successes. Mauduit himself had drawn attention to the mounting cost of the war as a whole, although he said he was opposed only to the German part.[70] In 1754–5 just over £4 million had been voted in supplies for the year. By 1761 the amount was over £19½ million: of this £12 million was raised by borrowing, in comparison with £2 million in 1756. The National Debt had almost doubled.[71] From late 1759 Newcastle's friends in the City had been anxious about the 'immense' debt, the 'frightfull' sums to be raised and expenses 'extended infinitely beyond our capacity'. Their gloom was sometimes belied by ready responses to loans but by mid-1761 serious difficulties in raising money were evident.[72] Tightening financial strains were shown in the drastic fall of Government stock prices in August, when it was suspected that France and Spain had joined in the Family Compact. Exchange rates were still unfavourable. The feelings of the moneyed interest were vividly reflected in the movement of stock prices upwards whenever peace seemed likely.[73] Moreover, by the latter part of 1761 it was obvious that the economic boom had ended. Merchants, manufacturers, tradespeople and their employees were all affected.[74]

However, there is little evidence of a general and urgent desire for peace. The death of George II interrupted any spate of addresses on the fall of Montreal which might, like that from the City,[75] have indicated attitudes to the continuation of the war. But addresses on the accession of the new King poured in from November 1760 well into 1761. They are a less direct test of public opinion because the occasion imposed some compunction about making political points. It is perhaps significant that fewer than half mention the happy circumstances of victory surrounding the accession. Most of these

[70] *Considerations On The Present German War*, pp. 56, 67–71.

[71] *Parl. Hist.* xv, cc. 513, 1006; memorandum, 12 Feb. 1761, Add. MSS 32918, f. 467; Williams, ii, p. 49. The supply figures for 1756–7, 1759–60, 1760–1 were £8,335,320, £12,761,310 and £15,503,563 (*Parl. Hist.* xv, cc. 782,938,966). The National Debt was £72 million in 1755; in 1762 after another £12 million loan, it was £150 million.

[72] Watkins to Newcastle, 19 Nov. 1759, 8 May (quotation), 7 Nov. 1760, 18 Mar, 1761, memorandum for Bute, 15 July, note (Barrington), 21 July 1761, Add. MSS 32898, f. 270, 32905, f. 341, 32914, f. 181, 32920, f. 301, 32925, ff. 86, 231.

[73] Ashton, pp. 124–5; on the Family Compact, see below p. 200; Lord Holland's Memoir, p. 41; Walpole to Mann, 14 May 1761, *Walpole's Corr.* xxi, p. 504.

[74] Ashton, pp. 150–1.   [75] See above pp. 151–2.

just echo the King's own words about an expensive but just and necessary war and hopes of an honourable and lasting peace. But occasionally subtleties of wording reveal more. Certainly there was a natural wish for peace, but there was also virtual unanimity that it should be advantageous and secure, and confidence that Britain could dictate the terms she wanted. The addresses that were anxious for relief from the burdens of war were at least balanced by others promising further cheerful contribution.[76] The nation was certainly desirous of, but not desperate for, peace.

Discussion in the newspapers confirms this. Discussion had hardly slackened since the failure of the negotiations of early 1760 and stipulations about terms remained high. Only the *Westminster Journal* seemed at all eager for peace.[77] By the time negotiations resumed in 1761 there was pretty general concern about the cost of the war and much talk about ways money might be raised. Some were confident that the cost was justified and could be met. Others argued convincingly about the economic and financial strains of war.[78] There was certainly more talk of peace and more now who thought that the aims of the war had been secured and that peace was necessary and not just desirable.[79] To this extent there had been a change of emphasis in discussion. But still the predominant demand was for a strong, advantageous, secure peace and for vigorous prosecution of the war until such a peace was possible.[80] Only on the German war, not on colonial matters, was there a marked division of opinion.

The relatively slight but significant change in the tone of discussion was shared by those City interests to which Pitt particularly looked for support. When the *Monitor* came back to the question from May 1761 onwards, it was much more favourably disposed to the need and desire for peace than it had been a year earlier. Indeed

[76] *London Gazette*, 31 Oct. 1760–28 Feb. 1761.

[77] e.g. *LC*, 5–7 Aug., 30 Aug.–2 Sept. 1760; *LEP*, 2–4 Sept. 1760; *Mon.* 258–9, 28 June–5 July, 261–8, 19 July–6 Sept., 270, 20 Sept., 275, 25 Oct. 1760; *Westminster Journal* in *Lloyd's EP*, 7–9 July, *LC*, 5–7 Aug. 1760.

[78] e.g. *LEP*, 17–19, 19–21 Mar. 1761; *LC*, 5–7 Feb., 21–4 Mar. 1761.

[79] e.g. *GM*, xxx, Dec. 1760, pp. 577–9, xxxi, Jan. 1761, pp. 3–6, 10–12 Feb., p. 71; *LC*, 16–18 Dec. 1760, 5–7, 17–19 Feb. 1761; *OWC*, 11–18 Apr. 1761. *LEP*, 17–19 Mar. 1761, admitted that there had been divisions of opinion over the continuation of the war.

[80] e.g. *Gaz.* 4 Dec. 1760 (none available 1761); *LM*, xxix, Dec. 1760, pp. 619–22; *Lloyd's EP*, 18–20 Feb., 16–18 Mar. 1761, *LC*, 21–4 Feb. 1761; *OWC*, 21–8 Feb., 14–21 Mar., 11–18 Apr. 1761.

it rejected the arguments of those who were still against a peace out of hopes for further victories or from fear that the distressed state of Britain's allies might endanger retention of her conquests. The aims of a just and necessary war had been achieved. The country should be relieved of the burden of war as soon as possible. The *Monitor* no longer emphasized Britain's ability to continue the war, except in absolute necessity. However, it still insisted that the peace must be an advantageous and secure one. It should be negotiated by those with a clear grasp of the nation's interest without too much attention to any clamour for peace, which might have been stirred up by the French. High terms, especially in the colonial field, were still demanded. Meanwhile, the war should be vigorously prosecuted.[81]

Other evidence confirms this as representative of much City opinion. Walpole reported despairingly to Mann in May that the Belle-Île expedition was attracting as much attention as the possibility of peace. This was certainly true in the newspapers. When the City congratulated the King on the fall of Belle-Île, it exulted in the hope that the conquest would force France to accept a prescribed peace while warmly assuring the King of its support in a just and necessary war in the meantime. Again Beckford and Beardmore helped to shape these views, those of Common Council rather than of the mercantile and financial élite. Rigby even thought 'the madness of the times' for holding on to all conquests had spread beyond the City, encouraged by new successes. However, only Bristol and York followed the City with addresses on Belle-Île.[82]

Renewal of negotiations inspired a renewal of the debate over the relative merits of Canada and Guadeloupe as permanent acquisitions. The pamphlets concentrated on this issue, with both numbers and quality on the side of Guadeloupe for the moment.[83] The debate was eagerly followed by the *London Chronicle* especially. The newspapers generally favoured the retention of all North America, including Louisiana, with Guadeloupe too, if possible.[84] The *Monitor* took up the pro-Canada position more clearly than ever, making it central to its consideration.[85] Although the fisheries featured in

---

[81] *Mon.* 303–4, 9–16 May, 307–8, 6–13 June, 313–14, 18–25 July 1761.

[82] Walpole to Mann, 14 May 1761, *Walpole's Corr.* xxi, p. 505; *London Gazette*, 16–20 June, 4–7 July 1761; Birch to Royston, 27 June 1761, Add. MSS 35399, f. 209; Rigby to Bedford, 27 Aug. 1761, *Corr. Bedford*, iii, pp. 42–3.

[83] Esp. *Reasons For Keeping Guadaloupe at a Peace*, London, 1761.

[84] e.g. *LEP*, 11–14 Apr. 1761; *Lloyd's EP*, 27–9 Apr. 1761; *LC*, 30 Apr.–2 May 1761.

[85] *Mon.* 304, 16 May, 314–16, 25 July–8 Aug., 319, 29 Aug. 1761.

these debates as part of the demand for all North America, they did not loom large. Perhaps Bute and Newcastle were wrong in their opinion that Pitt was determined on the fisheries to please his City friends.[86] However, throughout the period of negotiation the public demand for high terms was maintained. Even the *Westminster Journal* appears to have hardened its attitude. Despite the shift in emphasis towards the desirability of peace, notes of urgency diminished if anything. As it became clear that the negotiations might fail the reaction was to blame French duplicity and ambition and to argue that France must and could be brought to her senses by active prosecution of the war.[87]

It does not seem that public debate on the possibility or terms of peace constrained Pitt this time. Public opinion, even in the City, did not now dictate resistance to peace. Pitt could have made the kind of peace he wanted and still have kept his popularity. Yet the support of his City friends and others for a strong peace may have confirmed Pitt's inclination to assert his control over policy on this question. He could oppose his more lenient colleagues and still maintain his popular base. He might thus also escape some of the embarrassment the German war was causing to his reputation.

Whatever the relative weight of the influences determining Pitt's stand, this time he could not be blamed for the failure of negotiations. Although his arrogance undoubtedly nettled the French, it was less important in the final breakdown than the 'second-string' tactics of Choiseul. From late in 1760 France had been exploring the possibility of an agreement with Spain. By the time the peace negotiations seemed likely to go less easily than Choiseul had hoped, these explorations were reaching fruition. In mid-August the Family Compact and a special convention between France and Spain were signed. They were secret, of course, but already in July, in reply to British proposals, the French had formally associated themselves with the grievances the Spanish had been expressing since September 1760. The French now demanded satisfaction of these grievances and suggested that Spain be asked to guarantee the forthcoming treaty between Britain and France. The Cabinet was unanimous in rejecting these suggestions. As the evidence increased

[86] Namier, *England*, p. 290.
[87] e.g. *Lloyd's EP*, 19–22 June, 17–20 July 1761; *LC*, 8–11, 11–13, 13–15, 27–9 Aug., 3–5 Sept. 1761; *LEP*, 11–13, 13–15 Aug. 1761. If indeed Bussy did hire English writers to advocate French views they were remarkably ineffective (Williams, i, p. 100).

that the two powers had come to some agreement the peace negotiations gradually ground to a halt. In August, the other English Ministers prevailed over Pitt to offer France some share in the fisheries, but her attitude over Spain raised growing doubts over her sincerity. No Minister was prepared to extend the negotiations to include the Spanish grievances. In mid-September, after a last exchange of offers, a unanimous vote of the Cabinet ordered Stanley to ask for his passport. The negotiations were at an end.

Undoubtedly the course of the negotiations had increased the strains among Ministers, especially in the stormy meetings in August over the fisheries. Pitt in fact had little to complain of, especially from Bute. Although Bute had proposed the compromise over the fisheries, by the end of the negotiations he had still not committed himself to the 'peace party', suspect though his motives for not doing so might be.[88] Yet Pitt did complain that he had been led into difficulties by the negotiations with France and expressed regret to his colleagues, in his last interview with Bussy and later to the House of Commons, that he had been forced to concede over the fisheries.[89] The process of negotiation undoubtedly increased his bitter frustration over his waning control of policy. This frustration came to breaking point over the attitude Britain should take to the increasingly provocative stance of Spain, so closely connected with the breakdown of the peace negotiations.

To forestall the threat that the Bourbon union might restore French naval power, Pitt was for seizing the initiative by immediate and decisive action against Spain. He wanted at least the recall of the British Ambassador, at most the interception of the Spanish treasure fleet. He was supported only by Temple. Other Ministers, unready to add another war to the one they wanted to end, favoured a more cautious diplomatic approach to investigate Spanish intentions. Newcastle's caution was increased by reports from the City of the scarcity of money and the belief of financiers that peace was essential.[90] Now at last Bute was forced to choose between Pitt and the 'peace party', between war with Spain and the risk that Pitt would resign before the war was ended. Reluctantly he chose the latter. Continuing the war without Pitt would bring unwelcome

[88] e.g. Newcastle to Bedford, 13 Sept. 1761, *Corr. Bedford*, iii, pp. 44–5.
[89] Harwicke's notes, 24 Aug., Newcastle to Hardwicke, 21 Sept. 1761, Yorke, *Hardwicke*, iii, pp. 272, 326; Williams, ii, p. 100.
[90] Browning, p. 281.

responsibilities; but to widen it further would make Pitt indefinitely indispensable. The King was much less ambivalent. Amongst other Ministers there was something of a swell of long pent-up exasperation at Pitt's domineering arrogance.[91] This time he could not break the united front against him and no grounds of compromise could be found. On 18 September Pitt and Temple insisted on drawing up their advice in writing for presentation to the King. For days, as discussion continued and new reports were considered, anxious speculation grew about Pitt's reaction to the united front.[92] At last, on 2 October, Pitt announced his intention to resign, using the famous words which were to resound through the ensuing controversy. He was

called . . . by his Sovereign and he might say in some degree by the voice of the People, to assist the State, when others had *abdicated* the service of it; that he accordingly came, had gone through more difficulties than ever man did: . . . that it was called *his war*; that it had been a successful one, and more than hinted that the success was singly owing to him; that the case was otherwise now; he saw what little credit he had in the Council from an union of opinion of some of the greatest persons in this Kingdom; . . . that in his station and situation he was responsible and would not continue without having the direction; that this being his case, nobody could be surprised that he could go on no longer, and he would repeat it again, that he would be responsible for nothing but what he directed.[93]

Three days later, on 5 October, Pitt surrendered the seals to the King. On 9 October Temple followed him. In the end Pitt had been out-manœuvred by Choiseul's 'two-string' policy, which thus got rid of what he saw as the chief obstacle to peace.[94]

So came about the first major political upset of the new reign, ending the comparative calm of 1757–61. It revived major political controversy in Parliament and outside and affected political life for

---

[91] Bute to Dodington, 8 Oct. 1761, *Dodington*, p. 425; George III to Bute,? 19 Sept. 1761, *Letters from George III to Lord Bute*, p. 63; Newcastle to Hardwicke, 23, 26 Sept. 1761, *Memoirs of [the Marquis of] Rockingham [and His Contemporaries]*, ed. George Thomas, Earl of Albemarle, 2 vols., London, 1852, i, pp. 42, 44; Browning, p. 281.

[92] Jenkinson to Grenville, [29 Sept. 1761], *Grenville Papers*, i, p. 390; Newcastle to Hardwicke, 21, 23, 26 Sept. 1761, Yorke, *Hardwicke,* iii, p. 326, *Mems. Rockingham*, i, pp. 42, 44.

[93] Newcastle's Minutes of the Meeting of the Council, 2 Oct. 1761, Yorke, *Hardwicke,* iii, pp. 279–80.

[94] Corbett, ii, p. 207.

the rest of the 1760s. It is quite clear that of those at the heart of the affair no one except the King wanted or welcomed Pitt's resignation. However, a genuine difference of policy had arisen, evident in the flurry of meetings of late September over the Spanish issue.[95] In these circumstances Pitt found his situation so undermined that he no longer had any hope of that single control of policy which he had always regarded as essential. He had already felt challenged, and indeed had threatened resignation, over the peace negotiations.[96] Now he was sure—and 'would not continue without having the direction'.

This was at the heart of his reasons for resigning. But it does not make clear how he saw his political future. There are some grounds for thinking that perhaps his ill-health and disillusionment were leading him to retirement. Bute had thought so, probably on the basis of conversations during the attempted reconciliations of April and October 1760, and Newcastle wrote as though Pitt had so talked when he threatened resignation early in September 1761. Immediately after the resignation his talk and behaviour further suggested retirement.[97] His acceptance of 'some honourable Provision', a title for his wife and a pension for himself, adds some confirmation, although the title for his wife left him in the House of Commons. However, it is also possible that Pitt was 'throwing himself' on his popularity. From the beginning of the reign Egmont had believed he would do this. Several competent, if not entirely detached observers thought that Pitt had deliberately set his demands high, both on the peace and the Spanish question, in order to be able to 'retire with the Glory of our Success, and leave to others the Difficulty of carrying on or closing the War'. His resignation was, to them,

a piece of artful policy in him to get out of this administration at the Eve of a peace, which he knew it woud be impossible to make in such a Manner as to gratifie the extravagant Expectations of the Quixot politicians of this Age—Instead therefore of risquing his popularity with them, he is now in a

[95] Williams, ii, pp. 107–11.

[96] Newcastle to Bedford, 13 Sept. 1761, *Corr. Bedford,* iii, p. 44.

[97] Ibid.; Newcastle's account of a conversation with Bute, 10 Mar. 1761, Add. MSS 32920, f. 67; Hardwicke to Newcastle, 13 Oct. 1761, Yorke, *Hardwicke,* iii, p. 332; Hardwicke to Lyttelton, 17 Oct. 1761, *Mems. Lyttelton,* ii, p. 630; Birch to Royston, 12 Oct. 1761, Add. MSS 35399, f. 257; Williams, ii, pp. 65–6; Brewer, *Party Ideology,* pp. 103–4.

Situation of encreasing it, by joining with a disappointed populace in the Clamour which they will not fail to make against every peace of which he is not supposed the immediate author.[98]

Such observers were not entirely right. Given acceptance of his terms (and the peace finally made in 1762 was not so far from them) Pitt could probably have made peace without danger to his reputation. Fears of this kind were not the major reason for his resignation. Nevertheless, popular reactions to the peace negotiations may well have suggested to him that, having lost support in Cabinet and Closet, he still had another source of strength to turn to. War with Spain, with hopes of yet further commercial gain, was likely to be as popular in the City as a firm stand in peace negotiations.[99] It is possible to see the resignation at least in part as a gamble to revive the popular basis of his political power which he had given so many signs of valuing. Certainly, reactions to it and its accompanying rewards soon made an untroubled and honourable retirement impossible, and showed, if indeed it was such a gamble, what a desperate chance Pitt had taken. Whether intentionally or not, the resignation raised the biggest question yet about both the substance and the effectiveness of Pitt's popularity. How far could 'popularity' support an eighteenth-century statesman without the unique circumstances of 1756–7 or 1759?

---

[98] See above p. 193; Kinnoull to Newcastle, 24 Oct. 1761, Add. MSS 32930, f. 12 (first quotation); Edward Seeds to Royston, 11 Oct. 1761, Add. MSS 35606, f. 370 (second quotation); Lord Holland's Memoir, p. 46; *Mems. Rockingham*, i, p. 47, quoting Soame Jenyns to Royston (without date); Dodington to Bute, 8 Oct. 1761, *Dodington*, p. 426. Such accusations became commonplace in pamphlets. See below pp. 207, 215, 216, 221.

[99] Walpole to Conway, 25 Sept. 1761, *The Letters of Horace Walpole*, v, p. 114; cf. Walpole to Mann, 14 Nov. 1761, *Walpole's Corr.* xxi, p. 549; Williams, ii, p. 111, quoting Granville at the Cabinet meeting of 2 Oct. 1761.

VII

Aftermath of Resignation 1761–1762

Pitt's resignation was reported unofficially in the evening papers of 6 October 1761. The newspapers were at once agog with reports, speculations, and comment on its likely effects. Initially this comment was sympathetic, reflecting concern, even indignation, at the loss of Pitt.[1] Such feelings were strong in the City, despite reassuring first reports to Newcastle about the moneyed interest, and preparations began to bring the matter before Common Council.[2]

Within days, however, indignation changed to perplexity, when the delayed *Gazette* report of the resignation, dated 9 October, was coupled with the announcement that the King had conferred on Pitt a pension of £3,000 a year for his life and that of his wife and eldest son, with a barony for his wife. Rumours of these had already been reported in the morning papers just as the *Gazette* came out on 10 October. The *Gazetteer* treated the rumours with incredulity as merely 'calculated to throw a damp on a certain lustre'. The *Public Ledger* stated that Pitt had refused the offers.[3] When instead the rumours were confirmed, incredulity turned to confusion and anger. Strenuous efforts by Beckford to spread reports that Pitt had not yet accepted the offers had little effect. 'The city and the people are outrageous about Lady *Cheat'em*, as they call her, and her husband's pension,' reported Rigby; '. . . they say . . . that his Majesty has

[1] e.g. *PA*, 9 Oct. 1761; *LEP*, 6–8, 8–10 Oct. 1761; *St. JC*, 8–10 Oct. 1761; *Lloyd's EP*, 5–7, 7–9 Oct. 1761.

[2] Newcastle memoranda, 6, 8 Oct., Bute to Newcastle, 6 Oct., Birch to Royston, 12 Oct. 1761, Add. MSS 32929, ff. 83–4, 113–14, 74, 35399, f. 258; *LEP, LC*, 8–10 Oct. 1761.

[3] *London Gazette*, 6–10 Oct. 1761, repeated in morning papers of 12 Oct. and evening papers of 10–13 Oct. 1761; *PA, PL*, 10 Oct. 1761; *Gaz.* in *LC*, 8–10 Oct. 1761.

broke his word with them by this bounty to Pitt, for that he promised he would not govern by corruption.' When the Common Council met on 13 October, it broke up without taking any action over the resignation. Predictions that Pitt's patriot reputation would suffer the fate of Pulteney's if he accepted any reward seemed likely to be fulfilled.[4]

The *Monitor* fully reflected these initial confusions. Its paper of 10 October made no reference to the resignation. Yet its tone, markedly different from that of preceding papers, suggests shock, bewilderment, and an indignation which, uncertain of its precise object, was vented on its long-standing enemies, Newcastle and his associates. The paper of the next week was much more explicit about events but still uncertain in reactions. It spoke of the general 'damp upon the spirit of the nation' created by the resignation, and the 'hasty conjectures and dangerous resolutions amongst the people' it was likely to cause. There was no hint of dissatisfaction over the pension and peerage. Equally there was no defence of Pitt. The mood was still one of bewilderment taking refuge in instinctive anti-Newcastle reactions.[5] It amply suggests the embarrassment of Beckford and the confusion of others in the City.

The rewards, and particularly the manner of announcing them, were undoubtedly part of a deliberate effort to neutralize the impact of the much-feared resignation. At the time it was suspected that Bute's 'agents were not idle' in coffee houses and newspapers, a suspicion amply confirmed by evidence in the Bute papers. These 'agents' were almost certainly responsible for the early rumours of the intended rewards.[6] Their efforts were not unprovoked. Rumours intended to embarrass the remaining Ministers had also been circulated. The first reports of Pitt's resignation had been accompanied by suggestions, soon officially denied, that Bussy was to return to conclude an early peace. There were accounts, too, of the action

[4] Birch to Royston, 17 Oct., memorandum, 8 Oct., Touchit to Newcastle, 13 Oct., Watkins to Newcastle, 15 Oct. 1761, Add. MSS 35399, f. 260, 32929, ff. 113, 235, 293; Rigby to Bedford, 12 Oct. 1761, *Corr. Bedford*, iii, pp. 51–2 (quotation); Temple to Wilkes, 16 Oct. 1761, *Grenville Papers*, i, p. 404.

[5] *Mon.* 325–6, 10, 17 Oct. 1761.

[6] Hardwicke to Royston, 12 Oct., Bedford to Newcastle, 11 Oct. 1761, Add. MSS 35352, f. 198, 32929, f. 192; Walpole, *Geo. III*, i, pp. 63, 64; [John Almon], [*The History of the Late*] *Minority*, London, 1765, reprinted 1766, p. 79; Brewer, *Party Ideology*, p. 224 and fn. 23.

the 'Great Patriot' was supposed to have recommended against Spain and reports designed to confirm Spain's hostile intentions.[7]

Bute's agents were actively supported by the Yorkes and Newcastle.[8] Their hand can be seen at work very early, in a hostile comment in the *London Chronicle* of 10–13 October. This for the first time made the suggestion which was to become commonplace, that Pitt resigned in order to escape the difficulties of concluding the war satisfactorily. It added that 'the minister had acted more consistent with the high character he has for some years so well supported, had he refused the reward till he had *completed* his work'. Indeed the *London Chronicle* quickly became the vehicle of a sustained attempt to compromise Pitt's reputation by such insinuations, making the most of the change in 'the people's' attitude to him because of his acceptance of a pension.[9]

Even in its pages, however, such attacks were answered and comment in other papers, notably the City-oriented *Public Ledger* and the old stalwart, the *London Evening Post*, remained friendly. They praised Pitt's war policy and successes, regretted his loss, uneasily speculated on its causes, and defended his rewards as 'accepted' but not 'solicited'. Most interesting of all, the *St. James's Chronicle* clearly rejected an attempt, countenanced and perhaps initiated by Hardwicke, to swing it to the defence of the remaining Ministers. In a series of questions and answers on 13–15 October it provided a concise summary of the state of the attack and defence at this stage.[10] The first occasional publication on the resignation, a four-page defence entitled *A Certain Great Man Vindicated*,[11] was a warm defence of Pitt. His services, it said, deserved rewards more than most. Rewards were further justified by the injury to his private circumstances and health in the service of his country, the need to take care of his family and to make it clear that he did not retire in disgrace. He was still free to serve and advise in the House

[7] *PA*, 9, 10 Oct. 1761; *LEP*, 8–10 Oct. 1761; *St. JC*, 6–8 Oct. 1761; *LC*, 8–10 Oct. 1761; *PL*, 10 Oct. 1761.

[8] Royston to Hardwicke, 16 Oct., Hardwicke to Royston, 17 Oct. 1761, Add. MSS 35352, ff. 199–200, 202–3.

[9] e.g. *LC*, 10–13 Oct. (2 articles), 15–17 Oct. 1761.

[10] e.g. *PL*, 12, 13, 15 Oct. 1761; *LEP*, 13–15 Oct. 1761; *St. JC*, 10–13, 13–15 Oct. 1761 (copied *PL*, 16 Oct.)., cf. Hardwicke to Royston, 17 Oct. 1761, Add. MSS 35352, ff. 202–3.

[11] Advt. *PA*, 16 Oct. 1761. Full titles and publication details of pamphlets referred to in this chapter are given in the bibliography.

of Commons. The leaflet prompted the City to go ahead with its reported intention to thank Pitt and urged every community to follow their example. It is likely that Temple, who had declared his intention to defend the resignations publicly, had a hand in encouraging these publications.[12]

Yet Bute's agents had some success. These defences bore witness to the 'execration' of 'the people' against Pitt. Many people, the leaflet said,

do not scruple openly to declare, that all his former services are rendered now disservices, by leaving us in the lurch . . . and that the late honest P[atriot] is at last become a slave to venality . . . We hear now nothing but—*he was afraid to go through with what he undertook.—He sunk under the load.—He has sold himself.*

There was, as the *Monitor* later admitted, 'a general stagnation of sentiment' to Pitt's disadvantage at the thought that he had deserted his country for a pension. The *Monitor*'s own relative backwardness in defence of Pitt at this time emphasizes the seriousness of the threat to his standing in the City. As the *Annual Register* pointed out, Pitt also faced a wider dilemma as a result of the *Gazette* announcement. It would embarrass his future political activity, whether he opposed the Ministers and so laid himself open to charges of ingratitude, or concurred and appeared to have been bought.[13]

It is little wonder, then, that Pitt felt compelled to revise his initial 'temper and moderation' and defend himself. He had already explained the reasons for his resignation personally to the Lord Mayor. Now, on 17 October, there appeared in the *Public Ledger* a copy of a letter from Pitt in reply to the 'misrepresentation' in the City of the circumstances of his resignation. The published version did not name the recipient, but the letter was written to Beckford on 15 October. By explaining that the resignation resulted from differences of opinion over Spain and that the rewards followed it, the letter attempted to remove the imputation that Pitt had been bought off by the Court. Although Pitt was later to disavow any

---

[12] Rigby to Bedford, 12 Oct. 1761, *Corr. Bedford*, iii, pp. 52–3; Newcastle to Devonshire, 14 Oct. 1761, Add. MSS 32929, f. 256.

[13] *PL*, 13 Oct. 1761 (first quotations); *A Certain Great Man Vindicated*, pp. 1, 2; *Mon.* 330, 14 Nov. 1761; *AR*, iv, 1761, p. 45.

hand in its publication, the letter was obviously intended as some kind of public declaration. Naturally it attracted great attention. More than 3,000 copies of the *Ledger* were sold before noon, by which time the *Gazetteer* had reprinted its issue for the day with the letter in it, and all the other papers followed.[14]

The letter served its purpose in bringing back Pitt's 'mad noisy City friends, who were, for a time, displeased with him', however much the King and leading politicians indignantly criticized it. Despite the confirmation that Pitt had, contrary to his friend's denials, accepted the rewards, Beckford's efforts 'to form a Cabal in the City' in Pitt's favour now bore fruit. Soon the City was all '*Fire, and Flame*'.[15] On 22 October the Common Council again met and this time passed unanimously a vote of thanks to Pitt. He had, the vote said, aroused the 'ancient spirit' of the nation and greatly extended the sphere of trade and commerce. A further motion expressed sorrow at his loss at so critical a moment. Outspoken instructions to the City members of Parliament were also agreed to, urging them to continue Pitt's policies. They were to insist on no peace without the retention of all or nearly all conquests, especially in North America and the fisheries. The just and necessary war should be vigorously prosecuted to reduce France's remaining colonies (firmer attitudes than the City had shown in the months before the resignation). They were also to demand an inquiry into the application of supplies over recent years and into the accounts for forage in Germany.[16]

The proceedings were not without some debate. There was division over the motion regretting the loss of Pitt. A motion urging him to accept the Secretary of State's seals again whenever they were offered was defeated. Even Beckford spoke against it. Proposals

---

[14] Williams, ii, p. 120; Hardwicke to Lyttelton, 17 Oct. 1761, *Mems. Lyttelton*, ii, p. 630 (quotation); Newcastle to Devonshire, postscript 15 Oct., Birch to Royston, 12, 17, 19 Oct. 1761, Add. MSS 32929, f. 258, 35399, ff. 257–8, 259, 261; Pitt to Beckford, 15 Oct. 1761, *Corr Chatham*, ii, pp. 158–9; Royston to Hardwicke, [13 Nov. 1761], Yorke, *Hardwicke*, iii, p. 338; Walpole, *Geo. III*, i, p. 74. The text of Pitt's letter is printed in Appendix II.

[15] Birch to Royston, 17 Oct. 1761, Add MSS 35399, f. 259 (second quotation); Hardwicke to Royston, 17 Oct. 1761, George Harris, *The Life of Lord Chancellor Hardwicke*, 3 vols., London, 1847, iii, pp. 266–7; Newcastle to Hardwicke, 18, 20 Oct. (third quotation), to Bedford, 20 Oct. (first quotation), Add. MSS 32929, ff. 358, 406, 403; George III to Bath, *c.*17 Oct. 1761, *Letters from George III to Lord Bute*, p. 66.

[16] *LEP*, 22–4 Oct. 1761.

made at a preceding private meeting that an inquiry should be made into the circumstances of his resignation and that something be said about war with Spain were not raised. All these motions touched on the delicate question of the King's prerogative even more than the demands about the peace. Further, in the course of debate, several expressions in the instructions were softened, and the first City member of Parliament and 'father' of the City, Sir Robert Ladbroke, opposed that on supplies. Yet there was no doubt of the prevailing sentiments of Common Council. The divisions merely served to highlight the remarkable nature of this intrusion into the sphere of national government and the prerogative, more explicit than the gold boxes of 1757 and sharply resented by King and politicians. Nor was there any doubt about where the initiative lay in directing City sentiments. Beckford '*roared* prodigiously', treating opponents with great contempt. Moreover, the motion on supplies and the special attention to the forage accounts, though thought by some to have been made out of deference to Mauduit, clearly reflected Beckford's and Pitt's tactics in the previous parliamentary session of diverting blame to Newcastle for the expense of the German war.[17]

The alliance of Pitt and the City had been restored, sealed by Pitt's ostentatiously complimentary reply. As Newcastle righteously bewailed, 'they want mischief, violence and clamour; and, if Mr Pitt will join in that, they don't care what money, or what rewards he has'. The effects were soon felt in anxiety and caution among the moneyed men and the fears of politicians mounted that the clamour might grow and seriously disrupt business at a criticial time.[18]

The City lived up to Newcastle's fears even more riotously on 9 November, the day of the new Lord Mayor's banquet. According to custom in the first year of a new reign, the King and Queen attended. Temple and Pitt also attended at Beckford's special request. 'It is the Universal desire of people of all denominations', he wrote to Temple, 'and a refusal, at this Critical Juncture, would damp the ardour and publick Spirit of every well wisher to his Country.' Along the route and at Guildhall, they were greeted with greater acclaim than the King himself, sometimes in circumstances

[17] Newcastle to Devonshire, to Barrington, 22 Oct., account of Common Council meeting, 22 Oct., memorandum, 22 Oct. 1761, Add. MSS 32929, ff. 437, 446, 442, 435; Birch to Royston, 27 Oct. 1761, Add. MSS 35399, f. 262 (quotation).

[18] Memorandum, 23 Oct., Newcastle to Devonshire, 21 Oct. (quotation), 31 Oct., Kinnoull to Newcastle, 24 Oct. 1761, Add. MSS 32929, ff. 468, 428, 32930, ff. 222, 13.

contrived to point the contrast, while Bute was hissed and pelted by the crowds and only narrowly saved from worse harm. There was little doubt that the demonstration was organized by Beckford. The Lord Mayor's enquiries discovered that Beckford 'had visited several public-houses over night, and had appointed ringleaders to different stations, and had been the first to raise the huzza in the hall on the entrance of Mr Pitt', although he denied all knowledge of the mobbing of Bute. In hostile eyes he thoroughly deserved Fox's appellation, 'toad eater to the mountebank'. Again, resentment was expressed at these further 'excesses' of the City and there is even a suggestion that Pitt came to regret his part in them.[19]

Reactions to Pitt's resignation and its attendant circumstances were not confined to the City, although they are best documented there. Walpole's humorously exaggerated yet real disillusion was probably representative of the reactions of many observers. To them Pitt's actions seemed not only to compromise his patriot stance but also to be a precipitate desertion of the nation in a crisis.[20] 'Lord Talbot and his Tories' were reported to be angry over the rewards. Temple obviously felt the force of these initial reactions and took care to explain the circumstances very fully to Wilkes. In Buckingham, the heart of Temple country, the burgesses refused to drink Pitt's health. A club of tradesmen in Chichester were lukewarm. The publication of Pitt's letter somewhat modified these early unsympathetic reactions. It saved the situation in Buckingham, to Temple's evident relief. Newcastle began to fear that other places would follow London's example and vote thanks to Pitt, and took steps to forestall such action.[21]

---

[19] Beckford to Pitt, 6 Nov. 1761, with Lady Chatham's endorsement, Thomas Nuthall to Lady Chatham, 12 Nov. 1761, *Corr. Chatham*, ii, pp. 165 and fn., 166–8; Beckford to Temple, 6 Nov. 1761, PRO 30/8/19, f. 73; Walpole to Mann, 14 Nov. 1761, *Walpole's Corr.* xxi, p. 547; Walpole, *Geo III*, i, p. 70 (second quotation); Lord Holland's Memoir, p. 53 (third quotation).

[20] Walpole to Mann, 6, 10 Oct. 1761, *Walpole's Corr.* xxi, pp. 537–8, 541; Walpole to Montagu, to the Countess of Ailesbury, 10 Oct. 1761, *The Letters of Horace Walpole*, v, pp. 129–30, 131–2; Bath to Mrs Montagu, 8 Oct. 1761, *Elizabeth Montagu*, ii, pp. 263–4; cf. William Gray, quoted in Stanley Ayling, *The Elder Pitt Earl of Chatham*, London, 1976, p. 293.

[21] Rigby to Bedford, 12 Oct. 1761, *Corr. Bedford*, iii, p. 52 (quotation); Temple to Wilkes, 16, 22 Oct. 1761, *Grenville Papers*, i, pp. 404–5, 406; Temple to Lady Chatham, 25 Oct. 1761, PRO 30/8/62, f. 37; John Page to Newcastle, 13 Oct., Newcastle to Rockingham, 22 Oct. 1761, Add. MSS 32929, ff. 238–9, 444–5.

Yet this time there proved little to fear. Unlike that of 1757,' this flame . . . had much ado to spread'. By the middle of November only Exeter, Chester, York, and Stirling had thanked Pitt, to be followed in mid-December by the merchants and traders (but not the Corporation) of Dublin and by Pitt's own constituency of Bath. Later still came Cork and Norwich. Moves at Leicester and King's Lynn were rejected.[22] For Pitt, this response could only be called disappointing. True, a response similar to the great waves of addresses on the victories of war was scarcely likely. On such occasions addresses to the King were *de rigueur*. Addresses of thanks to a minister on his resignation were, in contrast, virtually unprecedented. Yet after the great successes of the war, which were generally credited to Pitt, a warmer response than the 'rain' of gold boxes of 1757 might have been expected. Instead, there were only nine addresses compared with thirteen gold boxes. The three cities gained since 1757, Dublin (although the 'ruling part' was still cool),[23] Cork, and York, were of some importance. Dublin and Cork, with the retention of Stirling in Scotland, gave additional substance to Pitt's claim to national British support. York, the county town of the greatest English county, was traditionally Tory but was coming increasingly under the influence of the Marquess of Rockingham. For all these reasons it was a considerable support.[24] It was doubtless gratifying to be able to hold Exeter, Chester and, belatedly, Norwich. The first two were also traditionally Tory, Exeter and Norwich were cities of first rank and all three indicated a wide spread of English support. The seven losses since 1757 were, however, even more significant. They included six Tory or Tory-influenced corporations, and confirmed the waning of wider Tory support for Pitt, whether of individual Tory members of Parliament (Boston and Worcester) or of independent Tory country gentlemen (Tewkesbury). These Tory losses included one city of first impor-

---

[22] Walpole to Mann, 14 Nov. 1761, *Walpole's Corr.* xxi, p. 546 (quotation), cf. *AR*, iv, 1761, p. 46; *Anecdotes of Chatham*, iii, pp. 219–34; Cork Address, 29 Dec. 1761, PRO 30/8/61, f. 60; Walpole, *Geo. III*, i, pp. 66, 96–9.

[23] *PL*, 12 Dec. 1761.

[24] Langford, 'William Pitt and public opinion, 1757', p. 59; C. Collyer, 'The Rockinghams and Yorkshire Politics 1742–1761', *Publications of the Thoresby Society*, xli, *Thoresby Miscellany*, xii (1954), pp. 369, 375; id., 'The Rockingham Connection and Country Opinion in the early years of George III', p. 252 and fn. 5; Rockingham to Newcastle, 29 Oct. 1761, Add. MSS 32930, f. 159.

tance, Newcastle, and two other substantial county towns, Worcester and Salisbury. Salisbury was lost despite the influence of the Beckfords. The loss of Great Yarmouth was probably largely due to the changing loyalties of George Townshend.[25]

Altogether, the response to London's lead suggests that popularity was likely to be a very uncertain support for Pitt now. The middling tradesmen of the City might still be in the grip of patriot fervour. Pitt's resignation made them fear that victories might be sacrificed and revived their long-standing suspicion of government. Elsewhere such people were far fewer and they had no means to make their views known. Symmer thought that 'the City and the Trading Part of the Nation' were for Pitt, while 'the Cooler part of the Nation, and the landed Interest' were sick of war and anxious for peace. Yet there was not much sign of a rallying of the 'trading part' outside London. Rockingham reported disillusionment among the merchants of Wakefield.[26] Those other bastions of popularity, the country Tories and independents, had been worn away by the necessary compromises of office and the demands of war policy. The wider popularity that victories had brought was indeed ephemeral and unreliable. Unless the Ministers made drastic mistakes in the continuation of war and the making of peace, attitudes were unlikely to change. If popularity was to be any use at all now, the continuing loyalty of the City was more important than ever.

No doubt the limited response to the City's example in addressing Pitt was due at least in part to the newspaper and pamphlet debate, which was in full swing by late October. The debate probably also prevented any attempt to inflate the significance of the few addresses that did eventuate, in the manner that had been so effective with the gold boxes of 1757.[27] In the last three months of 1761 the most sustained attack of all the war years was mounted against Pitt's policies and popularity. With the defences it provoked, it both brought to a climax the arguments that had never been long silent through the war and adumbrated new ones that

[25] Langford, 'William Pitt and public opinion, 1757' (for borough politics); the other Tory loss was Bedford. For George Townshend's changing loyalties see below p. 239.

[26] Symmer to Mitchell, 20 Nov. 1761, Add. MSS 6839, f. 239; Rockingham to Newcastle, 29 Oct. 1761, Add. MSS 32930, ff. 158–9.

[27] Langford, 'William Pitt and public opinion, 1757', pp. 58–9.

were to continue through the troubled 1760s. It certainly did much to shape reactions to Pitt's resignation and the effect on his reputation.

The first pamphlets supported Pitt. Appearing at the same time as his letter to Beckford, they elaborated on early newspaper defences. *An Earnest Address To the People of Great-Britain and Ireland* was full of glowing praise of Pitt's successes. It supported his resignation as a protest against the rejection of all his measures and the pension as a just reward which did not compromise his freedom to give his services in Parliament. *A Letter To His Grace the Duke of N[ewcastle]* also praised Pitt for the successes of the war and allowed him the title of the Great Commoner. But with devastating artlessness it admitted that in accepting the peerage and pension he had not stood up to the full test of patriotism. Indeed he must have made a bargain with the Ministers not to go into opposition. This admission was to be taken up by a vitriolic adversary as proof from one of Pitt's 'own Flock' of the force of its own attacks.[28] On the other side, one of Bute's pensioners, William Guthrie, produced an early substantial pamphlet addressed to Bute. It was a reasoned and moderate discussion of war measures designed to demonstrate the necessity of and general desire for peace and disentanglement from the Continent. It attempted to show that, despite the exaggerated reactions of the public, hopes of peace need not be upset by the resignations. Pitt and his friends, Guthrie argued, could surely not be suspected of intending to disturb public harmony by opposition, thus forfeiting 'the venerable appellation of patriots'.[29]

The publication of Pitt's letter may have saved the situation in the City but it provoked his opponents to yet greater efforts and gave grounds for further attack—as Bute and Newcastle well realized. It could be said to reveal Cabinet secrets, and Pitt could be further criticized for his complaint, made at his last Cabinet meeting and now repeated, that he 'was no longer allowed to guide' measures.[30] The tone of attack became more bitter and the balance in favour of Pitt turned on the whole against him.

[28] *An Earnest Address*, advt. *LC*, 13–15 Oct. 'to be published tomorrow noon'; *A Letter To His Grace the Duke of N[ewcastle]*, advt. *PA*, 17 Oct. 1761. See esp. pp. 28–30, quoted in *The Patriot Unmasked*, pp. 29–32.

[29] *A Letter To the Right Honourable The Earl of B[ute]*, advt. *PA*, 17 Oct. 1761 (quotation p. 73); Birch to Royston, 27 Oct. 1761, Add. MSS 35399, f. 263.

[30] Newcastle to Hardwicke, 18 Oct., Devonshire to Newcastle, Kinnoull to Newcastle, 24 Oct. 1761, Add. MSS 32929, f. 359, 32930, ff. 5, 13.

The renewed attack began as before in the newspapers, especially in the *London Chronicle*. For a time the forcefulness if not the number of hostile contributions to it outweighed the defence. One especially strong article on 22–4 October outlined the main arguments that were to dominate the attack. It criticized Pitt's Spanish policy, the presumption of his claim to 'guide' against the advice of the majority of the Cabinet, his desertion at a time of crisis, and the many inconsistencies and broken promises of his past career. It concluded by speculating again that the true motive for the resignation was fear of public resentment when expectations were not fulfilled. The next week, with the tide still against Pitt, a series of queries suggested criticism of the City for its thanks and Pitt for his pretensions to absolute power. *Owen's Weekly Chronicle* reacted angrily to the City instructions.[31]

However, opinion in the newspapers did not set firmly against Pitt. The *Public Ledger* and *London Evening Post* remained loyal. *Lloyd's Evening Post* was only briefly shaken from its original warmth. Even in the *London Chronicle* the attacks did not go unanswered. In particular the paper of 20–2 October reprinted from the *Public Ledger* an important defence of the constitutional propriety of Pitt's resignation on the grounds of the responsibility of ministers, particularly of that minister who by virtue of holding the seals and of public approbation was 'the chief Director of all measures'.[32] The *St. James's Chronicle* declared its impartiality in the debate and one of its correspondents reacted favourably to Pitt's letter, holding it to have answered all objections. Although it remained friendly on the whole, its columns were not without hostile notes and indeed it floated a spurious reply from Beckford to Pitt that did his cause no good. The *Gazetteer*'s initial reactions were similarly mixed.[33]

By early November the impetus of the newspaper debate was slackening somewhat. The volume of criticism in the *London Chronicle*

[31] *LC*, 22–4 Oct. (answered in *PL*, 28 Oct. which says it was also copied in *Gaz.*), 27–9 Oct. 1761; *OWC*, 24–31 Oct. 1761.

[32] *PL*, 21 Oct. 1761; *LC*, 20–2 Oct. 1761; see also *LEP*, 20–2 Oct. 1761.

[33] *St. JC*, 17–20, 22–4 Oct. 1761; for *Gaz.* see *GM*, xxxi, Oct. 1761, pp. 461, 463, and Birch to Royston, 19 Oct. 1761, Add. MSS 35399, f. 261. The spurious reply was referred to frequently in pamphlets and generally accepted as genuine e.g. by *AR*, iv, 1761, pp. 300–1 and initially by *GM*, xxxi, Oct. 1761, pp. 462–3, but *PL*, 30 Oct. 1761, dismissed it as a joke and by Nov. *GM* (p. 517 fn.) had realized its mistake. The wording and tone of the letter leave no doubt that even Beckford could not have perpetrated it. It is not printed in *Corr. Chatham*.

abated, although it may have increased in the *Gazetteer* and the criticism was still influential.[34] But other papers remained loyal and the initiative passed to pamphlets. In them the bitter tone became more obvious.

Already a change of tone in reaction to Pitt's efforts to defend himself had been shown in two pamphlets which appeared just as the City was responding to Pitt's letter—*The Patriot Unmasked* and *The Right Honourable Annuitant Vindicated*.[35] More fully than the newspapers, they show how Pitt's defence and the City response gave an added stimulus to attempts to undermine the popular reputation he was trying to defend. To this end, his acceptance of a pension gave devastating new weight to old arguments. It was, the second pamphlet maintained, just the last in a long series of inconsistencies in behaviour which showed Pitt to be only a mock or pretended patriot. It went on to restate shrewdly the slurs already cast on Pitt's motives in resigning. 'He *prudently* foresaw that there would be more trouble and difficulty in settling a peace to the liking of all ranks of people', so he prudently withdrew with a prudent pension. It then showed in detail how Pitt's letter with its arrogant claim to 'guide' could be used against him, especially when backed up by the supposed reply, quoted in full. Both gave support to the pamphlet's mocking criticism of that new and very singular character which only Pitt's remarkable excellence of 'temper and conduct' made possible, a 'PENSIONER IN OPPOSITION', a 'PATRIOT-PENSIONER' or a '*Right Honourable* ANNUITANT'. The City might well consider him a '*broken Patriot*', a '*Bankrupt* in Politics', yet, like many other bankrupts, likely to set up a more thriving trade than ever.[36]

The Patriot Unmasked extended the attack on Pitt's patriotism back over his whole career. His popularity, especially in the City, was

[34] *GM* summary of the papers, xxxi, Nov. 1761, pp. 514–21, still gives more weight to criticism. According to Brewer, *Party Ideology*, p. 224, Bute's agents were still very active, especially in *LC*, but the dates given for articles do not tally recognizably with the *LC* columns. Some may have appeared in *Gaz.*, which seems from references in other papers and pamphlets to have been the only exception in the general abatement of criticism. See *Mon.* 330, 14 Nov., 332, 28 Nov. 1761, 338, 9 Jan. 1762; *PL*, 19 Nov. 1761; *The Patriot Unmasked*, p. 16; *A Letter from the Anonymous Author*, p. 10. But Haig, p. 51, quotes Almon's claims to have written in defence of Pitt in *Gaz.*

[35] Advt. *PA*, 17 Oct. 'to be published Tuesday next' (20 Oct.), and 22 Oct. 1761 as 'Tomorrow will be published'.

[36] *The Right Honourable Annuitant Vindicated*, pp. 24, 49, 50, 66.

dismissed as mere sheep-like following of one who had 'the strength of a good Pair of Lungs' to clamour loudly for 'Liberty and Property'.[37] Criticism of Pitt's rewards and suggestions about his motives for resigning were again fully elaborated and all defences of them, particularly those of the *Monitor* and the *Gazetteer*, were rejected. Against Pitt's services had to be set their cost, his change of front on German measures and his projected ruinous war with Spain. The claim that he could still give his services and advice in the Commons was skilfully taken up to suggest the arrogance of the 'Dictator of the People'. This pamphlet was aimed at the City; the other was directed primarily to increasing the uneasiness of country gentlemen. The theme of both—that of false patriotism—is aptly summed up in the ballad that ends the first.

> Your Courtiers and *Patriots*, 'mong other fine Things,
> Will talk of their Country, and Love to their Kings,
> But their Mask will drop off if you shake but the Pelf,
> And show King and Country all centered in Self.[38]

In this first round of pamphlet exchanges, over by 24 October, there were as many defences of Pitt as attacks on him. But against such invective the defences seemed naïve and ineffective. *An Answer to A Letter to . . . B[ute]*,[39] for example, although it made a preliminary attempt to justify the peerage and pension, was predominantly a step-by-step rebuttal of the arguments of its antagonist on Pitt's measures, his successes, and the grounds for a strong peace. It was hardly an incisive contribution to a debate that now turned on Pitt's patriotism.

There was a lull in the pamphlet debate of almost a fortnight after 24 October, probably to reserve fire for the opening of the first session of the new Parliament. Only a poem which sharply illustrates the widening personal attack on Pitt's allegedly false patriotism, ranting oratory and haughty arrogance interrupted this lull.[40] Meanwhile, in the second half of October the *Monitor* had been jolted from its earlier uncertainties by Pitt's letter and the news-

---

[37] *The Patriot Unmasked*, pp. 4, 5. Beckford was one of the 'Bell-Weathers' who 'mouths it as well as any-body' in recommending Pitt to the City (pp. 4, 6).
[38] Ibid., p. 42.   [39] Advt. *PA*, 24 Oct. 1761.
[40] Parliament assembled on 3 Nov. for the election of the Speaker and the taking of oaths. The King's Speech was not delivered until 13 Nov. *The Conciliad or the Triumph of Patriotism*, advt. *PA*, 31 Oct. 1761, second edn. 2 Jan. 1762.

paper attacks. It now began a full-scale defence of the foreign and domestic achievements of the patriot minister who knew the best interests of the country and was opposed only by 'faction'. Amplifying the voices of supporters in the newspapers, it argued that, in face of the frustration of Pitt's firm measures which were fully justified by the enemy's arrogance in the peace negotiations, he had no alternative but to resign. True, his was only one voice in the Cabinet Council and majorities should normally prevail. But he had in fact been given full power to plan and execute measures and majorities could be abused and bribed. So his resignation only heightened the amiability of his character and filled with gloom the hearts of everyone except the enemy and the French-influenced 'faction' from whose hands he had delivered the country. Only they resisted the demand for Pitt's return, which was not 'clamour' but 'the language of every dispassionate person, of every true patriot in the British dominions'.[41]

The *Monitor* was supported early in November by the first effective pamphlet defence of Pitt, *The Conduct of a Rt. Hon. Gentleman . . . justified*. Without glossing over difficulties, it provided a positive, well-reasoned and comprehensive defence, covering Pitt's measures, the constitutional propriety of the resignation and its circumstances, and the moral and political propriety of his acceptance of rewards (a point as yet ignored by the *Monitor*). Pitt's conduct was, it maintained, defensible on three grounds, already outlined in the newspaper debate. First, resignation was the only possible action when, over Spanish affairs, he was forced to deviate from 'the great lines of conduct he had chalked out' when he first came into office and which had achieved so much. In maintaining this proposition the pamphlet made a careful defence of Pitt's German policy, not denying some unavoidable deviation from principle. Secondly, it argued that his resignation was in fact a great service to his country and entirely agreeable to the constitution. The role of directing minister or minister of state was, admittedly, not recognized by the constitution or the laws. But it was necessary in fact, the pamphlet said, and belonged to the office of Secretary of State, the only officer of the Crown whose powers were not delimited by laws, precedent, and practice. Pitt had been promoted to such an office by his sovereign's will and the public voice (and his own ambition). When

[41] *Mon.* 327–8, 24–31 Oct. 1761 (quotation from 328).

he was faced by unanimous opposition, his best service to his country was to retire, in order to avoid dissension and public debate. Retirement was the constitutional step left open to a directing minister who, since the Revolution, had been held answerable for commissions and omissions while in office. Finally, the pamphlet argued that Pitt was still at liberty to offer his opinion as freely as before. The attacks on the pension and title were directly turned about to argue that if he had refused them his idolizing public would have justly feared that they were offered as hush money. Thus animosities and even obstruction of supply might have been stimulated. The debate out of doors, the pamphlet concluded, should concentrate on Spanish measures, not on whether Pitt had 'guided' measures or should have received rewards. And, it claimed, the French account of the negotiations, which had just been published, was the best justification yet of Pitt's line.[42]

However, after this sophisticated and powerful statement of Pitt's case had renewed pamphlet debate, the balance of argument swung more strongly against him than ever.[43] The swing began early in November with Guthrie's *Second Letter To . . . B[ute]*[44] and was well under way by the middle of the month when debates in Parliament commenced. Now the attacks were concentrated less strongly on false patriotism and manipulated popularity, although the pension and the title were certainly not forgotten.[45] More often criticism fastened on Pitt's letter to Beckford, Beckford's supposed reply and the City's thanks and instructions.[46] Most notable was *A Letter From A Right Honourable Person And the Answer to it, Translated into Verse* by Philip Francis of *Test* fame, now making his court to Bute and urged on again by Fox. In the tradition of the *Test*, Francis brought an even more virulent personal tone into the controversy. His mocking versification and its sequel became the most noticed of all the

---

[42] Advt. *PA*, 7 Nov. 1761 (quotation p. 3).

[43] The November Reviews notice only two pamphlets in support of Pitt and eight against.

[44] Advt. *PA*, 5 Nov. 1761.

[45] e.g. in *Impartial Reflections upon the present State of Affairs*, advt. *PA*, 12 Nov. 1761.

[46] e.g. in *A Second Letter To . . . B[ute]*; *Remarks upon a Popular Letter*, advt. *PA*, 12 Nov.; *A Letter To The Right Honourable Author Of A Letter to a Citizen*, advt. *PA*, 24 Nov.; *The Box Returned, or, The City Satisfied*, advt. *PA*, 16 Nov. 1761.

attacks on Pitt.[47] At the same time other writers widened the attack to survey the whole of Pitt's record as a Minister, sometimes in response to praise of him, real, or spurious as in the supposed reply to Pitt's letter.

Pitt was criticized for rashness, presumptuousness, and arrogance both before and after the resignation, all of it attributed to his being 'too much actuated by the love of popularity'.[48] His complaint of not being allowed to 'guide' was particularly fastened on; following suggestions already made in newspapers, it was interpreted as aspiring to the unconstitutional role of a leading minister. A Secretary of State was a servant of the King and nation, of equal weight with other councillors, not a 'lord paramount of all public affairs'. To escape being held responsible for measures he did not approve he had only to disavow them, as in fact Pitt had done, in writing to the King.[49] Pitt's unconstitutional pretensions, his claims to a despotism over his colleagues and the people, were held to be the result of excessive and unthinking public adulation which had encouraged an 'inebriated' sense of his own importance. So, as first attempted by the *Test*, further efforts were made to neutralize Pitt's still generally accepted popularity, by suggesting not only that it was ill-founded and unthinking (and probably now declining), but also that it endangered the balance of the constitution. The support of the people, as well as that of the Court, could erect an overpowerful minister. Pitt's public explanation of his resignation was held to suggest that 'he is become ambitious of making a new stand on opposition, falsely called

[47] Advt. *PA*, 14 Nov. 1761. Sometimes attributed to Arthur Murphy, Francis's collaborator in the *Test* (*British Library Catalogue of Printed Books*), it can be definitely assigned to Francis on Fox's evidence (see letter from Ilchester, 10 June 1917, prefixed to one of the British Library copies; cf. Giles S. H. Fox-Strangeways, Earl of Ilchester, [*Henry*] *Fox*, [*First Lord Holland his Family and Relations*], 2 vols., London, 1920, ii, p. 154). This pamphlet was popularly known as *Mr Pitt's Letter Versified.* There is no evidence to support Brewer's assertion (*Party Ideology*, p. 224) that there were two separate works attributed respectively to Francis and Murphy. Francis's work went through five editions by Jan. 1762 (*PA*, 1, 12 Dec. 1761, 11 Jan. 1762). Walpole, *Geo. III*, i, pp. 96–7, attributes to it the stopping of an address to Pitt from Leicester.

[48] *Remarks upon a popular Letter*, p. 29; cf. *The Case of the Late Resignation Set in a True Light*, London, 1761, advt. *PA*, 14 Nov. 1761.

[49] *A Letter To The Right Honourable Author*, pp. 12 (quotation), 13; cf. *A Second Letter To . . . B*[ute], pp. 3, 4, 19; *Remarks upon a popular Letter*, p. 16.

Patriot-Ground, in order to secure himself in future, the *Despotism* he has, for the present, been deprived of'.[50]

In surveying the whole course of the war, the attack reiterated well-established lines of criticism, questioning the wisdom of some measures, doubting whether Pitt was the sole or even the main architect of success and, of course, raising all the issues about the German war.[51] Pitt's attitude to the peace negotiations was now discussed in much more detail than before his resignation.[52] Spanish policy provided new matter for consideration. It was important to deny that Spanish issues gave suitable grounds for resignation. This could be done one of two ways: an effort could be made to show that they arose out of long-standing grievances over which Pitt, if he was 'guiding', should have taken earlier action or resigned sooner; or it could be argued war with Spain was not in British interests or, even if it was, that Pitt's own German involvements made it ill-advised.[53]

In this widened attack, damaging insinuations continued about the 'real' reasons for Pitt's resignation.[54] Attempts were also made to neutralize the effects of the City's support for Pitt, which loomed so large in discussion. The City had no right, it was said, to speak on national affairs or intrude on the King's prerogative. Its support for Pitt through all his changes of front from 1757 to 1761 was dismissed as absurd. The claim of the Aldermen and Common Council (let alone Beckford in his supposed letter) to speak for the City as a whole was denied. The right to instruct, it was maintained, belonged to the constituency as a whole, that is, the Livery—if, indeed, instructions, except in times of dire emergency, were not unconstitutional. Elsewhere the content of the Instructions was critically examined. Beckford himself came in for some virulent abuse for his 'patriot ebulition . . . like small beer from a bottle just uncorked, hissing, striking and ending in a vapid liquor'. One who had learnt 'his notions of treating mankind from the maxims of negro-drivers in

[50] *A Letter From A Right Honourable Person*, pp. 18–19, 25; *The Case of the Late Resignation*, pp. 3–4, 8 (quotation); *Remarks upon a popular Letter*, pp. 29–30.

[51] *A Letter To The Right Honourable Author* and *Impartial Reflections* are the best examples of this wholesale wider attack. The latter's stirring call for a return to true British policies (pp. 63–6) suggests a Tory allegiance.

[52] Particularly in *A Letter To The Right Honourable Author*, pp. 67–75.

[53] *A Second Letter To . . . B[ute]*, pp. 23–55; *Impartial Reflections*, pp. 31–7.

[54] e.g. *The Case of the Late Resignation*, pp. 12–13; *A Letter To The Right Honourable Author*, pp. 76–7; *Impartial Reflections*, pp. 47–9.

the colonies' was hardly a fitting leader of the City. Both Pitt and the City were criticized for disturbing public harmony, and Francis held that Pitt's appeal to the public justified ridiculing him in public.[55]

In answer to such an onslaught Pitt's only defence in pamphlet form was the relatively lightweight *Reflections occasioned by the Resignation of a Certain Great Man*.[56] It freely admitted an 'extraordinary' change in public regard for Pitt, and sought to offset it by distinguishing between two transactions which were being wrongly associated. The first, Pitt's resignation, had been satisfactorily explained in his letter; the second, the rewards, were the just deserts of an honest and able minister who had rendered real services. In this and other ways it merely reiterated established defences. Likewise, the weak panegyric of the ballad *Chevy-Chase*[57] added little weight, much as it might rally less discerning supporters.

These weaknesses in Pitt's pamphlet defenders made the regular support of the *Monitor* even more important. This is borne out by the detailed accusations made against its two papers of late October by *The Case of the Late Resignation*. They were attempts 'to excite clamour and sedition' among the citizens of London (over whom the *Monitor*'s influence was acknowledged), unjustly insinuating that a French-influenced faction was behind the opposition to Pitt's policies.[58] Through November the *Monitor* continued to develop its defence of Pitt, especially in answer to the *Gazetteer* and the *Second Letter* to Bute. The emphasis was partly on foreign policy. In reply to the *Second Letter*, Pitt's stand on Spain was justified as properly conceived for Britain's interests. It was indeed the genuine reason for his resignation, or at least part of the reason, for Pitt, the *Monitor* said, resigned over a whole series of frustrations in peace negotiations as well as war policy. The constitutional propriety of Pitt's behaviour was also defended by the usual arguments with some distinctive additions. His claim to guide was not an attempt to dictate. He had not usurped royal power, as Walpole had done, by manipulation of patronage and corruption. He exercised only the power properly belonging to his station and office. The blame heaped on him for the German war, although he was in no position

---

[55] *A Letter From A Right Honourable Person*, pp. 11, 17; *A Second Letter To . . . B[ute]*, pp. 11–12, 67–8, 69–72; *A Letter To The Right Honourable Author*, pp. 63–6 (second quotation p. 63), 69–70 (first quotation).

[56] Reviewed *PL*, 17 Nov. 1761.   [57] Advt. *PA*, 24 Nov. 1761.

[58] *The Case of the Late Resignation*, pp. 13–16; cf. *LEP*, 21–4 Nov. 1761.

to control the 'great dissipation of the public treasures' on it, showed that he would in fact have been held accountable for policies whether or not he agreed with them. To resign 'from a post he could not defend, and at a crisis, in which he must have lost his honour, had he continued therein, is defensible by common reason and upon the principles of patriotism'. He was the true patriot, harried by faction but supported by the voice of the nation. His public explanation revealed no secrets not already known from the triumph of his opponents. And he had good reason to make it in order to stop a very real swing of opinion against him.[59]

Early in December the *Monitor* initiated the most important exchange of the whole resignation debate when it was provoked by the versifying efforts of Francis to take up at last the sensitive subject of the pension. The impact of Francis's attack can be sensed in the vehemence of the *Monitor*'s reply to what it called the falsehood, virulence and malice of the 'frenchified faction' and their 'political scriblers'. The *Monitor* had to admit that the annuity, as the paper called it, had weighed heavily with the people as evidence of a loss of patriotic virtue. In defence it could only parade the standard answers. There was no evidence of a secret bargain, or that Pitt had altered in his frequently professed indifference to money. Particularly there was no evidence that Pitt had solicited a pension from Newcastle five years before, as Francis had charged. In a daring attempt to take the sting out of the accusations of false patriotism, Pitt's behaviour was contrasted with that of Pulteney in 1742.[60]

In the next *Monitor* attention was moved to the insinuations, made by Francis in his 'General Reflections', that Pitt had adopted Hanoverian policies to pander to the King and further his own ambition. Again there could be little answer but denial and defence of ambition directed to the good of the nation, together with the now stock defence that it was not Pitt but the 'faction' that was responsible for the profusion of money on German measures, as part of their deliberate attempt to destroy him.

Alas! such was his situation, in this respect, that his popularity would never have supported his patriotism against the influence of the T[reasur]y, had he attempted to expose the iniquitous means, by which the increase of expence in Germany was made.[61]

Probably in response to Spanish attempts to place the blame on Pitt for

[59] *Mon.* 330–2, 7–21 Nov. 1761 (quotation from 331).
[60] Ibid. 333–4, 5–12 Dec. 1761.   [61] Ibid. 334.

worsening relations with England, a note of caution now entered the *Monitor*'s account of his Spanish policy. His advice had been merely cautionary and conditional, urging the need, in face of evidence of Spanish hostility, to deter her and prepare for defence. This was coupled with a denial of the veracity of Francis's account of proceedings in the Cabinet, probably because they highlighted Pitt's arrogance. In some detail, the *Monitor* also refuted the account, first floated by Francis, of the last interview with the King in which Pitt was alleged to have wept in gratitude. The attention devoted to it suggests how damaging this story was felt to be to Pitt, presumably because it suggested that he was a subservient courtier who might have been bought after all.[62]

A promise to defend the City against the sarcasms of the versifier was fulfilled in the next *Monitor*. By a survey of the history of the City, it attempted to justify the right of Common Council to address and instruct on behalf of the City although Common Council did not elect the City members of Parliament.[63] Apart from this, the *Monitor* took no notice of the frequent strictures made by Francis and others on the behaviour of the City and of Beckford. However, at least it was a more effective answer to Francis than *A Full Vindication of the Right Honourable Wm. Pitt and Wm. Beckford, Esqurs*,[64] a weak attempt to belittle Francis's annotated versification by providing an alternative version.

This was mockingly dismissed by Francis when, in *A Letter from the Anonymous Author of the Letters Versified*, he returned to the fray with the *Monitor*. With his usual vehemence, he gibed at 'The Right Honourable, and his *patriotic* Friends . . . the *well-instructed* Alderman, and that Flower of City Knighthood, Sir James [Hodges]'. The *Monitor* had indulged '*anonymously for half a dozen Years*, in universal Scandal'. Now it was 'hired to abuse, in bitterness of Calumny, whoever does not render a senseless, superstitious Worship to the Idol of Mr B[eckfor]d's Devotion'. Francis's main attack fell on the *Monitor*'s excessive adulation of Pitt, its denial that Pitt had ever asked Newcastle for a pension, its vague allegations about the activites of a 'Frenchified faction' against Pitt, and its attempts to justify Pitt's German measures and exculpate him (although he

---

[62] The accounts given by Francis (later much repeated e.g. *AR*, iv, 1761, pp. 43, 44–5) seem substantially correct. Cf. above p. 202 and Williams, ii, pp. 112–13, 115 and fn. 2.

[63] *Mon.* 335, 19 Dec. 1761.   [64] Advt. *PA*, 21 Dec. 1761.

was 'guiding') from blame for their expense. A further apparently discrediting episode, Barré's attacks on Pitt in the House of Commons and Pitt's and Beckford's unresponsiveness, was added to former anecdotes to defame Pitt.[65]

In this duel between the *Monitor* and Francis the scurrilously personal tone of attack and defence came to a height and the whole resignation debate reached its climax. Similar acrimonious personal attack continued to dominate the pamphlets that went on appearing through December and January.[66] The *Coalition*,[67] a satire on both Pitt and Newcastle, was much more sharply pointed against Pitt, his patriot pretensions and inconsistency, his Tory, country-gentlemen and City supporters, especially Beckford and Philipps, and his arrogance and greed. Even more extremely than its predecessors, *An Impartial Enquiry Into The Conduct Of A late Minister*, no more impartial than the earlier *Impartial Reflections*, expatiated on 'false Merit, uplifted by the foul Breath of little Emissaries' to gain 'an Esteem and Reputation among a Company of Grocers, low Booksellers, and Coblers' and on a deliberate affectation of public virtue and public spirit to promote political ambition. More fully than recent predecessors, it made use of the inconsistencies of the whole of Pitt's political career to undermine his 'affectation' of patriotism. Some interesting new reproaches were added to the usual ones. Pitt was accused of having been lukewarm to the Militia, then of using it, once established, as an excuse 'to smuggle away more *British* troops to *Hanover*'. He had kept it 'unnecessarily' embodied so that service became odious to every independent gentleman. The emptiness of Pitt's promises of economies was also dwelt on, while the parting gibe at the contractors and gentlemen of Change Alley who 'have reaped a Golden Harvest' from the war adds to the impression that this pamphlet reflects the bitter disillusion of the archetypal Tory squire.[68] The same new accusations were made in the later *Constitu-*

---

[65] Advt. *PA*, 30 Dec. 1761 (quotations from pp. 8, 19). Pitt's harsh letter to his sister Anne on her receipt of a pension in 1760, regretting that the name Pitt had appeared on a pension list, was now used to add fuel to the attack on Pitt's patriotism (p. 92). See Williams, i, p. 206. For Barré's attacks see below p. 236.

[66] In Dec. seven pamphlets are noticed in the Reviews, three in defence, four (the more powerful) against Pitt. In Jan. six are noticed, two for and four against.

[67] Advt. *PA*, 9 Dec. 1761 (second edn. 5 Jan. 1762).

[68] Advt. *PA*, 7 Dec. 1761 (quotations from pp. 1–2, 10, 38–9). Cf. similar criticisms of Pitt's attitude towards the Militia in *GM*, xxxi, Nov. 1761, p. 518.

tional Queries.[69] This also turned the old complaints against the German war to a new purpose in maintaining that it had left Britain so distressed as to invite Spanish insults while she was incapable of resisting them effectively. Another attack with a rather different point came in J. Massie's *Observations relating to British and Spanish proceedings.* German rather than Spanish policy was Massie's chief concern. He used the 1758 *Monitor* dialogue between Harry and Will on Continental involvement to show how Pitt had departed from the principles there enunciated. All justifications of his change of front were rejected as mere covers for the real motive, Pitt's subservience to West Indian interests. This, said Massie, had also prevented his making any real effort in North America or the West Indies since 1759 (a quite common complaint).[70] Beside these attacks, the moderation of *The Equilibrium*[71] is a strange and ineffectual contrast. It criticized Pitt's Spanish policy, the award of all praise for successes to him, and his precipitate resignation in time of need, but it regarded his rewards as deserved.

Meanwhile, the *Monitor* had once more taken up the German war issue in response to another blast from Mauduit's trumpet, *Occasional Thoughts On The Present German War,* published in December. This was a lengthy, diffuse and disjointed work designed to prove yet again that the war was entirely against the interests of Europe, Germany, or Britain. It made some reflections on Pitt's consistency and on the concessions he had made in peace negotiations but disavowed any part in 'the disputes about the merit or demerit of the late Minister'.[72] Despite its heaviness, Mauduit again stirred considerable public interest and immediately prompted two answers of substance as well as four supporters of no great merit although more pointed in attacks on Pitt.[73] This exchange created an embarrassing undercurrent to the main debate over Pitt's resignation, even becoming predominant at times. The *Critical Review* commented on

[69] Advt. *PA*, 13 Jan. 1762.

[70] See *Mon.* 158, 29 July 1758, and above p. 122. For other complaints about neglect of American and West Indian campaigns see above. p. 172.

[71] Advt. *PA*, 17 Dec. 1761.

[72] Advt. *PA*, 3 Dec., second edn. *PL*, 8 Dec., third edn. *PA*, 10 Dec. 1761 (quotation from pp. v–vi).

[73] See e.g. *GM*, xxxi, Dec. 1761, pp. 575–9, Supplement, pp. 619–24; *LM*, xxx, Appendix, pp. 677–81; *CR*, xii, Dec. 1761, pp. 473, 475, 476, 479; *MR*, xxv, Dec. 1761, p. 470, xxvi, Jan. 1762, p. 73, Feb., p. 148.

Mauduit's 'bold and melancholy truths, judicious remarks, and irrefragable arguments'. Symmer reported that the German war was 'the great Question now agitated', on which the mass of the people were 'inflamed and violent'.[74] The *Monitor*'s interest confirms his assessment. In four papers in December and January it provided a full answer on its usual lines to the charge that Pitt had tricked the nation into a ruinous Continental war inconsistent with his former principles. Rather, 'whatever share Mr Pitt took in the German war, he improved it for his country's interest'.[75]

The only other defences of Pitt of any substance in these months were *A Seventh Letter to the People of England*, an 'unthinking panegyric' on Pitt and all his policies, and *A Consolatory Epistle To the Members of the Old Faction*.[76] The latter, an answer to Francis's *Letter From A Right Honourable Person* and the *Impartial Reflections*, took up in quite effective ironical vein a version of the *Monitor*'s old 'faction' argument, applying it to the German war and Prussian alliance, the attribution of all credit to Pitt, and the resignation. On the first question, its suggestion that both Pitt and the people were deluded into the Continental war by the Machiavellian cunning of the old faction would seem to be somewhat two-edged.

By this time, despite the more pacific approach of Pitt's former colleagues, war with Spain had proved inevitable. The declaration of war on 4 January 1762 seemed, as the *Consolatory Epistle* pointed out,[77] to threaten a revival of Pitt's reputation. His supporters did all they could to encourage the revival. For example, false stories that, on the receipt of news from Madrid, he had been summoned again to the Cabinet and complimented by the King, appeared in the newspapers.[78] This threatened revival prompted a *Third Letter To . . . B[ute]* by Guthrie. Like his earlier efforts, this was not a personal attack but a careful, thorough—and prolonged—consideration of Pitt's measures on Spain, peace, Germany, the National Debt and the standing army. Guthrie's often reiterated major complaint was that although Pitt's Spanish policy appeared justified by the onset of

[74] *CR*, xii, Dec. 1761, p. 473; Symmer to Mitchell, 11 Dec. 1761, Add. MSS 6839, f. 242.

[75] *Mon.* 334, 12 Dec., 336, 26 Dec. 1761; 337, 2 Jan., 339, 16 Jan. 1762 (quotation).

[76] *CR*, xii, Dec. 1761, pp. 477–8 (quotation), *MR*, xxv, Dec. 1761, pp. 469–70; advt. *PA,* 18 Jan. 1762.

[77] *A Consolatory Epistle*, p. 14.

[78] *St. JC*, 26–8 Dec. 1761; Birch to Royston, 2 Jan. 1762, Add. MSS 35399, f. 267.

war, it was still open to serious objections. He would have had the British behave like lawless ruffians. Yet earlier they had failed to act decisively on complaints against Spain when success would have been much more likely.

What constructions can be put upon such an acquiescence, so long continued with our eyes open, and so suddenly interrupted, but that our minister found it convenient for him to make that a pretext for retiring from a post he no longer could hold with safety?

The most interesting lesser criticism was that Pitt should not have renewed the Prussian treaty in 1759–60 when Britain could easily have separated from Prussia and made peace.[79]

Such a solid attempt to prevent any revival of Pitt's reputation seems to have been unnecessary. In fact, despite Walpole's prediction to the contrary, the Spanish war was for him as much an embarrassment as an opportunity. There is strong evidence that, as the prospect became a reality, not only the moneyed interest but merchants grew wary, more fearful of disruption than hopeful of increase of trade. Others, including some of Pitt's 'greatest Admirers', shared this caution. The City was no longer easily confident, as Beckford had been two months before, about 'the *comfortable* state' of the nation. When the declaration of the departing Spanish Ambassador, published on 1 January, threw the blame on Pitt, his supporters felt it necessary to condemn it as a forgery perpetrated by 'the *hirelings*, employed to abuse the Patriot Minister'. Despite their efforts it was doubtful 'whether that [the declaration] will not lose him with the People, who do not relish the Legacy he has left them as a Minister'.[80] The *Monitor* naturally attempted to answer the charges of the Ambassador that Pitt had been implacably set on war against Spain and was guilty of unbounded ambition and haughtiness. On the contrary, it said, he had responded merely with the necessary firmness of a wise and steady statesman, sincerely conciliatory until convinced of his opponent's obduracy. Yet it gave only one paper to the question.[81] In marked contrast to its attitude to

[79] Advt. *PA*, 11 Jan. 1762 (quotation from p. 55).

[80] Walpole to Mann, 28 Dec. 1761, *Walpole's Corr.* xxi, pp. 557–8; Newcastle to Devonshire, 3 Dec., memorandum, 7 Dec., West to Newcastle, 29 Dec. 1761, Add. MSS 32931, ff. 388, 427, 32932, f. 404; Symmer to Mitchell, 1 Jan. 1762, Add. MSS 6839, f. 246 (third quotation); Birch to Royston, 2, 9 Jan. 1762, Add. MSS 35399, ff. 266–7 (second quotation), 270 (first quotation).

[81] *Mon.* 338, 9 Jan. 1762.

Francis's personal attacks, it did not take up Guthrie's concentration on measures.

By mid-January, with the Spanish war diverting rather than re-kindling interest, the main thrust of both attack on and defence of Pitt was over. Yet the great revival of public controversy did not die away as the issue passed, like lesser bouts of the last five or six years. Rather it found new issues on which to feed and grow—and debate over Pitt's policies was never far below the surface in discussion of them. This profound and continuing disturbance of the political nation is in itself one measure of the disruptive effect of Pitt's resignation.

The resignation controversy was of course far from entirely spontaneous. Certainly such an interesting event did prompt unsolicited contributions both in pamphlets and in newspapers. But the fierceness of the debate was the result of a deliberate attack, with a degree of Government support unequalled since the days of Walpole. The attack, a combination of personal abuse with substantial argument about policies, was designed to 'overwhelm Pitt's supporters and block off every channel of reply' and to destroy once and for all Pitt's popular reputation.[82] The argument over Spanish policy provided some new material. The discussion of the powers and responsibility of ministers provoked by Pitt's claim to 'guide' raised fundamental constitutional issues and foreshadowed the debate over Bute's position, soon to follow. Otherwise, there is little in the methods or substance of the attack that had not been adumbrated earlier. Its greatest force came from the new ammunition which the resignation and its circumstances supplied for use in well-tried ways against Pitt's patriot reputation, his consistency and the soundness of his claim to popularity.

For this study, the main interest of the debate lies in the effectiveness or otherwise of this new ammunition in overwhelming Pitt's defences. The attack seems to have had least effect in the more ephemeral forms of publicity. There is little sign in the prints of any reaction against Pitt.[83] Of the newspapers, the *Public Advertiser* kept itself consistently aloof from the controversy, the *London Evening Post* and *Public Ledger* were steadfastly loyal, and of those papers which

[82] Brewer, *Party Ideology,* pp. 223–4.
[83] George, pp. 119–20 but cf. Atherton, pp. 255–7, esp. p. 257, describing *Sic Transit Gloria Mundi.*

opened their pages to the attack only the *Gazetteer* appears to have remained hostile. It may be, however, that the impact of the initial attack, directed as it was chiefly through evening papers with a country circulation, was not wholly undone by its later slackening. The loyalty of the *London Evening Post* and *Public Ledger* merely reflected different elements of City opinion. In the pamphlets there is no doubt that attacks far outweighed defence of Pitt both in quality and quantity.[84] The volunteers on Pitt's side were no match for Bute's professional hacks. Without Beckford's hacks in the *Monitor* Pitt's defence in anything more sustained than letters and paragraphs in the papers would have been weak indeed. There seems no way to decide certainly which would have the greater impact, the generally favourable balance of the more ephemeral yet more regular newspapers or the clearly unfavourable balance of more weighty occasional writing.[85] It is, however, of some significance that it was the attacks and particularly the abuse that most attracted the comment of contemporaries. The *Monitor* was not alone in its wondering and increasing allusion to the bitter personal attacks on Pitt. John Almon, a bookseller and political writer sympathetic to Pitt, referred to 'prodigious streams of abuse . . . in all the channels of conveyance to the public', while Walpole, the *Critical Review,* and the *Annual Register* made similar comments.[86] Bute's writers may not have succeeded in blocking off 'every channel of reply' but they seem to have attracted most attention.

It would seem, further, that they succeeded in so damaging Pitt's reputation as to affect his political strength. Certainly their efforts suggest that they believed their attacks could achieve this result. Without exception commentators of varied loyalties admitted the initial effect of the attack on Pitt's popularity. Some thought that this initial repulse was followed by a reaction in Pitt's favour similar to that provoked by the very strength of the attacks of the *Test* in 1756–7.[87] The evidence, however, seems to be against them. The

[84] Neither *CR* nor *MR* was able to recommend for its quality any of the pamphlets in Pitt's defence.

[85] It is perhaps significant that *GM* in its quite extensive summaries of the controversy usually gives more space to extracts from the papers than to those from pamphlets. See xxxi, Oct. 1761, pp. 460–8, Nov., pp. 513–21, Dec., pp. 579–84.

[86] *Mon.* 330, 14 Nov., 333, 5 Dec. 1761, 354, 1 May 1762; Haig, p. 50, quoting Almon; Walpole, *Geo III,* i, pp. 83, 85; *CR,* xii, Oct. 1761, p. 304; *AR,* iv, 1761, p. 47.

[87] e.g. Walpole, *Geo. III,* i, p. 66; *Anecdotes of Chatham,* i, pp. 371–2, 378–9; the introductory essay to the collected edn. (1765) of the *Contrast* (1763) speaks of a strong

compromises of the years in office and the satiety brought by success in war meant that sympathy for Pitt was less readily forthcoming now. The *Monitor* was clearly forced on to the defensive, its early ebullient attempts to whip up the people and claim their support soon forgotten. The *Monthly Review*, although it might deplore extreme abuse, was sympathetic to the pamphlet attacks from the beginning. Most significant is the trend of the *Critical Review*'s reactions. At first hostile to attacks although not entirely happy about Pitt's actions, it became steadily more critical of him until it was sorrowfully siding with the critics.

We are sorry to find the enemies of Mr P[itt] in a condition to supply so many plausible arguments against the conduct of that celebrated m[iniste]r. We are still more sorry, that we cannot altogether justify a resignation so made, at such a juncture, so attended with circumstances, and so likely to revive those animosities and heart-burnings, which were so happily extinguished.[88]

Such a reaction was reflected in a tangible way in the limited response of the corporations to London's example of thanks to Pitt. As the *Annual Register* remarked in its judicious account of these 'violent conflicts', 'the popular cause was worse sustained, and the ministerial better, (that is, with greater effect) than is usual in such discussions' and

the barriers that were opposed against that torrent of popular rage, which it was apprehended would proceed from the resignation . . . answered their end perfectly; this torrent for some time was beaten back, almost diverted into an opposite course; and when afterwards it returned . . . it was no longer that impetuous and irresistible tide, which in the year 1757 had borne down every thing before it; it was weakened, divided, and ineffective.

Fox, indeed, speculated that if Bute had been able to make peace and prevent rather than provoke war with Spain, Pitt's popularity would have been at an end.[89]

Already the first session of the new Parliament was providing a pertinent test of the effects of the resignation and the consequent

reaction against the *Letter . . . Translated into Verse*, causing Pitt's popularity to return 'with redoubtable lustre'.

[88] e.g. *MR*, xxv, Oct. 1761, pp. 317–18; *CR*, xii, Oct. 1761, pp. 304–10, 311–12, Nov., p. 394 (quotation).

[89] *AR*, iv, 1761, pp. 44, 45; Lord Holland's Memoir, pp. 75–6.

popular clamour. Before its opening Newcastle had anxiously rallied support to avoid repercussions indoors of the ferment he feared was developing outside. Kinnoull supported his fears that a general uproar would create difficulties. Bute, Newcastle and Hardwicke all treated the King's Speech as part of the contest for popularity.[90] Certainly, when the real business of the session opened on 13 November, the effects of the resignation were seen in a series of great debates which broke the relative calm of the period of the Coalition Ministry, brought to the surface issues which before had simmered below, and introduced new ones. On four occasions of major debate before Christmas[91] argument turned on four main themes: the situation which occasioned Pitt's resignation, its political effects and the propriety of his letter of explanation; relations with Spain and Spanish intentions; the merits or otherwise of the German war; and the course of the peace negotiations and especially the fisheries question. After Christmas, the coming of war with Spain occasioned further debate on Spanish policy.[92] On all themes Pitt defended himself skilfully in substantial speeches, in a way which suggested an intention to remain active in politics. Yet for him the results of this defence were to be disappointing.

On the first theme, the least thoroughly debated, there was much reference to the uncertainties of the political situation, and to unfortunate new divisions and factions. Pitt repeated his contention that he resigned 'in order not to be responsible for measures he was no longer suffered to *guide*'. This led to some heated exchanges over the necessity and desirability of a 'first minister' in such troubled times. In these Beckford took a prominent part. Rigby, among others, rubbed home the irony that the Opposition should now claim for Pitt the dominance for which Walpole was so criticized. 'But what! had the city instructed its representatives to demand a First Minister? He had heard the Excise adopted by a sort of First

[90] Newcastle to White, 20 Oct., to Rockingham, 22 Oct., to Hardwicke, 23 Oct., Hardwicke to Newcastle, 23 Oct., Kinnoull to Newcastle, 24 Oct. 1761, Add. MSS 32929, ff. 409, 444, 470, 472, 32930, ff. 12–13.

[91] On the Address in Reply, 13 Nov., on the estimates for the land forces later in Nov., on the vote for the Army in Germany, 9, 10 Dec., and on a private motion for papers relating to the Spanish claim to a share in the North American fisheries, 11 Dec. 1761, Walpole, *Geo. III*, i, pp. 71–7, 79–83, 85–96.

[92] On the King's message announcing the declaration of war, 19 Jan. 1762, ibid., pp. 103–6.

Minister.' At this Pitt was provoked to explain his claim. He somewhat disingenuously repudiated Beckford's interpretation of it as a claim to be a 'single' minister and explained that he demanded only the right to control the correspondence of his own office, not to direct that of others.[93]

On the two occasions before Christmas when questions concerning Spain were given a full airing,[94] Pitt defended at length his call for vigorous measures. They were based, he said, on conviction and information, and he hinted that he had more knowledge than he could properly reveal. He denied that he had courted war and called for full information to be placed before Parliament. On the closely connected question of the peace negotiations, the main point that arose was the concession to France over the fisheries. Pitt, taxed by Beckford for yielding this, regretted that he had been overborne by numbers although he admitted that the concession had been necessary to keep the hope of peace alive. He declared he would support Britain's sole control of the fisheries as a *sine qua non* in renewed negotiations.[95]

The German war was still the most controversial issue of all, especially in view of renewed debate outside. On the three occasions it was debated[96] Pitt firmly maintained its usefulness in diverting France, preventing invasion and making possible all Britain's colonial conquests. In the debate on the Address in Reply he made his famous claim that 'America had been conquered in Germany'. Later attacks, especially from Rigby, put him more on the defensive and caused him to admit that he had been driven into German measures for reasons of Hanoverian rather than English policy. He maintained still that he had not agreed until the measures were modified to allow for the defence of Britain and America and until every other service had been provided for. He had, he said, so modified German policy as to make it a millstone round the neck of France rather than round that of Britain, as formerly. He got firm support for his 'divine plan' from Charles Townshend, now Secretary at War.[97] Altogether the issue was not as embarrassing to Pitt

[93] Ibid., pp. 72, 75 (Pitt), 89 (Beckford), 91 (Rigby), 92.

[94] On the Address in Reply and the motion for papers.

[95] Walpole, *Geo. III*, i, pp. 74, 76, 77; Royston to Hardwicke, [13 Nov. 1761], Yorke, *Hardwicke*, iii, p. 338.

[96] On the Address in Reply, the vote for the land forces, and especially on the vote for the Army in Germany.

[97] Walpole, *Geo. III*, i, pp. 75–6 (quotation), 79 (Townshend), 80, 82–3.

as it might have been because the Ministry was itself divided on the question and not in a position to push home the attack on him.[98] But it would seem that Pitt did not fully realize the depth of feeling on this matter, especially outside.[99]

In the debates after Christmas on the declaration of war against Spain, Pitt exploited the opportunities offered him. These were increased by an injudicious attack by Lord North. Pitt appeared to praise the Ministers while drawing attention to his own foresight and successes. He defended himself against the charge of having provoked Spain yet disavowed any wish for papers to be produced to support his claims unless it would benefit national affairs. He urged unanimity despite the 'cruel attacks on him', and contrasted the 'wide connections' of the Ministers with his own individual status.[100] Yet after this he took no further part in debates until May. This was not for lack of opportunity or provocation. In late January, motions on the German war were made by Bedford and Rigby in the Lords and Commons respectively. These motions were designed at least in part out of hostility to Pitt, but revealed embarrassing divisions in the Ministry which redounded to his credit and were ripe for exploitation.[101]

Pitt's part in these debates provides the only available evidence of his intentions about his future. Certainly he had defended himself with some skill and with apparent restraint, especially in his explanation of his claim to 'guide', which had given such offence. To most observers, friendly or otherwise, his speech on the Address in Reply showed moderation. He seemed, then and later, to be assuming the role of the responsible elder statesman, detachedly offering advice, opposing only what he would have opposed 'with the Seals in his hand', and speaking of himself only when necessary to defend his reputation. Indeed he disavowed any intention to 'inflame', making much of the claim (taken up by some pamphlets) that he had resigned in order not to breach the unanimity of the Administration. Further, he 'hoped never to be a public man again. He never would come into place again.'[102]

[98] Walpole, *Geo. III*, i, pp. 79–80, 81.

[99] See above p. 227 and Watkins to Newcastle, 10 Nov. 1761, Add. MSS 32930, f. 398.

[100] Walpole, *Geo. III*, i, pp. 104–6.   [101] Ibid., pp. 107, 108.

[102] Royston to Hardwicke, [13 Nov. 1761], Newcastle to Hardwicke, 15 Nov. 1761, Yorke, *Hardwicke*, iii, pp. 338, 339; Symmer to Mitchell, 20 Nov. 1761, quoted *Corr. Chatham*, ii, p. 169 fn.; *AR*, iv, 1761, p. 48; Walpole, *Geo. III*, i, pp. 74, 75 (second quotation), 76, 91–2, 93 (first quotation).

On the other hand, Walpole saw Pitt's speech on the Address as 'artful and inflammatory', and he was probably right. Bute realized that Pitt's call for papers concerning Spain was designed to procure evidence 'in order to try the cause between the King and his late Secretary'. Hints about fears of misrepresentation, hints that he knew more that was disturbing than he would reveal and was silent out of delicacy rather than obligation, expressions of confidence in the present Ministers which could only be ironical, these indeed were inflammatory. Pitt's conduct hardly supported his claim that he wanted to maintain unanimity. His declaration that he would not push for papers concerning the Spanish claim to the fisheries if the Ministers would declare that the claim had not been intended to impede peace negotiations was clearly designed to embarrass the Ministry.[103] Equally, his expression of regret for conceding a share in the fisheries to France was angling for City support. His disavowals of intention to inflame and his declaration that he would never hold office again were both made in the context of bitter laments over lack of support, which suggests that they are not entirely to be taken at face value.[104]

There are more positive indications that at least early in the parliamentary session Pitt intended to take no merely passive role. He showed every sign of intending to exploit the question of the extension of the Militia Act, sidetracked in 1760–1 but now made unavoidable by the prolongation of the war. This was apparently a good issue on which to arouse an active opposition. Possibly Charles Townshend could be recruited, for he was aggrieved at the advancement of Grenville, although he was himself still Secretary at War. The lack of any reference to the Militia in the King's Speech was noted by several speakers in the debate on the Address, including Pitt and Temple, and, when a meeting of supporters of the Militia at the St. Albans Tavern on 25 November resolved to move for a bill to make the Militia perpetual, Pitt took a prominent part. All seemed set for an effort to make political capital out of the issue which Pitt while Minister had carefully sought to avoid.[105]

So whatever Pitt's calculations previous to resignation, his behaviour in the early weeks of the parliamentary session suggests that by

[103] Walpole, *Geo. III,* i, pp. 77 (quotation), 93, 94; Bute to Grenville, [12 Nov. 1761], *Grenville Papers,* i, p. 417.

[104] They are strikingly similar in tone and context to complaints made at his last Cabinet meeting. Cf. Yorke, *Hardwicke,* iii, pp. 279–80.

[105] See above p. 161; Walpole, *Geo. III,* i, pp. 68, 69, 72, 74, 78; Walpole to Mann, 12 Dec. 1761, *Walpole's Corr.* xxi, pp. 552–3; Western, pp. 184–5.

then he had no intention of giving up political activity and would marshall what resources he could in active opposition. Yet the response to his skilful and sustained defence was hardly encouraging. Grenville had told Hardwicke before the session opened that he 'did not imagine that Mr Pitt would have any great following of the Tories . . . and that Sir Charles Mordaunt and the soberer part of them were sick of Mr P[itt']s measures of war, more especially continental, and of the immense expence'. His forecast proved to be correct. Two Tories answered Beckford in the debate on the Address on just these points. Rigby, when attacking the German war, claimed to speak for the country gentlemen, and the tone of the House seemed clearly with him. The divisions in the Ministry prevented too much overt embarrassment to Pitt on this issue. But when he backed the private motion of Cooke and Beckford for papers relating to the Spanish claim to the fisheries, the lack of Tory support was obvious. The defeat of the motion without a division was a humiliation. Pitt was further mortified by lack of support from the House in face of the vicious and unexpected attacks of a new and unknown member, Colonel Barré, who, in the language of the pamphlets, called him 'a profligate minister, who had thrust himself into power on the shoulders of the mob'; 'variations, inconsistencies, arts, popularity, ambition, were all pressed upon Pitt with energy and bitterness.' The attacks provoked much unfavourable comment but no rallying of support to Pitt within the House. Pitt, absent on the first but not on the next occasion, seemed by some accounts to have been disconcerted. Certainly he disdained to reply.[106]

It was after the last debate on Spanish papers that Fox reported exultantly to Devonshire

Never did Man make a more miserable Figure than Mr Pitt. He found, He felt, He owned, He had hardly one Friend in the House of Commons . . . Death to Mr Pitt and Mr Pitt looked dying . . . and had it been in the prelude to his natural not political Death, He could not have looked otherwise than He did.

West and Onslow concurred, if in more sober terms, 'that it was all

[106] Hardwicke to Newcastle, 15 Oct. 1761, giving Grenville's views, quoted Namier, *England*, pp. 298–9; Walpole, *Geo. III*, i, pp. 73, 80, 86 (first quotation)–7, 94 (second quotation)–6; Walpole to Mann, 12 Dec. 1761, *Walpole's Corr.* xxi, p. 553; Lord Holland's Memoir, p. 54; John Millbanke to Rockingham, 28 Dec. 1761, *Mems. Rockingham*, i, pp. 81–2.

over with him'. There was justification, indeed, for the King's remark, 'I suppose his party consist of that Lord [Strange], Mr Beck[ford], Mr Cooke, and perhaps a very few more who are of the same hot headed stamp.'[107]

After this humiliating defeat Walpole saw the Militia question as Pitt's only chance of rallying his forces. It was to prove a vain hope. The Militia Bill was effectively taken out of the arena of factious politics by the union of its moderate supporters against both Newcastle's hostility on one side and the hopes of making political capital out of it on the other. An extension for seven years rather than in perpetuity was agreed on and amendments were accepted to improve the Militia's practical efficiency and reduce its burden. Some of Pitt's supporters, including Beckford, continued to press for perpetuity but with little effect. Altogether the progress of the Bill suggested 'the declining importance and usefulness of the militia as an issue in political warfare'.[108] The *Monitor's* complete silence on the question confirms this and it figures only slightly in the pamphlet controversy, usually in complaints about prolonged embodiment.[109]

Despite Pitt's skilful exploitation of the announcement of war against Spain, which kept the attention of the House on him, this turn of events did not appear to rally support for him inside Parliament any more than without. If even his closest supporters outside were wavering over this issue, it was hardly likely that opinion within would see the extension of the war as anything but a regrettable necessity, hardly requiring his return to office. Only if it was disastrously mismanaged would they look to him as a saviour. It was probably his sense that the issue was not likely to change the discouraging response of the House that made him speak 'languidly and meekly' and, in contrast to his energy hitherto, to take no further part in debates until May. In the general lull which followed 'a certain great man is now very little heard of, though not yet forgot'.[110]

[107] Fox to Devonshire, 17 Dec. 1761, quoted Brewer, *Party Ideology*, p. 102; George III to Bute, 11 Dec. 1761, Newcastle reporting West and Onslow, Add. MSS 32932, f. 149, quoted in *Letters of George III to Lord Bute*, p. 73.

[108] Walpole to Mann, 12 Dec. 1761. *Walpole's Corr.* xxi, p. 553; Western, pp. 185–93 (quotation); West's account, 20 Mar. 1762, Add. MSS 32935, f. 494.

[109] See above pp. 225–6.

[110] Fox to Ilchester, 20 Jan. 1762, Ilchester, *Fox,* ii, p. 161 (Fox's letter suggests Pitt may have been ill); Symmer to Mitchell, 19 Mar. 1762, Add. MSS 6839, f. 259.

In May the tempo of debate revived in response to the King's message concerning aid to Portugal, under attack from Spain. Pitt grasped the opportunity of this new issue and the associated divisions in the Ministry over the future of the German war, which were soon to lead to Newcastle's resignation.[111] Pitt's speech, highly praised by Walpole, favoured vigorous prosecution of the war everywhere. He warmly supported aid to Portugal but deprecated suggestions of withdrawal from Germany. He disdained to turn the whole blame for the cost of the German war on the Treasury now that Newcastle was its chief proponent in the Ministry. Pitt could again disavow opposition in such a way as to highlight the disarray of the Ministry, claiming that he alone agreed with the whole Administration, being for war both in Portugal and in Germany. Wilkes, Legge, and Beckford gave preliminary support, but circumstances were hardly ripe for the House to react favourably to this full-blooded war-mongering. As Grenville effectively pointed out, victories were continuing; the accession of a new Czar friendly to Prussia made support of Prussia seem no longer necessary and set opinion even more against the German war and in favour of peace. In any case, the prorogation was too near for any response in the House to have much effect. Beckford might boldly claim—on what authority is not clear—that the City demanded to have 'their *old minister*' again. There was no evidence that anyone else did, and it became obvious that the Ministry would be reconstructed without him after Newcastle's resignation later in the month. Any revival of Pitt's fortunes would now have to wait on other developments.[112]

Pitt must have known that unless he intended retirement, to resign was to gamble with his political future. It is doubtful, however, whether he realized the serious tests and crises it would create. Instead of the general revival of his somewhat tarnished popularity that he probably expected,[113] his reputation was more in danger of serious compromise than it had been at any time since 1757. His various mistakes had been seized on with glee by skilful opponents. Despite his energy and skill in his own defence he had been unable to retrieve the situation. In the House the Great Commoner and war Minister had been humiliated. Many of the

[111] See below pp. 240–1.
[112] Walpole, *Geo. III*, i, pp. 128–31, 127 (quotation), 122, 108.
[113] As Kinnoull did (to Newcastle, 24 Oct. 1761, Add. MSS 32930, ff. 12–13).

Tories in Parliament and in the country were lost. Some of his erstwhile supporters like Richard Glover and George Townshend were now disillusioned with him and rested their hopes on the new King.[114] In Parliament, among Pitt's committed supporters Beckford stood out as the most vocal and energetic. He, with Cooke and the now more active Wilkes, hardly comprised impressive support. Outside Parliament, Beckford's backing was more effective. In the City he was now prominent as a popular leader. His awkward personality was not always conducive to co-operation, perhaps, but with Beardmore as his loyal henchman and with the help of Hodges he held the City—or at least Common Council—firmly for Pitt. To a wider audience his paper, the *Monitor*, had championed Pitt against attack. Yet the debate had run against Pitt, and his popular support was now, as several observers noted, very one-sided.

Thus Pitt was 'not only low at Court, but sinks in the public Esteem, and meets with but little Respect in the House of C[ommo]ns'; he was without office; the Grenville connection was divided; Legge had long since been alienated. What political future could he hope for? Could 'Mr Pitt and the Common Council on one hand' hope to prevail against 'the great lords on the other', especially when the latter seemed to have the support of the 'the Cooler part of the Nation, and the landed Interest'?[115] What use could or would Pitt make of the remaining bastion of his popularity in the City?

---

[114] See above p. 191; *Dodington*, p. 441 fn. 1; George III to Bute, [*c.* 18 Dec.] 1761, *Letters of George III to Lord Bute*, pp. 73–4.

[115] Symmer to Mitchell, 20 Nov. 1761, 29 Jan. 1762, Add. MSS 6839, ff. 239, 251 (first and fourth quotations); Walpole to Conway, 26 Oct. 1761, *The Letters of Horace Walpole*, v, p. 139 (second and third quotations); cf. Seeds to Royston, 11 Oct. 1761, Add. MSS 35606, f. 370.

VIII

The End of the War 1762–1763
—the Decline of a Patriot

The main debate over Pitt's resignation had ended by January 1762, both in Parliament and outside. He seemed to have suffered a crushing defeat; a correspondent in the *London Chronicle* considered him 'politically dead'.[1] Yet the effects of the resignation were far from finished. The 'violent fermentation in the political world'[2] in 1762 was a direct result of the anxieties, frustrations, and uncertainties it caused.

In March the official publication of papers relating to the break with Spain brought renewed controversy over Pitt's Spanish policy. John Wilkes made his début in occasional propaganda in a criticism of the official papers, maintaining that some had been deliberately held back to justify the Ministers and destroy Pitt's reputation. The *Monitor* fully supported Wilkes's argument while the five answers to him all reflected more or less pointedly on Pitt's Spanish policy.[3]

In May divisions in the Ministry over the German war at last reached their climax. When aid was granted to Portugal against Spain, at the expense of Britain's subsidy to Prussia, Newcastle

---

[1] In Mar. *An Address To The City of London* and *A Continuation Of The Address* attacked Pitt. They provoked *Mon.* (348–9, 20–7 Mar. 1761) and occasioned the *LC* comment (9–11 Mar.).

[2] Mrs Montagu to Bath, May 1762, *Mrs Montagu, ['Queen of the Blues'],* ed. Reginald Blunt, 2 vòls., London, [1923], p. 20.

[3] *Papers relative to the Rupture with Spain, MR*, xxvi, Mar. 1762, pp. 228–9; [John Wilkes], *Observations On The Papers Relative To The Rupture with Spain, MR*, xxvi, Mar. 1762, p. 230, *CR*, xiii, Mar. 1762, pp. 263–4; *Mon.* 352–3, 17–24 Apr., 358–9, 29 May–5 June 1762; for further pamphlets see *MR*, xxvi, Apr. 1762, pp. 317–18, May, p. 383; *CR*, xiii, Apr. 1762, p. 359, May, p. 438. The newspapers followed the exchange.

resigned. The resignation, at last made public on 26 May, fastened all attention on Bute. Now as First Lord of the Treasury he was formally head of the Administration. As a relatively unknown intruder into the position of leadership vacated by familiar figures, he now became the target for all the resentments and fears bred by political upheaval and well-publicized policy divisions. Over the next eleven months he was to endure an adverse propaganda campaign of unprecedented virulence which gave him an unpopularity he never overcame.[4] With fine dramatic irony, the controversy begun over Pitt's resignation rebounded against its prime mover.

This remarkable campaign was begun by the *Monitor*. On 22 May it published a daring article on favourites, headed by a quotation referring to Tiberius and Sejanus. The paper attracted immediate attention. In the sacred precincts of the King's drawing room a courtier asked Mrs Montagu her opinion of it. It was the work of a new hand in the writing of the *Monitor*, John Wilkes.[5] Soon, on Temple's initiative, Wilkes's rather too provocative energies were diverted from the established *Monitor*. The first issue of his own essay paper, the *North Briton*, appeared on 5 June. He continued to write for the *Monitor*, however, and indeed provided, in a continuing series on favourites, its distinctive contribution to the attack on Bute.[6] Meanwhile, Bute had taken a hand against his adversaries. On 29 May the first issue of the *Briton*, written by Tobias Smollett, appeared as an answer to the *Monitor*. It was joined on 12 June, after the appearance of the *North Briton*, by the *Auditor*, written by Arthur Murphy. Soon a great battle of the weeklies was raging, surpassing that of 1756–7 in vehemence and virulence. 'The new administra-

---

[4] There had been some hints of uneasiness about Bute early in the reign but these had soon subsided, except in the prints. See e.g. Walpole, *Geo. III*, i, p. 13; *Cat. Prints and Drawings*, iv, pp. 3–4, 22–4, 29, 31–2, 36–7. The renewed campaign is described in John Brewer, 'The Misfortunes of Lord Bute: [A Case-Study in Eighteenth-Century Political Argument and Public Opinion]', *Historical Journal*, xvi, i, Mar. 1973, esp. pp. 5–17. The following account differs from Brewer in some details about its timing and balance.

[5] *Mon.* 357, 22 May 1762; Mrs Montagu to Lord Bath, May 1762, *Mrs Montagu*, i, p. 20. The paper has the same initial signature, O.P., and is headed by the same quotation as the paper printed as 361, 19 June 1762, but never published, and clearly identified as by Wilkes. George Nobbe, *The North Briton, a study in political propaganda*, New York, 1939, pp. 44–5.

[6] Nobbe, pp. 44–5; *Mon.* 360, 12 June, 363, 3 July, 366, 24 July, 371, 28 Aug., 372, 4 Sept., 377, 9 Oct., 380, 30 Oct. 1762.

tion begins tempestuously,' wrote Walpole to Mann. 'My father was not more abused after twenty years than Lord Bute is in twenty days. Weekly papers swarm, and like other swarms of insects, sting.'[7]
    Quickly in June and July the battle absorbed public attention. The *Monitor*'s first articles aroused some indignant replies in the newspapers.[8] The *London Chronicle*'s columns were soon dominated by letters in defence of Bute. The *Gazetteer*'s correspondents also quickly entered the fray, on both sides. *Lloyd's Evening Post* and the *St. James's Chronicle* were rather more detached, often deploring or mocking all the contention, although both carried more comprehensive extracts from the weeklies than did other papers. Surprisingly, the *London Evening Post* was at first distinctly uneasy about the attack on Bute and concerned above all about the break of national unanimity and its possible consequences. Only with the loss of Newfoundland and later in discussion of a possible peace was it jolted into taking sides against him. The *Public Advertiser*, alone among the papers, as yet remained serenely almost untouched.[9] In June, the *Gentleman's Magazine* began a new feature, a regular report on the political papers, with the comment that 'Political Disputes which have for a long time been suspended, seem, upon the late Change of Ministry, to be revived with greater Virulence than ever'. Other magazines began, if they did not all long persist with, similar features.[10] Pamphlets were not important in the debate until September or later, when they were mainly hostile to Bute.[11] The

[7] Walpole to Mann, 20 June 1762, *Walpole's Corr.* xxii, p. 42; cf. Symmer to Mitchell, 18, 29 June, 30 July 1762, Add. MSS 6839, ff. 272, 274, 279; Lord Holland's Memoir, p. 68; *MR*, xxvi, June 1762, p. 472. Other weeklies made short-lived appearances, e.g. the pro-Pitt *Patriot*, which ran for five issues from 19 June. Various newspapers started their own essays, e.g. *Gaz.*, 22 June 1762, *Lloyd's EP*, 28–30 June 1762.

[8] *LC*, 29–31 May, copied in *Lloyd's EP*, 31 May–2 June 1762; *Gaz.*, 1 June 1762.

[9] e.g. *Gaz.*, 11, 18, 19, 21, 26, 29 June, 1, 2, 6, 13, 14 July 1762; *Lloyd's EP*, 28–30 June, 26–8 July 1762, *St. JC*, 26–9 June 1762; *LEP*, 26–9 June, 29 June–1 July, 15–17, 24–7, 27–9 July 1762; *PA*, 30 June 1762. Early reaction in the newspapers to the attack on Bute deserves more attention than is possible here. My reading of the evidence does not support Brewer's claim that contributions were overwhelmingly hostile ('Misfortunes of Lord Bute', pp. 12, 16).

[10] *GM*, xxxii, June 1762, p. 269; *LM*, *Royal Magazine*, and *Scots Magazine* began similar features.

[11] e.g. *MR*, xxvii, Sept. 1762, pp. 221–2, Oct., p. 311, xxviii, Feb. 1763, p. 159; *CR*, xiv, July 1762, p. 76, Sept., p. 238, Oct., p. 315, Dec., pp. 476–7. Contrast Brewer, 'Misfortunes of Lord Bute', p. 12. The pamphlet he cites in fn. 48 is much more a defence of Pitt than an attack on Bute. See above p. 217.

prints, which had been unhappy about him since the beginning of the reign and especially since Pitt's resignation, stepped up their campaign much more rapidly and thoroughly. Altogether there were to be more prints attacking Bute than there had been against Walpole in his long years of office, and they were more scandalous and virulent.[12]

The heart of the controversy clearly remained the exchange of the weeklies. Only the *Gazetteer*, and perhaps the defence in the *London Chronicle*, can rival their cover of the issues involved. Much of it was personal attacks on Bute as a Scotsman, favourite, and worse. In the *North Briton* Wilkes developed the anti-Scottish theme, while in the *Monitor* he continued to discourse on favourites, using the well-tried device of historical parallels. The most daring of all, on Isabella, the mother of Edward III, and Mortimer (both favourite of the King and his mother's lover) allowed Wilkes to suggest that Bute owed his influence to a similar relationship to the Princess Dowager. The prints developed this insinuation much more crudely.[13]

But there was more to the campaign against Bute than just personal attack. Its wider development brought out clear contrasts between Bute and Pitt. The attack on favourites raised important constitutional issues, in discussion of which the basis of Bute's power in royal favour, supposedly deviously won, was by implication contrasted with Pitt's support from the people and even Newcastle's from property and connection. The *Auditor* conveniently drove the point home when it unflatteringly compared the favourite of the venal and the favourite of the mob with the favourite of the prince. Questions concerning the proper exercise of the King's prerogative to choose ministers and the consequences for the status of those ministers, first raised in the resignation debate, were clearly involved.[14] Pitt, according to the attack, was a legitimate directing minister, but Bute a monopolizing royal favourite.

The debate became more clearly one about the relative merits of Pitt and Bute when it considered Bute's policies and success as a minister. The contrast with Pitt became insistent as argument ranged over all the major issues, especially of foreign policy, since the beginning of the war. The colonial war, anyway, continued to

---

[12] *Cat. Prints and Drawings*, iv, pp. 51 ff; Atherton, pp. 208–27.

[13] See above fn. 6, esp. *Mon.* 377, 9 Oct. 1762, cf. *North Briton* 5, 3 July 1762; Atherton, pp. 217–20.

[14] The *Auditor* 2, 17 June, 5, 8 July 1762; e.g. *Gaz.*, 11, 16, 18, 22 June, 3 July 1762.

bring successes—Martinique fell in February, followed by most of the remaining West Indian islands, Havannah in August, Manila in October. The *Monitor* and *North Briton* steadily refused to allow the present Ministry any credit for these successes, which were, they said, the fruits of Pitt's policies. But they blamed the Ministers fully for any setbacks such as the temporary loss of Newfoundland in June. (It was reconquered in September).[15] The dropping of the Prussian subsidy kept alive debate over the German war, providing the ministerial papers with their strongest grounds of attack.[16]

Especially from September, the most important issue in the Pitt–Bute debate was the question of peace. Hopes of peace were uppermost in the minds of the Ministers and secret approaches had been resumed within ten days of Pitt's resignation. By the beginning of April direct formal negotiations could begin. In early September plenipotentiaries were exchanged. The Duke of Bedford left for Paris while the duc de Nivernois came to London. The hammering out of terms was somewhat delayed by the fall of Havannah and the embarrassing necessity of demanding some compensation for its return. At last, the preliminary terms were signed in Paris on 3 November and arrived in London on the 9th, the opening of Parliament having been delayed until the 25th to allow for their consideration. By them Canada, Cape Breton, lands east of the Mississippi, Senegal and some lesser West Indian islands were recognized as British, Minorca was returned in exchange for Belle-Île, and the French were much restricted in India. Spain gave up Florida in exchange for Havannah. But in the West Indies, Martinique, Guadeloupe, Marie Galante and the strategically important island of St. Lucia were returned to France. The Newfoundland and St. Lawrence fisheries were open to her, with two island bases. Gorée was returned. The terms relating to Germany were far from unsatisfactory to Frederick. On 1 December the cessation of arms by sea and land was formally proclaimed in Britain.

These negotiations were accompanied by more public discussion than ever before, stimulated in part by the continued successes of British arms but even more by the acrimony born of political division. Bute's dilemma was neatly summed up by Walpole:

[15] See e.g. *Mon.* 361, 19 June, 367, 31 July, 368, 7 Aug. 1762.

[16] e.g. the *Briton* 3, 12 June, 30, 18 Dec. 1762, 38, 12 Feb. 1763; the *Auditor* 2, 17 June, 22, 21 Oct. 1762; *Mon.* 361, 19 June, 365, 17 July, 374, [18] Sept., 376, 2 Oct. 1762; *St. JC,* 3–15, 29–31 July 1762.

'misfortunes would remind us of Mr Pitt's glory; advantages will stiffen us against accepting even such a peace as he rejected'.[17] Pitt's measures and Pitt's successes were at the heart of discussion. His resignation had been immediately associated with moves for a peace at any price. The publication of the French account of the previous negotiations in November 1761, at the height of the resignation controversy, stimulated a debate in which the merits of Pitt's firm stand against French duplicity were never far from sight. Some opinion, at least, stiffened again in favour of a strong peace which had been the cry for most of the war.[18] The revival of negotiations in 1762 gave marvellous scope to Pitt's followers to heighten fears that without Pitt British victories would not be properly protected.

The *Monitor* began the renewed discussion of the prospect of peace. It was, the paper said, the chief reason for its uneasiness about the new Ministers, whose 'partisan scribblers' were decrying the war. Driven by the political motive to find the Ministers lacking, it forgot its readiness to contemplate peace in 1761 in order to elaborate once again the long-established themes of French duplicity and aggressiveness and to reiterate the absolute necessity of breaking the threat of the Family Compact to British trade. It stood out for ever-stronger terms—Florida and Louisiana as well as the retention of virtually all conquests—and clamoured for the continuation of the war if necessary to secure them. The *Auditor* had little difficulty in finding material out of the *Monitor*'s own mouth to convict it of inconsistency, particularly over the peace terms.[19] From September onwards the *North Briton* gave the *Monitor* occasional support on the peace question, while it was persistently answered by both the *Briton* and the *Auditor*. The newspapers, too, turned to discussion of peace in August and September. Predictably, the *London Evening Post* followed a strong line and the *Gazetteer*, too, wanted a peace of few concessions. True to its new loyalty, the *London Chronicle* defended the Ministry's peace efforts. Elsewhere

[17] Walpole to Mann, 1 July 1762, *Walpole's Corr.* xxii, pp. 47–8.

[18] Beckford claimed in Nov. 1761 that the 'middling rank of men' were set 'to demand peace sword in hand'. Walpole, *Geo. III*, i, p. 72. Much pro-Bute propaganda admitted a change in attitudes from those shown during the earlier negotiations e.g. *A Political Analysis Of The War* and the Trinobantian 2, quoted in *GM*, xxxii, Oct. 1762, pp. 457–8, Sept., pp. 429–31.

[19] e.g. *Mon.* 361–2, 19–26 June, 364–5, 10–17 July, 369–70, 14–21 Aug., 374–6, [18] Sept.–2 Oct., 383–4, 4–11 Dec. 1762; the *Auditor* 18, 25 Sept., 22, 21 Oct. 1762.

there was rather more support for peace than before, although comment was mixed.[20]

In September, one of Bute's occasional publicists, Edward Richardson, created quite a stir with a four-page broadside, *A Letter to a Gentleman in the City*, commonly known as the 'Wandsworth letter'. This, according to the *Monitor* and other witnesses, was distributed free at the Royal Exchange and sent free by post all over the country. It was also widely reprinted, noticed in the newspapers and parodied in verse by Charles Churchill, co-author of the *North Briton*.[21] It does in fact effectively summarize the arguments being advanced for peace. It deplored the outcry in the City against a peace reported to be better than the terms of 1761, negotiated by a Ministry which was the first to prefer British interests and to end a war which had been diverted from its proper objectives in North America to expensive involvement in Germany. The cry to keep all conquests was, it maintained, based on the mistaken conviction that France was ruined and on lack of appreciation of the burden of war on Britain. This cry prompted the suspicion that the City had selfish motives, inflamed by Prussian emissaries, in seeking the continuation of the war. Not surprisingly, the *Monitor* was provoked to a lengthy rebuttal.[22]

Bute's publicists also had some success in that most of the many pamphlets on the subject supported peace.[23] But the pamphlets on both sides were generally trivial, with little solid debate on the terms to be hoped for, their polemical purpose clearly predominant. They were almost all disparagingly received by both Reviews for their 'hackneyed and commonplace' content and their factious tone, and seen as merely echoing the disputes of the weekly papers.[24] The only

---

[20] e.g. *LEP*, 21–4, 24–6 Aug., 18–21, 21–3, 23–5 Sept. 1762; *Gaz.*, 23, 24 Aug., 21, 22, 23 Sept., 18 Oct. 1762; *LC*, 24–6 Aug., 31 Aug.–2 Sept., 2–4 Sept. 1762; *Lloyd's EP*, 20–2, 22–4 Sept., 18–20, 20–2 Oct. 1762; *St. JC*, 21–3 Sept., 19–21 Oct. 1762.

[21] *Mon.* 374, [18] Sept. 1762; Birch to Royston, 11, 18 Sept. 1762, Add. MSS 35399, ff. 348, 355; *GM*, xxxii, Sept. 1762, pp. 405–6; *LM*, xxxi, Sept. 1762, pp. 502–4; *PA*, 9 Sept. 1762; *Gaz.*, 22, 23 Sept. 1762; *CR*, xiv, Sept. 1762, p. 239 (the parody); Brewer, *Party Ideology*, p. 223.

[22] *Mon.* 374–6, 18 Sept–2 Oct. 1762. On Prussian emissaries see below fn. 32.

[23] Nineteen pamphlets which appear to deal mainly with peace were reviewed in *CR* and *MR* from Sept. to Nov. 1762. Eight were clearly against, ten in favour of peace.

[24] e.g. *MR*, xxvii, Sept. 1762, pp. 222–4, Oct., pp. 310–11; *CR*, xiv, Sept. 1762, pp. 239–40, Oct., pp. 316–17.

one to receive significant commendation and notice elsewhere was *A Political Analysis Of The War*, an attempt to see the best in both Pitt and Bute and urging a coalition between them.[25] One that can be clearly identified as the work of one of Bute's hacks, yet another attempt to influence City opinion, apparently had little impact. It was certainly less noticed than another pamphlet addressed to the City from the opposite side by a former Tory Alderman and Lord Mayor, Gilbert Heathcote, which attacked in detail 'so dishonourable and shameful a Peace' and urged firm support of Pitt.[26] Otherwise the pamphlets attracted little comment. It was the more ephemeral propaganda that made the running. If in the pamphlets the bias was for peace, the prints, in tune with their traditional opposition to peace-making and major treaties, were almost uniformly against it.[27]

The predominant polemical purpose behind this vigorous public debate makes it even more difficult than usual to determine the balance of public opinion on the controversy. At times the *Monitor* claimed that the terms it was proposing were based on the unanimous and precise voice of the nation.[28] As far as popular opinion in the City was concerned, such claims were largely justified. There were contradictory reports at first about the City's attitude but by early September, when Bedford left for Paris, it was by all accounts settling into definite hostility to negotiations. Its sentiments were expressed in violent language in coffee houses, papers posted up in public places, and 'an Inundation of such Infamous, obscene and Shocking Prints as were never before known in England', while Bedford was hissed as he passed through the streets. There was talk that 'the old Agitators in the Common Council' were planning an

[25] *MR*, xxvii, Oct. 1762, pp. 312–13; *CR*, xiv, Sept. 1762, pp. 226–35; *LM*, xxxi, Oct. 1762, pp. 531–2, Nov. 1762, pp. 573–5; *GM*, xxxii, Oct. 1762, pp. 457–8; *LC*, 28–30 Sept. 1762; *Lloyd's EP*, 24–7 Sept. 1762.

[26] *A Letter To The Right Honourable The Lord Mayor, Aldermen, Common Council, and Citizens, of London*, London, 1762; attributed to Hugh Baillie by Brewer, *Party Ideology*, p. 223; [G. Heathcote], *A Letter To the Right Honourable The Lord Mayor, The Worshipful Aldermen, and Common-Council; . . . From an Old Servant*, London, 1762, esp. pp. 4 (quotation), 34; *LM*, xxxi, Nov. 1762, pp. 614–16; *LEP*, 16–18 Nov. 1762; *St. JC*, 18–20 Nov. 1762; for two answers, see *MR*, xxvii, Nov. 1762, pp. 385–6; *CR*, xiv, Nov. 1762, pp. 394–6. On Heathcote, see Rogers, 'The City Opposition . . . 1725–47', pp. 14, 16, 19, 20, 21, 22.

[27] Atherton, pp. 188–90, 185–7.

[28] e.g. *Mon.* 373, 11 Sept., 375, 25 Sept., 376, 2 Oct. 1762.

address to congratulate the King on the prospect of peace 'but expressing their hopes, that no Terms will be admitted in the Treaty inconsistent with the Honour and Interest of his Kingdoms, or unsuitable to the extraordinary Successes of the War'.[29] The fall of Havannah merely excited the City's demands. This time an address did eventuate, lavishly praising the value of the conquest, asking for a vigorous pursuit of the war until the Family Compact was dissolved and promising warm support and contributions until a peace 'adequate to our glorious successes' could be obtained. Similar sentiments had been expressed in April, on the fall of Martinique.[30] When the peace preliminaries finally became public knowledge in November it was soon clear that they fell far short of such expectations.[31]

There is little doubt about where the leadership came from in forming City views.[32] Both Beckford and Beardmore were on the committee which drew up the Martinique Address and Beckford was on that for Havannah. His views against a separate peace, which he was said to have expressed to Pitt, were reported to Newcastle. The frequency with which Beckford and Beardmore were the butts of the ministerial papers confirms that they were recognized as the instigators of the City attitudes, and the *Auditor* once acknowledged the *Monitor* as 'the maker of a political creed for a particular sett of men in the city'.[33]

[29] Newcastle to Devonshire, 15, 17 Aug., to Barrington, 15 Aug. 1762, Add. MSS 32941, ff. 243, 264, 245; Newcastle to Devonshire, 4 Sept. 1762, quoted Nobbe, p. 87; Birch to Royston, 4 Sept. 1762, Add. MSS 35399, f. 341 (second and third quotations); Walpole to Conway, 9 Sept., 4 Oct. 1762, *Letters of Horace Walpole*, v, pp. 243, 261; Symmer to Mitchell, 10 Sept. 1762, Add. MSS 6839, ff. 284–5 (first quotation); Lord Bath to Mrs Montagu, 13 Sept. 1762, *Mrs Montagu*, i, p. 34; Walpole, *Geo. III*, i, p. 151.

[30] *London Gazette*, 6–10 Apr., 2–5 Oct. 1762.

[31] Walpole to Mann, 9 Nov. 1762, *Walpole's Corr.* xxii, p. 95; Bute to Bedford, *Corr. Bedford*, iii, p. 152.

[32] They are sometimes attributed to the work of Prussian emissaries in the City. Despite the indignant denials of *Mon.* 376, 2 Oct., there is little doubt they were active. See Symmer to Mitchell, 10 Sept. 1762, Add. MSS 6839, f. 285; Yorke, *Hardwicke*, iii, p. 299; Corbett, ii, pp. 334, 353, 359–60. It is unlikely, however, that they significatnly influenced the City in a stand all its past conduct made likely.

[33] Jour. Common Council, 62, ff. 330–1, 63, ff. 14–15; Newcastle to Devonshire, 5 Nov. 1762, Add. MSS 32944, f. 282; e.g. the *Auditor* 2, 17 June, 4, 1 July, 7, 22 July, 12, 26 Aug., 16, 18 Sept., 18, 25 Sept. (quotation), 19, 30 Sept. 1762; the *Briton* 15, 4 Sept., 25, 10 Nov. 1762. See also *Cat. Prints and Drawings*, iv, p. 213, no. 3985.

Moreover it was just at this time that Beckford was elected Lord Mayor. The election, with only one vote against, probably his own, was in the normal order of seniority, so cannot be taken at face value as evidence of City support for his views. However, it did take place in odd circumstances. In August 1762 and again the day before the Michaelmas election, Beckford had attempted unsuccessfully to resign his alderman's gown, only to be elected at Michaelmas without opposition. Beckford certainly had a strong streak of perversity and may have been truly intending to throw in the sponge. But in view of his greater activity in the City over the last two years or so it seems more likely that his tactics were designed to bring out into the open and decisively defeat undercurrents of opposition to him. In making his first attempt to resign his gown, Beckford himself raised the complaints made against him in 1761 that his Militia and parliamentary duties were incompatible with those of a City magistrate. There may also have been opposition because of his stand against the malt distillery.[34] More dangerous, Bute was proving attractive to City Tories. In August, just when Beckford was making his first attempt to resign, Bute had been assured of the esteem of the members of the Half Moon Club for his advice to the King not to limit his favours to Whigs (although at the same time he was told of their doubts of his ability to make a strong peace). The *London Evening Post*'s uneasiness about attacks on Bute reflects this ambivalence towards him. Through his secretary, Charles Jenkinson, and his City contact, Edward Richardson, Bute was establishing a warm relationship with the immediate past Lord Mayor, Sir Matthew Blakiston, a Tory, and even with Sir James Hodges, who was said to have used his influence to defend the peace. These moves were apparently connected with approaches from Bute to Pitt on the eve of the meeting of Parliament.[35] Even Beckford

[34] Birch to Royston, 7 Aug., 4 Oct. 1762, Add. MSS 35399, f. 319, 35400, f. 4; *PA*, 29, 30 Sept. 1762; *GM*, xxxii, Oct. 1762, p. 499; John Entick, *A New and Accurate History and Survey of London, Westminster, Southwark, and Places Adjacent . . .*, 4 vols., London, 1766, pp. 217–18.

[35] Brewer, *Party Ideology*, pp. 48, 223, citing Baillie to Bute, 8 Aug. 1762; Richardson to Jenkinson, 20, 22, [29] Oct. 1762, Add. MSS 38200, ff. 53–4, 55, 74; *The Jenkinson Papers, 1760–1766*, ed. N. S. Jucker, London, 1949, pp. xii, 69. Despite his apparent change of front, Hodges was still linked with Beckford and Beardmore by the ministerial papers. See above fn. 33. On Blakiston see above p. 71 fn. 55.

himself was later not to be immune to this curious ambivalence of the City Tory-patriots towards Bute.[36]

According to Birch, however, Beckford was entirely successful in outmanœuvring the opposition to his election. Despite considerable exasperation at his earlier attempts to avoid the office, his speech of acceptance, by emphasizing the '*Independency* of the City, regained the popular Voice in loud acclamations' so that he 'seems likely to have interest enough again to add new Vigour to the Spirit of Faction there'. This prophecy seemed justified when Bute received yet another rough reception when he ill-advisedly attended the Lord Mayor's banquet on 9 November.[37]

There was little doubt, then, about the prevailing City attitude to the prospect of peace or to Bute as its main instigator. Other trading cities expressed objections to the peace, too.[38] About wider opinion it is difficult to draw conclusions. Only Edinburgh had followed London in addressing the King in congratulation on the fall of Martinique, and then with nothing like London's bellicosity. Many more places, substantial and otherwise, noticed the fall of Havannah. Most did so at the same time as they congratulated the King on the birth of the Prince of Wales. That at first there was a political point in doing so is made obvious by the *London Evening Post*, but the practice became so general as to lose any special significance.[39] Some observers thought the City's ill-humour against the supposed terms and its high expectations of advantages to be won from standing firm were general throughout the kingdom. Others differed. The *London Chronicle* challenged the *Monitor*'s contention that the voice of the nation was against peace.[40] The attitudes of the Reviews provide some evidence of a swing of opinion in favour of peace. The writers in both were clearly for peace. Although the

---

[36] See below pp. 257–8 and fn. 61.

[37] Birch to Royston, 4 Oct. (quotations), 13 Nov. 1762, Add. MSS 35400, ff. 4, 27.

[38] Burke to Charles O'Hara, 30 Oct. 1762 [*The*] *Correspondence* [*of Edmund*] *Burke*, ed. Thomas W. Copeland, 9 vols., Cambridge, 1958–70, i, p. 152; [John Almon], *A Review of Lord Bute's Administration. By the Author of the Review of Mr Pitt's*, London, 1763, p. 88. fn.

[39] *London Gazette*, 6 Apr.–1 July, 2 Oct.–6 Nov. 1762; *LEP*, 16–19, 19–21 Oct. 1762.

[40] Symmer to Mitchell, 10 Sept. 1762, Add. MSS 6839, f. 284; Temple to Wilkes, 11 Sept. 1762, *Grenville Papers*, i, p. 469; Newcastle to Hardwicke, 18 Sept. 1762, Add. MSS 32942, f. 289; Royston to Birch, 30 Sept. 1762, *Mems. Rockingham*, i, p. 124; Collyer, 'The Rockingham Connection and Country Opinion', p. 257. But cf. Walpole, *Geo. III*, i, pp. 152–3; Bath to Lyttelton, 26 Aug. 1762, *Mems. Lyttelton*, ii, pp. 636–7; *AR*, v, 1762, p. 45; *LC*, 4–7 Sept. 1762.

Monthly Review insisted that the terms should be good, it thought that they were likely to be so. By October the *Critical Review* judged from the works it was reviewing that 'the popular tide seems to have taken a turn favourable to the pacific measures of the present administration'. The reaction of the *Critical Review* to partisan attacks on the prospect of peace is particularly interesting. It showed increasing irritation with 'that blaze . . . kindled by sedition and faction', made disparaging references to patriotic letters in the weekly papers, and displayed open hostility to the *Monitor*, the City and even to Pitt.[41] Once again it was probably reflecting the changing loyalties of the Tory country gentlemen. The *Monthly Review*, by contrast, was much more sceptically detached from the partisan battles.

Yet if wider opinion seemed less set against peace there were disturbing signs of hostility to Bute. In London, theatre audiences applauded attacks on favourites and roared out against Scots. Newcastle, anyway, felt as early as July that the campaign against Bute was having a wider effect in the country although Hardwicke was more cautious about the effects of the 'Run and a Cry' kept up by the *Monitor* and *North Briton*. Later reports tended to confirm Newcastle's view and to show effects among more substantial opinion. The gentlemen at the High Sheriff's dinner in Surrey were the cause of much attention and conflicting stories when they refused to drink Bute's health. By 1763 there was evidence of hostility in Yorkshire. In November 1762, at the opening of Parliament, Bute had yet another taste of mob violence when, despite efforts at concealment, he was hissed and pelted on his way both to and from the House.[42] That Bute appreciated the part played by propaganda, especially the weeklies, in creating this uncomfortable situation is demonstrated by the attempts made to

[41] *MR*, xxvii, Oct. 1762, p. 310, Nov., p. 386; *CR*, xiv, Sept. 1762, p. 239 (second quotation), Oct., pp. 316 (first quotation), 317, Nov., pp. 393–4, 396.

[42] Hardwicke to Newcastle, 29 July, Newcastle to Hardwicke, 31 July 1762, Add MSS 32941, ff. 94, 129; Newcastle to Hardwicke, 11 Aug. 1762, Yorke, *Hardwicke*, iii, p. 407; Birch to Royston, 2 Oct., 13 Nov. 1762, Add. MSS. 35400, ff. 2–3, 27; Walpole to Mann, 30 Nov. 1762, *Walpole's Corr.* xxii, p. 102; *Boswell's London Journal 1762–1763 together with Journal of My Jaunt, Harvest, 1762*, ed. Frederick A. Pottle, London, 1951, p. 146, 8 Dec. [1762]; Brewer, 'The Misfortunes of Lord Bute', pp. 6, 9, 10.

silence the *Monitor* and the *North Briton* as the session of Parliament approached.[43]

To such a climax grew the 'violent fermentation in the political world', swelling directly from the uncertainties and fears prompted by the resignation of Pitt. After the setback to Pitt's reputation of the resignation debate and the disappointments of the last session of Parliament, the ferment appeared to create circumstances ripe for him to exploit. The resignation of Newcastle opened other opportunities, as did the arrangements Bute made in mid-October with Fox for him to lead the House for the Administration in the new session (George Grenville having made himself unacceptable by his firm stand in the last stages of the peace negotiations). This arrangement seemed likely to increase the unpopularity of the Administration especially with the Tories, some of whom might now be won back from Bute.[44]

Yet over the summer Pitt had made no move. No one knew what he intended to do in Parliament. If he was still implacably opposed to Bute's 'transcendency of power', as his rejection of approaches from Bute suggested,[45] alliance with Newcastle was one possibility. Newcastle, slowly adapting to the unaccustomed situation of being out of office, was, under Cumberland's influence, moving towards opposition, and had, like Pitt, rejected the amateurish approaches made by the dithering Court. Newcastle could bring some support

---

[43] Attempts were made to scare off the printers of the *North Briton* (Nobbe, pp. 132–3) and possibly also of the *Monitor*, whose printer, Jonathan Scott, refused to publish one of the controversial articles on favourites (377, 9 Oct. 1762), broke with the authors and ran three numbers of a spurious *Monitor*. Within two days of the appearance of 377, Scott was giving information to the Administration (*A Complete Collection of State Trials,* xix, c. 1033), who were certainly considering legal action against the *Monitor* at this time (Jenkinson to Weston, 14 Oct. 1762, HMC, *Tenth Report,* pt. i, p. 346). On 6 Nov. warrants were issued for the arrest of the known authors, printers, and publishers, and arrests were made on 11 Nov. The defendants were bailed but the cases against them were not proceeded with (PRO, SP 44/87, pp. 153–5, 157–8; *AR,* vi, 1763, p. 82; *GM,* xxxiii, June 1763, p. 312). After a two weeks' break the *Monitor* resumed publication undeterred.

[44] Devonshire to Fox, 14 Oct. 1762, *Letters to Henry Fox, Lord Holland: With a few addressed to his brother Stephen, Earl of Ilchester,* ed. Earl of Ilchester, London, 1915, p. 163; Hardwicke to Newcastle, 17 Oct. 1762, Yorke, *Hardwicke,* iii, p. 422; Walpole to Mann, 28 Oct. 1762, *Walpole's Corr.* xxii, p. 93.

[45] T. Walpole's account of conversation with Pitt, 13 Nov. 1762, Yorke, *Hardwicke,* iii, pp. 430–1; Newcastle to Devonshire, 20 Nov. 1762, quoted Namier, *England,* p. 389.

of numbers, although exactly how much was far from clear and certainly dwindling. Fox's skilful influence would hasten the dwindling. By the time Parliament met Newcastle's own estimates of his support had fallen to 142.[46] Yet significant though this support could be to Pitt, alliance with Newcastle had serious disadvantages. Pitt was still bitterly aggrieved by a sense that Newcastle had deserted him at the time of his resignation when 'out-Toried by Lord Bute and out-Whigged by the Duke of Newcastle, he had nobody to converse with but the clerk of the House of Commons'. More than this, he realized that to commit himself to Newcastle would, as in the past, risk compromising his political independence: 'he . . . must do it in his own way; he could not appear to take that part, in order to bring in the D[uke] of Newcastle; he would come with his own handful of people.' Alliance with Newcastle could endanger any Tory support he could hope for, especially if Newcastle insisted on a proscription of Tories in a new administration. So Pitt persistently discouraged any alliance and a series of meetings early in November, including one between Pitt and Cumberland, did nothing to change his attitude. By 30 November Newcastle was committed to opposition to the peace, chiefly on the initiative of his 'Young Friends', but independently of Pitt.[47]

The terms of Pitt's rejection of the Newcastle approaches suggested an intention not to retire from politics but to explore the possibilities of an independent line such as he had taken in the past. Success would require support from the Tories and independents. Their attitudes were variously assessed. They were thought likely to be shaken by the appointment of Fox, and Newcastle received confident accounts from Cumberland and Legge. Temple had reports that Pitt could 'stagger' the Tories and even that the whole party would go against the Administration.[48] Certainly, if they were disillusioned with Bute, they would be likely to rally to Pitt rather than to Newcastle. Perhaps vigour in opposition could still bear fruit

[46] Frank O'Gorman, *The Rise of Party in England. The Rockingham Whigs 1760—82*, London, 1975, pp. 40–4.

[47] T. Walpole's account of conversation with Pitt, 13 Nov. 1762, Yorke, *Hardwicke*, iii, p. 430 (first quotation); Namier, *England*, pp. 388–9 and Newcastle to Devonshire, 20 Nov. 1762, quoted there (second quotation); Newcastle, 22 July 1762, quoted *Letters from George III to Lord Bute*, p. 129; O'Gorman, pp. 48–9.

[48] Newcastle to Devonshire, 5 Nov. 1762, Add. MSS 32944, f. 282; Namier, *England*, pp. 389–90; Temple to Lady Chatham, [Nov.] 1762, *Corr. Chatham*, ii, p. 193.

without Newcastle's numbers. Beckford was for going it alone (and news of Pitt's intended meeting with Cumberland was apparently kept from him). So was Temple. Outsiders, too, were urging Pitt for his reputation's sake to speak against an ignominious peace on behalf of 'the patriot band' who still 'beloved and reverenced' him. So he would keep firm the 'glorious basis' of his popularity.[49] On the other hand Fox was wooing the Tories as never before. They were consulted over finance, summoned to the pre-session Cockpit meeting, and a Tory was chosen to second the Address. Hardwicke's assessment that they were disillusioned with the little that Pitt had done for them in comparison with Bute and the King might well turn out to be more correct than Temple's optimistic expectations. Moreover, even if they were not enamoured of Bute it was inherently unlikely that they would oppose the peace. It was perhaps for this reason that Pitt promised them not to be in the House on the first day of the session. Other specific issues over which any dislike of Bute could be exploited were not likely to be raised.[50]

As the session of Parliament approached Pitt was again afflicted with an attack of the gout which looked like being protracted.[51] Uncertainty about his intentions persisted. Despite the clamour outside and the expectations of a similar storm within,[52] with Pitt absent the first day of the session passed uneventfully. The Address in Reply was passed unanimously without any attempt to provoke a debate, despite a lengthy reference in the King's Speech to the peace. Beckford alone took the opportunity to abuse it. He won Temple's warm praise, and for once was well-received in the Commons.[53] Expectations rose again, however, for the first real test

[49] T. Walpole to Newcastle, 17 Nov. 1762, Add. MSS 32945, f. 68; Temple to Lady Chatham, 23 Nov. 1762, PRO 30/8/62, f. 57; Hon. Thomas Hervey to Pitt, 5 Dec. 1762, *Corr. Chatham*, iii, pp. 197–9 (quotations). Hervey was a somewhat eccentric character (Sedgwick, *House of Commons*, ii, p. 135) but his views may perhaps be taken to reflect those of Pitt's admirers beyond the heart of politics.

[50] O'Gorman, p. 42; Brewer, *Party Ideology*, p. 102; Hardwicke to Newcastle, 27 Nov., to Yorke, 9 Sept. 1762, Yorke, *Hardwicke*, iii, pp. 436, 415; Namier, *England*, p. 389.

[51] Temple to Wilkes, 25 Nov. 1762, *Grenville Papers*, ii, p. 7.

[52] T. Walpole to Newcastle, 17 Nov. 1762, Add. MSS 32945, f. 68; Walpole to Montagu, 14 Oct., to Mann, 28 Oct. 1762, *Walpole's Corr.* x, p. 45, xxii, p. 93.

[53] Rigby to Bedford, 26 Nov. 1762, *Corr. Bedford*, iii, p. 160; Temple to Wilkes, 28 Nov. 1762, *Grenville Papers*, ii, p. 8; Newcastle to Hardwicke, 29 Nov. 1762, Yorke, *Hardwicke*, iii, p. 438.

for the Opposition on 9 December, when, after a delay to enable Pitt to be present, the preliminary peace terms were considered. It proved a fiasco. Grafton, Newcastle, Hardwicke, and Temple spoke in opposition in the Lords but the preliminaries were approved without division. In the Commons, Beckford took the lead, proposing the reference of the preliminaries to a committee of the whole House, but the House would not hear him. Then debate was interrupted by the dramatic arrival of Pitt. Dressed in black velvet and swathed with flannel, he was borne in the arms of his servants and accompanied by the acclamation of the crowd out of doors. His three-and-a-half hours' speech considered in detail whether the preliminaries lived up to the successes of the war. It was quite ineffective, 'very tedious, unconvincing, heavy, and immethodical', delivered without his usual fire and with obvious signs of the strains of illness. He left before the division, having further dispirited his supporters by declaring himself unconnected and speaking as though his political career might well be over.[54] Unexpected and effective support for the peace terms came from Charles Townshend. He had just resigned and was expected to be violent in opposition but was probably affected by the attitude of Pitt. When a division was unwisely forced on a motion to thank the King, the figures were 319 to 65 in support of the preliminaries. Next day, in the same debate, the Opposition fared no better (227–63). 'But how astonished the Public was! when the explosion of this bomb proved to be but the bursting of a bubble.' 'I think I have in no day for two months past heard less said against the peace than this day,' one observer reported.[55]

The manner of Pitt's speech may again have given some grounds for believing that he intended retirement. Most of its matter, however, uncompromising in criticism of the peace, spoke for active opposition, despite the public avowal of independence from Newcastle. The peace, Pitt said, was both insecure, because it restored to

[54] Walpole, *Geo. III*, i, pp. 175–7, 178, 183; Burke to O'Hara, 12 Dec. 1762, *Corr. Burke*, i, p. 160 (quotation).

[55] George III to Bute, [10 Nov. 1762], *Letters from George III to Lord Bute*, p. 161; Colebrooke, *Retrospection*, i, p. 63; Lady Temple to Temple, 17 Dec. [1762], *Grenville Papers*, ii, p. 22; Symmer to Mitchell, 31 Dec. 1762, Henry Ellis, *Original letters [illustrative of English History]*, 11 vols., London, 1824–46, 2nd series, iv, pp. 452–4 (first quotation); James Hayes to Neville, 10 Dec. 1762 (second quotation), Rigby to Bedford, 13 Dec. 1762, *Corr. Bedford*, iii, pp. 168–70.

the enemy the means to future greatness, and inadequate, because the conquests retained were no equivalent for those surrendered nor adequate recompense for the expenses of war. He could approve only the acquisition of Canada and the restoration of Minorca; otherwise the terms did not secure the advantages to British trade made possible by the victories of the war. Instead of being the foundation for a lasting peace, which one more campaign might have secured, they laid the basis for further war. The concession of the fisheries was most castigated. There had been no need to make such concessions to 'manage' France. She had proved her duplicity in the last negotiations and anyway was losing everywhere. In fact, Pitt claimed, better terms had been offered the previous year although British circumstances had then been worse. Again he discoursed at length on the value of the Prussian alliance and pilloried the desertion of Prussia as 'insidious, tricking, base, and treacherous'.[56] The speech was the language of those outside (like the *Monitor*) who had for so long spoken out for a peace of no concessions and the vigorous prosecution of war to the finish. It was a speech careless of consistency with what Pitt had been prepared to do in office, forgetful of his promise to the King of no factious opposition, with none of the hints of the previous session of the elder statesman standing above the battle. Pitt had made a declaration of independent and uncompromising opposition.

But as a rallying call it dismally failed. The divisions of 9 and 10 December, poor as they were, were predominantly Pelhamite votes. Very few of the minority could be attributed to Pitt. There were some Tories (twelve) but only about the same proportion as there were Tories in the whole House, a fact which amply demonstrated that they had not been won back to their traditional opposition. The *Annual Register* noted their general support for the peace. The same tendency away from habitual opposition has been detected amongst the overlapping group of independent knights of the shire.[57] In the vote of 1 December on the move to postpone the date for the consideration of the peace preliminaries to ensure Pitt's presence, the lack of Tory support had been even more evident. Sir John

[56] Walpole, *Geo. III*, i, pp. 179–82; *Corr. Chatham*, ii, pp. 198–9 fn. (quotation).

[57] O'Gorman, p. 52; Namier, *England*, p. 398; *AR*, v, 1762, p. 62; J. B. Owen, 'The Survival of Country Attitudes [in the Eighteenth-Century House of Commons]', *Britain and the Netherlands*, iv, *Metropolis, Dominion and Province*, ed. J. S. Bromley and E. H. Kossmann, The Hague, 1971, p. 56.

Philipps's waverings were now such that he had been invited to the pre-session Government meeting and was asked to second the Address. Temple might rejoice and the King express concern that he did not accept the latter invitation but there was no doubt that he now looked more to the Crown than to Pitt. Hardwicke's assessment of the attitude of the Tories had indeed been proved right.[58]

Pitt, still incapacitated by illness, did nothing to retrieve the situation. Another effort to get him to put himself at the head of a united opposition failed. Despite continuing hopes that a 'great flame' would soon rise out of the 'general discontent' the Opposition never recovered. Instead it 'died in the birth'. The Peace of Paris was finally signed in definitive form on 10 February. 'There does not, indeed, seem to be any kind of materials in the Opposition to obstruct or delay business,' wrote Rigby in February.[59]

It seems that on the question of peace the vote in the House of Commons reflected and affected public opinion. Having made an independent assessment of the peace terms, general opinion found them not short of the main objects of the war—or desperately wanted peace—and would have nothing to do with Pitt's attack. The economic depression was now at its worst and affecting the whole country. In late November Hardwicke was convinced that 'the generality of the Parliament and of the nation (abstracted from the interested or wild part of the City of London)' was strongly for peace, while Symmer noted at the end of December that the 'Public talk very differently of the Peace from what they did a month ago'. Others confirmed these views.[60] There were even some hints of changing opinions in the City. Moneyed men and merchants wanted relief from the financial strains of war more urgently than ever. Even the bellicose patriotism of the middling men which still dominated Common Council could be moderated. Almon com-

---

[58] Namier, *England*, p. 393; Betty Kemp, *Sir Francis Dashwood, An Eighteenth-Century Independent*, London, 1967, p. 53; Temple to Wilkes, 25, 28 Nov. 1762, *Grenville Papers*, ii, pp. 6, 8; George III to Bute, 1 Dec. 1762, *Letters from George III to Lord Bute*, p. 170; for Hardwicke's views see above p. 254.

[59] Lady Temple to Temple, 17 Dec. 1762, *Grenville Papers*, ii, p. 22 (first two quotations); Walpole to Mann, 28 Jan. 1763, *Walpole's Corr.* xxii, p. 116 (third quotation); Symmer to Mitchell, 21 Jan. 1763, Add. MSS 6839, f. 309; Rigby to Bedford, 3 Feb. (fourth quotation), Neville to Bedford, 16 Feb. 1763, *Corr. Bedford*, iii, pp. 185–6, 202; Walpole, *Geo. III*, i, p. 109.

[60] Ashton, p. 151; Hardwicke to Newcastle, 27 Nov. 1762, Yorke, *Hardwicke*, iii, p. 436; Symmer to Mitchell, 31 Dec. 1762, Ellis, *Original letters*, 2nd series, iv, p. 454.

mented on the failure of the City to petition against the preliminaries and attributed it to a secret understanding between Beckford
and Bute about approaches to Pitt in January (of which Newcastle
also heard rumours). The *North Briton*, too, ironically attacked
Beckford about the City's failure to do anything about the preliminaries.[61]

Any change there may have been in the City was, however, much
less marked than elsewhere. In December merchants were still
agitating against the West Indian terms and Boswell reported a
coffee house conversation of the same time in which a citizen spoke
in favour of continuing the war and on the whole against the peace.
Although the Court of Aldermen did at length congratulate the
King on having relieved his people from 'the increasing Burthens of
a long and expensive though glorious and successful War', the
Common Council ostentatiously said nothing, now or later.[62] And
the public debate certainly continued. The *Monitor* kept up its
campaign after the peace had gone through Parliament. After the
crucial debate of 9–10 December, it made a detailed examination of
the preliminaries in a series of thorough if hardly fiery papers. Like
Pitt, it found the peace to show great and unjustified generosity to
France and discovered something to criticize about every article
with (unlike Pitt) nothing to praise. These papers show the extremes
to which some City sentiment could go in criticizing the treaty and
demanding the full fruits of war. Almost at the end of the *Monitor*'s
preoccupation with the subject of the peace came two papers which
made abundantly clear its political objectives. More pungently than
ever, the *Monitor* applied the criterion of success in foreign and
domestic policy in order to form 'candid and just sentiments in the
present political controversy and to adjust the merits of the late and
present administration'. As well as his successful foreign policy, the

[61] Rogers, 'London Politics', pp. 268–71; Newcastle to Thomas Walpole, 4 Jan.
1763, Add. MSS 32946, f. 50; Barrington to Mitchell, 18 Jan. 1763, Ellis, *Original
letters*, 2nd series, iv, p. 458; [Almon], *Minority*, p. 214; the *North Briton* 39, 26 Feb.
1763. Such suggestions about Beckford are made more credible by Beckford's part in
approaches from Bute to Pitt in Aug. 1763 (Beckford to Pitt, [25 Aug. 1763], *Corr.
Chatham*, ii, pp. 235–6). See below p. 261.

[62] Burke to Charles O'Hara, 9 Dec. [1762], *Corr. Burke*, i, p. 159; *Boswell's London
Journal*, p. 149, 11 Dec. 1762; the *North Briton* 35, 29 Jan. 1763; Corporation of London
Record Office, City addresses from 1760 to 1812 (MSS), p. 11; Sharpe, iii, pp. 72–3.
A later address of merchants in May in support of the peace did receive more than
900 signatures. *PA*, 12, 18 May 1763.

merits of Pitt's domestic measures were revived in his praise. In contrast, the foreign policy and peace-making of his successor, together with his boasted attempts at 'economy' in the public offices, were described most disparagingly. Those proved unfit for public office should resign, the *Monitor* concluded.[63]

The *North Briton* supported the *Monitor* with its own particular slants, seeing the peace as a treaty of friendship between France and Scotland, effectively if rather belatedly contrasting the terms of 1761 and 1762. At the same time, especially through late November and December, the *Auditor* and *Briton* engaged in equally detailed and persistent defence of the preliminaries, both having to admit, at times, the volume of criticism being raised against them. The *Auditor* again made effective use of the previous stands of its opponents to convict them of inconsistency in opposing these terms, claiming with some justification that this peace was based on that proposed by Pitt in 1761 to which no objections had been made.[64] Again the arguments of the weeklies were echoed in the newspapers. Britannicus in the *London Evening Post* furiously backed up the *Monitor* in November and December. At first the *Gazetteer* seemed satisfied with the preliminaries and tired of dispute, but in December it carried a lengthy critique of the terms.[65] Other comment was mixed and the *London Chronicle* seemed less interested. The balance in the still-proliferating pamphlets was more clearly than ever in support of the peace, although again they were of no great quality. Once more the main interest of the pamphlet debate was the attitude of the Reviews, particularly the *Critical Review*, towards it. It showed increasing impatience with any opposition to the peace and a marked hostility to Beckford.[66] So the continuing public debate clearly reflected divided responses to the peace: on the one hand the heated reactions of the City, on the other a more general acceptance in line with that of Parliament.

[63] *Mon.* 384, 11 Dec., 385–8, 18 Dec. 1762–8 Jan. 1763, 389, 15 Jan., 390, 22 Jan. (all quotations), 391, 29 Jan. 1763.

[64] e.g. the *North Briton* 27, 4 Dec., 28, 11 Dec. 1762, 35, 29 Jan. 1763; the *Briton* 27–9, 27 Nov.–11 Dec. 1762; the *Auditor* 28, 2 Dec., 30, 9 Dec., 31, 18 Dec. 1762.

[65] e.g. *LEP*, 16–18, 18–20 Nov., 4–7, 7–9, 9–11 Dec. 1762; *Gaz.*, 15, 16, 20 Nov., 6–11 Dec. 1762.

[66] Of sixteen pamphlets reviewed between Dec. and Feb. thirteen were clearly for the peace and only two against. *CR*, xiv, Dec. 1762, pp. 472–3, 476, [4] 80. *MR* was noticeably less partisan.

At the same time, headed by another major sally of Philip Francis, *A Letter From The Cocoa-Tree To The Country Gentlemen*, the main thrust of the pamphlet debate was being turned away from the peace, with all its implications for Pitt, towards the emerging opposition to Bute with which he had refused to co-operate. Francis's sally, an attack on Cumberland, Newcastle and Devonshire, attracted much comment and several replies as well as some support.[67] The new debate was taken up with vigour by the weeklies and newspapers.[68] The whole exchange is of considerable importance in the Bute debate, especially in illustrating the redefinition of party labels. It also confirms the importance attached to the Tory country gentlemen in a fluid political situation. But it is of direct interest for Pitt's position only because he figures in it in a relatively small way. The continuing debate over the peace and especially the continuing firmness of the City suggests that there was still support that Pitt could have rallied if he would. Yet he offered neither the vicarious satisfaction of effective opposition in Parliament in co-operation with others nor encouragement to his admirers out of doors by more overt links with them. At the end of the war and the concluding of peace the winner of victories seemed bypassed, a spent force.

The events of 1762 had further illustrated the political dilemma posed for Pitt by the new reign and the dying war in effectively preserving his unusual political position. He was still determined, on the whole for sound reasons, to stand independent of either Bute and the King in government or Newcastle in opposition. Yet normal peacetime conditions were not likely to provide the issues to revive the popular basis on which he had founded his independence. One important support of that popular basis, the Tories, he had now clearly lost. They were to be recovered only by some *rapprochement* with Bute and the Court which he was not yet prepared to contemplate, although there is some reason to think that such a *rapprochement* might not have been as intolerable to his other allies as

[67] *MR*, xxvii, Dec. 1762, pp. 466–9, 469–71, Appendix, p. 508, xxviii, Feb. 1763, pp. 159–60; *CR*, xiv, Dec. 1762, pp. 473–5, xv, Jan. 1762, pp. 68–9; *GM*, xxxii, Supplement 1762, pp. 620–5.

[68] e.g. the *Auditor* 32, 25 Dec. 1762, 33, 1 Jan. 1763; the *Briton* 31, 25 Dec. 1762, 37, 5 Feb. 1763; the *North Briton* 30, 25 Dec. 1762, 34, 22 Jan. 1763; *St. JC*, 4–7 Dec. 1762, 4–6 Jan. 1763; *LEP*, 6–8, 8–11 Jan. 1763; *LC*, 27–30 Nov., 11–14, 14–16 Dec. 1762, 1–4, 6–8 Jan. 1763.

the propaganda made it seem. There was as yet little doubt of the City. Common Hall now as well as Common Council was held by Beckford, with the *Monitor* as their voice. But if the City was to maintain in peacetime the unusually consistent interest in national politics natural only in time of war, it would have to be courted with something more positive than the arrogant detachment affected by Pitt. New means of mobilizing outside support were needed if popularity was to give political strength in more normal conditions. There was little to suggest that Pitt had any notion of such new means.

* * * * * *

The next few years were to see Pitt still caught in his political dilemma, moving uneasily between the options open to him, and in doing so heightening political instability. In the last weeks of the 1762–3 parliamentary session, perhaps prodded by the ineffectiveness of opposition to the peace, he at last explored the possibilities of joint action with Newcastle. The result was a brief burst of co-operation and vigour, led by Pitt, against Bute's cider tax. The vigour achieved relatively little. Bute's dramatic resignation, its apparent result, in fact had deeper causes, and the Opposition had no immediate part in the reconstruction of the Ministry round Grenville, Halifax, and Egremont.[69] In August, when, as one of a number of moves to strengthen the narrowly based Ministry, an approach was made to Pitt through Bute, leading to two interviews with the King, Pitt acted very much as the party leader, ostentatiously consulting his colleagues and demanding extensive changes. But he soon became disillusioned with this role, apparently convinced by this experience that storming the Closet was no sure way back to office, let alone to royal confidence.[70] Although there were to be later bursts of co-operation, and Pitt was never averse to winning over individuals from the Old Corps, he became less and less enthusiastic about putting himself at the head of a united Whig opposition. Not only did he doubt its effectiveness as a way back to office; despite some earnest courting of him, he was not convinced that his independence could be protected in such an

---

[69] O'Gorman, pp. 59–63.

[70] Walpole, *Geo. III*, i, pp. 227–30; Namier and Brooke, iii, p. 296; Brewer, *Party Ideology*, pp. 80, 106.

arrangement—and the varying attitudes to him of the leaders of the remnants of the Old Corps provided some grounds for such fears.[71] So despite some promising issues between 1763 and 1764, particularly those arising out of Government action against Wilkes and the *North Briton*, opposition remained weak, fragmented and ineffectual.

On the other hand, Pitt paid very little attention in these years to his popular base and his independent support, either inside the House or out. His energy over the cider tax may have been designed to win the Tories[72] but on other matters he seemed deliberately to offend. Again in the last weeks of the 1762–3 session the Tories, both those now inclined to the Court and those still firmly in opposition, moved to revive their traditional concerns. Sir John Philipps, seconded by Beckford, proposed a motion for a commission of accounts to enquire into the disposition of the money voted during the war, and the Tories generally supported a peacetime Army smaller than that proposed by the Administration. Yet Pitt gave only general support to the demand for 'economy' and in fact backed the Government on the size of the Army, even wishing it were larger because the peace was so precarious.[73] He had apparently no interest in a revived 'country' opposition.

Nor did Pitt make any special effort to court the City. There, the popular opposition, under Beckford's active leadership, on the whole retained the upper hand, despite increasing divisions over political issues such as the spate of addresses of congratulation on the peace in the spring and summer of 1763 and the ramifications of the *North Briton* affair.[74] But Pitt did nothing to satisfy the City's continued interest in the cider tax in 1763–4 and although he took up the general issues of principle raised by the *North Briton* affair he carefully detached himself from support for Wilkes personally. In contrast, Beckford was prominent in much less temperate support for Wilkes both in the City and the House.[75] According to New-

[71] Brewer, *Party Ideology*, pp. 80–1.   [72] As Brewer suggests, ibid., p. 103.

[73] Walpole, *Geo. III*, i, pp. 191–2, 193–5; Rigby to Bedford, 23 Feb., 10 Mar. 1763, *Corr. Bedford*, iii, pp. 208–10, 218–19.

[74] Marie Peters, 'The *Monitor* 1755–1765: [A Political Essay Paper and Popular London Opinion]', unpublished Ph.D. thesis, University of Canterbury, New Zealand, 1974, pp. 343–5, 351, 357–7; Rogers, 'London Politics', pp. 265–9.

[75] Peters, 'The *Monitor* 1755–1765', pp. 338, 341–2, 350–1, 352, 355, 369. The *Monitor*, however, was relatively cool in response to Wilkes, see e.g. ibid., pp. 342–3, 351–3.

castle, Pitt now 'spoke with much less respect of the City and regard for popular applause than I have ever heard him before'.[76]

The vagaries of Pitt in refusing either to lead a vigorous opposition or to cultivate popularity with his former finesse (or even to take opportunities to return to office), accentuated the natural relapse of the City from the close interest in national politics of the war years. As the excitement of the war, the contentions of the peacemaking and then the Wilkes issues died down, there was little to form and invigorate a specific or dominant City view. Contrary tendencies and other interests could come to the fore; popular opinion, so far as it retained a political interest, looked elsewhere for its inspiration. Grenville had foreseen this in December 1763 when he told Charles Yorke that the clamour of the people could not be appeased by any change of ministers 'since it was no longer a cry for the Duke of Newcastle, Lord Hardwicke, or even Mr Pitt, but for Pratt and Wilkes'.[77] In these circumstances Beckford lost the political purpose which had led him to cultivate an influence in the City in the late fifties and early sixties so that he could bring it to bear on national politics in the interest of the leader to whom he had committed himself in 1756. Increasingly isolated by Pitt's waywardness, divided from his former Tory friends by his continuing loyalty to Pitt, yet not at the heart of opposition, Beckford allowed his activity in the City to decline markedly after the end of his mayoralty in November 1763.[78]

Nowhere is the increasing disjunction between City and national politics more clearly reflected than in the decline of the *Monitor*. Its commentary became increasingly divorced from present events and issues, it lost its heated sense of close involvement, and other political writing passed it by. It lapsed into senility and a mood of impotent pessimism about the drift of contemporary politics, bringing on itself well-deserved strictures for dullness from friend and foe alike. At last, in March 1765, it fell silent.[79] When the City was aroused again in 1769–70, it was to be by more radical appeals.

[76] Quoted Namier and Brooke, iii, p. 296.

[77] Grenville diary, 17 Dec. 1763, *Grenville Papers*, ii, p. 239. There is some evidence to suggest that in 1765 the popular party, under the leadership of Beardmore, rather than Beckford, was still strong. Peters, 'The *Monitor* 1755–1765', pp. 372, 21–2.

[78] From Nov. 1763 to Nov. 1764 he attended only two Common Councils, in the year beginning Nov. 1764 none.

[79] Peters, 'The *Monitor* 1755–1765', pp. 340–1, 351–4, 358–9, 360–3, 365, 369, 370–1, 373–4.

Yet Pitt was to have another chance to dominate politics, despite the apparently missed opportunites of 1763–5. The chance came more out of the weaknesses and mistakes of others than his own strength. He won it, in July 1766, not by vigorous opposition or popularity, but by a careful mending of his bridges to the King in accordance with the lessons of August 1763.[80] More than ever before, in much more favourable circumstances than 1756 or 1757, the cards seemed all in his hands. Yet almost at once he threw them all away. His decision to accept a peerage not only took him out of his natural stronghold, the House of Commons, leaving no competent lieutenant there; it set off against him once again the popular cry against a false patriot and further dimmed his reputation.[81] His present and past arrogance robbed him of able colleagues and prevented his co-operating with those he had. Within months, his nerve had broken under the strain of the one constant factor in his political career, his ill-health. After this, despite one more brief burst of energy in 1769–70 which brought a revival of his alliance with the City, his career was virtually over. He was never entirely to lose the lustre of his popularity and reputation. In a sense they shone with a more congenial light in the twilight years of the elder statesman in the 1770s, but they were spent forces as far as real political strength was concerned. As John Brooke has aptly said, North did not fear Chatham as Newcastle had feared Pitt.[82]

An explanation of why Pitt was not able to make better use of his political resources in the 1760s lies beyond the scope of this study and deep in his complex personality. Yet the reasons are closely connected with the support and image Pitt had chosen to cultivate in the war years. Some final reflections on the lessons of those years may suggest the outlines of an explanation of his later career.

---

[80] Brewer, *Party Ideology*, pp. 106–7; Namier and Brooke, iii, p. 298.
[81] Brewer, *Party Ideology*, pp. 107–8.   [82] Namier and Brooke, iii, p. 298.

IX

Popularity and the Eighteenth-Century Statesman

His power, as it was not acquired, so neither was it exercised in an ordinary manner. With very little parliamentary, and with less court influence, he swayed both at court and in parliament with an authority unknown before to the best supported ministers. He was called to the ministry by the voice of the people; and what is more rare, he held it with that approbation; and under him for the first time, administration and popularity were seen united.

So the *Annual Register* gave its considered opinion of Pitt's political achievement after his resignation in 1761, in the midst of a not uncritical panegyric of his successes as a war minister.[1] Even those more sceptical of Pitt's virtues, like John Douglas, acknowledged this achievement, if partly ironically and as a means of embarrassment. He addressed Pitt as

Not tutored in the School of Corruption, but listed, from your earliest Years, under the Banner of Patriotism; called into Power, by popular Approbation, and still uniting, the uncommon Characters of *Minister* and *Patriot*; favourite of the Public, and Servant of the Crown.[2]

In Boswell's famous words Pitt was 'a minister given by the people to the King'.[3] Together these judgements highlight the three

---

[1] *AR*, iv, 1761, p. 47.

[2] *A Letter Addressed To Two Great Men*, p. 50; cf. Walpole to Mann, 4 Mar. 1759, *Walpole's Corr.* xxi, p. 277, where he comments 'that it is as much the fashion to couple [the two words *ministerial* and *patriot*] now as it was formerly to part them', and *GM*, xxxi, Dec. 1761, pp. 579–80, which noted that it had not been true for the last four years as it usually was that 'An opposition to government will always please, and gain the people of *England*, who are great levellers.'

[3] Quoted Langford, 'William Pitt and public opinion, 1757', p. 54.

constant elements in contemporary assessments of Pitt in the period of the Seven Years' War: that he owed his strength to popularity; that he enjoyed that popularity because he was a 'patriot'; and that he was unusual, indeed unique, in maintaining his patriot image and popularity in office, as the hitherto unknown phenomenon, the 'patriot minister'.

This book assesses the validity of these contemporary judgements by using some of the variety of evidence described in the introduction. With particular reference to the City of London and the metropolitan press, an attempt is made to define the nature and substance, to chart the course and to assess the influence of that popular reputation which Pitt was universally acknowledged to enjoy. After the only mediocre fortunes of his early career, the disappointments of 1754–5 propelled him to cultivate not only the alliance of Leicester House but also the image of a patriot. He initiated a popular opposition, to which the crisis of 1756 brought fortuitous success. With success came 'popularity', but not yet in the sense of the general good opinion of the political nation. Instead popularity meant high expectations of one who had now been firmly cast in the patriot mould, and brought the support of those who habitually responded to the patriot appeal, notably the Tories and the middling sort of the City. This support, if carefully handled, could give some independent standing in politics. Miraculously saved from dissipation by the meagre record of the brief Devonshire–Pitt Administration of 1756–7, these tangible fruits of popularity helped Pitt to force a new alliance with the Pelhamite Old Corps in 1757. This gave him a much more secure hold on power.

Yet that very alliance ran the risk of offending the popular support which had helped to secure it and without which Pitt could have found his standing in the alliance seriously weakened. This danger was increasd by the necessary compromises of office and the chequered fortunes of war. It was averted only by Pitt's ostentatious support for popular measures and careful disguise of his responsibility for unpopular ones, with the opportune assistance of the first successes in war. Then in the flush of victories of 1759–60, almost universally ascribed to Pitt, his popular support was widened into a much more general good standing with the political nation. Newspapers other than the Tory-popular *Monitor* and *London Evening Post* now reflected this general opinion. In the City, the merchant oligarchy was attracted by the opportunities for profit out of successful war and joined the Tories and middling sort in support of Pitt.

Pitt's widened popularity, generously acknowledged by his colleagues, did much to increase his political strength and give him pre-eminence. Without the careful protection of his independence and skilful cultivation of his patriot image in the years of waiting, his effectiveness as a war minister would have been the less, this pre-eminence might well have been much reduced and the glory of victory not so exclusively his. Instead, now he was

A Man Honoured by his King, Revered by the People, Dreaded by our Enemies; Under whose Administration All Parties united for the Common Good, Confidence between the Court and Country was restored, a respectable Militia was established, the natural Strength of the Nation was exerted by Sea and Land, the Terrors of an Invasion were removed, Public Credit was carried to the greatest Height, the British Arms triumphed in every Quarter of the Globe, Trade and Navigation were promoted and protected, and France was humbled, and reduced to the Necessity of suing for a Peace.[4]

Political propaganda vividly illustrates the potency of this patriot image. In its terms Pitt was constantly both attacked and defended. The *Monitor*, for example, uses it both positively, in continued glowing praise of Pitt's supposed achievements, and negatively, in ready attribution of all disappointments to 'faction'. Not just propagandists but also Walpole and others reacting to Pitt's resignation, Pitt's colleagues and even Pitt himself, in his last speech to the Cabinet, interpreted situations and events in the light of this propaganda.

Yet Pitt's pre-eminence was to be brief and its popular foundations uncertain. Already he had discovered that the patriot pose could be a liability as well as an asset, making it difficult and embarrassing to do things that had to be done. Even in victory he was never free from harassment for his now manifest disloyalty to one of the main planks of the patriot programme, its hostility to Continental connections. This harassment may have been 'only' propaganda artfully spread by political enemies, rather than substantial criticism, but it could strike at the patriot image, itself the product of propaganda. In the light of victory, hostile propaganda

[4] John Entick and others, *The General History of the Late War* . . ., 5 vols., London, 1763–4, i, dedication.

had little influence over Pitt's general popularity and only slightly affected those in the City who could sate themselves on the fruits of victory. But it had potent effects on those on whom the burdens of war weighed heavy, among them the country Tories who had been so important to Pitt. The *Critical Review* often echoed their uneasiness. Even the *Monitor* and *London Evening Post* were not immune to it, but the issues mattered little to commentators with no Tory bias. The difficulties of managing popularity became the more acute as the question of peace came to the fore. The general popularity born of victory was very liable to attrition from war-weariness. Yet it seemed almost impossible to make the peace that might halt this attrition while at the same time satisfying the extravagant expectations of Pitt's most ardent supporters, especially those in the City. The victorious war minister seemed unlikely to carry his popularity beyond the war.

The changed circumstances of the new reign, coinciding with some swing of opinion against a war in which Britain seemed to have already won all the necessary victories, soon made Pitt's vulnerability apparent. To this uncomfortable situation his not unforeseen reaction was, eventually, resignation. This simply highlighted Pitt's reliance on 'popularity' for political strength and at the same time emphasized with particular intensity how fragile that popularity was. The attack on him which followed his resignation (merely the most sustained and ferocious of a series since 1756–7) certainly weakened him politically and hindered him in rallying his support in the House of Commons and the country. Together with the initial shaping of Pitt's patriot image, this setback provides striking evidence of the influence of propaganda in eighteenth-century politics—and weeklies and pamphlets, the latter especially in 1761, were still more important than newspapers. Altogether the resignation clearly posed the question whether popularity could still be useful to Pitt. His attitudes in the next few years suggested that he thought not.

The chief stronghold of Pitt's popularity was the City of London. Yet throughout the war its actions and attitudes vividly portrayed both the vicissitudes of Pitt's reputation and the complexities of City politics. Not even the Tory-patriots, Pitt's most ready supporters, let alone the full range of City interests, were united in opinion on national affairs. There were conflicting, or at least diverse, elements among the Tories over the whole period. When a popular opposition to the Government began to rise again in the City in 1756 and at length supported Pitt in 1756–7, the initiatives came from Hodges, Blakiston, Scott, and Blachford, as well as Beckford, and were not always in harmony. Nor was the support reliable. Whatever Beckford may have wished, the *Monitor*, unlike the short-lived *Con-Test*, could not be a mere mouthpiece for Pitt in face of the shocks of the Coalition and the failure of the Rochefort expedition in 1757, and the sending of British troops to Germany in 1758. Rather than a mouthpiece, it is a record of the stormy dialogue between Beckford and the supporters he still had to secure for Pitt.

From the latter months of 1758, indeed, the Tories were reconciled to Pitt by victories and by the opportunity created for them to re-establish their leadership in City affairs in the general swing of opinion to Pitt. Political divisions in the City were now temporarily muted by the profits of war. Beckford became more active in leadership, with Beardmore, his attorney and manager of the *Monitor*, often as his lieutenant in Common Council. But Beckford was still not Pitt's only link with the City. Sir James Hodges, the Town Clerk, was an ally but no mere auxiliary. Moreover, impressive though the City's formal declarations of support were, its unanimity was brief. By mid-1760 and even more after Mauduit's blast in November, not only many wealthy merchants but also some Tories were becoming anxious about the cost of the war. These Tories began to look to Sir John Philipps, whose influence among them was of some long standing, rather than to Beckford. Beckford's difficulties in the 1761 election showed how transient was the unity of the City for Pitt. Beckford was able to rally popular support for Pitt in the crisis of October–November 1761, and hold it in 1762–3, because Pitt's resignation again stirred deep fears among the middling men of collusion at Court against the interests and influence of City and nation. But the curious ambivalence of some of them towards Bute showed again the complexities of popular opinion. And throughout the war the degree of City support for Pitt had been exaggerated by the dominance of Common Council as its political voice. Because of its composition, Common Council was pretty readily controlled by patriot opinion and did not fairly reflect the views of the merchant and moneyed oligarchy or the strength of the Court interest in the City. Nor did it always show the Livery's instinctive distrust of politically minded City members of Parliament like Beckford.[5]

In fact Beckford owed his rise in the City to Pitt's growing reputation at least as much as Pitt owed his City support to Beckford. This raises doubts about the wisdom of Pitt's extravagant commitment (much noticed by contemporaries)[6] to Beckford and his narrow self-interest in the sugar duty and distillery issues of 1759 and 1760. Pitt's support on these issues unnecessarily aggravated the alienation of the country Tories, to say nothing of others. It did not even please all City interests friendly to Pitt. Certainly Beckford was a prominent speaker in the House of Commons but his speeches were often ill-considered or ill-delivered and the objects more often of mirth or boredom than serious attention.[7] He could be useful among the considerable West Indian interest both in the House and in the City. His influence (with the help of the *Monitor*) with popular interests in the City was valuable especially in the early 1760s when Pitt most needed help. To some extent he also had links with the Tories generally. Whether all this was sufficient to justify Pitt's apparently high assessment of his importance at the expense of others is questionable. The attachment to Beckford was not the only way Pitt showed himself strangely careless about others who had helped him to pre-eminence. Leicester House, too, was lost with little effort to keep it, regardless of George II's advancing years.

Despite such carelessness, and the vicissitudes of Pitt's reputation, this study of his popularity largely bears out the assessments of contemporaries. Popularity, cultivated through appeal to the patriot image at least as much as it was won by success in war, was the major foundation of Pitt's political strength. It helped to establish

[5] On the political dominance of Common Council in the mid-eighteenth century see Rogers, 'London Politics', pp. 351–2. Between 1756 and 1763 no attempt was made to use Common Hall for political initiatives, as was to happen at the end of the 1760s (George Rudé, *Wilkes and Liberty*, Oxford, 1962, pp. 108, 150, 153, 180). The views of other City interests were shown in the 1761 general election, for example, and the aldermanic Address on the Peace of Paris in 1763, and are reflected frequently in the comments of observers like Birch and Gordon.

[6] e.g. Walpole, *Geo. II*, ii, p. 350. Mauduit as quoted in Grant, 'Canada Versus Guadeloupe', p. 742; Hardwicke to Newcastle, 2 Apr. 1762, Add. MSS 32936, f. 310.

[7] e.g. Walpole to Conway, 24 Jan. 1756, *The Letters of Horace Walpole*, iii, pp. 388–9; John Yorke to Royston, 20 Feb. 1758, Add. MSS 35374, f. 144; Symmer to Mitchell, 24 Nov. 1758, Add. MSS 6839, f. 115; Lady Anne Egerton to Bentinck, 13 Mar. 1759, Eg. 1719, ff. 32–3; Walpole, *Geo. II*, ii, pp. 350–1.

his firm hold on high office in 1756–7 and shaped his distinctive reputation which, lingering long in memory, gave him a pre-eminence in eighteenth-century politics unparalleled by anyone except Walpole. Even his son was not known, as they were, as the 'great man'.[8] Winning his reputation as he did, Pitt was indeed unique among eighteenth-century politicians. It was not that others did not recognize the possibilities. Opponents of Walpole in the 1730s, for example, made vigorous efforts to mobilize popular support by appeal to the patriot rhetoric and 'country' ideas. They proved the power of such an appeal by rousing the country gentleman, against their self-interest, to oppose the Excise Bill.[9] Yet no one politician was able to focus that success on himself. It was not their popularity that hoisted some opposition politicians into office in 1742 and certainly no one proved able to exploit it in office. After Pitt, the Rockinghams were to value reputation with 'the people' and to seek means of mobilizing support out-of-doors, yet they reaped little benefit from their efforts. Again it was not popularity that helped to hoist them into office or maintain them there. In contrast, Pitt's son enjoyed a popular reputation which contributed something to his political strength, at least in the critical months of 1783–4. Then, for once, the 'country' suspicion of apparently self-interested professional politicans swung opinion strongly for the King and his Minister and against Charles James Fox. Indeed, in changing circumstances, Pitt the Younger was to wean the independent country gentlemen in the House from opposi-tion to government more permanently than his father did.[10] Yet the Younger Pitt's reputation, unlike his father's, owed little to deliber-ate cultivation (though not a little, at least initially, to the reflected glory of his name). His political pre-eminence rested primarily on other bases. Fox might have effectively used a revived popularity in the 1790s but circumstances were too adverse. Pitt the Elder was the only true patriot minister. Historians of eighteenth-century politics must take account of his methods as well as those of Walpole.

Yet this study has also shown that popularity was not all strength. It placed constraints on Pitt's actions, made him peculiarly vulner-able to damaging propaganda attacks and was in many ways an unreliable support which he was unable to exploit to good purpose

---

[8] Cf. Langford, *The Excise Crisis*, p. 5.   [9] Ibid., esp. pp. 156–8.
[10] Owen, 'The Survival of Country Attitudes', pp. 63–4.

in the sixties. Indeed sometimes it seems that the deference paid to him then was a reflection more of the weaknesses and confusion of others than of his own strength. The very uniqueness of his earlier use of popularity, together with the fact that popularity was not all strength to him, raises the general question of how useful this peculiar support could be to an eighteenth-century politican of leading rank. Was it only exceptional circumstances that enabled Pitt to make the use of it he did in the fifties, against the grain of normal eighteenth-century realities, or was it his mistakes and flaws of personality that prevented a more effective and continuing exploitation?

It can indeed be argued that it was only the peculiar circumstances of war, the crisis of 1756–7 and then the perhaps fortuitous successes, which enabled Pitt to overcome the substantial obstacles in the way of maintaining popularity in office, to square the circle and parade as the patriot minister. The experience of most of the rest of the century seemed to show that it was much easier to mobilize public opinion against rather than in support of government. This was largely because the public's perception of politics was often limited and unrealistic, its interpretation moulded by the patriot stereotype rather than formed by responses to reality. Particularly this is shown in the relatively limited discussion of war issues, dominated by the argument over Continental connections and then by insatiable greed for victories. To some extent these were arguments over real strategic considerations and the objects of the war. The relationship of the Continental and colonial theatres was an important issue, probably the major one. The advantages to be expected from victory deserved discussion. Yet the debate does not often escape the straitjacket of propaganda and become a realistic consideration of the validity of Pitt's strategy. It is always easier to attack than to defend the government; the 'country' bent of the patriot stereotype gave the advantage even more to opposition.

In any case, popularity was likely to be ephemeral and unreliable, at the mercy of changing circumstances. The patriot pose could win the independents and Tories, and the middling sort in the City, but they were not the stuff of which steady and reliable support was made. Neither group was in any sense a party; they were not usually united in attitude and did not have clearly accepted and capable leaders. Nor could they be easily led. Both were to some extent outsiders in national politics, instinctively suspicious of those in office and not readily committed to any one political figure. Nor, because of their conflicting social and economic interests, were they easily combined for any length of time. Moreover, popularity needed issues to stimulate and focus it and issues were the exception in eighteenth-century politics. Only in unusual circumstances was public opinion on issues a major factor in swaying the votes of electors or members of Parliament. The issues that could be exploited for popular purposes—Continental connections and the question of Hanover, 'corruption', the peace, Bute, Wilkes—were likely to be offensive to those whose support was even more necessary for political effectiveness, especially the King. It was certainly political suicide, as the Rockinghams were to discover in 1765–6, to sacrifice all to the hope of 'popularity'.[11] Finally, and for all these reasons, it was not easy to bring the pressure of popularity regularly to bear where it could most count for political success, on voting in the House of Commons, in Cabinet, and in the Closet. As Walpole remarked, when describing the 'pungent little paper war' provoked by the *Letter From The Cocoa-Tree* in 1762–3, 'no citadel was ever taken by pop-guns'.[12] Perhaps it was rather the mediocrity of Pitt's competitors—Bute as well as Newcastle and the others—than the effectiveness of his popular support which explains the deference paid to him.

On the other hand, there are strong reasons for suggesting that the forces of public opinion are not just to be dismissed as 'pop-guns' and that the influence of popularity was not just a mirage seen only by those far from the oases of Court favour. After the brief quietness of the Pelham years, the boundaries of the political nation were widening again, extended by a flourishing press increasingly interested in substantial political discussion. Indeed in the turbulent sixties, on the evidence of the press and the frequent references of contemporaries, it is possible to speak of 'an all-embracing "political nation"', a 'substantial political nation, far larger than the parliamentary classes', which historians have not generally led us to expect.[13] Wilkes, especially, brought into focus this wide interest in politics. It was apparently in these years that the term 'public opinion' came to be used in something approaching its modern

---

[11] Cf. Paul Langford, *The First Rockingham Administration 1765–1766*, London, 1973, pp. 56–60.

[12] Walpole to Mann, 28 Jan. 1763, *Walpole's Corr.* xxii, p. 116.

[13] Brewer, *Party Ideology*, chs. 8 and 9 *passim* (quotations, pp. 141 and 160).

sense.[14] Certainly they were of particular importance in the evolution of City attitudes to national politics. An increasing resentment at exclusion from what was felt to be the City's due influence could have fostered not only the disillusion and radical leanings which eventuated.[15] It could also, given the right leadership, have brought a more continuous interest and involvement. And, despite the hold of the patriot stereotype, there were signs that this interest was becoming more realistic in its view of politics. Opinion in the City, at least, could escape the prejudice against Continental connections and recognize that colonial and commercial advantage was indeed the chief objective of Pitt's strategy and could be assisted by some intervention in Europe. Further, the views of the *Monthly Review* and some of the newspapers on these questions and the making of peace suggest that a wider body of opinion was prepared to make a more realistic assessment. These modifications of ingrained attitudes could make it more easy to combine a popular reputation with office. Furthermore, encouraged first by the war and then by political instability, interest in politics was coming to be more continuous and steady, not simply a series of outbursts in crises like the loss of Minorca or the fiasco at Rochefort. Perhaps Pitt's reputation could not have been won without the special circumstances of war; but having been won it did not necessarily need crises to sustain it.

There is plenty of evidence that politicians were concerned about public opinion and not only in crises, impossible though it may be to measure its influence precisely. They were well aware that government was not merely a matter of manipulation of Court, Cabinet, and Commons. None felt easy without some sense of public confidence; otherwise votes could slide away, colleagues equivocate, and public credit tremble. Newcastle's correspondence is full of anxiety (his City advisers' as well as his own) that movements of opinion would affect the raising of money. Perhaps the most telling evidence comes from the increasing attempts of politicians to control the press for their own ends.[16] Public opinion had conditioned

---

[14] Paul Kelly, 'Radicalism and Public Opinion in the General Election of 1784', *Bulletin of the Institute of Historical Research*, xlv, May 1972, p. 83; cf. *OWC*, 28 July–4 Aug. 1759.

[15] Lucy S. Sutherland, *The City of London and the Opposition to Government . . . 1768–1774*, London, 1959, pp. 5–9, 12.

[16] Brewer, *Party Ideology*, ch. 11.

eighteenth-century politics on occasion before; even more so now, as the interest of the political nation became more informed and sustained, calculations about public attitudes could affect the behaviour of Court and Cabinet as well as the Commons. Not just the career of Pitt, but those of Newcastle, Bute and, later, the Rockinghams, bear witness to this.

It can therefore be argued that the support of the political nation could have been more effectively mobilized than Pitt mobilized it in the sixties as an important strength of a politician of leading rank. Popularity was certainly not enough by itself. Pitt could not have stormed back into office by opposition to a peace which most wanted anyway, or even by careful exploitation of the Wilkes affair. There is some degree of perception of, or at least unconscious adaptation to, political realities in Pitt's indifference to popularity in the sixties, a recognition that the key to power was in the Closet, not outside. Yet popularity could have strengthened his hand; the way in which, because of his reputation, he was considered essential to any stable political arrangement is some indication of that. Had he taken care to protect his popular standing by resigning without accepting compromising rewards, for example, or by a more considered expression of his relatively moderate views on the peace, had he taken opportunities to strengthen his standing on later issues, had he maintained and developed links with the City and the press, and then combined this popularity with other supports such as alliance with Bute or Newcastle, his position could have been unassailable. Bute would probably have been the better partner in the 1760s, at least after 1763 when he had been forced to realize his own limitations. He could sway the King but could not challenge Pitt in any other way, and there is much to suggest that alliance with him could have been made acceptable to Pitt's City supporters, despite the hostile propaganda. Pitt could have dominated either Bute or Newcastle as he controlled Newcastle in the Coalition. Thus he could have solved his dilemma of the sixties and created the circumstances in which his undoubtedly creative vision could have continued to find realization.

Certainly such a combination of political strengths would have required great skill. Popularity now needed to be cultivated by means other than Pitt's high-handed detachment and contempt for the means whereby it was sustained, such as the press. Appeal from the distant heights to popular applause may have been effective, even an advantage, in the fifties. By the sixties the mood was changing, especially in the City, always sensitive to the slights of unscrupulous politicians from the landed establishment. The cultivation of popularity now needed one who could break out of the cautious and condescending attitude to 'the people' characteristic of most eighteenth-century politicians[17] into a more equal, direct, and confident relationship. Otherwise popularity would be taken over by outsiders such as Wilkes. Charles James Fox could perhaps have made the change had circumstances given him another chance. Such a change of attitude would not easily be made, however, without offence to the other equally necessary political supports.

Such skill had not been beyond Pitt before. Even before victories came to his aid he had laid the foundations of popularity in office in coalition with Newcastle. Now it would seem that the flaws in his character[18] prevented the full exploitation of his resources. There is nothing to suggest, despite the importance of Beckford's *Monitor* in his defence, that Pitt ever paid even such attention to the press as other politicians did, even less that he appreciated the skills of Wilkes. Indeed he expressed his contempt for 'party-papers'.[19] His arrogance and disdain, his distaste for allies of equal status as well as his aloofness from his popular supporters, compromised his opportunities. These flaws, rather than the 'realities' of eighteenth-century politics, prevented his continuing to demonstrate that a politician of imagination could use popularity in office as well as in opposition. Realities were beginning to change, even if the change was not to be fully apparent until the next century.

[17] Brewer, Party Ideology, pp. 235-9.

[18] Recognized by *AR*, iv, 1761, p. 47, in its assessment of Pitt, part of which is quoted at the beginning of this chapter.

[19] Walpole, *Geo. III*, i, p. 75. The context suggests that the disdain may not have been entirely sincere, but it is in accord with everything known of Pitt's attitudes.

Appendix I: List of Newspapers Used

The following newspapers have been used in this study, and are available in complete runs unless otherwise stated. Locations are given in the bibliography.

Dailies

The *Gazetteer* from the beginning of the period had more political comment than the *Public Advertiser* and was widely read in the City. It was frequently referred to in controversy but copies survive only for 1756, Jan.–June 1759, Sept.–Dec. 1760, and June 1762 onwards, with a few other isolated copies. However, its letters were quite often copied in other papers. It shows no signs of Tory ideological scruples. By 1759 it was warmly for Pitt but apparently turned against him in the resignation controversy in 1761. It opposed the proposed peace terms late in 1762.

The *Public Advertiser* carried some letters but little political comment before 1762–3. As a widely-read paper, however, it is of some use as a test of fluctuations of political interest. It showed no political bias.

The *Public Ledger* from its foundation in Jan. 1760 competed for the commercial City readership of the *Gazetteer*, chiefly by its advertising policy. No files survive for 1762–3. Not strongly political to begin with, it was staunchly pro-Pitt by the time of his resignation in Oct. 1761.

Tri-weeklies

The *London Evening Post,* the most clearly political of all the newspapers, regularly carried paragraphs of comment (embryo editorials) under its 'London' head, as well as letters, many of them over a long period over the pseudonym 'Britannicus'. From Dec. 1756 it was strongly pro-Pitt, although sometimes initially embarrassed by moves which offended Tory-popular susceptibilities.

The *London Chronicle* (founded Jan. 1757), *Lloyd's Evening Post* (founded July 1757) and the *St. James's Chronicle* (founded Apr. 1761) all included in their varied content for country readers a fluctuating amount of political comment, often copied, for example from the *Monitor*. In the *London Chronicle* and *St. James's Chronicle* the volume of comment grew in the 1760s and included more that was original; in *Lloyd's Evening Post* (for which no copies survive July 1759–June 1760) comment declined and it did not develop its own. These general evening papers are useful as a rough test of political interest and as an indication of the political comment available to a wider readership. The *London Chronicle* generally supported Pitt at first but after the accession of George III leant increasingly to the new Court. It carried much criticism of Pitt in the resignation debate and defended Bute in 1762. The *St. James's Chronicle* claimed impartiality and generally lived up to its claim. *Lloyd's Evening Post* was also not strongly political but usually warm towards Pitt.

The *Whitehall Evening Post*, almost entirely a news and advertisement paper, and the *General Evening Post*, of which few copies survive, have not been used.

Weeklies

Read's Weekly Journal, with scarcely any direct political comment, has been used to 1761, after which it lapsed. Although not strongly political it supported Pitt through to 1761, despite a penchant for a 'British' war strategy. The *Universal Chronicle* and *Owen's Weekly Chronicle*, both founded in April 1757, provide examples of more varied weeklies, carrying a fluctuating amount of comment, some of it political but to begin with little original. In the *Universal Chronicle* (for which the run is complete only to Apr. 1760) the political comment was slight, although sometimes significant, until it amalgamated with the *Westminster Journal* in Jan. 1760. Then it seemed to turn against Pitt. *Owen's Weekly Chronicle* (for which there are copies only for 1758, 1759, and 1761) developed its letters and other political comment more quickly, at least in the 1750s, but had only a little political comment in 1761 and showed no strong commitment.

It is unfortunate that copies of the elusive *Westminster Journal* survive only for Dec. 1759, because it was apparently the most overtly political of the weekly newspapers, carrying regular essays, letters, and paragraphs of comment. It gave this political bent, by this time strongly critical of Pitt, to the *Universal Chronicle* after the merger of 1760. It appears in *Owen's Weekly Chronicle* in 1763 and 1764 but also survived independently. It was sometimes copied by other papers.

Appendix II: Pitt's letter to Beckford, 15 October 1761[1]

Dear Sir,

Finding, to my great surprise, that the cause and manner of my resigning the seals are grossly misrepresented in the city, as well as that the most gracious and spontaneous marks of his Majesty's approbation of my services, which marks followed my resignation, have been infamously traduced, as a bargain for my forsaking the public, I am under the necessity of declaring the truth of both these facts, in a manner which I am sure no gentleman will contradict. A difference of opinion with regard to measures to be taken against Spain, of the highest importance to the honour of the crown, and to the most essential national interests, and this founded on what Spain had already done, not on what that court may further intend to do, was the cause of my resigning the seals. Lord Temple and I submitted in writing, and signed by us, our most humble sentiments to his Majesty; which being over-ruled by the united opinion of all the rest of the King's servants, I resigned the seals on Monday, the 5th of this month, in order not to remain responsible for measures which I was no longer allowed to guide. Most gracious public marks of his Majesty's approbation of my services followed my resignation. They are unmerited, and unsolicited; and I shall ever be proud to have received them from the best of sovereigns.

I will now only add, my dear Sir, that I have explained these matters only for the honour of truth, not in any view to court return of confidence from any man, who, with a credulity as weak as it is injurious, has thought fit hastily to withdraw his good opinion from one who has served his country with fidelity and success; and who justly reveres the upright and candid judgment of it; little solicitous about the censures of the capricious and the ungenerous. Accept my sincerest acknowledgments for all your kind friendship, and believe me ever, with truth and esteem, my dear Sir,

Your faithful friend.

W. Pitt.

[1] *Corr. Chatham*, ii, pp. 158–9. See above pp. 208–9.

Bibliography

Primary sources

Manuscript

British Library

Bentinck Papers	—	Egerton MSS 1719.
Bute Papers	—	Add. MSS 36796–7.
Calcraft Papers	—	Add. MSS 17493–6.
Coxe Papers (Etough)—		Add. MSS 9201.
Hardwicke Papers	—	Add. MSS 35351–3, 35374, 35398–401, 35415–22, 35593–7, 35606–7.
Holland House Papers—		Add. MSS 51398, 51407, 51416, 51420.
Liverpool Papers	—	Add. MSS 38197–201, 38331–6.
Mitchell Papers	—	Add. MSS 6839.
Newcastle Papers	—	Add. MSS 32858–947, 33035.
Wilkes Papers	—	Add. MSS 22131–2, 30867–9, 30877–8, 30883–6, 30891.

Corporation of London Records Office

Common Hall Minute Book No. 8, 1751–88.
Common Hall Minute Papers, 1755–63.
Journals of the Court of Common Council, vols. 61–3, 1755–65.
Repertories, vols. 160, 164, 165–7, 1755–6, 1759–60, 1761–3.
City Addresses from 1760 to 1812.
Lists of Common Councilmen in chronological order within the Wards.
Index to Common Councilmen prior to 1880.

Guildhall Library, London

Wilkes Papers — MSS 214, vols. 1–4, 2892.

Typescript calendars to MSS 2739, 2892, 3332, 3724.

History of Parliament Trust
Transcripts of Sir Roger Newdigate's Diary and Manuscripts.

Public Record Office
Chatham Papers — PRO 30/8.

Reading, Berkshire Record Office
Richard Aldworth Neville's parliamentary diary, Neville (Aldworth) Papers.

Printed

Parliamentary Records
Journals of the House of Commons
The Parliamentary History of England from the Earliest Period to the Year 1803, [ed. William Cobbett], 36 vols., London, 1806–20.
The History, Debates and Proceedings of Both Houses of Parliament . . . 1743 . . . 1774, [ed. John Debrett], 7 vols., London, 1792.

Periodical Publications
The dates given are those of issues consulted, not necessarily the full run of the publication.
One location for each title is indicated by the following abbreviations:
BL — British Library
B — Bodleian Library
G — The Goldsmiths' Library, University of London
Gu — Guildhall Library, London
H — Henry E. Huntington Library, San Marino, California
UC — University of Canterbury Library
The Annual Register, Or A View of The History, Politicks, and Literature, Of the Year, 1758–63 (UC).
The Auditor, 1762–3 (BL).
The Briton, 1762–3 (BL).
The Champion, 1763 (BL).
The Con-Test, 1756–7 (BL).
The Contrast, 1763 (B).
The Crab-Tree, 1757 (BL).
The Critical Review: Or, Annals of Literature, 1756–63 (BL).
The Gazetteer and London Daily Advertiser, 1756–63, incomplete (BL).
The Gentleman's Magazine, And Historical Chronicle, 1756–63 (UC).
The Herald; Or, Patriot Proclaimer, 1757–8 (B).

The Literary Magazine: Or, Universal Review, 1757 (BL).

Lloyd's Evening Post, and British Chronicle, 1757–63 (BL).

The London Chronicle: Or, Universal Evening Post, 1757–63 (BL).

The London Evening Post, 1756–63 (BL).

The London Gazette, 1756–63 (BL).

The London Magazine: Or, Gentleman's Monthly Intelligencer, 1756–63 (UC).

The Lying Intelligencer, 1763 (BL).

The Moderator, 1763 (BL).

The Monitor, Or British Freeholder, Nos. 1–403 (BL except nos 404–29, 431–3
436–45, 488, 504, on microfilm from Yale University Library).

The Monthly Review, Or, Literary Journal, 1756–63 (BL).

The North Briton, 1762–3 (BL).

The New (Owen's) Weekly Chronicle, Or, Universal Journal, 1758–63 (B).

The Patriot, 1762 (BL).

*The Political Controversy: Or, Weekly Magazine of Ministerial and Anti-Ministeria
Essays* . . ., 1762–3 (BL).

The Protestor, On Behalf of the PEOPLE, 1753 (BL).

The Public Ledger, (Or, DAILY REGISTER of Commerce and Intelligence)
1760–1 (BL).

The Public Advertiser (1756–63 (BL).

Read's Weekly Journal, Or, British Gazetteer, 1756–61 (BL).

The Reformer, 1756 (B).

The St. James's Chronicle; Or, The British Evening-Post, 1761–3 (BL).

The Schemer. Or, Universal Satirist, 1760–2 (BL).

The Test, 1756–7 (BL).

The (Payne's) Universal Chronicle, Or Weekly Gazette (and Westminster Journal)
1758–60 (BL).

The Westminster Journal: Or, New Weekly Miscellany, 1759, incomplete (BL).

Pamphlets, Broadsheets and Ballads, 1756–62

Listed chronologically as far as possible. Locations are given as for
periodical publications. Only those pamphlets used for this study are listed,
not all those located or read.

1756

[Shebbeare, John], *A Third Letter To The People of England. On Liberty, Taxes,
And the Application of Public Money*, London, 1756 (BL).

*A New System of Patriot Policy Containing The Genuine Recantation of The British
Cicero*, London, 1756 (BL, G)

[Shebbeare, John], *A Fourth Letter To The People of England. On The Conduct of
the M[iniste]rs in Alliances, Fleets, and Armies, since the first Differences on the
Ohio, to the taking of Minorca by the French*, London, 1756 (BL, G)

*A Serious Call to the Corporation of London to address his M[ajest]y to remove from his
Councils and Person for ever Weak, and Wicked M[inister]s, &c. Humbly addressed*

to The Right Honourable the Lord Mayor, Aldermen, Common Council and Liverymen of the said City [broadsheet, London, 1756] (BL)

A Letter to the Gentlemen of the Common Council By a Citizen and Watchmaker, London, 1756 (BL)

A Letter to the Livery-Men of the City of London, on account of their late choice of a Lord-Mayor, London, 1756 (Gu)

The Wonder of Surry! The Wonder of Surry! or the genuine Speech of an old British oak, being a true and faithful Narrative of what passed between an Oak and a certain great Minister [ballad, London, 1756] (BL)

Wonder upon Wonder: Or The Cocoa Tree's Answer to the Surrey Oak. To The Tune of William and Margret [ballad, London, 1756] (BL)

Admiral B[yn]g's Answer to the Friendly Advice, Or The Fox out of the Pit And The Geese in [broadsheet, London, 1756] (BL)

The Resignation: Or, The Fox Out of the Pit, And The Geese In, with B[yn]g at the Bottom, London, 1756 (BL)

The Test Pro-Tested; Or, the Pudding saved [broadsheet, London, 1756] (BL)

The Ministry Changed: Or, The clean contrary Way. A New Song, To an Old Tune [ballad, London, 1756] (BL)

A Letter to the Rt. Hon. William Pitt, Esq; Being An Impartial Vindication of the Conduct of the Ministry, from the Commencement of the present War to this Time. In Answer to the Aspersions cast upon them by Admiral Byng and his Advocates, London, 1756 (BL)

A Political Treatise on National Humour. In which the Character and Conduct of a Statesman is Generally and Impartially Considered, Addressed to the Rt. Hon. William Pitt, Esq., London, 1756 (BL)

1757

The Constitution. With An Address To A Great Man, London, 1757 (BL)

A Letter From A Merchant of the City of London, To The R[igh]t H[onoura]ble W[illiam] P[itt] Esq; Upon The Affairs and Commerce of North America, and the West-Indies; Our American Trade; the Destination of Our Squadrons and Convoys; New Taxes, and the Schemes proposed for raising the extraordinary Supplies for the current Year, London, 1757 (G)

Two Very Singular Addresses To The People of England: Faithfully printed from the Originals, 'after performing a Quarantine of more than Forty Days', London, 1757 (BL)

The Enquiry is not begun! When will it? [broadsheet, London, 1757] (BL)

Essential Queries Relating to the Condemnation and Execution of Admiral Byng [broadsheet, London, 1757] (BL)

To the worthy Merchants and Citizens of London [broadsheet, London, 1757] (BL)

A Morning's Thoughts On Reading The Test And Contest, London, 1757 (BL)

A Full and Particular Account Of a most dreadful and surprising Apparition, Which appeared to a certain Great Man, at his Great House, on Monday last, at Midnight [broadsheet, London, 1757] (BL)

Past twelve o'clock, or Byng's Ghost [broadsheet, London, 1757] (BL)

[Shebbeare, John], *A Fifth Letter To The People of England, On The Subversion of the Constitution: And, The Necessity of it's being restored*, London, 1757 (BL)

The Constitution. With A Letter to the Author. Number II. To be continued occasionally, London, 1757 (BL)

The Constitution. With Some Account of a Bill lately rejected by the H[ouse] of L[ords]. Number III. To be continued occasionally, London, 1757 (BL)

The Speech of William the Fourth, to both Houses of P[arliament], [broadsheet, London, 1757] (BL)

The Father of the City of Eutopia, Or the Surest Road to Riches, Dedicated to the Rt. Hon. Wm. P[itt], Esq., London, 1757 (G)

For our Country. An Ode As Presented To The Right Honourable William Pitt. . . . Published by Order of the Managers and Proprietors of the Antigallican Private Ship of War, And Laudable Association of Antigallicans, held at the Lebeck's Head in the Strand. By a Member of the said Association, London, 1757 (BL)

The Chronicle of the Short Reign of Honesty. In four Chapters. Addressed to the Lord-Mayor, Aldermen, and Common-Council of the City of London, London, 1757 (G)

Political Truths Humourously Delineated, In A Letter From A Young Gentleman in Town To His Patriot Friend in the Country, London, 1757 (G)

A Letter To the Right Honorable H[enr]y F[o]x, Esq, London, 1757 (B)

A Letter From A Porter in the City, To The Lords and Commons of Great Britain, Assembled in Parliament at Westminster, On Thursday, December the First, 1757, London, 1757 (B)

An Essay on Political Lying, &c, London, 1757 (BL)

A Seasonable Reply To A Scurrilous Pamphlet, Called An Essay On Political Lying. By A Citizen of London, London, 1757 (BL)

An Appeal To The People: Part the Second. On the Different Deserts and Fate of Admiral Byng and his Enemies: The Changes in the last Administration: The Year of Liberty or Thraldom, London, 1757 (BL)

A Letter To His Grace the D[uke] of N[ewcastl]e, on The Duty he owes himself, his King, his Country and his God. At This Important Moment, London, 1757 (BL)

A Short History Of Late Administrations, Shewing their Spirit And Conduct; From whence it is made evident, That England is to be saved by the Virtue of the People Only. In a Letter to the Constituents by a Friend to the Constitution, London, 1757 (BL)

An Account Of The Facts which appeared on the late Enquiry into the Loss of Minorca, from Authentic Papers. By the Monitor, London, 1757 (BL)

[Shebbeare, John], *A Letter To The People of England upon the Militia, Continental Connections, Neutralities, and Secret Expeditions*, London, 1757 (BL)

The Secret Expedition. A New Hugbug Ballad. To the Tune of God prosper long our noble King [broadsheet, London, 1757] (BL)

A New Historical, Political, Satyrical, Burlesque Ode, On That Most Famous Expedition, of all Expeditions, Commonly called, The Grand Secret Expedition, As it was Performed By the Author, At a late High Borlace, London, 1757 (BL)

A Genuine Account of the Late Grand Expedition to the Coast of France, Under the Conduct of the Admirals Hawke, Knowles, and Broderick, General Mordaunt, &c. By a Volunteer in the said Expedition, third edn., London, 1757 (BL)

An Appeal to the Nation. Being A Full and Fair Vindication of Mr Mordaunt, and the other Gentlemen employed in the Conduct of the late Secret Expedition. In which The Circumstances relating to the Miscarriages of that Affair, are set in a just and satisfactory Light, London, 1757 (BL)

Public Injuries Require Public Justice: Or, an Enquiry into the Causes of the Miscarriage Of the late Secret Expedition to the Coast of France, London, 1757 (G)

1758

[Shebbeare, John], *A Sixth Letter To The People of England, On The Progress of National Ruin; In Which It is shewn, that the present Grandeur of France, and Calamities of this Nation, are owing to the Influence of Hanover on the Councils of England*, London, 1758 (BL)

Candid Reflections on the Report (As Published by Authority) of the General-Officers, Appointed by his Majesty's Warrant of the First of November last, to enquire into the Causes of the Failure of the late Expedition to the Coasts of France. In a Letter to a Friend in the Country, London, 1758 (BL)

[Potter, Thomas], *The Expedition against Rochefort Fully Stated an Considered. In a Letter To the Right Honourable the Author of the Candid Reflexions On the Report of the General Officers, &c. By a Country Gentleman*, London, 1758 (BL)

Considerations on the Proceedings of a General Court-Martial, Upon the Trial of Lieutenant-General Sir John Mordaunt (As published by Authority) With an Answer to the Expedition against Rochefort, fairly stated. In a Letter to the Right Honourable the Author of the Candid reflections, &c. To which is added, An Appendix, Being a Reply to the Monitor of Saturday the 21st Instant. By the author of the Candid Reflections, London, 1758 (BL)

An Address to the Great Man: With Advice to the Public, London, 1758 (BL)

A Letter To The Citizens Of London, London, 1758 (G)

A Vindication of Mr Pitt. Wherein all the Aspersions thrown out against that Gentleman, relative to the Affair of Rochefort, are unanswerably confuted. By a Member of Parliament, London, 1758 (BL)

[Perceval, John, Earl of Egmont], *Things As They Are*, London, 1758 (BL)

Things Set In A Proper Light. Being A full Answer to a Noble Author's Misrepresentation of Things As They Are, London 1758 (BL)

A Letter to His E[xcellenc]y L[ieutenan]t G[enera]l B[lig]h, second edn., London, 1758 (G)

An Examination of a Letter Published under the Name of L[ieutenan]t G[enera]l B[li]gh and addressed to the Hon. W[illia]m P[it]t, Esq, London, 1758 (BL)

1759

Expedition An Ode, To the Tune of the British Grenadiers, London, [1759?] (BL)

An Apology for W[illiam] P[itt], Esq; In which The Conduct of L[ieutenant] G[eneral] B[lig]h is vindicated from all the Cavils thrown out against him, London, 1759 (BL)

A Letter From A Member of Parliament In Town, To A Noble Lord In the Country, In regard to the Last Expedition to the Coast of France, London, 1759 (G)

Corrinna Vindicated, To which is added, An Answer to the Simile, London, 1759 (BL)

[Carlyle, Alexander], *Plain Reasons For Removing A certain Great Man From His M[ajest]y's Presence and Councils for ever. Addressed To The People of England. By O. M. Haberdasher*, London, 1759 (BL)

The Honest Grief of a Tory, Expressed in A Genuine Letter From A Burgess of [Calne], in Wiltshire, To The Author of the Monitor, Feb. 17, 1759, London, 1759 (BL)

A Second Letter From Wiltshire To The Monitor, On the Vindication Of His Constitutional Principles, London, 1759 (BL)

A Letter From The Duchess of M[a]r[lborou]gh, In The Shades, To The Great Man, London, 1759 (BL)

A Defence Of The Letter from the Dutchess of M[arlboroug]h in the Shades to the Great Man. Addressed to the Public, In Answer to The Monitor's Two Papers, Of the 23d and 30th of June, 1759, London, 1759 (BL)

Considerations On The Importance of Canada, And The Bay and River of St. Lawrence; And of the American Fisheries dependent on the Islands of Cape Breton, St. John's, Newfoundland, and the Seas adjacent. Addressed to the Right Hon. William Pitt, London, 1759 (BM)

[Douglas, John], *A Letter Addressed To Two Great Men, On The Prospect of Peace; And on the Terms necessary to be insisted upon in the Negociation*, London, 1759 (BL)

1760

An Ode, In Two Parts, Humbly Inscribed To The Right Honourable William Pitt, London, 1760 (B)

Remarks On The Letter Addressed To Two Great Men. In a Letter to the Author of that Piece, London, 1760 (BL)

[Ruffhead, Owen], *Reasons Why The Approaching Treaty of Peace Should Be Debated in Parliament: As a Method most Expedient and Constitutional. In a Letter addressed to a Great Man. And Occasioned by the Perusal of a Letter addressed to Two Great Men*, London, 1760 (BL)

A Letter From A Gentleman In the Country To His Friend in Town, On his Perusal of a Pamphlet Addressed to Two Great Men, London, 1760 (BL)

[Ruffhead, Owen], *Ministerial Usurpation Displayed, And The Prerogatives of The Crown, with the Rights of Parliament and of the Privy Council, considered. In an Appeal to the People*, London, 1760 (BL)

A Letter To The People of England, On The Necessity of putting an Immediate End to the War; And The Means of obtaining an Advantageous Peace, London, 1760 (BL)

General Reflections Occasioned by the Letter addressed to Two Great Men, And The Remarks on that Letter, London, 1760 (BL)

[Franklin, Benjamin], *The Interest Of Great Britain Considered, With Regard to her Colonies And the Acquisitions of Canada and Guadaloupe. To which are added, Observations concerning the Increase of Mankind, Peopling of Countries,* &c., London, 1760 (BL)

The Voice of Peace: Or, Considerations Upon The Invitation of the Kings of Great Britain and Prussia for holding a Congress. Together With A Plan of Pacification. In Six Letters. By the Secretary to the Spanish Embassy at the Hague, London, 1760 (BL)

[Mauduit, Israel], *Considerations On The Present German War,* London, 1760 (BL)

[Ruffhead, Owen], *The Conduct Of The Ministry Impartially Examined. And The Pamphlet entitled Considerations On The Present German War, Refuted from its own Principles,* London, 1760 (BL)

A Full and Candid Answer to a Pamphlet, entitled, Considerations On The Present German War, London, 1760 (G)

A Vindication Of the Conduct of the Present War, In A Letter To xxxxxx, London 1760 (BL)

Remarks On Two Popular Pamphlets, Viz. The Considerations on the present German War. And The Full and Candid Answer to the Considerations, London, 1760 (BL)

1761

Reasons In Support of the War in Germany, In Answer to Considerations on the Present German War, London, 1760 (G)

The Plain Reasoner: Or, Further Considerations On The German War, London, 1761 (BL)

[Perceval, John, Earl of Egmont?], *Things As They Are Part the Second. By the Author of the First,* London, 1761 (BL)

A Word To A Right Honourable Commoner, London, 1761 (H)

[Douglas, John], *Seasonable Hints From An Honest Man On the Present Important Crisis Of A New Reign And A New Parliament,* London, 1761 (BL)

[Massie, J], *General Propositions relating to Colonies,* broadsheet, London, 1761 (BL)

[Massie, J], *Brief observations concerning the Management of the War, and the Means to prevent the Ruin of Great Britain. Most humbly offered to the Consideration of the Parliament and the People thereof,* second edn., London, 1761 (G)

Reasons For Keeping Guadaloupe at a Peace, Preferable to Canada, Explained In Five Letters From A Gentleman in Guadaloupe To His Friend in London, London, 1761 (BL)

A Detection Of The False Reasons and Facts, Contained in the Five Letters, Entitled, Reasons for keeping Guadaloupe at a Peace, preferable to Canada; in which The Advantages of both Conquests are fairly and impartially stated and compared. By a Member of Parliament, London, 1761 (BL)

The Importance Of Canada Considered. In Two Letters To A Noble Lord, London, 1761 (BL)

October 1761

The Crisis: Or, Considerations On The Present State of Affairs, London, 1761 (G)

A Certain Great Man Vindicated. By a Lover of his Country, London, 1761 (BL)

A Letter To His Grace the Duke of N[ewcastle]. On The Present Crisis In The Affairs of Great Britain. Containing Reflections on a late Great Resignation, London, [1761] (BL)

An Earnest Address To the People of Great-Britain and Ireland: Occasioned by the Dismission of William Pitt, Esq. From the Office of Secretary of State, London, 1761 (B)

The Patriot Unmasked, Or, A Word to his Defenders. By John Trott, Cheese-monger and Statesman, London, 1761 (BL)

A Letter To the Right Honourable The Earl of B[ute], On A late important Resignation, and its probable Consequences, London, 1761 (BL)

The Right Honourable Annuitant Vindicated. With A Word or two in Favour of the other Great Man, in Case of his Resignation. In a letter to A Friend in the Country, London, 1761 (BL)

An Answer to A Letter to the Right Honourable The Earl of B[ute], In which the false Reasoning and absurd Conclusions, in that Pamphlet, are fully detected and refuted. Addressed to the Right Hon. Earl Temple, London, 1761 (BL)

The Conciliad or the Triumph of Patriotism. A Poem. Translated from the Latin of Tertius Quartus, Quintus, third edn., London, 1762 (BL) (first edn. advt. *PA,* 31 Oct. 1761)

November 1761

The Conduct of a Rt. Hon. Gentleman In resigning the Seals of his office, justified, by Facts, And upon the Principles of the British Constitution. By a Member of Parliament, London, 1761 (BL)

A Second Letter To the Right Honourable The Earl of B[ute]. By the Author of the First, London, 1761 (BL)

Impartial Reflections upon the present State of Affairs. With incidental Remarks upon certain recent Transactions. In a Letter to a Friend, London, 1761 (BL)

Remarks upon a popular Letter. By a Citizen of London, London, 1761 (BL)

The Case of the Late Resignation Set in a True Light, London, 1761 (BL)

[Francis, Philip], *A Letter From A Right Honourable Person And the Answer to it, Translated into Verse, as nearly as the different Idioms of Prose and Poetry will allow, With Notes Historical, Critical, Political, &c,* London 1761 (BL)

Reflections occasioned by the Resignation of a Certain Great Man. Particularly addressed to the Citizens of London, London, 1761 (BL)

The Statesman: Or, The Constitutional Advocate. Number I, London, 1761 (BL)

[Shebbeare, John], *A Letter To The Right Honourable Author Of A Letter to a Citizen, with Animadversions on the Answer thereto, And on the Behaviour of the Corporation of the City of London. In Which His Reasons for resigning; the Conduct, Success and Advantages of his Administration; His Fidelity to his Country; Capacity for directing the Transactions of War, Commerce and Pacification, are fairly stated and freely considered*, London, 1761 (BL)

The Unhappy Memorable Old Song, (As It Is Called) of the Hunting of Chevy-Chace; Imitated; In a Spick and Span New Ballad, accommodated to the Present Times, London, 1761 (BL) (reissued 1762 with comment on Newcastle's resignation)

December 1761

Occasional Thoughts On The Present German War. By the Author of the Considerations on the same Subject, London, 1761 (BL)

The Coalition: or, An Historical Memorial Of The Negotiations for Peace, Between His High Mightiness of C[lare]m[oun], and His Sublime Excellency of H[a]y[e]s. With the Vouchers. Published by Authority of One of the Contracting Powers, London, 1761 (BL)

An Impartial Enquiry Into The Conduct Of A late Minister, London, 1761 (Wren Library, Trinity College, Cambridge)

A Letter From A Patriot in Retirement, To the Right Honourable Mr. William Pitt, Upon Resigning his Employment, London, [1761] (BL)

A Fair and Compleat Answer To The Author of The Occasional Thoughts On The Present German War, with a Reply to the Considerations on the same Subject, London, [1761] (BL)

The Equilibrium: Or, Balance of Opinions, on a late Resignation. By A Citizen of the World, Residing In London, London, 1761 (B)

A Full Vindication of the Right Honourable Wm. Pitt and Wm. Beckford, Esqurs. In Answer to A scurrilous Pamphlet, intituled, A Letter from a Right Honourable Person, and the Answer to it, translated into Verse. With Counter-Notes Historical, Critical, Political, &c. In Which Every Argument of that boasted Performance is subverted, and the Conduct of those Gentlemen Set in a true Light, London, 1761 (G)

[Francis, Philip], *A Letter from the Anonymous Author of the Letters Versified to the Anonymous Writer of the Monitor*, London, 1761 (BL)

1762

A Third Letter To The Right Hon. The Earl of B[ute]. In Which The Causes and Consequences of the War between Great Britain and Spain, are fully considered; And The Conduct of a certain Right Honourable Gentleman further examined, London, 1762 (BL)

Constitutional Queries, Humbly Addressed to the Admirers Of a late Minister, London, 1762
(BL)

*A Consolatory Epistle To the Members of the Old Faction; Occasioned by the Spanish War. By
the Author of The Consolatory Letter to the noble Lord dismissed the Military Service*,
London, 1762 (BL)

[Massie, J], *Observations relating to British and Spanish proceedings, &c. Wherein Due
Notice is taken of a memorable Dialogue between Harry and Will. on the Expediency of A
Continental War* . . . *To which is added, A Proposal for replacing the New Taxes on Malt
and Beer. Most humbly submitted to the Consideration of the Parliament and People of Great
Britain*, London, 1762 (G)

An Address To The City of London, London, 1762 (H)

A Continuation Of The Address To The City Of London, London, 1762 (H)

[Wilkes, John], *Observations On The Papers Relative To The Rupture with Spain, Laid
Before Both Houses of Parliament, On Friday the Twenty-ninth Day of January, 1762, By
his Majesty's Command. In a Letter from a Member of Parliament, to a Friend in the
Country*, London, 1762 (BL)

An Answer To The Observations On The Papers relative to the Rupture with Spain, London,
1762 (BL)

*A Full Exposition Of a Pamphlet entitled, Observations On The Papers Relative To The
Rupture with Spain* . . . *In An Answer from the Country-Gentleman, To The Member of
Parliament's Letter*, London, 1762 (BL)

[Shebbeare, John], *Invincible Reasons for the Earl of Bute's immediate Resignation of the
Ministry. In a Letter to a Nobleman*, London, 1762 (BL)

A Letter to a Gentleman in the City, [London, 1762] (BL)

*The True Briton, A Letter Addressed to the Right Honourable Sir Samuel Fludyer, Bart. Lord
Mayor*, London, 1762 (B)

*A Letter To A Member Of The Honourable House of Commons, On The Present Important
Crisis of National Affairs*, London, 1762 (BL)

*A Letter To The Right Honourable The Lord Mayor, Aldermen, Common Council, and
Citizens, of London, Concerning The Peace now in Agitation between Great Britain and
France*, London, 1762 (BL)

*A Political Analysis Of The War: The Principles of the present political Parties examined; And
A just, national and perfect Coalition proposed between Two Great Men, whose Conduct is
particularly considered*, London, 1762 (Widener Library, Harvard University).

[Heathcote, George], *A Letter to the Right Honourable The Lord Mayor, The Worshipful
Aldermen, and Common-Council; The Merchants, Citizens, and Inhabitants of the City of
London. From an Old Servant*, London, 1762 (BL)

*A Reply To Mr. Heathcote's Letter, From An Honest Man. In Which The Arguments are proved
to be delusive; and the Facts untrue*, London, 1762 (BL)

*A Letter To the Right Honourable William Pitt, Esq; On the Present Negotiations for a Peace
with France and Spain*, London, 1762 (BL)

[Marriott, James], *Political Considerations; Being A Few Thoughts Of A Candid Man At
The Present Crisis. In a Letter to a Noble Lord retired from Power*, London, 1762 (BL)

One More Letter to the People of England. By their old Friend, London, 1762 (BL)

[Francis, Philip], *A Letter From The Cocoa-Tree To The Country-Gentlemen,* London, 1762 (BL)

[Almon, John], *A Review of Mr. Pitt's Administration,* London, 1762 (BL)

Later Pamphlets

1763

[Almon, John], *A Review of Lord Bute's Administration. By the Author of the Review of Mr. Pitt's,* London, 1762 (BL)

1765

[Almon, John], *The History of the Late Minority. Exhibiting the conduct, principles, and views, of that party during the years 1762, 1763, 1764 and 1765,* London, 1765 (reprinted with some additions 1766) (BL)

A Letter To The Common-Council Of London On Their Late Very Extraordinary Address To His Majesty, London, 1765 (BL)

Memoirs and Correspondence

ALMON [John Almon], *Biographical, Literary, and Political Anecdotes, of Several of the Most Eminent Persons of the Present Age,* 3 vols., London, 1797.

John Almon, *Memoirs,* London, 1790.

BEDFORD *Correspondence of John, fourth Duke of Bedford . . . with an introduction by Lord John Russell,* 3 vols., London, 1842–6.

BOSWELL *Boswell's London Journal 1762–1763 together with Journal of My Jaunt, Harvest, 1762,* ed. Frederick A. Pottle, The Yale Editions of the Private Papers of James Boswell, London, 1951.

BURKE *The Correspondence of Edmund Burke,* ed. Thomas W. Copeland, 9 vols., Cambridge, 1958–70.

CHESTERFIELD *Letters to His Son by the Earl of Chesterfield,* ed. Oliver H. Leigh, 2 vols. in one, New York, [n.d.].

COLEBROOKE Sir George Colebrooke, *Restrospection: Or Reminiscences Addressed To My Son—Henry Thomas Colebrooke, Esq.,* 2 pts., London, 1898, 1899.

An Eighteenth Century Correspondence, ed. Lilian Dickins and Mary Stanton, London, 1910.

DODINGTON *The Political Journal of George Bubb Dodington,* ed. John Carswell and Lewis Arnold Drallé, Oxford, 1965.

Ellis, Henry, *Original letters illustrative of English history . . .,* 11 vols., London, 1824–46.

EGMONT Egmont's account of events 25 Oct.–3 Dec. 1760, 'Leicester House Politics, 1750–1760, from the papers of John, Second Earl of Egmont', ed. A. N. Newman, *Camden Miscellany,* xxiii, fourth series, vii.

FOX *Letters to Henry Fox, Lord Holland: With a few addressed to his brother Stephen Earl of Ilchester,* ed. Earl of Ilchester, London, 1915.

'Lord Holland's Memoir on the Events attending the death of George II And the Accession of George III', *The Life and Letters of Lady Sarah Lennox*

1745–1826, ed. Countess of Ilchester and Lord Stavordale, 2 vols., London, 1901, i.

GEORGE III *Letters from George III to Lord Bute 1756–1766*, ed. Romney Sedgwick, London, 1939.

The Correspondence of King George the Third from 1760 to December 1783, ed. the Hon. Sir John Fortescue, 6 vols., London, 1927–8.

GLOVER [Richard Glover], *Memoirs by a Celebrated Literary and Political Character from . . . 1742 to . . . 1757*, second edn., London, 1814.

GRAFTON *Autiobiography and Political Correspondence of Augustus Henry, Third Duke of Grafton, K.G.*, ed. Sir William R. Anson, London, 1898.

GRENVILLE *The Grenville Papers: being the Correspondence of Richard Grenville Earl Temple, K.G., and the Right Hon. George Grenville, their Friends and Contemporaries*, ed. William James Smith, 4 vols., London, 1852–3.

HARDWICKE George Harris, *The Life of Lord Chancellor Hardwicke; with Selections from his Correspondence, Diaries, Speeches, and Judgments*, 3 vols., London 1847.

Philip C. Yorke, *The Life and Correspondence of Philip Yorke, Earl of Hardwicke, Lord High Chancellor of Great Britain*, 3 vols., Cambridge, 1913.

HISTORICAL MANUSCRIPTS COMMISSION

Third Report, London, 1872. Appendix. Manuscripts of the Most Honourable the Marquis of Lansdowne, at Lansdowne House.

Fourth Report, London, 1874. Appendix, Part i. Manuscripts of the late Colonel Macaulay.

Eighth Report, London, 1881. Appendix, Part i. Manuscripts of George Wingfield Digby, Esq.

Ninth Report, London, 1883. Appendix, Part ii. The Manuscripts of Alfred Morrison, Esq., of Fonthill House, Hindon, Wilts, and Carlton House Terrace, London.

Tenth Report, London, 1885. Appendix, Part i. Manuscripts of Charles Fleetwood Weston Underwood, Esq., of Somerby Hall, Lincolnshire.

Eleventh Report, London, 1887. Appendix, Part iv. Manuscripts of the Marquess Townshend.

Fourteenth Report, London, 1894. Appendix, Part iv. Manuscripts of Lord Kenyon.

Report on the Manuscripts of Mrs Stopford–Sackville, Drayton House, Northamptonshire, 2 vols., London, 1904, 1910.

Report on the Manuscripts of the Marquess of Lothian preserved at Blickling Hall, Norfolk, London, 1905.

Report on Manuscripts in Various Collections, vol. vi, Dublin, 1909. Manuscripts of Miss M. Eyre Marcham.

Report on the Manuscripts of Lord Polwarth, 5 vols., London, 1911–61.

JENKINSON *The Jenkinson Papers, 1760–1766*, ed. N. S. Jucker, London, 1949.

LYTTELTON *Memoirs and Correspondence of George, Lord Lyttelton, from 1734 to 1773*, ed. Robert J. Phillimore, 2 vols., London, 1845.

MONTAGU *The Letters of Mrs Elizabeth Montagu with some of the Letters of her Correspondents*, ed. Matthew Montagu, 4 vols., London, 1809–13.

Elizabeth Montagu, the Queen of the Bluestockings. Her Correspondence from 1720 to 1761, ed. Emily J. Climenson, 2 vols., London, 1906.

Mrs Montagu "Queen of the Blues", ed. Reginald Blunt, 2 vols., London, [1923].

PITT *Anecdotes of the life of the Right Honourable William Pitt, Earl of Chatham; and of the Principal Events of his Time; with his Speeches in Parliament, from the year 1736 to the year 1778*, [John Almon], third edn., corrected, 3 vols., London, 1793.

Correspondence of William Pitt, Earl of Chatham, ed. William Stanhope Taylor and John Henry Pringle, 4 vols., London, 1838–40.

'Letters from William Pitt to Lord Bute: 1755–1758', Romney Sedgwick, *Essays presented to Sir Lewis Namier*, ed. Richard Pares and A. J. P. Taylor, London, 1956.

ROCKINGHAM *Memoirs of the Marquis of Rockingham and His Contemporaries*, ed. George Thomas, Earl of Albemarle, 2 vols., London, 1852.

SHELBURNE *Life of William Earl of Shelburne, afterwards First Marquess of Lansdowne with Extracts from his Papers and Correspondence*, ed. Lord Edmond Fitzmaurice, 3 vols., London, 1875–6.

WALDEGRAVE James, Earl Waldegrave, *Memoirs from 1754 to 1758*, London, 1821.

WALPOLE Horace Walpole, Earl of Orford, *Memoires of the Last Ten Years of the Reign of George the Second*, 2 vols., London, 1822.

Horace Walpole, *Memoirs of the Reign of King George the Third; first published by Sir Denis Le Marchant bart.*, ed. G. F. Russell-Barker, 4 vols., London, 1894.

The Letters of Horace Walpole Fourth Earl of Orford, ed. Mrs Paget Toynbee, 16 vols., London, 1903–5.

The Yale Edition of Horace Walpole's Correspondence, ed. W. S. Lewis, 39 vols., in progress, New Haven, Conn., 1937–[74].

WILKES *The Correspondence of the Late John Wilkes, with his Friends, printed from the original Manuscripts, in which are introduced Memoirs of his Life*, ed. John Almon, 5 vols., London, 1805.

The Correspondence of John Wilkes and Charles Churchill, ed. Edward H. Weatherley, New York, 1954.

Wyndham, Maud, *Chronicles of the Eighteenth Century Founded on the Correspondence of Sir Thomas Lyttelton and his Family*, 2 vols., London, 1924.

Miscellanea

A Complete Collection of State Trials and Proceedings for High Treason and other Crimes and Misdemeanours from the Earliest Period to the Present Time with Notes and Other Illustrations, ed. T. B. Howell, 33 vols., London, 1809–26.

The English Reports, 176 vols., reprint, Edinburgh and London, 1900–30.

Entick, John, *A New and Accurate History and Survey of London, Westminster, Southwark, and Places Adjacent* . . ., 4 vols., London, 1766.

The General Biographical Dictionary . . ., ed. Alexander Chalmers, new edn., revised and enlarged, 32 vols., London, 1812–17.

Guildhall Library, Noble Collection of Newspaper Cuttings.

Lysons, Daniel, *The Environs of London, being an historical account of the towns, villages, and hamlets, within twelve miles of that capital* . . ., 4 vols., London, 1792–6.

Maitland, William, *The History of London from its Foundation to the Present Time* . . . *Continued to the year 1772 by the Rev. John Entick M.A.* . . ., 2 vols., London, 1772.

Nichols, John, *Literary Anecdotes of the Eighteenth Century; comprizing Biographical Memoirs of William Bowyer, Printer, F.S.A. and Many of his learned friends;* . . . *and Biographical Anecdotes of a considerable number of Eminent Writers and Ingenious Artists*, 9 vols., London, 1812–15.

—— *Illustrations of the Literary History of the Eighteenth Century. Consisting of Authentic Memoirs and Original Letters of Eminent Persons; and intended as a sequel to The Literary Anecdotes*, 8 vols., London, 1817–58.

Political Ballads Illustrating the Administration of Sir Robert Walpole, ed. Milton Percival, Oxford, 1916.

Secondary Works. A select list

Bibliographies, Catalogues and Lists—Periodicals and Prints

The Cambridge Bibliography of English Literature, ed. F. W. Bateson, 4 vols., Cambridge, 1940.

Catalogue of Prints and Drawings in the British Museum. Division I. Political and Personal Satires, ed. Frederick George Stephens and Mary Dorothy George, 11 vols., London, 1870–1954.

Crane, R. S. and Kay, F. B., *A Census of British Newspapers and Periodicals, 1620–1800*, Chapel Hill, N.C., 1927.

Milford, Robert Theodore and Sutherland, D., *Catalogue of Newspapers and Periodicals in the Bodleian Library, 1622–1800*, Oxford, 1936.

[Muddiman, J. G.], *The Times, London, Tercentenary Handlist of English and Welsh Newspapers, Magazines and Reviews*, London, 1920.

Weed, Katherine K. and Bond, R. P., *Studies of British Newspapers and Periodicals from their Beginnings to 1800. A Bibliography, Studies in Philology*, Extra Series, 2, Chapel Hill, N. C., 1946.

General: Books

Ashton, T. S., *Economic Fluctuations in England 1700–1800*, Oxford, 1959.

Atherton, Herbert M., *Political Prints in the Age of Hogarth. A Study of the Ideographic Representation of Politics*, Oxford, 1974.

Ayling, Stanley, *The Elder Pitt Earl of Chatham*, London, 1976.

Beaven, Alfred B., *The Aldermen of the City of London*, 2 vols., London, 1908, 1913.

Bond, Richmond P., ed., *Studies in the Early English Periodical*, Chapel Hill, N.C., 1957.

Bourne, H. R. Fox, *English Newspapers*, 2 vols., London, 1887.

Brewer, John, *Party Ideology and Popular Politics at the Accession of George III*, Cambridge, 1976.

Brooke, John, *King George III*, London, 1972.

Brown, Peter Douglas, *William Pitt Earl of Chatham The Great Commoner*, London, 1978.

Browning, Reed, *The Duke of Newcastle*, New Haven, Conn., 1975.

Carlson, C. Lennart. *The First Magazine: A History of the Gentleman's Magazine*, Providence, R. I., 1938.

Corbett, Julian S., *England in the Seven Years' War: a study in combined strategy*, second edn., 2 vols., London, 1918.

Cranfield, G. A., *The Development of the Provincial Newspaper 1700–1760*, Oxford, 1962.

Dickinson, H. T., *Liberty and Property. Political Ideology in Eighteenth-Century Britain*, London, 1977.

Fox-Strangeways, Giles S. H., Earl of Ilchester, *Henry Fox, First Lord Holland His Family and Relations*, 2 vols., London, 1920.

George, M. Dorothy, *English Political Caricature*, 2 vols., Oxford, 1959.

Graham, Walter, *English Literary Periodicals*, New York, 1930.

Haig, Robert L., *The Gazetteer 1735–1797. A Study in the Eighteenth-Century English Newspaper*, Carbondale, Ill., 1960.

Hanson, Laurence, *Government and the Press 1695–1763*, Oxford, 1936, reprinted 1967.

Hotblack, Kate, *Chatham's Colonial Policy: A Study in the Fiscal and Economic Implications of the Colonial Policy of the Elder Pitt*, London, 1917.

Kemp, Betty, *Sir Francis Dashwood. An Eighteenth-Century Independent*, London, 1967.

Langford, Paul, *The First Rockingham Administration 1765–1766*, London, 1973.

—— *The Excise Crisis. Society and Politics in the Age of Walpole*, Oxford, 1975.

McKelvey, James Lee, *George III and Lord Bute. The Leicester House Years*, Durham, N.C., 1973.

Midgley, Graham, *The Life of Orator Henley*, Oxford, 1973.

Morison, Stanley, *The English Newspaper, Some Account of the Physical Development of Journals Printed in London between 1622 and the Present Day*, Cambridge, 1932.

Namier, Sir Lewis, *The Structure of Politics at the Accession of George III*, second edn., London, 1960.

—— *England in the Age of the American Revolution*, second edn., London, 1966.

Namier, Sir Lewis, and Brooke, John, *The History of Parliament. The House of Commons 1754–1790*, 3 vols., London, 1964.

―― ―― *Charles Townshend*, London, 1964.

Nangle, Benjamin C., *The Monthly Review First Series 1749–1789. Indexes of Contributors and Articles*, Oxford, 1934.

Nobbe, George, *The North Briton, a study in political propaganda*, New York, 1939.

O'Gorman, Frank, *The Rise of Party in England. The Rockingham Whigs 1760–82*, London, 1975.

Pares, Richard, *War and Trade in the West Indies, 1739–1763*, Oxford, 1936.

―― *Colonial Blockade and Neutral Rights, 1739–1763*, Oxford, 1938.

Perry, Thomas W., *Public Opinion, Propaganda, and Politics in Eighteenth-Century England: A Study of the Jew Bill of 1753*, Cambridge, Mass., 1962.

Pope, Dudley, *At 12 Mr Byng was Shot . . .*, London, 1962.

Rea, Robert R., *The English Press in Politics 1760–1774*, Lincoln, Nebraska, 1962.

[Redding, Cyrus], *The Memoirs of William Beckford of Fonthill, Author of Vathek*, 2 vols., London, 1859.

Rosebery, Lord, *Chatham, His Early Life and Connections*, London, 1910.

Sedgwick, Romney, *The History of Parliament. The House of Commons 1715–1754*, 2 vols., London, 1971.

Sharpe, Reginald, *London and the Kingdom*, 3 vols., London, 1895.

Sherrard, O. A., *Lord Chatham. A War Minister in the Making*, London, 1952.

―― *Lord Chatham. Pitt and the Seven Years' War*, London, 1955.

―― *Lord Chatham and America*, London, 1958.

Spector, Robert Donald, *English Literary Periodicals and the Climate of Opinion During the Seven Years' War*, The Hague, 1966.

Sutherland, Lucy S., *The East India Company in Eighteenth-Century Politics*, Oxford, 1952.

―― *The City of London and the Opposition to Government. A Study in the Rise of Metropolitan Radicalism, 1768–1774*, London, 1959.

Thackeray, Francis, *A History of The Right Honourable William Pitt, Earl of Chatham*, 2 vols., London, 1827.

Torrens, W. M., *History of Cabinets: from the Union with Scotland to the Acquisition of Canada and Bengal*, 2 vols., London, 1894.

Tunstall, Brian, *Admiral Byng and the Loss of Minorca*, London, 1928.

―― *William Pitt Earl of Chatham*, London, 1938.

Von Ruville, Albert, *William Pitt Earl of Chatham*, 3 vols., London, 1907.

Western, J. R., *The English Militia in the Eighteenth Century. The Story of a Political Issue 1660–1802*, London, 1965.

Wiggin, Lewis M., *The Faction of Cousins. A Political Account of the Grenvilles, 1733–1763*, New Haven, Conn., 1958.

Wiles, R. M., *Freshest Advices. Early Provincial Newspapers in England*, [Columbus, Ohio], 1965.

Williams, Basil, *The Life of William Pitt Earl of Chatham*, 2 vols., London, 1915.

General: Articles

Adams, Thomas R., 'The British Pamphlets of the American Revolution for 1774: A Progress Report', *Proceedings of the Massachusetts Historical Society*, lxxxi (1969).

Brewer, John, 'The Faces of Lord Bute: a Visual Contribution to Anglo-American Political Ideology', *Perspectives in American History*, vi (1972).

—— 'The Misfortunes of Lord Bute: A Case-Study in Eighteenth-Century Political Argument and Public Opinion', *Historical Journal*, xvi, 1 (Mar. 1973).

Christie, Ian R., 'British Newspapers in the Later Georgian Age', *Myth and Reality in Late-Eighteenth-Century British Politics and Other Papers*, London, 1970.

Collyer, C., 'The Rockingham Connection and Country Opinion in the Early Years of George III', *Proceedings of The Leeds Philosophical and Literary Society*, vii, 3 (Mar. 1955).

—— 'The Rockinghams and Yorkshire Politics 1742–1761', *Publications of the Thoresby Society*, xli, *Thoresby Miscellany*, xii (1954).

Cranfield, G. A., 'The *London Evening Post*, 1727–44: A study in the Development of the Political Press', *Historical Journal*, vi, 1 (1963).

—— 'The *London Evening Post* and the Jew Bill of 1753', *Historical Journal*, viii, 1 (1965).

Davis, Ralph, 'English Foreign Trade, 1700–1774', *Economic History Review*, xv, 2 (Dec. 1962).

Foster, J. R., 'Smollett's Pamphleteering Foe Shebbeare', *Publications of the Modern Languages Association*, lvii (1942).

Fraser, Peter, 'Public Petitioning and Parliament before 1832', *History*, xlvi (Oct. 1961).

Grant W. L., 'Canada versus Guadeloupe, an Episode of the Seven Years' War', *American Historical Review*, xvii, 4 (July 1912).

Jones, Claude E., 'Contributors to the *Critical Review* 1756–1785', *Modern Language Notes*, lxi, 7 (Nov. 1946).

—— 'The *Critical Review*'s First Thirty Years (1756–1785)', *Notes and Queries*, iii (1956).

Kemp, Betty, 'Patriotism, Pledges and the People', *A Century of Conflict 1850–1950. Essays for A. J. P. Taylor*, ed. Martin Gilbert, London, 1966.

Langford, Paul, 'William Pitt and public opinion, 1757', *English Historical Review*, lxxxviii (Jan. 1973).

Middleton, Richard, 'Pitt, Anson and the Admiralty, 1756–1761', *History*, lv (June 1970).

Mitchell, A. A., 'London and the Forty-Five', *History Today*, xv, 10 (Oct. 1965).

Namier, Sir Lewis, 'Country Gentlemen in Parliament, 1750–84', *Crossroads of Power. Essays on Eighteenth-Century England*, London, 1962.

Owen, J. B., 'The Survival of Country Attitudes in the Eighteenth-Century House of Commons', *Britain and the Netherlands*, iv, *Metropolis, Dominion and Province*, ed. J. S. Bromley and E. H. Kossmann, The Hague, 1971.

Pares, Richard, 'American versus Continental Warfare, 1739–63', *English Historical Review*, li (July 1936).

Penson, Lilian M. 'The London West India Interest in the Eighteenth Century', *English Historical Review*, xxxvi (July 1921).

Peters, Marie, 'The *Monitor* on the constitution, 1755–1765: new light on the ideological origins of English radicalism', *English Historical Review*, lxxxvi (Oct. 1971).

Rogers, Nicholas, 'Popular Disaffection in London during the Forty-Five', *London Journal*, i, 1 (May 1975).

—— 'Resistance to Oligarchy: The City Opposition to Walpole and his Successors, 1725–47', *London in the Age of Reform*, ed. John Stevenson, Oxford, 1977.

Sedgwick, Romney, 'William Pitt and Lord Bute. An Intrigue of 1755–58', *History Today*, vi, 10 (Oct. 1956).

Smith, D. Nichol, 'The Newspaper', *Johnson's England. An Account of the Life and Manners of his Age*, ed. A. S. Turberville, 2 vols., Oxford, 1933.

Sutherland, Lucy, 'The City of London in Eighteenth-Century Politics', *Essays presented to Sir Lewis Namier*, ed. Richard Pares and A. J. P. Taylor, London, 1956.

—— 'The City of London and the Devonshire–Pitt Administration, 1756–7', *Proceedings of the British Academy*, xlvi (1960).

Unpublished works

Fraser, E. J. S., 'The Pitt–Newcastle Coalition and the Conduct of the Seven Years' War 1757–1760', D. Phil. thesis, University of Oxford, 1976.

Harris, Michael, 'The London Newspaper Press, ca. 1725–1746', Ph.D. thesis, University of London, 1973.

Peters, Marie, 'The *Monitor* 1755–1765: A Political Essay Paper and Popular London Opinion', Ph.D. thesis, University of Canterbury, New Zealand, 1974.

Rogers, Nicholas, 'London Politics from Walpole to Pitt: Patriotism and Independency in an Era of Commercial Imperialism 1738–63', Ph.D. thesis, University of Toronto, 1975.

Watson, Derek Herbert, 'The Duke of Newcastle, the Marquis of Rockingham, and Mercantile Interests in London and the Provinces 1761–68', Ph.D. thesis, University of Sheffield, 1968.

Index

Only those pamphlets named in the text have been indexed